Feedback Control
of Computing Systems

Feedback Control
of Computing Systems

Joseph L. Hellerstein
Yixin Diao
Sujay Parekh
Dawn M. Tilbury

IEEE PRESS

A JOHN WILEY & SONS, INC., PUBLICATION

For general information on our other products and services please contact our Customer Care Department within the U.S. at 877-762-2974, outside the U.S. at 317-572-3993 or fax 317-572-4002.

Wiley also publishes its books in a variety of electronic formats. Some content that appears in print, however, may not be available in electronic format.

Library of Congress Cataloging-in-Publication Data:

Feedback control of computing systems / Joseph L. Hellerstein ... [et al.].
   p. cm.
  "A Wiley-Interscience publication."
  Includes bibliographical references and index.
  ISBN 0-471-26637-X (cloth)
  1. Feedback control systems. 2. Control theory. 3. Electronic data processing. I.
Hellerstein, Joseph, 1952-

TJ216.F44 2004
629.8′3–dc22

                             2004040490

10 9 8 7 6 5 4 3 2 1

To Our Families

Contents

PART II SYSTEM MODELING

Preface

This book is intended primarily for practitioners engaged in the analysis and design of computing systems. Analysts and designers are extremely interested in the performance characteristics of computing systems, especially response times, throughputs, queue lengths, and utilizations. Although steady-state characteristics can be well understood using queueing theory (e.g., as is done with capacity planning), practitioners lack the conceptual tools to address the *dynamics of resource management*, especially changes in workloads and configuration. The focus of this book is to distill and make accessible the essentials of control theory needed by computing practitioners to address these dynamics.

The dynamics of computing systems are important considerations in ensuring the profitability and availability of many businesses. For example, e-commerce sites frequently contend with workloads that change so rapidly that service degradations and failures result. Experienced designers know that leaving the management of dynamics to operators is not acceptable because many changes occur too rapidly for humans to be able to respond in a timely manner. As a result, ad hoc automation is frequently deployed with surprising results, such as wild oscillations or very slow responses to changes in workloads. Our belief is that by understanding the essential elements of control theory, computing practitioners can design systems that adapt in a more reliable manner.

A second audience for this book comprises researchers in the fields of computer science and controls. Today, very few computer science researchers have familiarity with control theory. As a result, many resource management schemes fail to address concepts that are well understood in control, such as the effect of measurement and system delays on stability and other aspects of control performance. Similarly, researchers in control fields rarely appreciate the issues particular to computing systems, such as considerations for policy-based management, service-level agreements, and the implications of modifying computing systems to provide sensors and actuators that are appropriate for control purposes. To address this second audience, we show through numerous examples how control theoretic techniques can be applied to computer systems, and describe the many challenges that remain.

Much effort has been devoted to making this book accessible to computer scientists. First, the examples focus on computer systems and their components, such as Web servers, caching, and load balancing. Second, our approach to modeling draws heavily on insights from queueing systems and their dynamics (as opposed to Newton's laws). Third, we focus almost entirely on discrete-time systems rather than continuous-time systems (as is traditional in controls books). There are two reasons for this: (1) performance measurements of computer systems are solicited on a sampled basis, which is best described by a discrete-time model; and (2) computer scientists are quite comfortable thinking in terms of difference equations, and much less comfortable thinking in terms of differential equations.

Prerequisites

The book assumes background in series and their convergence, all of which is common in an undergraduate engineering and mathematics curriculum. Some prior exposure to Z-transforms (or Laplace transforms) is also of benefit, although not required. Also helpful is experience with developing statistical models, especially using linear regression.

Having appropriate software tools is immensely helpful in developing statistical models as well as for control analysis and design. Throughout the book, we use MATLAB®, a very powerful analysis environment that is arguably the standard for control engineers[1]. In Appendix E we provide an introduction to MATLAB (including the Control System Toolbox). However, access to MATLAB is not required for the vast majority of the book, only the optional section (indicated by *) at the end of each chapter.

Outline of the Book

The book is divided into three parts. Part I, Background, consists of one chapter introducing the control problem and giving an overview of the area. Part II, Modeling, contains six chapters and covers modeling of dynamic systems in discrete time using difference equations, Z-transforms, block diagrams, transfer functions, and transient analysis. The focus is on single-input, single-output first- and second-order systems, although Chapter 7 is devoted to multiple-input, multiple-output (MIMO) systems. Part III, Control, has four chapters. In the first chapter we describe proportional control and pole placement design. In the next chapter we consider integral and differential control as well, including PID

---

[1]MATLAB is a registered trademark of The MathWorks, Inc.

(proportional–integral–differential) control tuning techniques. In the third chapter we address state-space feedback control, including the application of pole placement to MIMO systems and design using linear quadratic regulators. In the last chapter we discuss a variety of advanced topics, such as adaptive control, gain scheduling, minimum-variance control, and fuzzy control. In all three parts, examples are used extensively to illustrate the problems addressed, the techniques employed, and the value provided by the techniques.

Several appendixes are provided to make the book more useful as a reference and more self-contained. Appendix A summarizes the mathematical notation used, Appendix B lists key acronyms, and Appendix C contains key results developed in the book. Anothertwo appendixes contain supplemental material. Appendix D describes results from linear algebra that are used in Chapters 7 and 10. In Appendix E we provide an overview of the facilities in MATLAB for doing control analysis and design along with a brief MATLAB tutorial.

Considerable thought was given to the choice of examples. We sought examples that both aid in communicating key concepts and provide a basis for modeling systems encountered in practice (especially based on our experience at IBM and that of colleagues elsewhere in industry and academia). Our most basic example is a single-server queueing system with exponential interarrival and service times and a finite-size buffer ($M/M/1/K$), which provides a means to study the dynamics of admission control and proportional scheduling. The e-mail example based on the IBM Lotus® Domino™ Server[2] provides insight into challenges faced in system identification. The Apache HTTP Server[3] example serves as a vehicle for studying MIMO control. Additional examples include caching with differentiated service and load balancing.

Roadmaps of the Book

The book may be approached in many ways depending on the interests of the reader. As depicted in Figure P.1, computer scientists interested in the basics of control theory should read Chapters 1 and 4 in detail. Chapters 2, 3, and 5 should be skimmed to gain insight into the nature of control system modeling, and Chapter 8 can be read in modest detail to understand the essence of control system design. Chapter 11 will also be of interest since it discusses other areas of control theory that are potentially applicable to computing systems.

Designers of computing systems who want to apply control theory in practice should proceed as shown in Figure P.2 by readying Chapters 1 through 6 and Chapters 8 and 9. State-space techniques, which are described in Chapters 7 and 10, should be approached only after there is a solid understanding of the other chapters. Considerable effort has been made to include worked examples that can be the basis for more extensive analysis and design studies. Also, all of these chapters include a section of extended examples that should stimulate ideas about the range of applications of control theory to computing systems.

---

[2] IBM Lotus Domino is a registered trademark of IBM Corporation.

[3] Apache is a trademark of The Apache Software Foundation and is used with permission.

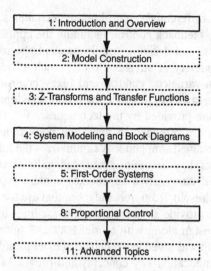

Fig. P.1 *Roadmap for computer scientists interested in the basics of control theory. Dashed boxes indicate chapters that should be skimmed.*

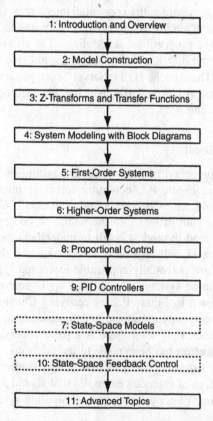

Fig. P.2 *Roadmap for computer scientists interested in applying control theory. Dashed boxes indicate chapters that should be skimmed.*

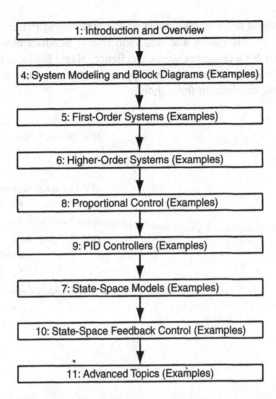

Fig. P.3 *Roadmap for control theorists interested in applications to computing systems. The focus should be on the examples, both the short in-chapter examples and the extended examples at the end of each chapter.*

Control theorists interested in computing system applications should proceed as depicted in Figure P.3. Desirable properties of controllers in computing systems and many examples of computing systems are described in Chapter 1. Chapters 4 through 11 contain a rich set of control problems based on these examples, especially the extended examples at the end of chapters.

Errata and Additions

We intend to post errata and various additions to the book on the Web site *http://www.research.ibm.com/fbcs/*. For example, several of us are currently teaching a class based on the book at Columbia University. This has resulted in a number of new ideas about how to present the material.

Acknowledgments

We wish to acknowledge the many colleagues who have helped with this book in various ways. Xichu Chen at the University of Michigan, Freeman Rawson at IBM Research in Austin, Texas, and Jose Renato Santos at Hewlett-Packard

Laboratory provided detailed comments on the text. David Patterson at the University of California–Berkeley and Armando Fox at Stanford aided us in better focusing the book for a computer science audience. Nagui Halim at IBM Research in Hawthorne, New York, gave strong support for this project from the start and provided constant enthusiasm throughout.

J.L. Hellerstein
IBM Thomas J. Watson Research Center
Hawthorne, New York

Y. Diao
IBM Thomas J. Watson Research Center
Hawthorne, New York

S. Parekh
IBM Thomas J. Watson Research Center
Hawthorne, New York

D.M. Tilbury
Mechanical Engineering Department
University of Michigan
Ann Arbor, Michigan

Part I

Background

1

Introduction and Overview

This book is about feedback control of computing systems. The main idea of feedback control is to use measurements of a system's outputs, such as response times, throughputs, and utilizations, to achieve externally specified goals. This is done by adjusting the system control inputs, such as parameters that affect buffer sizes, scheduling policies, and concurrency levels. Since the measured outputs are used to determine the control inputs, and the inputs then affect the outputs, the architecture is called *feedback* or *closed loop*. Almost any system that is considered automatic has some element of feedback control. In this book we focus on the closed-loop control of computing systems and methods for their analysis and design.

1.1 THE NATURE OF FEEDBACK CONTROL

Feedback control is about regulating the characteristics of a system. We begin with some key concepts: the measured output, which is the characteristic to be regulated to a desired value; the control input, which is what influences the measured output; and a disturbance, which affects the way in which the input affects the output. These are illustrated in a later section.

The reader may be familiar with everyday feedback control systems, such as cruise control in an automobile, a thermostat in a house, or the human sensorimotor system. A cruise control system achieves the desired speed by adjusting the accelerator pedal based on a velocity measurement from the speedometer. Here,

Feedback Control of Computing Systems, by Joseph L. Hellerstein, Yixin Diao, Sujay Parekh, and Dawn M. Tilbury
ISBN 0-471-26637-X   Copyright © 2004 John Wiley & Sons, Inc.

the accelerator pedal adjustments are the control input that provides a means to regulate speed, the measured output. The desired speed is maintained even when the car goes up or down hills or encounters head or tail winds, all of which are examples of disturbances that affect the relationship between the control input and the measured output. A thermostat achieves the desired temperature (output) by adjusting the furnace cycle and fan (input). The desired temperature is maintained even when the outside temperature increases or decreases (disturbance). The sensorimotor system achieves the desired hand position (output) to pick up an object by adjusting the muscle tensions (inputs) based on the current position sensed by the eyes and touch.

These concepts of feedback control apply to computing systems as well. Consider a computing system with a desired output characteristic. For example, operators of computing systems, or *administrators*, may want each of three Apache HTTP Servers [24] to run at no greater than 66% utilization, so that if any one of them fails, the other two can immediately absorb the entire load. Here, the measured output is CPU utilization. In computing systems, the measured output typically depends on the nature of the requests being served, or *workload*. Workload is often characterized in terms of the arrival process (e.g., Poisson, self-similar), and the distribution of service times for the resources used (e.g., CPU, memory, and database locks) [20]. In our studies of the Apache HTTP Server, CPU utilization depends on the workload and the control input. The workload is characterized by the request rate and whether the requests are for static or dynamic hypertext pages. The control input is the maximum number of connections that the server permits as specified by the MaxClients parameter. The workload is uncontrolled and so can be viewed as a disturbance. The control input MaxClients can be manipulated by an administrator or an automatic controller to affect CPU utilization.

Much of feedback control deals with understanding how the control input and disturbance affect the measured output. Continuing with the Apache HTTP Server example, as MaxClients increases, the CPU utilization increases. However, the effect is not instantaneous. A larger MaxClients only *allows* more users to connect; the system must wait some time for the users to arrive. Similarly, when MaxClients is decreased, current users are not disconnected until their sessions have timed out. Further, the value of MaxClients that results in a 66% utilization depends on the current workload, which may be unknown *a priori* and/or may change over time. Feedback control provides a method for setting MaxClients *automatically* to achieve the desired utilization that takes into account these dynamics and the effects of disturbances.

With this context we can describe feedback control in more detail. However, before doing so, a change in perspective is required. In computing systems we think in terms of the flow of work units or data through a system. Thus, input–output relationships reflect how work is done and/or data are transformed. Control theory also relies heavily on input–output relationships. However, the semantics are different. In control analysis, the inputs and outputs are metric values (e.g., CPU utilization) and/or control settings (e.g., MaxClients).

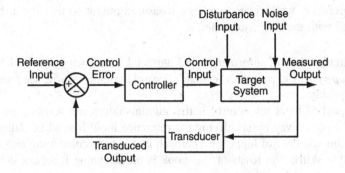

Fig. 1.1 *Block diagram of a feedback control system. The reference input is the desired value of the system's measured output. The controller adjusts the setting of control input to the target system so that its measured output is equal to the reference input. The transducer represents effects such as unit conversions and delays.*

Figure 1.1 is an example of a single-input, single-output *SISO* control system, a control system that has a single control input (i.e., MaxClients) and a single measured output (i.e., CPU utilization). More commonly in computing we deal with *MIMO* systems, which have multiple control inputs (e.g., settings of configuration parameters) and multiple measured outputs (e.g., response times and throughputs by service class). For pedagogical purposes, the sequel focuses on SISO systems, although MIMO considerations are addressed in passing.

The essential elements of feedback control system are depicted in Figure 1.1. These elements are:

- *Control error*, which is the difference between the reference input and the measured output.
- *Control input*, which is a parameter that affects the behavior of the target system and can be adjusted dynamically (such as the MaxClients parameter in the Apache HTTP Server).
- *Controller*, which determines the setting of the control input needed to achieve the reference input. The controller computes values of the control input based on current and past values of control error.
- *Disturbance input*, which is any change that affects the way in which the control input influences the measured output.
- *Measured output*, which is a measurable characteristic of the target system, such as CPU utilization and response time.
- *Noise input*, which is any effect that changes the measured output produced by the target system. This is also called *sensor noise* or *measurement noise*.
- *Reference input*, which is the desired value of the measured outputs (or transformations of them), such as CPU utilization, should be 66%. Sometimes, the reference input is referred to as *desired output* or the *setpoint*.
- *Target system*, which is the computing system to be controlled (see the examples of target systems in Section 1.6).

- *Transducer*, which transforms the measured output so that it can be compared with the reference input.

The circular flow of information in Figure 1.1 motivates our use of the term *closed-loop system* to refer to a feedback control system. We will use these terms interchangeably.

An appeal of feedback control is that administrators can achieve the desired output in a direct way by specifying the reference input instead of indirectly by manipulating the control input (an approach that is time consuming and requires considerable skill). The focus of this book is on designing feedback controllers to achieve a desired output.

The disturbance inputs are factors that affect the measured output but for which there is no governing control input. The disturbance input is depicted as a second input to the target system in Figure 1.1. An example of a disturbance input in the Apache HTTP Server is the executions of tasks such as backups and virus scans (collectively referred to as *administrative tasks*) that affect the relationship between the control input MaxClients and the measured output CPU utilizations and response times. One reason that feedback control is so powerful and so widely used is that it can ensure that the measured output is very close to the reference input even in the presence of disturbances.

The *transducer* transforms the measured output into the values used by the controller. An example of a transducer is a moving-average filter that smooths the stochastics of computer system measurements. Another example is a measurement sensor, especially if the sensor introduces time delays because of the manner in which measurements are collected. A third example is unit conversions, such as converting from queue lengths into response times using formulas such as Little's result [35] in systems that do not measure response times directly. Not all feedback systems contain a transducer. However, in other systems, the transducer is a complicated element that performs multiple functions.

Before closing this section, we note that systematic construction of controllers requires a model of the input–output relationships of the target system. We refer to this as the *system model*. Because of the central role that the system model plays in controller design, a significant fraction of the book is devoted to modeling techniques (especially based on linear system theory) and their application to computing systems.

1.2 CONTROL OBJECTIVES

Controllers are designed for some intended purpose. We refer to this purpose as the *control objective*. The most common objectives are:

- *Regulatory control.* Ensure that the measured output is equal to (or near) the reference input. For example, the utilization of a Web server should be maintained at 66%. The focus here is on changes in the reference input, such as changing the target utilization from 66% to 75% if a fourth server becomes available. The term *tracking control* is used if the reference input changes frequently.

- *Disturbance rejection.* Ensure that disturbances acting on the system do not significantly affect the measured output. For example, when a backup or virus scan is run on a Web server, the overall utilization of the system is maintained at 66%. This differs from regulatory control in that we focus on changes in the disturbance input, not in the reference input.

- *Optimization.* Obtain the "best" value of the measured output. For example, in Chapter 11 we describe a fuzzy controller that adjusts MaxClients in the Apache HTTP Server so as to minimize response times.

Much of the book is about regulatory control with disturbance rejection. The need for regulatory control arises in three ways in computing systems. First, as already noted, regulation arises when there is a need to maintain reserve capacity (sometimes referred to as *head room*). Second, regulatory control is used for a kind of constrained optimization, such as "maximize throughput subject to response time being no greater than 1 second." A common heuristic for such an objective is to accept as many requests as possible without exceeding the response-time constraint (e.g., regulate response time to be 1 second). Third, regulation is important in the enforcement of service-level agreements. Disturbance rejection addresses the fact that the foregoing must be done in the presence of time-varying loads and changes in hardware and software configurations.

To elaborate on the last point, *service-level agreements* (or *SLAs*) are a contract between a service provider and its customers. Such agreements consist of one or more *service-level objectives* (*SLOs*). Examples of service providers include Internet service providers, application service providers, and internal IT organizations. An example of an SLO is: "Gold customer response times should be no greater than 2 seconds." There are three parts to an SLO: the metric (e.g., response time), the bound (e.g., 2 seconds), and a relational operator (e.g., less than). Intuitively, service providers want to have sufficient resources to meet their SLOs. But they do not want to have more resources than required since doing so imposes unnecessary costs. As a result, SLO enforcement often becomes a regulation problem. In terms of the architecture in Figure 1.1, the SLO metric is the measured output, and the SLO bound is the reference input.

The choice of control objective typically depends on the application. Indeed, with multiuse target systems, the same target system may have multiple controllers with different SLOs.

1.3 PROPERTIES OF FEEDBACK CONTROL SYSTEMS

There are several properties of feedback control systems that should be considered when comparing controllers for computing systems. Our choice of metrics is drawn from experience with the commercial information technology systems.

Other properties may be of interest in different settings. For example, [43] discuss properties of interest for control of real-time systems.

Below, we motivate and present the main ideas of the properties considered. More formal definitions are given later in the book.

- A system is said to be *stable* if for any bounded input, the output is also bounded. (We discuss stability in detail in Chapter 3 .) Stability is typically the first property considered in designing control systems since unstable systems cannot be used for mission-critical work.

- The control system is *accurate* if the measured output converges (or becomes sufficiently close) to the reference input. Accurate systems are essential to ensuring that control objectives are met, such as differentiating between gold and silver classes of service and ensuring that throughput is maximized without exceeding response-time constraints. Typically, we do not quantify accuracy. Rather, we measure inaccuracy. For a system in steady state, its inaccuracy, or *steady-state error*, is the steady-state value of the control error.

- The system has *short settling times* if it converges quickly to its steady-state value. Short settling times are particularly important for disturbance rejection in the presence of time-varying workloads so that convergence is obtained before the workload changes.

- The system should achieve its objectives in a manner that *does not overshoot*. Consider a system in which the objective is to maximize throughput subject to the constraint that response time is less than 1 second, which is often achieved by a regulator that keeps response times at their upper limit so that throughput is maximized. Suppose that incoming requests change so that they are less CPU intensive and hence response times decrease to 0.5 second. Then, by avoiding overshoot, we mean that as the controller changes the control input that causes throughput to increase (and hence response time to increase), response times should not exceed 1 second.

Much of the focus of the book is on these *SASO* properties: stability, accuracy, settling time, and overshoot.

We begin with what constitutes a stable system. For computing systems we want the output of feedback control to converge, although it may not be constant due to the stochastic nature of the system. To refine this further, computing systems have operating regions (i.e., combinations of workloads and configuration settings) in which they perform acceptably and other operating regions in which they do not. Thus, in general, we refer to the stability of a system within an operating region. Clearly, if a system is not stable, its utility is severely limited. In particular, the system's response times will be large and highly variable, a situation that can make the system unusable.

Figure 1.2 displays an instability in the Apache HTTP Server that employs an improperly designed controller. The horizontal axis is time, and the vertical axis is CPU utilization (which ranges between 0 and 1). The solid line is the

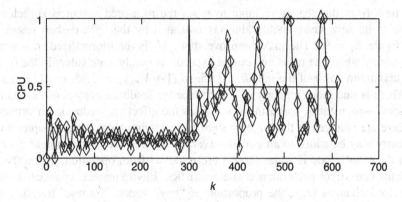

Fig. 1.2 *Example of an unstable feedback control system for the Apache HTTP Server. The instability results from having an improperly designed controller.*

reference input for CPU utilization, and the line with markers is the measured value. During the first 300 seconds, the system operates in open loop. When the controller is turned on, a reference input of 0.5 is used. At this point, the system begins to oscillate and the amplitude of the oscillations increases. This is a result of a controller design that overreacts to the stochastics in the CPU utilization measurement. Note that the amplitude of the oscillations is constrained by the range of the CPU utilization metric.

If the feedback system is stable, it makes sense to consider the remaining SASO properties: accuracy, settling time, and overshoot. The vertical lines in Figure 1.3 plot the measured output of a stable feedback system. Initially, the (normalized) reference input is 0. At time 0, the reference input is changed to its steady value $r_{ss} = 2$. The system responds and its measured output eventually converges to $y_{ss} = 3$, as indicated by the heavy dashed line. The steady-state error e_{ss} is -1, where $e_{ss} = r_{ss} - y_{ss}$. The settling time of the system k_s is

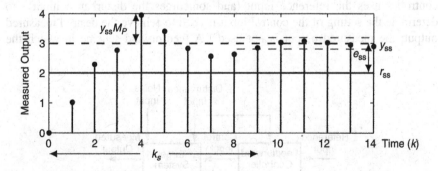

Fig. 1.3 *Response of a stable system to a step change in the reference input. At time 0, the reference input changes from 0 to 2. The system reaches steady state when its output always lies between the lightweight dashed lines. Depicted are the steady-state error (e_{ss}), settling time (k_s), and maximum overshoot (M_p).*

the time from the change in input to when the measured output is sufficiently close to its new steady-state value (as indicated by the light dashed lines). In the figure, $k_s = 9$. The maximum overshoot M_P is the (normalized) maximum amount by which the measured output exceeds its steady-state value. In the figure the maximum value of the output is 3.95, so $(1 + M_P)y_{ss} = 3.95$, or $M_P = 0.32$.

There is one more property of importance for feedback control of computing systems—robustness. Robustness addresses the effect on feedback performance if there are changes in the target system or its environment. For example, more memory may be added to an e-mail server, a clustered Web server might operate in a degraded mode if some servers are removed from operation, and software updates can affect performance characteristics. Environmental changes include workload changes (e.g., the proportion of "buy" versus "browse" transactions) and the location of network access points. Informally, a controller is robust if such changes have little effect on the control system properties, especially stability and accuracy.

The properties of feedback systems are used in two ways. The first relates to the analysis. Here, we are interested in determining if the system is stable as well as measuring and/or estimating its steady-state error, settling time, and maximum overshoot. The second is in the design of feedback systems. Here, the properties are *design goals*. That is, we construct the feedback system to have the desired values of steady-state error, settling times, and maximum overshoot.

1.4 OPEN-LOOP VERSUS CLOSED-LOOP CONTROL

Although closed-loop control has considerable appeal, its use requires, among other things, online measurements and careful design to ensure desirable system properties, especially stability, accuracy, short settling times, and small overshoot.

An alternative is *open-loop control*, a technique that avoids using the measured output to adjust the control input. (Open-loop control is sometimes referred to as *feedforward control*.) Figure 1.4 depicts such a system. The feedforward controller uses the reference input (and sometimes the disturbance input) to determine the setting of the control input needed to achieve the desired measured output; the measured output is not used. A feedforward scheme in which the

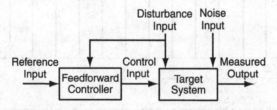

Fig. 1.4 *Block diagram of feedforward control. In contrast to Figure 1.1, the measured output is not used by the (feedforward) controller to determine the control input needed to achieve the reference input.*

TABLE 1.1 Comparison of Open- and Closed-Loop Control

	Open Loop	Closed Loop
Avoids using measured outputs	Yes	No
Cannot make stable system unstable	Yes	No
Simple system model	No	Yes
Adapts to disturbances	No	Yes

control input is a deterministic function of the reference (and/or disturbance) input is stable if the target system is stable. However, to construct such a system, we must have an accurate model of the target system (e.g., as a result of detailed experiments) from which the setting of the control input is determined. This model must be robust to changes in the system and its operating environment (including disturbances such as the execution of administrative tasks).

To illustrate these points, consider the Apache HTTP Server. The administrator may experiment with several different MaxClients and find one that results in a CPU utilization of 66%. However, if the workloads are time varying (e.g., by time of day, day of week), MaxClients may need to be adjusted to maintain the desired CPU utilization. Unlike closed-loop control, open-loop control cannot compensate for disturbances or noise. In contrast, closed-loop control can provide such compensation. Also, closed-loop systems do not require an accurate system model, something that is difficult to obtain in practice.

Table 1.1 summarizes the comparison of open- and closed-loop systems. Although open-loop systems have appeal in terms of reducing design complexity (e.g., avoiding the use of measured outputs) and ensuring stability, they are rarely used in practice because they cannot adapt to change and it is almost impossible to obtain an accurate system model. The remainder of the book focuses on closed-loop systems, especially on designing feedback controllers that are stable, minimize steady-state error, and have short settling times and small overshoot.

1.5 SUMMARY OF APPLICATIONS OF CONTROL THEORY TO COMPUTING SYSTEMS

Since the early 1990s, there has been broad interest in the application of control theory to computing systems, especially in the areas of data networks operating systems, middleware (e.g., Web servers, database servers), multimedia, and power management. Below we summarize these efforts, although we make no claim that this is a comprehensive survey.

In the area of data networks, there has been considerable interest in applying control theory to problems of flow control. One of the first, [34], develops the concept of a Rate Allocating Server that regulates the flow of packets through queues. Others have applied control theory to short-term rate variations in TCP (e.g., [40]) and some have considered stochastic control [5]. More recently, there have been detailed models of TCP developed in continuous time (using fluid flow approximations) that have produced interesting insights into the operation of buffer management schemes in routers (see [29], [28]). The area of Asynchronous Transfer Mode (ATM) Networks has been an area of intensive exploitation of control theory in the 1990s (e.g., [10], [58], [32], [63], [56], [46]). However, the limited success of ATM technology and the use of continuous time and/or advanced control techniques (e.g., stochastic control) meant that there was little adoption of control theory by computing practitioners.

Although not nearly as prodigious, there has been considerable interest in applying control techniques to operating systems as well. [6] describes the details of control techniques widely used in IBM's Multiple Virtual Storage (MVS) operating system to achieve several kinds of service level objectives. The foregoing is based primarily on detailed knowledge of the operating system's control inputs and measured outputs. Others have proposed approaches that require little knowledge of details, relying instead on learning algorithms (e.g., [11]).

One of the most recent areas in which control theory has been applied to is middleware. Middleware are software systems that facilitate the development of robust, enterprise level applications. Examples include application servers (e.g., Apache HTTP Server), database management systems (e.g., IBM's Universal Database Server), and e-mail servers (e.g., IBM Lotus Domino Server). There are three types of control problems that are typically addressed. The first is to provide a capability for enforcing service level agreements in that customers receive the service levels for which they contracted. Often referred to as *service differentiation*, this is achieved by enforcing relative delays [2], preferential caching of data [44], or in special cases modifying application codes to insert effectors (e.g., [54]). The second problem is to regulate resource utilizations so that they are not excessive, either because of reliability considerations (e.g., some software systems become fragile at heavy loads) or because of system design (e.g., to allow spare capacity for fail overs). Examples here include a mixture of queueing and control theory used to regulate the Apache HTTP Server [62], regulation of the IBM Lotus Domino Server [53], and multiple-input, multiple-output control of the Apache HTTP Server (e.g., simultaneous regulation of CPU and memory resources) [17]. The third problem that is often addressed is to optimize the system configuration, such as to minimize response times [18].

Management of multimedia streams has also been an area of focus for applying control theory to computing systems. The challenge here is that end-user performance is related to receiving a regular flow of correlated streams of data (e.g., voice and video), whereas the underlying systems operate more on a contention basis (e.g., execution priority). One solution to this is to regulate process priorities in accordance with the desired service levels (e.g., [61]). Another approach is to develop a control framework in which to build the capabilities for providing these service levels (e.g., [39]).

There is one last area we mention in passing—dynamic power management. The expense and engineering complications associated with supplying power to computational elements have motivated intensive investigations into how power can be managed within computing elements. Considerations here include addressing nonstationary service requests [15], the success of which largely depends on being able to model dynamics (a key concern in any control system). More extensive discussions of power-aware computing can be found in [65] and related articles in the same issue.

We close this discussion by pointing to an overview of the application of control techniques to computing in [60] and related articles in the same issue.

1.6 COMPUTER EXAMPLES OF FEEDBACK CONTROL SYSTEMS

In this section we present several examples of feedback control in computing systems to illustrate the kinds of dynamics that must be addressed, along with possible approaches and technical challenges. Many of these examples are used in later chapters to demonstrate techniques for control analysis and design. Each example begins by describing the computing system, such as the flow of Web requests through the Apache HTTP Server. Then the control problem is presented in terms of Figure 1.1, and we discuss the issues in control design and implementation. A common theme is the difference between the computing systems perspective and the control perspective. In particular, the former emphasizes the flow of work though functional components of a target system. The latter focuses on regulating measurement values that characterize the operation of the target system.

1.6.1 IBM Lotus Domino Server

Today's corporate information technology environment typically devotes a substantial fraction of its budget to e-mail service. This example considers a specific e-mail server in detail—the IBM Lotus Domino Server. We also refer to this as the *Notes Server*.

As shown in Figure 1.5, Lotus Notes is a client–server application. Client machines interact with end users to provide access to e-mail and other applications

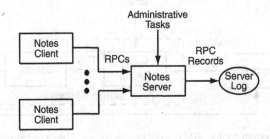

Fig. 1.5 *Components and data flows in a system with the IBM Lotus Domino Server. End users interact with Lotus Notes client software, which sends remote procedure calls (RPCs) to the IBM Lotus Domino Server. Records of RPCs processed are written to the server log.*

enabled by the IBM Lotus Domino Server. The server uses a database abstraction to provide an application computing environment. For example, clients access e-mail by opening an e-mail database, obtaining a view of the elements in the database, and then reading, updating, deleting, and inserting entries in the database. The interaction between the client and server is in the form of remote procedure calls (RPCs). The IBM Lotus Domino Server maintains a server log of statistics on RPCs once they have completed. In addition to end-user-initiated RPCs, the IBM Lotus Domino Server handles various administrative tasks.

Administrators responsible for the IBM Lotus Domino Server pay considerable attention to the number of RPCs currently being processed by the server. We refer to this as *RIS*, the number of RPCs in the server. RIS is closely related to the number of active users, those users with an RPC being processed by the server. If RIS becomes too large, there may be excessive use of CPU, memory, and other resources, thereby causing poor performance.

One way to limit RIS is by the `MaxUsers` parameter, which can be adjusted dynamically through a console interface. `MaxUsers` constrains the number of concurrent sessions, that is, the number of client connections to the IBM Lotus Domino Server. It is important to note that the number of connections is *not* the same as RIS since (1) connected users may be thinking and hence have no RPC in the server, and (2) there are administrative tasks that are treated in a manner similar to user RPCs but for which there is no connection. Thus, the relationship between `MaxUsers` and active users is approximate at best. In practice, this is resolved by having administrators monitor server resource use and adjust `MaxUsers` so as to achieve the desired value for RIS.

From the foregoing we see that one control objective for the IBM Lotus Domino Server is regulating RIS. Figure 1.6 shows how a controller can be used to achieve this regulation. The target system is the IBM Lotus Domino Server in combination with a sensor that uses the server log to obtain RPC statistics. The administrator specifies a reference input for RIS. The control error is the difference between this reference input and measured RIS (as obtained from the sensor). From this, the controller computes settings of the control input

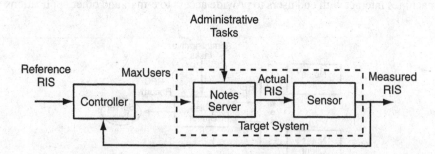

Fig. 1.6 Control system for the IBM Lotus Domino Server. The target system encompasses both the IBM Lotus Domino Server and the sensor. The reference input is the desired number of RPCs in the server (RIS). The measured output is obtained through the server log. The control input is `MaxUsers`.

MaxUsers. Note that the sensor is not treated as a transducer since it affects the measured output.

One subtlety in this design is that the sensor introduces a delay due to waiting for the RPC to complete so that the server log can be written. As we show in later chapters, such delays can have a dramatic effect on the properties of the feedback control system. Further details of feedback control of the IBM Lotus Domino Server can be found in [53].

1.6.2 Queueing Systems

Queueing systems are widely used to model the performance of computing systems. As such, queueing models provide an excellent way to study a variety of control issues in computing systems. Consider an elementary queue, as shown in Figure 1.7. Work requests (or customers) arrive and are placed in a queue or buffer (the rectangle with multiple vertical lines), where they are selected for processing by the server (the circle). Requests may be distinguished as belonging to difference service classes. Examples of Web services are *browsing* (which may only require searching the online catalog) and *buying* (which typically involves a secure server and a third-party payment system). E-commerce sites would like to use these class distinctions to allocate resources in a more favorable way to those users who have the most potential to make a purchase.

The queueing model can be applied to the problem of meeting service-level objectives. Consider the SLO "Response time for a credit card inquiry should be less than 5 seconds." One approach to handling this constraint is to reduce the delay experienced by credit card inquiries by limiting the number of "other" requests that are accepted into the queue; the other requests are directed elsewhere (e.g., using the HTTP REDIRECT verb). In terms of the queueing system example, response time can be regulated using as a control input the size of the buffer (in units of the number of requests that can be queued), with the understanding that requests that do not fit into the buffer are redirected.

Figure 1.8(a) depicts a feedback control system that regulates response times for the queueing system described above. The implicit objective of this system can be expressed as a service-level objective—maximize the number of requests processed subject to constraints on response times. One example of such an objective is service providers who obtain revenue from subscriber transactions but must abide by SLOs. In the system depicted, the reference input is the

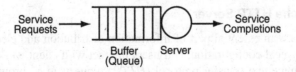

Fig. 1.7 *Single-server queueing system. Requests are placed in a buffer, where they await service. Completed requests depart the system.*

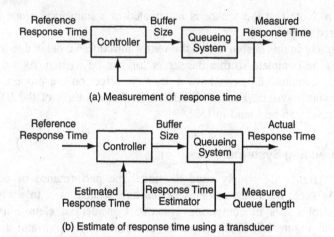

(a) Measurement of response time

(b) Estimate of response time using a transducer

Fig. 1.8 Use of a transducer to estimate response times in a queueing system.

desired response time, and the control input is the buffer size. The control error is computed by subtracting measured response times from the reference response time.

Figure 1.8(a) can be extended in many ways. First, it may be difficult or undesirable to use measured response times, especially for long-running transactions. The issue here is that for long-running transactions the use of response-time measurements introduces delay into the feedback loop since work must complete before its response time is recorded. Figure 1.8(b) depicts an alternative approach that is appropriate if arrival rates are fairly constant. Here, a transducer is used to estimate response time from the queue length (which can be measured instantaneously) using Little's result (e.g., [35]).

Some other extensions to Figure 1.8(a) are also worthy of note. There may be other control inputs, such as the fraction of the server devoted to each service class, a technique that is referred to as *generalized processor sharing*. Thus, if a gold customer is about to exceed its response-time constraints, and a silver customer is well below its constraint, a larger fraction of the server may be devoted to gold. Other generalizations include having multiple measured outputs (e.g., queue length, utilization) and using a moving-average filter to smooth stochastics in the output. Further details on queueing systems can be found in [35] and [4].

1.6.3 Apache HTTP Server

Web servers are an essential part of information distribution and electronic commerce. In a typical configuration, end users interact with client workstations that in turn send hypertext transfer protocol (*HTTP*) requests (e.g., browse a page or download a file) to one or more Web servers. The Web server replies with the appropriate information.

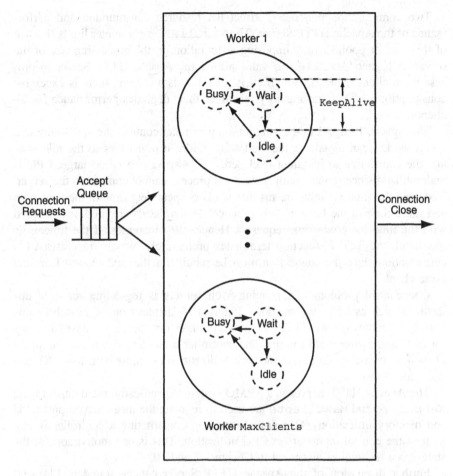

Fig. 1.9 *Apache architecture and session flow.* MaxClients *is the maximum number of workers; there is one worker devoted to each connection.* KeepAlive *is the maximum time that a worker remains in the wait state before the connection to its client is closed. While in the wait state, workers accept requests only from their connected client.*

The Apache HTTP Server [24] is structured as a pool of workers (either threads or processes, depending on the specific software release), as shown in Figure 1.9. Requests enter the server at the accept queue, where they wait until a worker (indicated by the large circles) is available. A worker is available if it is in the "idle" state. While the worker is processing a request, it is in the "busy" state. The widely used HTTP 1.1 protocol provides for persistent connections. That is, the worker does not close the connection after the request has been processed. Instead, the worker enters the "wait" state, and the connection remains open so that subsequent requests from the same client can be processed more efficiently. Note that while the worker is in the wait state, it cannot process requests from clients other than the one to which it is connected.

Two configuration parameters affect the resource consumption and performance of the Apache HTTP Server. The MaxClients parameter limits the size of this worker pool, thereby imposing a limitation on the processing rate of the server. A higher MaxClients value allows the Apache HTTP Server to process more client requests. But if MaxClients is too large, there is excessive consumption of CPU and memory resources that degrades performance for all clients.

The Apache KeepAlive configuration parameter controls the maximum time that a worker can remain in the wait state before it transitions to the idle state and the connection to its client is closed. If KeepAlive is too large, CPU is underutilized since clients with requests to process cannot connect to the server. Reducing the timeout value means that workers spend less time in the wait state and more time in the busy state (if connection overheads are modest compared with the time for processing requests). Hence, CPU increases. If the timeout is too small, the TCP connection terminates prematurely, which increases CPU consumption since the connection must be rebuilt for the next request from the same client.

One control problem in managing Web servers is regulating resource utilizations such as CPU and memory. Figure 1.10 displays one approach to this regulation in the Apache HTTP Server. Administrators specify the desired values for CPU and memory utilizations. The controller uses these two reference inputs as well as measured CPU and memory utilizations to adjust both KeepAlive and MaxClients.

The Apache HTTP Server is a MIMO system. Specifically, the control inputs KeepAlive and MaxClients are used to regulate the measured outputs CPU and memory utilizations. One complication in constructing a controller is that both of the control inputs affect CPU utilization. This is one motivation for the state-space techniques discussed in Chapters 7 and 10.

Further discussion of the Apache HTTP Server can be found in [24] and [2], [42], and [17] provide examples of applying linear feedback control to the Apache HTTP Server. A more elaborate scheme that includes nonlinear control is described in [57].

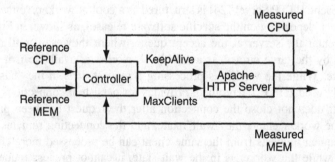

Fig. 1.10 Regulatory control of utilization for the Apache HTTP Server target system.

1.6.4 Random Early Detection of Router Overloads

A central element of the Internet is TCP, the transmission control protocol, which provides end-to-end communication across network nodes. The designers of TCP were concerned about regulating traffic flows in the presence of network congestion. One way in which this regulation occurs is at routers that direct packets between endpoints. In particular, routers have finite-size buffers. Thus, to prevent buffer overflows during congestion, routers may discard packets (which results in their later retransmission as part of the TCP protocol).

Unfortunately, by the time that buffer overflows occur, it may be that the network is already congested. The idea behind random early detection (RED) is to take action before congestion becomes severe. RED measures how much of critical buffers are consumed, a metric that is referred to as the *buffer fill level* (BFL). As depicted in Figure 1.11, RED introduces the capability of randomly dropping packets even if buffer capacity is not exceeded. If BFL is small, no packets are dropped. However, as BFL grows larger, progressively more packets are dropped.

RED has been shown to reduce network congestion and to improve network throughput [23]. However, one challenge with using RED in practice is specifying its configuration parameters, especially the BFL at which packets start being dropped and the maximum drop probability. One approach to this tuning has been to view RED as a feedback control system with a regulation objective in which the reference input is a desired BFL and the control input is drop probability. Figure 1.12 depicts this perspective. Control theory is used to study the impact on stability and other properties for different settings of RED configuration parameters [28]. Finally, proportional–integral (PI) control has been used for management of the accept queues of network routers [29].

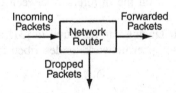

Fig. 1.11 *Router operation under random early detection. Incoming packets are dropped based on an adjustable drop probability. Drop probability controls the buffer fill level inside the router.*

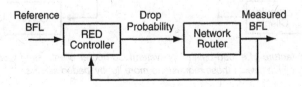

Fig. 1.12 *Feedback control of buffer fill level in a router. The reference input is the desired BFL, and the drop probability is the control input.*

1.6.5   Load Balancing

One of the most common techniques for constructing high-performance computing systems is to use a collection of similarly configured servers (often called a *server farm* or *cluster*) and balance the load between the servers. There is a vast literature on load balancing, including its use in multiple source routing [68], implementations for L4 switches [30], techniques for balancing loads in data warehouses [45], and redirection algorithms for web-server systems [13]. There have also been studies that analyze general strategies, especially static load balancing (which makes use of long-term trends) versus dynamic load balancing (which exploits current changes in state) [33]. Herein, we describe how load balancing can be viewed in terms of control theory.

Figure 1.13 displays the architecture of a load-balancing system. There are multiple computer clients that generate work requests such as Web page accesses and files to download. Instead of sending these requests to a specific server, they are sent to a work router that selects an appropriate server based on its server load levels. Work routers may use a round-robin scheme in which servers are chosen in sequence as requests arrive. To account for differences in loads on the servers as well as differences in their processing capabilities, a routing weight is employed. Servers with a larger weight receive more requests.

Figure 1.14 depicts a feedback control system for achieving balanced utilizations (or other metrics) across the servers in a load-balancing system. The target system encompasses multiple blocks, as indicated by the dashed rectangle. The work router and servers appear in Figure 1.13. The block "computed balance level" is added to calculate the degree to which the servers are balanced for one or more metrics. For example, the balance level might be the difference between the maximum and minimum utilization of the servers. The control input is the routing weight, and the measured output is the balance level. The controller computes routing weights based on the difference between the reference input and computed balance level.

More details on load balancing can be found in [31] and [7]. An application of load balancing to peer-to-peer networks is described in [52].

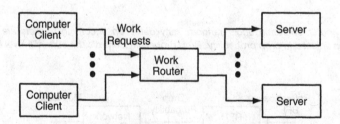

Fig. 1.13 *Architecture of a load-balancing system. Computer clients send work requests to the work router, which directs these requests to more lightly loaded servers.*

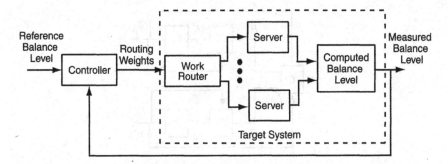

Fig. 1.14 *Feedback control for load balancing. The target system encompasses the work router, the servers, and an element that computes the balance level. The reference input is how closely utilizations (or other metrics) should match between servers. The control input to the work router are routing weights, the relative fraction of load that should be routed to the servers.*

1.6.6 Streaming Media

A rapidly growing area of interest is that of streaming media. Examples include Internet radio, Internet TV, and live music. Such applications require the continuous delivery of information at a predetermined rate. This is a considerable challenge in conventional computer systems that are more oriented toward maximizing throughput rather than a guaranteed rate of delivery. In particular, the service-level objectives are to keep response times below specified levels to avoid "jerky" video, interrupted audio, and so on.

Providing support for streaming media can be viewed as regulating response times for these applications. One way of doing this is to control the amount of nonstreaming work on the streaming resources so as to (1) ensure that the streaming work complies with its service-level objectives, and (2) maximize the throughput of the resources. Figure 1.15 displays a simple illustration of these ideas. In Figure 1.16 there are two resources (e.g., CPU and disk) that are required to process streaming requests. Other work may enter the system as

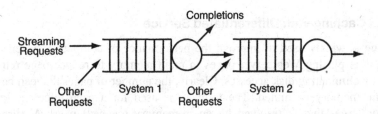

Fig. 1.15 *Simple example of streaming media. The example consists of two queueing systems in tandem, such as CPU and disk. There are two classes of customers, streaming requests and other requests. Streaming requests must traverse both queues within a constrained time if service-level objectives are to be met.*

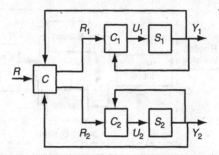

Fig. 1.16 Feedback control to enforce streaming service-level objectives. S_1 and S_2 correspond to systems 1 and 2 in Figure 1.15. Each system is controlled separately using a scheme such as that shown in Figure 1.8(a). A higher-level controller regulates the reference inputs for these control systems so as to achieve an end-to-end throughput that complies with the service-level objective.

well. The service-level objective is to ensure that the load carried (throughput) in the streaming system is sufficient for the application (e.g., 30 frames/second for streaming video).

Figure 1.16 translates this into regulatory control. A convenient approach is to employ a control hierarchy. That is, the individual systems use a scheme such as in Figure 1.8(a). Here R_1, C_1, S_1, and Y_1 correspond to the reference input, controller, queueing system, and measured output in Figure 1.8(a). Here, C_1 is a local controller for resource 1 (e.g., CPU). The reference input specifies the S_1 throughput required to achieve the overall service-level objective; the controller adjusts the resource allocation U_1 used by S_1 (e.g., CPU allocation), which results in the measured throughput of Y_1. R_2, C_2, U_2, S_2, and Y_2 are defined in the same way for a second queueing system. A higher-level controller, C, determines the setting for the reference inputs R_1 and R_2 based on their outputs and the service-level objective specified by R. An example of controlling streaming media is contained in [1], and more details on the connections with queueing theory can be found in [26].

1.6.7 Caching with Differentiated Service

Caching is widely used to improve the performance of computing systems. An example is placing Web server pages in main memory to reduce page retrieval times by eliminating disk accesses. Clearly, the number of pages that can be kept in main memory is limited. The term *hit* is used for a page reference (either read or write) that is resolved by an in-memory (cached) page. A *miss* is a memory access that requires reading disk memory for a noncached page. A good caching system keeps in memory those pages with the highest probability of being accessed next.

The performance of a caching system is measured in terms of average access time. Since the access time to a cached page is typically much less than accessing a page in backing store, performance is determined largely by the hit probability.

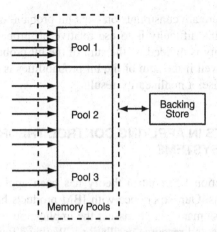

Fig. 1.17 *Caching system that supports differentiated service. Requests are directed to the storage pools that correspond to their service class. Requests for data that are not in a memory pool require physical I/O from the backing store.*

If reasonable algorithms are used to manage cache memory, the hit probability increases with the size of cache memory.

Now consider a variation on the caching problem. A Web content service provider has several classes of customers, differentiated by how much they pay for the service. Providing service differentiation requires having a caching system that can deliver desired hit probabilities for each customer class. Figure 1.17 displays an architecture for how this can be accomplished. Requests, which are indicated by the arrows, are made to specific cache pools (blocks of memory) of different sizes. Requests that cannot be satisfied by in-memory data require access to the backing store, which takes considerably longer (often by a factor of 1000).

Once again, we have a regulation problem. The reference inputs are the desired response times for each class of service, and the control input is the pool size. Figure 1.18 displays a diagram of a feedback control system for differentiated caching. Note that there are multiple control inputs since each pool is controlled separately. Also, there are multiple outputs since there is a measured output for each service class.

Further details on differentiated service for caching can be found in [44]. In particular, the authors address a couple of challenging problems in applying control theory. For example, with multiple customer classes and a finite amount

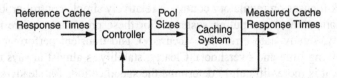

Fig. 1.18 *Feedback control to enforce differentiated service in a caching system. The target system is the caching system.*

of cache memory, there are constraints on what hit probabilities are feasible. One way to circumvent this difficulty is to use relative hit probabilities. That is, the absolute hit probability is divided by the sum of the hit probabilities of the other classes. This works well if the sum of the hit probabilities is constant or changes very slowly. Otherwise, a nonlinearity results.

1.7 CHALLENGES IN APPLYING CONTROL THEORY TO COMPUTING SYSTEMS

As discussed in Section 1.5, control theory has been applied to a wide range of computing systems. Our experience with IBM products has been that control theory provides a systematic way to assess the implications of controller designs such as settling times and resource oscillations. We have found these insights to be of great value in designing real world systems.

Unfortunately, control theory is rarely used by computing practitioners. A central goal of this book is to distill from control theory those techniques that are most important for computing systems and make them accessible to computing researchers and practitioners. Much as there is only a small subset of queueing theory that is essential to deal with steady-state stochastics of computing systems (e.g., Little's result, $M/G/1$, product form networks), we believe that control theory can be used to address dynamics in computing systems.

Control theory has developed a wide range of very sophisticated tools. Our philosophy is to start with the simplest tools and assess their value for controlling computing systems. In this book, "simple tools" means linear, deterministic, time-invariant systems. This approach is consistent with current research in applying control theory to computing systems in that the research contributions have focused on appropriate models of target system and/or novel ways of applying existing control theory. Very little innovation has been done with extending control theory or even the choice of controller designs. For example, most of the existing work uses a proportional–integral controller, which has been the standard industrial controller in the electromechanical and chemical industries for more than 40 years.

With this in mind, we see three broad areas of challenges in applying control theory to computing systems: (1) developing evaluation criteria for feedback controllers, (2) constructing models of the target system and controller, and (3) designing the feedback controllers.

The most fundamental question concerns the criteria for evaluating controllers. This book focuses on regulatory control, a relatively simple control problem with broad application to computing systems. For these problems, we are interested in stability, steady-state error (i.e., accuracy), and transient performance (especially, settling time and overshoot). Clearly, stability is almost always desirable. However, it is more difficult to determine the specifications for steady-state error and transient performance in computing systems. Exploring this further, we note that today, regulation is done by administrators as an informal way to achieve some kind of optimization. For example, service providers may regulate the request rate to servers to avoid excessive resource utilizations that could lead to long response times that violate service-level objectives. Thus, the broader problem is optimizing the profits of service providers, not regulating request rates.

There are many aspects to modeling the target system and controller. One of the most basic considerations is the decision to model in discrete time or continuous time. Continuous time facilitates certain kinds of modeling, especially fluid models (a very powerful tool for modeling characteristics of computing systems). However, discrete time is consistent with the way that measurements are obtained from computing systems and, in our experience, is conceptually more digestible to the computer science community. For these reasons, the book focuses on discrete time. We note that ignoring continuous time is somewhat of an "unnatural act" from a controls perspective, in that all introductory books on control theory that we know of begin with continuous time.

Another aspect of modeling is the manner in which the model is constructed. A first-principles approach starts with known properties of the target system. In mechanical systems, the starting point is Newton's laws. There are a few such laws that apply to computing systems. For example, the number of requests in the system at time k is equal to the number in the system at time $k-1$ plus the number of arrivals in $(k-1, k]$ minus the number of departures. Another example is flow balance: The time-averaged request rate must equal the time-averaged completion rate to achieve stability in steady state. Although considerable sophistication has been developed in some applications (e.g., TCP/IP Window size in [28]), requiring that such models be developed in order to apply control would be a significant impediment to its exploitation in computing systems. Thus, we have emphasized "black-box" models that use statistical techniques to relate inputs to outputs.

Still another modeling consideration relates to nonlinearities inherent in computing systems. For example, response times increase exponentially with utilizations at heavy loads. Another nonlinearity is saturation. There are two types. Output saturation occurs if the output metric is confined to a range, such as utilizations (which must lie between 0 and 1). Input saturation happens if the configuration parameter being manipulated has a finite range. An example of the latter is the MaxClients parameter in the Apache HTTP Server. Max-Clients cannot be less than 1 since at least one worker must be present to receive HTTP requests. While MaxClients can be set quite high (although it is constrained by operating system limits), it has no effect unless there is offered load that allows the demand for slave processes to grow as MaxClients is increased.

A final modeling challenge we have encountered is dealing with stochastics. Although there is a well-developed area of stochastic control, it is addressed only briefly in Chapter 11 because we (and others) have been very successful with applying deterministic control to real systems. However, there are shortcomings. In particular, it is sometimes difficult to distinguish between effects related to controllers and those that are a result of stochastics. In essence, ignoring stochastics introduces little error if variability is small compared to the effect of the control action. The simulation studies in Chapter 5 address this point in more detail.

A third area of challenge is controller design. In many cases, the goal of control design coincides with the Hippocratic admonition "at least do no harm."[1] We interpret this to mean that the closed-loop system should be stable. Thus, techniques such as gain and phase margins work well. However, as we learn more about the true control requirements, we discover that transient response matters. For simple (low-order) systems, pole placement works well. Indeed, that is the primary approach used in this book. However, as complexity grows, it may well be that frequency response techniques are needed. If this is the case, considerably more sophistication will be required to do control design.

Research is under way in applying control theory to computing systems, especially in caching, Web servers, and e-mail servers. In particular, there has been a recent flurry of interest in using control theory to evaluate and design algorithms for congestion control of routers (via RED, as described in Section 1.6.4). We fully expect these efforts to identify new control problems. One likely area is hybrid systems that combine discrete and continuous control, a combination that may prove effective for computing systems.

1.8 SUMMARY

1. The key elements of a control system are:

   (a) The reference input, which specifies the desired value of the measured output to be achieved by the control system.

   (b) The target system (e.g., the Apache HTTP Server) whose performance is to be controlled. The target system has one or more control inputs (e.g., `MaxClients` in the Apache HTTP Server) that are adjusted dynamically to control performance.

   (c) Measured outputs, which are metrics that quantify the performance characteristics to be controlled (e.g., response time).

   (d) The controller, which adjusts the control inputs of the target system based on the control objectives.

2. Two kinds of controllers are commonly used:

   (a) Feedforward controllers use a model of the target system to adjust control inputs.

   (b) Feedback controllers use the difference between the desired and measured output to adjust control inputs.

3. Feedforward control does not suffer from stability problems, but it requires an accurate model of the target system. Feedback control does not require an accurate model of the target system (which makes it robust to changes in the target system), but it can introduce instabilities.

---

[1] Hippocrates, *Epidemics*, Book I, Sect. XI.

4. There are several kinds of control objectives: regulation, disturbance rejection, and optimization.

5. Desirable properties of feedback control systems are (a) stability (e.g., a bounded input produces a bounded output); (b) accuracy (e.g., achieves its objectives for service differentiation); (c) speed (short settling time) in that changes in the system or workloads are handled quickly; and (d) small overshoot.

1.9 EXERCISES

1. What control objectives and properties of feedback control systems apply to the following:

   (a) A video player used exclusively by a single person.

   (b) A video server that can deliver multiple video streams concurrently to many clients.

   (c) A city street.

   Could the objectives of these systems be satisfied with open-loop control?

2. A cruise control system in an automobile keeps the vehicle at a constant speed.

   (a) What is the controller and the target system?

   (b) What is the reference input, control input, and measured output?

   (c) What is an example of a disturbance?

   (d) Draw a block diagram of a cruise control system.

3. Identify the components (i.e., target system, controller) and data (i.e., reference input, control input, disturbance input, and measured output) in the systems in Exercise 1.

4. A somewhat comical explanation for yawning being contagious is based on the following principles:

   (a) People yawn because they need more oxygen.

   (b) Yawning consumes more oxygen than normal breathing consumes.

   Thus, one person yawning consumes more oxygen, which in turn causes other people to yawn. Describe a system that regulates yawning by raising and lowering windows. What is the controller? The target system? What are the reference inputs, control inputs, and measured outputs?

5. Cyclic behavior, often referred to as "boom and bust" cycles is common in industrial economies. One reason for these cycles may be that consumer behavior changes more rapidly than it is possible to develop and staff new plants and services. Using this explanation, describe a simple control system that explains cyclic oscillations.

Part II

System Modeling

2

Model Construction

All models are wrong–but some models are useful.
—G.E.P. Box [12]

The systematic design of feedback systems requires an ability to quantify the effect of control inputs (e.g., buffer size) on measured outputs (e.g., response times), both of which may vary with time. Indeed, developing such models is at the heart of applying control theory in practice. The approach employed throughout this book is to start simple. This does not mean that the target system is simple! Rather, if simple models suffice, there is no need to develop complex models.

Our starting point is queueing theory, a widely used conceptual framework in which computing systems are viewed as networks of queues and servers. Over the last 30 years, queueing theory has proven quite effective at modeling the steady-state behavior of computing systems. Unfortunately, queueing models become complicated if dynamics are considered. In this chapter we introduce linear difference equations to model the dynamics of computing systems and employ insights from queueing theory to construct such models. We discuss briefly how difference equations can be constructed from first principles. Our focus, however, is to construct models using statistical or black-box methods, a process that is referred to as *system identification*.

2.1 BASICS OF QUEUEING THEORY

A queueing system consists of one or more buffers (queues) in which work requests wait for one or more servers. Figure 1.7 displays a queueing system

Feedback Control of Computing Systems, by Joseph L. Hellerstein, Yixin Diao, Sujay Parekh, and Dawn M. Tilbury
ISBN 0-471-26637-X   Copyright © 2004 John Wiley & Sons, Inc.

with a single queue and a single server. This system operates as follows:

- When a request arrives, it is placed in the queue.
- When the server completes a request, another request is selected from the queue.
- If the queue is empty, the server remains idle until the next request arrives.

Consider a queueing system in which requests are selected in a first-come, first-served manner from the queue. Figure 2.1 depicts the dynamics of this system. The horizontal line is time, which is numbered 0 through 9. The vertical axis indicates the state of a request. The states are:

- *Arrived:* has arrived and is waiting in the queue
- *Serving:* is in service
- *Departed:* has departed the system

We see that request 21 arrives at time 0 and immediately goes into service since the system is empty upon its arrival. This request begins a busy period, a time interval during which the server is busy. When request 22 arrives at time 1, it must wait until time 2 to enter service since that is when request 21 completes its service and departs. The busy period extends until time 7, when request 24 departs. Then the server enters an idle period until the next request arrives at time 9.

Several metrics can be used to quantify the performance of a queueing system. The *number in system* at time t is the number of requests that have arrived and whose service has not completed. For example, at time 3 in Figure 2.1, there are

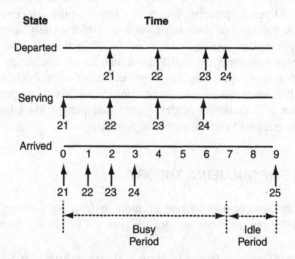

Fig. 2.1 Dynamics of a single-server queueing system with a first-come, first-served scheduling policy.

three requests in the system (22 through 24). The *utilization* of a server is the fraction of time that the system is busy over an interval. This is computed as the busy time divided by the sum of busy and idle times. Typically, utilization is denoted by ρ. In Figure 2.1, $\rho = 7/9$. The response time for a request is the elapsed time from the arrival of the request until its departure. The *response time* of request 22 is 3 since it arrives at 1 and departs at 4. The *waiting time* of a request is the time during which it is in the queue and not receiving service. Its *service time* is defined as the time when the request is being processed by the server. For example, request 22 has a waiting time of 1 since it arrives at 1 and enters service at 2, and its service time is 2. The rate at which requests are received by a system is the *arrival rate*. Sometimes, we also refer to the time between arrivals, or the *interarrival time* (which is the reciprocal of the arrival rate). Response time is the sum of service time and waiting time. The *throughput* of a queueing system is the rate at which requests leave; that is, the number of completions divided by the time over which the completions occur. For example, in Figure 2.1, throughput is 4/9.

The queue is typically implemented as a finite-size buffer. Requests that arrive when the buffer is full do not enter the queue and are not processed by the server. Such requests may be routed elsewhere, held in a separate queue (e.g., on disk), or discarded. Buffer size is often used as a control input.

The *steady-state* analysis of queueing systems can be done by making appropriate assumptions about the distribution of interarrival times and service times. Doing so allows us to compute metrics such as utilization, response time, and number in system (e.g., see [35] for details). Suppose that (1) service times are exponentially distributed with mean $1/\mu$, (2) the time between the arrival of requests is exponentially distributed with mean $1/\lambda$, and (3) both of the foregoing processes are independent and identically distributed and mutually independent of each other. These assumptions define an $M/M/1/K$ queueing system. The two M's refer to the exponential (memoryless) distribution, the 1 indicates a single server, and K is the size of the buffer. A little manipulation of the $M/M/1/K$ results in [35] allows us to compute key metrics. For example, utilization is 1 minus the probability that the server is idle, which is

$$\rho = 1 - \frac{1 - \lambda/\mu}{1 - (\lambda/\mu)^{K+1}}$$

The expected number in the system is

$$N = \frac{(\lambda/\mu)[1 - (\lambda/\mu)^K - K(\lambda/\mu)^K + K(\lambda/\mu)^{K+1}]}{(1 - \lambda/\mu)[1 - (\lambda/\mu)^{K+1}]} \tag{2.1}$$

From Little's result [35], we know that $R = N/\lambda$, where R is steady-state response time.

Control analysis focuses on the effect of the control input on the measured output. In $M/M/1/K$, buffer size can be used as a control input. That is, we can vary the buffer size dynamically to obtain desired response times, number in system, or other metrics. As discussed in Section 1.6.2, requests that arrive when the buffer is full can be handled in many ways, such as redirecting requests to less busy servers.

From Equation (2.1) we know that the metrics N, ρ, and R are nonlinear functions of the control input K. Figure 2.2 plots these relationships for different values of λ. Observe that each curve can be partitioned into three regions of buffer size, as specified below.

- *Region I* [e.g., for N and $\lambda = 3.5$, this is approximately $K \in [0, 25)$]. There is a linear relationship between K and the metrics, although the slope depends on the metric. Note that for a specific metric, the slope is fairly consistent across different values of λ.
- *Region II* [e.g., for N and $\lambda = 3.5$, this is approximately $K \in [25, 40)$]. This is the transition between regions I and III. This clearly is nonlinear. Also, it tends to be a relatively small region for lower values of λ than for larger values of λ.
- *Region III* [e.g., for N and $\lambda = 3.5$, this is approximately $K \in [40, \infty)$]. The slope is zero. That is, K has no effect on the metric since the buffer size is large enough so that requests are never discarded.

We underscore that the foregoing are steady-state results and so do not include transient effects, an important consideration for feedback control. Section 5.7

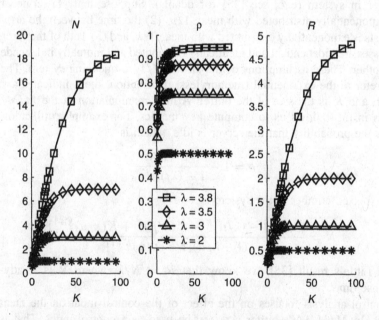

Fig. 2.2 *Effect of buffer size (K) on the steady-state characteristics of an $M/M/1/K$ queueing system. The service rate $\mu = 4$. Arrival rates (λ) are indicated in the box. The steady-state metrics are number in system N, utilization ρ, and response time R.*

presents simulation studies of the transient effect of adjusting buffer sizes in $M/M/1/K$.

2.2 MODELING DYNAMIC BEHAVIOR

In this section we introduce concepts that are central to modeling dynamic behavior in computing systems. We begin by discussing the variables used, especially their characterization as signals. Also addressed are considerations of discrete and continuous time as well as difference equations. Finally, we address nonlinearities present in computing systems.

2.2.1 Model Variables

We use the term *target system* to refer to the computing system (e.g., the Apache HTTP Server, the IBM Lotus Domino Server) or computing system element (e.g., a memory cache) that is to be controlled. Figure 2.3 displays the relationship between the input and output of a target system. The control input can be characteristics such as configuration parameters (e.g., buffer size) that are adjusted dynamically to regulate the measured output we want to control (e.g., response time, throughput, utilization). Disturbances are uncontrolled factors such as a change in workload (e.g., an increase in service times or arrival rates).

In addition, there may be *state variables*. These are possibly unmeasured quantities that aid in modeling input–output relationships. For example, consider a tandem queueing system in which the output of one queue is input to the next queue. Suppose that we are only interested in the end-to-end response time from entry into the first queue until exit from the second queue. One way to model such a system is to employ as state variables the response times at each queueing system, an approach that is detailed in Chapter 7. These individual response times are state variables in that they aid us in estimating the measured output.

2.2.2 Signals

The analysis of feedback control systems includes considerations of time-domain properties such as stability and transient response. Thus, it is essential that the

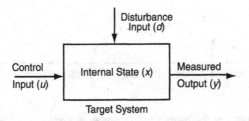

Fig. 2.3 *Relationships between the input, output, and state variable for a target system. The input affects the behavior of the system, and the output quantifies this effect. The internal state variables provide a way to characterize the effects of the input and the output produced.*

models we construct consider time. A variable that changes over time is called a *signal*. A *complete signal* takes on a value at each instant of time (e.g., utilization, number in system). A *partial signal* may be undefined at some time instants (e.g., response time).

There are several signals of interest in computing systems, especially number in system, utilization, and response time. We denote these time-varying metrics by $n_c(t)$, $\rho_c(t)$, and $r_c(t)$. The subscript c indicates that these are *continuous signals* in the sense that they are measured at time t, an instant in continuous time. Figure 2.4 displays an illustrative example of how these signals change as requests arrive at and depart from the queueing system. $n_c(t)$ increases by one when an arrival occurs, and it decreases by one when there is a departure. If multiple arrivals and departures occur simultaneously (at least within the resolution of the time granularity used), $n_c(t)$ is changed by the difference between the number of arrivals and the number of departures. For example, at $t = 0.6$ in Figure 2.4, there is one arrival and one departure, so $n_c(t)$ does not change. $\rho_c(t) = 1$ if $n_c(t) > 0$ and is 0 otherwise. $r_c(t)$ is measured when there is a service completion and hence is a partial signal. In Figure 2.4 there are 10 service completions, so there are 10 values of response times, each of which is indicated by an "×" (although two are overlaid with a solid circle).

A *discrete signal* has a value only at specific instants in time. For our purposes, we assume that these instants can be indexed by an integer; typically, we use k.

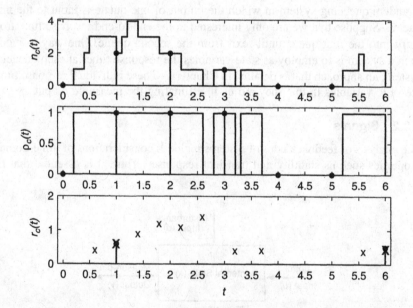

Fig. 2.4 Time evolution of the metrics $n_c(t)$ (number in system), $\rho_c(t)$ (utilization), and $r_c(t)$ (response time). Circles at $t = 1, 2, \ldots$ represent sampling points. Each "×" in the response-time graph corresponds to a departure of a request, at which time a response time is recorded. Note that at $t = 0.6$, an arrival and a departure occur simultaneously.

For computing systems, it is usually more convenient to work with discrete-time signals rather than continuous signals. There are several reasons for this. Measurement tools used in computing systems typically report values at regular intervals. Also, the overhead of continuous measurement is considerable, often requiring special hardware. Thus, even if continuous outputs are available, they are costly to obtain. Last, control actions are usually taken at discrete times, and it is much more natural to work with discrete output signals if the input signal is discrete.

Discrete signals can be constructed from continuous signals in many ways. One approach is sampling. Here, there is a fixed *sample time*, denoted by T_s, such that $x(k) = x_c(kT_s)$. Such an approach is illustrated in Figure 2.4 by the vertical lines with filled circles. An issue here is that for highly variable data, sample times must be sufficiently short to capture the dynamics of the continuous-time signal in the discrete-time signal. Also, for discrete signals, sampling times should coincide with instants at which the signal is defined. For example, in Figure 2.4 only two of the samples of $r(t)$ have a value.

An alternative approach is to compute average values. Consider response times. We define the kth interval of an output to be $(T_s(k - 1), T_s k]$. Suppose that there are N_k departures during the kth interval, with response times of $(y_{1,k}, \ldots, y_{N_k,k})$, where the subscript j, k indicates the jth departure in the kth interval. We define the average value $y_a(k)$ as

$$y_a(k) = \frac{1}{N_k} \sum_{j=1}^{N_k} y_{j,k} \qquad (2.2)$$

For example, as shown in Figure 2.5, $y_a(4)$ is the average of the two response times in the interval $(3, 4]$. Note that even though we average response times, we may still have missing values unless sample times are sufficiently large.

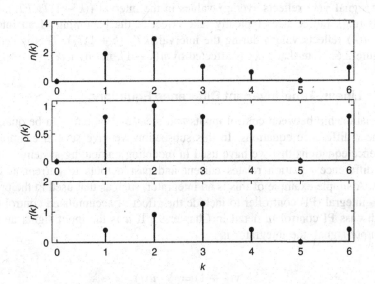

Fig. 2.5 *Average values of signals in Figure 2.4. T_s is 1 second.*

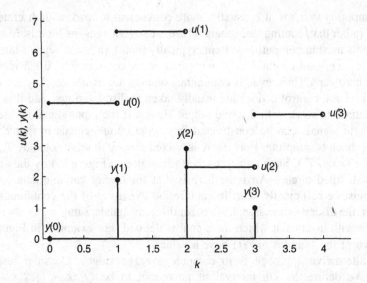

Fig. 2.6 *Relationship between input signal $u(k)$ and output signal $y(k)$. $u(k)$, the horizontal lines, reflect values in $[kT_s, (k+1)T_s)$. $y(k)$, the vertical lines, reflect values in $((k-1)T_s, kT_s]$. The solid dots indicate the starting value of $u(k)$. The open circle indicates the point at which $u(t)$ changes.*

Averaging can result in more representative values than sampling. For example, we see that in Figure 2.4, *sampled* utilization is 0 at time $k = 4$. However, the server is busy for much of (3, 4]. Figure 2.5 shows that average utilization at $k = 4$ is 0.6, which more accurately portrays utilization during the fourth interval.

In the remainder of the book we consider only discrete-time systems. The output signal $y(k)$ reflects average values in the interval $((k-1)T_s, kT_s]$. Input signals (e.g., buffer size) typically take effect at the beginning of an interval. Thus, $u(k)$ reflects values during the interval $[kT_s, (k+1)T_s)$. This is depicted in Figure 2.6. Note that $y(k)$ is affected by $u(k-1)$, not by $u(k)$.

2.2.3 Linear, Time-Invariant Difference Equations

The relationship between control inputs and measured outputs can be quantified by linear difference equations. In this subsection we give several examples of difference equations that we have used in modeling computing systems.

A difference equation relates current and past outputs to current and past inputs. A simple example of this is an integrator, such as that used in the proportional–integral (PI) controller to include the effect of accumulated control error. (We discuss PI control in detail in Chapter 9.) If u is the input signal and y is the output signal, the integrator is

$$y(k+1) = \sum_{i=0}^{k} u(i)$$

This relationship can be rewritten as a *difference equation* by subtracting successive values of y. That is, $y(k+1) - y(k) = u(k)$. Typically, we assume that initial conditions are zero, but this is not required. More commonly, we express this difference equation as

$$y(k+1) = y(k) + u(k) \tag{2.3}$$

Another commonly used model is the moving-average *filter*. Such filters are particularly useful when there is a signal that is extremely variable, such as CPU or disk utilization. Here, the input is a raw signal [denoted by $u(k)$ as before], and the output is a filtered or smoothed value $y(k)$:

$$y(k+1) = cy(k) + (1-c)u(k) \tag{2.4}$$

As with Equation (2.3), Equation (2.4) expresses $y(k+1)$ as a linear combination of $y(k)$ and $u(k)$. Here, the coefficients are c and $1-c$, where $0 \leq c < 1$. For values of c close to 1, we discount current measurements and rely more on the previous estimate. For values of c close to 0, we give more weight to the current measurement. If $c = 0$, then $y(k+1) = u(k)$. This is a one-step delay. We note that in some cases, we can avoid this delay, in which case the filter is defined as

$$y(k+1) = cy(k) + (1-c)u(k+1)$$

We can generalize Equations (2.3) and Equations (2.4) by having separate constants for $y(k)$ and $u(k)$:

$$y(k+1) = ay(k) + bu(k) \tag{2.5}$$

where a and b are scalars. We have found Equation (2.5) to be very useful in practice. For example, it turns out that the relationship between `KeepAlive` and CPU in the Apache HTTP Server can be expressed in terms of such a difference equation, as discussed in Section 2.6.2. Equation (2.5) is a *first-order model*, a model in which the next output depends only on the inputs and outputs from one time unit in the past. Equation (2.5) is also an example of a single-input, single-output or *SISO model*, since there is only one input u and one output y.

Equation (2.5) can be extended to consider n past output values $y(k), \ldots, y(k-n+1)$ in combination with m past input values $u(k), \ldots, u(k-m+1)$:

$$y(k+1) = a_1 y(k) + \cdots + a_n y(k-n+1) + b_1 u(k) + \cdots + b_m u(k-m+1) \tag{2.6}$$

This more general form is an *ARX model*.[1] Using such a model requires that we specify n and m in addition to the coefficients a_k and b_k. It is common to refer to

---

[1] Readers familiar with time-series models will note that the mathematical definition of ARX is identical to that of an autoregressive moving-average (ARMA) model. The distinction between ARX and ARMA is that u in an ARX model is controllable, whereas in an ARMA model, u is uncontrolled white noise.

n and m as the *model structure* and to the coefficients as the *model parameters*. Also observe that Equation (2.6) is equivalent to

$$y(k) = a_1 y(k-1) + \cdots + a_n y(k-n) + b_1 u(k-1) + \cdots + b_m u(k-m)$$
$$(2.7)$$

since all we did was shift k by one time unit.

We can generalize further by considering multiple inputs and multiple outputs, which we refer to as a *MIMO model*. For example, in the Apache HTTP Server described in Section 1.6.3, the inputs are KeepAlive and MaxClients and the outputs are CPU and MEM. One way to quantify the relationships between inputs and outputs is

$$\text{CPU}(k+1) = a_{11}\text{CPU}(k) + a_{12}\text{MEM}(k) + b_{11}\text{KA}(k) + b_{12}\text{MC}(k) \qquad (2.8)$$

$$\text{MEM}(k+1) = a_{21}\text{CPU}(k) + a_{22}\text{MEM}(k) + b_{21}\text{KA}(k) + b_{22}\text{MC}(k) \qquad (2.9)$$

(Section 2.6.2 provides more details.) In general, a MIMO model has one difference equation for each output. As such, writing these equations becomes tedious, especially if the MIMO model is a higher-order system with inputs (and/or outputs) from many time periods in the past. For these systems, it makes more sense to use a state-space model. State-space models are discussed in Chapter 7.

2.2.4 Nonlinearities

As with most real-world systems, computing systems are nonlinear, which is apparent in Figure 2.2. Despite this, our experience (and that of other researchers as well) has been that linear models work surprisingly well for many control applications (a statement that is consistent with the quote from G.E.P. Box at the beginning of this chapter). Here, we discuss the kinds of nonlinearities present in computing systems and how to approach their linearization.

The first source of nonlinearities is the *functional effect of the control input on the measured output*. Our starting point is Section 2.1, where we discuss the $M/M/1/K$ queueing system, in which buffer size has a nonlinear effect on utilization, number in system, and response time. Similar nonlinearities are common in production systems. For example, in the Apache HTTP Server, the parameter MaxClients has a nonlinear effect on response times, a relationship that is detailed in our discussion of fuzzy control in Section 11.6.

Another source of nonlinearities are constraints on metric values. For example, consider the effect of request rate on utilizations. Utilization is a linear function of request rate until the request rate equals the service rate. At that point, increasing the request rate does not increase utilization, since utilization cannot exceed 1.

Utilization is an example of a *constrained metric*, one whose value has prescribed limits. Such constraints are a very common form of nonlinearity in computing systems. For example, most metrics cannot be negative. Many have upper limits for semantic reasons (e.g., utilizations). Others are limited by configuration. For example, we cannot increase disk input–output rates beyond the capacity of the disk drives, and we cannot have queue lengths that exceed the capacity of the buffers in which requests are held.

Nonlinearities can also arise if the *control objective is optimization*. Consider load balancing, as discussed in Section 1.6.5. A common approach to determining the reference value of load for a work server is to compute the total load across all servers and then determine what *fraction* of this load should be handled by specific servers. Doing so requires dividing by the total load, which introduces a nonlinearity. If total load is fairly constant, this is not a problem. However, if total load varies considerably, we must be concerned with how well we can approximate this nonlinear function with a linear function.

The foregoing can potentially be handled in a very general way. A commonly used approach is to express the nonlinear function as a Taylor series (e.g., [50]) and then construct a linear approximation by including only the linear terms. In this very general framework, the control inputs are vectors denoted by $\tilde{\mathbf{u}}$, and the measured outputs are $\tilde{\mathbf{y}}$. $\mathbf{f}$ describes the relationship between inputs and outputs:

$$\tilde{\mathbf{y}}(k + 1) = \mathbf{f}(\tilde{\mathbf{y}}(k), \tilde{\mathbf{u}}(k)) \tag{2.10}$$

We know from the discussion of $M/M/1/K$ in Section 2.1 that the linear approximation very much depends on the range of control inputs considered. The *operating region* of a system is the range of control inputs (and their associated outputs) that are observed in operation. The *operating point* of a system is the desired steady values of $\overline{\mathbf{y}}$ and $\overline{\mathbf{u}}$ such that

$$\overline{\mathbf{y}} = \mathbf{f}(\overline{\mathbf{y}}, \overline{\mathbf{u}}) \tag{2.11}$$

This means that if the input is held constant at $\overline{\mathbf{u}}$, the output will be constant at $\overline{\mathbf{y}}$.

Most commonly, we linearize about an operating point. Doing so relies on the assumption that nonlinear functions can be approximated accurately by a linear function in regions that are sufficiently close to the operating point. Thus, the accuracy of the approximation depends on the operating region and the shape of $\mathbf{f}$ around the operating point. For regulatory control, the operating point is typically chosen to lie close to the reference value. This ensures that we have an accurate model of the target system in its desired region of operation, which is important if we hope to regulate the control input so that the system stays in this region.

The Taylor series is constructed as follows using the *offset value*, which is the deviation from the operating point. The offset value of the control input $\tilde{\mathbf{u}}(k)$ and the measured output $\tilde{\mathbf{y}}(k)$ are computed as follows:

$$\mathbf{u}(k) = \tilde{\mathbf{u}}(k) - \overline{\mathbf{u}}$$
$$\mathbf{y}(k) = \tilde{\mathbf{y}}(k) - \overline{\mathbf{y}} \tag{2.12}$$

Assuming that **f** is smooth, we have

$$\tilde{y}(k+1) = f(\tilde{y}(k), \tilde{u}(k))$$

$$\overline{y} + y(k+1) = f(\overline{y} + y(k), \overline{u} + u(k))$$

$$\overline{y} + y(k+1) = f(\overline{y}, \overline{u}) + \left(\frac{\partial f}{\partial y}\right)_{\overline{y},\overline{u}} y(k) + \left(\frac{\partial f}{\partial u}\right)_{\overline{y},\overline{u}} u(k) + \cdots$$

$$y(k+1) \approx \mathbf{A} y(k) + \mathbf{B} u(k)$$

The second equation substitutes for $\tilde{u}$ and $\tilde{y}$ using Equation (2.12). The third introduces the Taylor series expansion. The fourth subtracts the value of the operating point based on the equality in Equation (2.11), where $\mathbf{A} = (\partial f/\partial y)_{\overline{y},\overline{u}}$ and $\mathbf{B} = (\partial f/\partial u)_{\overline{x},\overline{u}}$

Unfortunately, it is rare that we can use this kind of linearization in practice since we do not know **f**. However, the foregoing strongly suggests that a linear approximation works well if we choose the appropriate operating point and operating region. If a linear approximation works poorly, more sophisticated techniques may be required, such as those described in Chapter 11.

2.3 FIRST-PRINCIPLES MODELS

Mechanical and electrical systems abide by a number of physical laws that can be expressed as mathematical relationships. For example, Newton's laws are widely used to characterize mechanical systems. A few such laws exist for computing systems as well. These laws are primarily a consequence of queueing relationships.

To illustrate, we develop a first-principles model for the system in Section 2.1 for the measured output number in system. For ease of presentation, we assume a fixed sample time (although this is not required). Let $n(k)$ be the number observed in the system at time k. Further, suppose that we can count the number of arrivals to and departures from the queue during the kth interval. Let $v(k)$ be the difference between the number of arrivals and departures during the kth interval (which we might manipulate through admission control):

$$n(k+1) = n(k) + v(k) \qquad (2.13)$$

Note that this is a linear difference equation that has the form of Equation (2.5), where $a = 1$ and $b = 1$. Further, this is a very general expression in that we do not specify the number of servers, the scheduling policy, or anything about the statistics of interarrivals or service times.

At first glance, it may seem counterintuitive that we obtain a linear model for the dynamics of number in system since we know from Figure 2.2 that the long-run average of the number in system for an $M/M/1/K$ queue is nonlinear. The reason for this apparent contradiction is the nature of the relationships being characterized. In Figure 2.2 we plot the number in the system as a function of buffer size (K). However, the expression above relates the number in the system to the difference between arrivals and departures in the previous interval.

For response times, we make assumptions that are more restrictive than the foregoing but still less constrained than the $M/M/1/K$ queueing system described previously. We assume a first-come, first-served scheduling policy and a single-server queueing system. Thus, requests depart in the same order in which they arrive. No restriction is imposed on the interarrival and service-time distributions. Let y_i denote the response time of the ith request, u_i^I denote the time between the arrival of the $(i-1)$st request and the ith request, and u_i^S be the service time of the ith request. We can relate these variables using Equation (1.120) from Kleinrock [36]:

$$y_i = \left(y_{i-1} - u_i^I\right)^+ + u_i^S \qquad (2.14)$$

To explain, request i arrives during either a busy period or an idle period. In the former case, it has a wait equal to the response time of request $(i-1)$, except for the interarrival time. In the latter case, $u_i^I > y_{i-1}$, so its response time is simply u_i^S. Relationships such as Equation (2.14) can be useful if we control u_i^I (e.g., through admission control) and/or u_i^S (e.g., through execution priorities if there are multiple classes of work). In the following, we focus on controlling service times. In particular, we use the approximation

$$y(k+1) \approx ay(k) + u(k) \qquad (2.15)$$

where $y(k)$ is the average response time during $((k-1)T_s, kT_s]$ and $u(k)$ is the average service time during $[kT_s, (k+1)T_s)$. Here, a depends on the utilization of the server. Indeed, $a \approx 1$ if the system is always busy, and $a = 0$ if a request never arrives when another request is in service.

Whereas our first example Equation (2.13) yields an exact relationship, the second example Equation (2.15) results in a linear difference equation that approximates the true relationship between the control input and the measured output. The latter approach is much more common than the former in practice.

Others have developed more sophisticated first-principles models. Misra et al. [48] develop a system of coupled differential equations that approximate the relationship between TCP/IP window size and router queue lengths under RED (random early detection) queue management. Lu et al. [44] use continuous-time techniques to model the allocation of storage to cache memory pools.

Although these efforts suggest that first-principles approaches can yield success, they also indicate that considerable sophistication is required to do so. Further, for complex computing systems, constructing first-principles models may be extremely difficult, if not impossible. In that case, we have to rely on empirical models, that is, models based on data collected from an actual system. In the next section we discuss some techniques for building these models.

2.4 BLACK-BOX MODELS

The difficulty of constructing first-principles models of computing systems motivates an approach that requires a less detailed knowledge of the relationships between inputs and outputs. Statistical techniques have considerable appeal since we reduce the knowledge required for model construction. That is, instead of employing detailed knowledge of the target system, we infer relationships between inputs and outputs by applying statistical techniques to data collected from the target system. The term *black-box model* is used since only the inputs and outputs of the target system need be known. In general, we employ an ARX model [as in Equation (2.6)] to describe the relationship between inputs and outputs.

In order to develop a black-box model, several steps must be followed. These steps are outlined in Figure 2.7 and described in detail in the following subsections. In summary, these steps are:

1. Specify the scope of what is to be modeled in the form of the inputs and outputs considered.
2. Design experiments and collect data that are sufficient to estimate the parameters of a linear difference equation of the desired order.

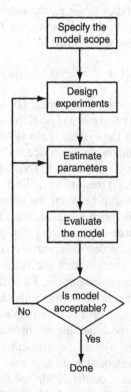

Fig. 2.7 Steps in black-box system identification.

3. Estimate the parameters of the model using least-squares techniques.

4. Evaluate the quality of the model fit. If the model quality must be improved, one or more of the foregoing steps are revisited.

2.4.1 Model Scope

There are many dimensions to the scope of the model. These are discussed below.

Stochastics   For control purposes, we focus on the effect of control inputs on the measured outputs. Unfortunately, it is frequently the case that measured outputs are highly variable, due to the stochastic nature of computing systems (e.g., randomness in interarrival times and service requirements). This can make it difficult to ascertain the effect of the inputs. Smoothing the output reduces variability, so can make the effect of the input signal more pronounced.

One way to smooth the outputs is to use longer sample times. This has the advantage of reducing the overheads for measurement collection on the target system. If sample times cannot be controlled, another approach is to use a filter, such as a running average. Note that both of these approaches mean that the system reacts slower to changes, such as a workload surge. Another approach to smoothing outputs is to use Equation (2.4), or techniques such as computing averages or medians within samples.

Model Structure   To apply the black-box approach, the model structure [m and n in Equation (2.6)] must be specified. In general, a better model is obtained if larger values of m and n are used. However, there is a danger of *overfitting*. By overfitting we mean that the model uses such large values of m and/or n that the model generalizes poorly to data other than those used to build the model. Overfitting results in poor model accuracy in practice. In general, overfitting is a problem with small data sets, those with the number of values close to $m + n$. To avoid overfitting, we initially consider a first-order model ($m = 1 = n$) and then see if higher-order models provide significantly greater accuracy. The best model is the one with the smallest values of m and n that provides a reasonable level of accuracy. (In Section 2.4.4 we discuss metrics for quantifying accuracy.) A lower-order model has the additional advantage of simplifying controller design. A more detailed discussion of how to choose a model structure is provided in [19].

Workloads   The *workload* of a computing system is the characteristic of requests that affect the performance metrics of the target system, such as throughputs, response times, and number in system. Examples of workload characteristics are the distributions of interarrival times and service times. Indeed, a major focus of queueing theory is estimating performance metrics based on workload characteristics.

The perspective taken in control analysis is different. We focus on the control input, not the workload. Workload is typically considered a disturbance that affects the way that control inputs affect the outputs. One implication for a black-box approach is that it is important to collect measurement data using representative workloads so that we correctly estimate the effect of control inputs on measured outputs in the operating environment.

If the typical (or worst-case) workload is known, it may suffice to build a single model that applies to this workload. However, better controller performance can sometimes be achieved by constructing separate controllers from workload-specific models and then switching to the appropriate controllers as workloads change. This is referred to as *gain scheduling* and is discussed in more detail in Section 11.2.

Example 2.1: M/M/1/K Workloads and sample times   The choice of sample time (T_s) often depends on workload. Consider an $M/M/1/K$ queueing system in which the service rate (customers per second) is $\mu = 4$ and the arrival rate (requests per second) is $\lambda \in \{2.8, 3.8\}$, so that $\rho \in \{0.7, 0.95\}$. Figure 2.8 displays average response time for a sine-wave input signal (buffer size) with a period of 35 minutes. The figure shows six plots that are structured into two rows of workloads in combination with three columns of sample times $T_s \in \{0.5, 2, 15\}$ minutes. The circles are individual response times, and the dashed line is the input signal (which is scaled to a second vertical axis).

There are several features of interest in this figure. First note that as sample time increases, the output becomes less variable, which is consistent with our

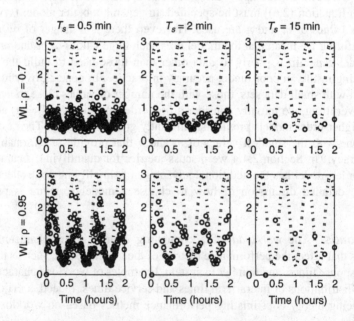

Fig. 2.8 *Effect of workload and sample times on response times of $M/M/1/K$. Measured response times are shown by the open circles; the dotted lines represent buffer size (which is scaled to a second vertical axis).*

expectations. However, if sample times get too large, it is difficult to see the effect of buffer size on response time. For example, when $T_s = 15$ minutes, sample times are nearly half the period of the input signal. As a result, measured response times peak and dip at times that do not correspond to the input.

We also see that the best choice of T_s depends on workload. Consider the first row in which $\rho = 0.7$. When $T_s = 0.5$, the input signal is barely discernible in the output signal, due to the large variability of the response times. This variability results from the load being light enough so that buffer size has less effect at larger values. The effect of the input signal is somewhat more clear if $T_s = 2$, since we average the impact of buffer size across more observations. A disadvantage, however, is that the output signal is flattened compared to that at $T_s = 0.5$. For $\rho = 0.95$, the choice of T_s is more of an issue. At $T_s = 0.5$, we clearly see the effect of the buffer size on response times since load is so heavy that small changes in buffer size affect the dynamics of the queueing system. At $T_s = 2$ we still get a sense of the input signal. However, the peaks are lower and more shifted in time from the input, due to measurement delays.

2.4.2 Experimental Design

Constructing black-box models requires data to estimate model parameters such as a and b in Equation (2.5). Such *training data* take the form of output signals (e.g., number in system and response times) and the corresponding input signals (e.g., buffer size) used to produce the output signals. Experimental design addresses how to construct input signals so that it is possible (although not guaranteed) to construct models that are sufficiently accurate for control purposes. To this end, three considerations are of importance in terms of the input signal:

- Range of values of the input signal
- Coverage of values within the operating region
- "Richness" in exciting the dynamics of the target system

We begin with the range of the input signal. We want to choose a range of control inputs that are representative of the operation of the feedback system. To do this, we work backward. Assume that the control objective is regulation (which is often the case in computing systems). Thus, we have some knowledge of the operating point of the target system in that outputs should be close to the reference values during operation. This means further that during operation the control inputs should be close to those values that result in the desired values of the outputs. Now consider the range of measured values that occur during operations (e.g., due to changes in the reference values). Here, too, we need to work backward from the associated control inputs that yield this range around the operating point.

At first glance, it may appear that there is a "chicken and egg" problem in that we cannot quantify the relationship between inputs and outputs without knowing the relationship between inputs and outputs. We address this by conducting exploratory experiments. These experiments not only assess the functional relationship between inputs and outputs but also consider (1) how large the operating region should be to moderate the effect of stochastics, and (2) how narrow the operating region must be to address nonlinearities (at least for the operating point chosen). Once the operating point and region have been specified, experiments must be conducted to determine the range of inputs needed to produce these outputs.

A second consideration is the coverage of values within the range of the inputs signals. To avoid biasing the parameters of black-box models, data should be collected uniformly across the range of inputs. This is particularly important if the target system has significant nonlinearities, since if data come predominantly from smaller (or larger) values of the input signal, there may be substantial inaccuracies in prediction.

Finally, we address the dynamics of the input signal. Intuitively, the input signal should be able to excite the target system so that its dynamics are apparent. Typically, this means that the input must contain at least as many frequencies (i.e., different rates of signal variation) as the order of the linear model. (See [41] for more details.) Our experience has been that for low-order models (e.g., first order), it suffices to use a low-frequency, discretized sine wave.

The issues associated with the dynamics of the input signal are best illustrated by example. Consider the MaxClients control parameters in the Apache HTTP Server. MaxClients determines the number of worker processes, which in turn determines the number of possible concurrent connections. Increasing MaxClients causes the Apache HTTP Server to increase the number of workers, and decreasing MaxClients causes the Apache HTTP Server to kill one or more workers. Creating a new process can be done with minimal delay. However, killing a process may take some time since the master process must wait until an existing worker completes so that its current request is not lost. Further complicating these dynamics is the fact that if MaxClients is large, it is more likely that at least one worker process completes its current request within a short period. From the foregoing, we see that (1) MaxClients's dynamics are asymmetric in that the transients associated with increasing MaxClients are not the same as with decreasing MaxClients, and (2) the dynamics change as MaxClients is varied. Thus, a linear model is only a rough approximation to the dynamics of the true system. However, our experience has been that this approximation suffices for regulatory control.

Example 2.2: $M/M/1/K$ Input signal We show the effect of different input signals (buffer size, K) on the operating point, operating region, and coverage of the input space. Figure 2.9 displays response times (open circles) and the input signals considered (the dashed lines) for an $M/M/1/K$ system in which $\lambda = 3.8$ and $\mu = 4$. Two factors are explored: (1) the type of input signal is either a step (top row) or a sine wave (bottom row), and (2) the range of the input signal is structured by column with values of $[21, 31]$ (left), $[1, 51]$ (center), and $[1, 101]$ (right). Note that for both input signals we see more effect if the range is larger.

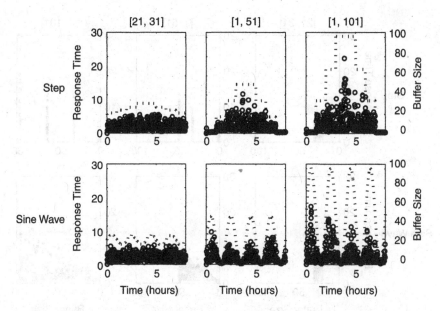

Fig. 2.9 *Time-serial effect of buffer size on response time in $M/M/1/K$. The circles are response times, and the input signals are indicated by dashed lines (which are drawn to the second vertical axis).*

Figure 2.10 presents the same data in a slightly different way in order to show issues of coverage and the potential for obtaining accurate models. Here, response times are plotted against buffer size. Note that for small ranges of the input signal, there is little difference between the step and the sine wave. However, as the range increases, the coverage provided by the steps is not nearly as good as that provided by the sine wave, as evidenced by the large gaps between values on the horizontal axis in the first row of plots.

The effect of signal range (columns) is most noticeable in the second row. At [21, 31], the range is so small that the effect of buffer size is not noticeable. At [1, 51], the impact of buffer size is clear, although there is considerable variability at the higher end of the range. In [1, 101], the variance at the high end of the range makes constructing an accurate model quite difficult.

2.4.3 Parameter Estimation

In this section we describe how to estimate model parameters once data have been collected. We focus on a commonly-used method called *least squares* regression. Our treatment is brief since this material is covered in detail in most introductory texts on applied statistics (e.g., [19]). There exist many other techniques for estimating model parameters from experimental data, but the discussion is beyond the scope of this text. In what follows, the focus is estimating a and b in Equation (2.5).

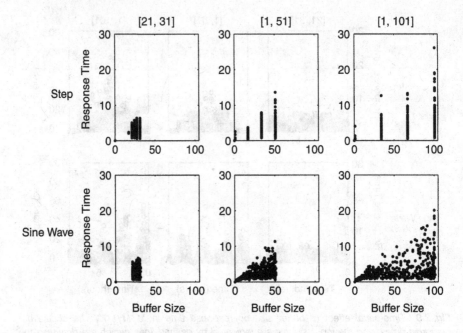

Fig. 2.10 *Effect of the input range in an $M/M/1/K$ queueing system. The input is buffer size, with the signals shown in Figure 2.9. The output is response time.*

The training data consists of a set of observations of the control input(s) supplied to the system and the corresponding output. Let the raw data be represented by a sequence of tuples $\{\tilde{u}(k), \tilde{y}(k)\}$, $1 \leq k \leq N + 1$. We begin by normalizing the input and output around their operating points. Let $\bar{u}$ be the mean input value and $\bar{y}$ be the mean output value. We assume that $(\bar{y}, \bar{u})$ is the operating point. That is, if $\tilde{y}(k + 1) = f(\tilde{y}(k), \tilde{u}(k))$, then $\bar{y} = f(\bar{y}, \bar{u})$. Then, the offset values are $y(k) = \tilde{y}(k) - \bar{y}$ and $u(k) = \tilde{u}(k) - \bar{u}$.

First, observe that Equation (2.5) provides a way to predict $y(k+1)$ from $y(k)$ and $u(k)$. We denote this predicted value by $\hat{y}(k + 1)$. That is,

$$\hat{y}(k + 1) = ay(k) + bu(k) \tag{2.16}$$

The $(k + 1)$st residual is $e(k + 1) = y(k + 1) - \hat{y}(k + 1)$. This is also known as the *prediction error*. We want to choose a and b so as to minimize the sum of the squared errors (residuals)–hence the name "least squares". More formally, we want to minimize the function

$$J(a, b) = \sum_{k=1}^{N} e^2(k + 1) = \sum_{k=1}^{N} \left[y(k + 1) - ay(k) - bu(k) \right]^2 \tag{2.17}$$

where $N + 1$ is the total number of observations.

We can find the values of a and b that minimize $J(a, b)$ by taking partial derivatives and setting them to zero. This results in

$$\frac{\partial}{\partial a} J(a, b) = -2 \sum_{k=1}^{N} y(k) \left[y(k+1) - ay(k) - bu(k) \right] = 0 \quad (2.18)$$

$$\frac{\partial}{\partial b} J(a, b) = -2 \sum_{k=1}^{N} u(k) \left[y(k+1) - ay(k) - bu(k) \right] = 0 \quad (2.19)$$

We can now solve these simultaneous equations for a and b. For convenience of notation, define the following quantities

$$S_1 = \sum_{k=1}^{N} y^2(k) \quad (2.20)$$

$$S_2 = \sum_{k=1}^{N} u(k)y(k) \quad (2.21)$$

$$S_3 = \sum_{k=1}^{N} u^2(k) \quad (2.22)$$

$$S_4 = \sum_{k=1}^{N} y(k)y(k+1) \quad (2.23)$$

$$S_5 = \sum_{k=1}^{N} u(k)y(k+1) \quad (2.24)$$

Manipulating the normal equations (2.18) and (2.19), we have

$$a = \frac{S_3 S_4 - S_2 S_5}{S_1 S_3 - S_2^2} \quad (2.25)$$

$$b = \frac{S_1 S_5 - S_2 S_4}{S_1 S_3 - S_2^2} \quad (2.26)$$

These are fairly easy computations to program. (See [41] for more details of the computations.) Alternatively, commercially available software such as MATLAB and Excel provide packaged solutions for least-squares regression.

Example 2.3: Parameter estimates for $M/M/1/K$ We fit a first-order model to data collected from an $M/M/1/K$ queueing system for which $\lambda = 3.8$, $\mu = 4$, $\tilde{y}(k)$ is response time, and $\tilde{u}(k)$ is buffer size. The sample data are shown in Table 2.1. Note that $N = 10$ since $N + 1 = 11$ is the number of samples. Figure 2.11 plots the raw data in the space of y and u. Our goal is to

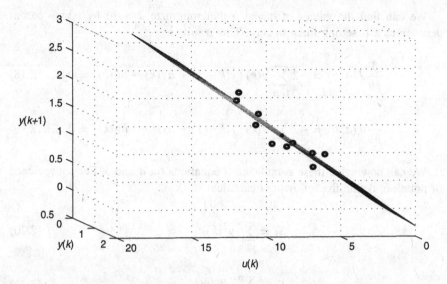

Fig. 2.11 *Fit of regression in Example 2.3. This is a three-dimensional space defined by $u(k)$, $y(k)$, and $y(k+1)$. The points are observed values, and the plane is $\hat{y}(k+1)$. The least-squares method estimates a and b so that the $\hat{y}$ plane lies in the middle of the observed values.*

estimate a and b so as to estimate y as indicated by the plane fitting the raw data.

We proceed as follows:

1. The mean buffer size and response time are computed. The former is computed over [1, 10] (since the last value is not used in the estimates produced) and the latter over [2, 11] [which is the mean of the $y(k+1)$'s]. The result is $\overline{u} = 7.7$ and $\overline{y} = 1.17$.
2. y and u are computed as shown in Table 2.1.

TABLE 2.1   Data Used in Example 2.3

k	$\tilde{u}(k)$	$\tilde{y}(k)$	$u(k)$	$y(k)$
1	4	0.62	−3.7	−0.55
2	5	0.72	−2.7	−0.45
3	5	0.76	−2.7	−0.41
4	6	0.52	−1.7	−0.65
5	7	0.91	−0.7	−0.27
6	8	0.92	0.3	−0.25
7	9	0.97	1.3	−0.20
8	10	1.52	2.3	0.35
9	11	1.42	3.3	0.26
10	12	1.99	4.3	0.82
11	13	1.95	5.3	0.78

**TABLE 2.2   Values of S_i
Estimates for the Data in
Example 2.1**

i	S_i
1	2.12
2	10.47
3	68.10
4	1.85
5	12.16

3. Using Equations (2.20) through (2.24), we compute the S_i as shown in Table 2.2. Note that the S_i are computed using $k \in [1, 10]$ since we estimate $\hat{y}(2), \dots, \hat{y}(11)$.

4. From the S_i just calculated and Equations (2.25) and (2.26), we have $a = -0.087$ and $b = 0.19$.

5. With this, we can calculate $\hat{y}(k + 1) = ay(k) + bu(k)$ and $\hat{\bar{y}}(k + 1) = \hat{y}(k + 1) + \bar{y}$.

We note in passing that with different data, we get different estimates. For example, repeating Example 2.3 with a data set consisting of 480 observations and $u(k) \in [1, 51]$, we obtain $a = 0.49$ and $b = 0.033$. This differs considerably from the estimates $a = -0.045$ and $b = 0.19$ obtained in Example 2.3 with 11 observations. In general, having more observations decreases the variability of parameter estimates, although other factors must be considered as well (e.g., linearity of the region over which the experiments are conducted).

2.4.4 Model Evaluation

Model evaluation quantifies the extent to which the model structure can explain the data collected. If the data are not well explained by the model, then various adjustments should be considered (e.g., employing a higher-order model is needed). Examples of the latter include adjusting how much the output signals are smoothed and changing the range of inputs considered in the design of experiments.

The accuracy of a model can be quantified based on the training data or a separate set of test data. In general, the latter provides better insight and guards against overfitting (although techniques such as cross validation can be used on the training data [49]).

One widely used metric for assessing accuracy is the root-mean-square error (*RMSE*). This is defined as

$$\text{RMSE} = \sqrt{\frac{1}{N} \sum_{k=1}^{N} [y(k + 1) - \hat{y}(k + 1)]^2} \qquad (2.27)$$

In essence, RMSE estimates the standard deviation of the residuals and so provides insight into the accuracy of predictions based on the model.

A second way to quantify accuracy is by computing the variability explained by the model. This is denoted by R^2 and

$$R^2 = 1 - \frac{\text{var}(y - \hat{y})}{\text{var}(y)} \tag{2.28}$$

where var(y) is the variance of the $y(k)$. R^2 ranges from 0 to 1. A value of 0 means that the model does no better than using the mean value of y to estimate $y(k)$. A value of 1 suggests (but does not guarantee) a perfect fit. In general, we look for models with $R^2 \geq 0.8$.

A third measure of model quality is the *correlation coefficient* (CC) between the input and the residuals. This is computed as

$$\text{CC} = \frac{\sum_k e(k)u(k)}{\sqrt{\text{var}(e(k))\text{var}(u(k))}}$$

A small correlation coefficient (CC) shows that most of the information in the control input (e.g., buffer size) has been extracted by the model, so little can be done to refine the model further.

Although RMSE, R^2, and the correlation coefficient have appeal, they can be misleading. For example, a very large R^2 can be obtained if data are clustered around extreme values. For this reason it is advisable to use residual analysis plots to confirm the insights provided these metrics. Such plots often provide insight into how the model should be changed to improve accuracy. An example of a residual analysis plot is a scatter plot of measured versus predicted values as used in the following example. (See [16] for more details on residual analysis.)

Example 2.4: Assessment of model for $M/M/1/K$ Using a step-up and step-down input signal as used in the upper middle plot of Figure 2.9, test data were collected to evaluate the first-order model whose parameters are estimated in Example 2.3 with 480 points. Table 2.3 displays the results. The R^2 values are fairly small, and RMSE is fairly large compared to the range of data values of response time. Putting the latter in perspective, we view RMSE as residual standard deviation. Thus, a 95% prediction interval around an estimate would have a width of approximately four times RMSE. Hence, in this data set, the 95% prediction interval is roughly half the range of the observed data, which is extremely wide. Note that the R^2 is slightly smaller for the test data than for the training data. We expect that a and b should explain more variability in the data

TABLE 2.3   Model Assessment for the $M/M/1/K$

Model Evaluation	RMSE	R^2	CC
Training data	1.62	0.34	0.006
Test data	1.53	0.33	0.030

from which they are estimated. The RMSE is smaller in the test data than the training data due to randomness in the way the data sets are generated.

One reason why the fit is poor may be that we need a higher-order model. We tried a model in which $m = 2 = n$, but this model increases R^2 by less than 0.01 on both the training and test data. To gain more insight into the underlying difficulties, Figure 2.12 plots measured versus actual values. This plot is particularly effective at identifying issues in system identification. Note that if we had a perfect model, all points would lie on the line of unit slope. However, this does not occur in Figure 2.12, even at small values of response times, where a linear model works well. The latter is because we used a very large operating region and least-squares fit a plane to the entire range of values, which included nonlinear regions. Further, we see that as response times increase, variance increases as well. This is called *heteroschedasticity*. Heteroschedasticity is common in queueing systems, as evidenced by the queueing formulas for metrics such as response times and number in system. Heteroschedasticity undermines an assumption needed for prediction based on least-squares regression, that residuals are realizations of independent and identically distributed random variables. Common ways of addressing heteroschedasticity are to model the square root or log of the raw data instead of the raw data itself (e.g., [19]).

One more consideration in model evaluation relates to the values used to calculate $\hat{y}(k+1)$. Consider Equation (2.5). The parameters a and b are obtained from least squares, and $u(k)$ is known by experimental design. However, there are two choices for the value of the measured output at k. In the first, we produce estimates as

$$\hat{y}(k + 1) = ay(k) + bu(k)$$

This is referred to as *one-step prediction*, in that it extrapolates only one step ahead of the measured outputs since a is multiplied by $y(k)$. The second choice, which is called *multistep prediction*, constructs estimates as

$$\hat{y}(k + 1) = a\hat{y}(k) + bu(k)$$

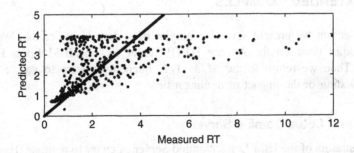

Fig. 2.12 Comparison of measured and predicted data for $M/M/1/K$.

Here, the measured outputs are not used at all [or possibly only at $y(0)$] in that a is multiplied by the previous *estimate* of the measured output. In general, multistep prediction is a more challenging assessment of the model than one-step prediction. Multistep prediction is often used in practice for controller design since the true system and controller may not be available. Hence, we use multistep prediction in this book.

2.5 SUMMARY

1. Signals are variables that are a function of time. Examples of signals are time-series measurements of response times, number in system, and utilization.

2. Queueing theory provides a way to estimate steady-state metrics of computing systems (e.g., response time, throughput) based on characteristics of workloads and other factors.

3. Difference equations provide a way to express dynamic relationships between variables, such as the transient effect on response times in the Apache HTTP Server when the value of MaxClients is changed.

4. ARX models are difference equations that relate linear functions of one variable's history to a linear function of another variable's history.

5. First-principles models are developed based on knowledge of how a system operates. Black-box models require minimal knowledge of the system, relying instead on statistical techniques (e.g., to construct ARX models).

6. The operating point of a system is the values of the input and output variables that are expected when the system is in steady state.

7. Constructing ARX models using black-box methods requires conducting appropriate experiments so that the data are representative of the region in which the model will be used.

8. The parameters of an ARX model can be estimated using least-squares regression, and the model accuracy can be assessed by using R^2, RMSE, and/or the correlation coefficient.

2.6 EXTENDED EXAMPLES

In this section we present several examples of system identification. We begin with studies done on the Apache HTTP Server and the IBM Lotus Domino Server. Then we return to the $M/M/1/K$ queueing system to gain a deeper understanding of the impact of nonlinearities.

2.6.1 IBM Lotus Domino Server

Administrators of the IBM Lotus Domino Server often try to regulate the number of remote procedure calls (RPCs) in the server, a quantity that we denote by RIS.

This regulation is accomplished by using the MaxUsers tuning parameter. Thus, for system identification, we construct a model whose input is MaxUsers and the output is RIS. A standard workload was applied to a IBM Lotus Domino Server running product-level software to obtain training and test data. In all cases, values are averaged over a 1-minute interval. The operating point is $\overline{\text{MaxUsers}}$ =165, $\overline{\text{RIS}}$ =135. The offset values are $u(k) = \text{MaxUsers}(k) - \overline{\text{MaxUsers}}$, $y(k) = \text{RIS}(k) - \overline{\text{RIS}}$. The input signal employed is a discretization of a ramp in which MaxUsers is increased by 20 every 20 minutes.

Figure 2.13(a) displays the input signal (solid line) and the corresponding output signal ("×"s). The model for this system is

$$y(k + 1) = 0.43y(k) + 0.47u(k) \tag{2.29}$$

The R^2 value is 0.98. Figure 2.13(b) plots the measured and predicted RIS. Note that most points line on or near the solid line of unit slope [where $y(k) = \hat{y}(k)$]. This confirms that the fit is quite good. More details can be found in [53].

2.6.2 Apache HTTP Server

Web server administrators frequently want to regulate resource utilizations since excessive utilizations can result in long response times and possibly system failures (e.g., due to queue overflows). Two resources of particular interest are CPU and MEM. The Apache HTTP Server exposes two controls that we have used: KeepAlive (which controls how long an idle HTTP connection is held) and MaxClients (the number of concurrent connections to the Web server). Here we explore the extent to which KeepAlive can be used to control CPU.

Experiments were conducted using a session-oriented workload considered to be a realistic workload for Web applications. KeepAlive was varied as a discrete sine wave with a period of 1200 seconds, a mean of 11, and an amplitude

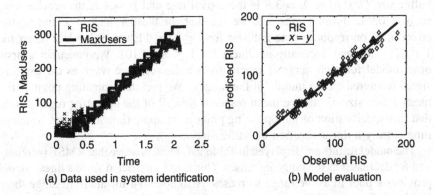

(a) Data used in system identification

(b) Model evaluation

Fig. 2.13 *Data and model evaluation for the IBM Lotus Domino Server. Part (a) displays the relationship between* MaxUsers *and RIS in system identification experiments. Part (b) shows that predicted RIS lie close to the observed values.*

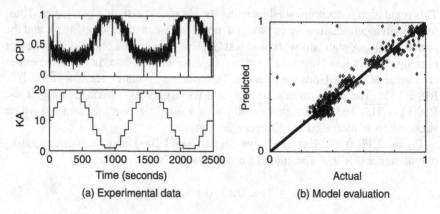

(a) Experimental data   (b) Model evaluation

Fig. 2.14   Model of how KeepAlive affects CPU in Apache HTTP Server.

of 10. The mean value of CPU was 0.58. Figure 2.14(a) shows the input and output signals. Thus, we use the operating point $\overline{\text{CPU}} = 0.58$, $\overline{\text{KA}} = 11$.

We use a first-order model to quantify the relationship between KeepAlive and CPU. Here $y(k) = \text{CPU} - 0.58$ and $u(k) = \text{KeepAlive} - 11$. The estimates of the model parameters are $a = 0.6$ and $b = -0.014$, and hence

$$y(k + 1) = 0.6y(k) - 0.014u(k) \tag{2.30}$$

(b is negative since a larger KeepAlive decreases carried load and thereby reduces utilizations.) $R^2 = 0.93$. Figure 2.14(b) confirms that the model is very accurate over the operating region studied. Further details can be found in [17].

2.6.3 $M/M/1/K$ Comparisons

We investigate the effect of operating region on model accuracy for $M/M/1/K$. As before, y is the offset value of response time, and u is the offset value of buffer size (K). Also, $\lambda = 3.8$ is the arrival rate and $\mu = 4$ is the service rate, so $\rho = 0.95$. From Figure 2.2, we see that for these values of λ and μ, the effect of K on response time is linear for $1 \leq K \leq 11$, somewhat less linear for $1 \leq K \leq 51$, and decidedly nonlinear for $1 \leq K \leq 101$. We construct a first-order model for each range of inputs using a discrete sine wave as the exciting signal (centered on the middle of the range). We pick the operating point as the mean buffer size $\overline{K}$ and the mean response time $\overline{R}$ of the operating region. Note that this specification of the operating point is an approximation unless response time is truly a linear function of buffer size.

The model results are displayed in Table 2.4. First, observe that RMSE increases and R^2 decreases as the range increases. This is to be expected since a linear model provides a poor fit as the range increases. Also note that for the third range there is a large difference between the results obtained using test data and those using training data. Most likely, this is due to the much greater variability when K is large. Last, observe the relationship between a and b as the range increases. In the

TABLE 2.4   System Identification of $M/M/1/K$ for Various Input Ranges[a]

Input Range	$(\overline{K}, \overline{R})$	(a, b)	Evaluation	RMSE	R^2
[1, 11]	(6, 0.85)	(−0.040, 0.11)	Training data	0.20	0.78
			Test data	0.18	0.77
[1, 51]	(26, 2.7)	(0.49, 0.033)	Training data	1.62	0.34
			Test data	1.53	0.33
[1, 101]	(51, 4.01)	(0.52, 0.014)	Training data	2.09	0.20
			Test data	2.62	0.17

[a] $\lambda = 3.8$, $\mu = 4$. $(\overline{K}, \overline{R})$ is the operating point for buffer size and response time.

[1, 11] range, $a \approx 0$, since response time is a linear function of K. Specifically, we obtain the model

$$y(k+1) = -0.04y(k) + 0.11u(k)$$

for the operating point $\overline{K} = 6$ and $\overline{R} = 0.85$. In [1, 51], b is smaller and a is larger:

$$y(k+1) = 0.49y(k) + 0.033u(k) \qquad (2.31)$$

for the operating point $\overline{K} = 26$ and $\overline{R} = 2.7$. This suggests that response times are highly autocorrelated, thereby providing state information that can aid in modeling the dynamics of the system. (The larger autocorrelation results from having higher utilizations because of larger buffer sizes.) The foregoing effect is even more pronounced for [1, 101]:

$$y(k+1) = 0.52y(k) + 0.0014u(k)$$

for the operating point $\overline{K} = 51$ and $\overline{R} = 4.01$.

We note in passing that the middle row, in which $(\overline{K}, \overline{R}) = (26, 2.7)$, is used as a running example in the remainder of the book.

*2.7   PARAMETER ESTIMATION USING MATLAB

MATLAB is a powerful software tool that is widely used in technical computing [67]. In particular, MATLAB is a very common environment for doing system identification and control design. Appendix E provides a brief introduction to the MATLAB environment.

Below we show how Example 2.3 can be solved using MATLAB. We begin by defining variables for $\tilde{y}$ and $\tilde{u}$. These values are taken from Table 2.1.

```
yp = [0.62 0.72 0.76 0.52 0.91 0.92 0.97 1.52];
yp = [yp 1.42 1.99 1.95]';
up = [4 5 5 6 7 8 9 10 11 12 13]';
```

Next, we compute the mean of the input and output values.

```
mu = mean(up(1:end-1));
my = mean(yp(2:end));
u = up - mu;
y = yp - my;
```

We can see the values computed by entering the following lines:

```
mu
my
[u y]
```

which produces the output

```
mu =
      7.7000

my =
      1.1680

u =
   -3.7000
   -2.7000
   -2.7000
   -1.7000
   -0.7000
    0.3000
    1.3000
    2.3000
    3.3000
    4.3000
    5.3000


y =
   -0.5480
   -0.4480
   -0.4080
   -0.6480
   -0.2580
   -0.2480
   -0.1980
    0.3520
    0.2520
    0.8220
    0.7820
```

Now, we compute the S_i. We do this by creating a variable S that is initially a vector of 0's. Note that these computations differ somewhat from Equations (2.20)–(2.24) because there are assumed to be $N + 1$ data points (that is, end= $N + 1$).

```
S = zeros(5,1);
S(1) = sum(y(1:end-1).^2);
S(2) = sum(u(1:end-1).*y(1:end-1));
S(3) = sum(u(1:end-1).^2);
S(4) = sum(y(1:end-1).*y(2:end));
S(5) = sum(u(1:end-1).*y(2:end));
```

We can view the results by entering S:

```
S =

    2.1177
   10.4650
   68.1000
    1.8419
   12.1740
```

The parameters a and b are computed as

```
a = (S(3)*S(4)-S(2)*S(5))/(S(1)*S(3)-(S(2))^2);
b = (S(1)*S(5)-S(2)*S(4))/(S(1)*S(3)-(S(2))^2);
```

and [a b] results in the output

```
ans =

   -0.0567    0.1875
```

Note that the estimate for a obtained here differs from that computed in Section 2.4.3 because of the rounding done in the calculations in Section 2.4.3.

MATLAB has facilities for doing multiple variable regression that can make the foregoing more convenient and allow us to scale to a larger number of variables. This facility is invoked using the `mldivide` function, which is also accessed with the backslash operator. For example, a and b can be estimated as follows:

```
H = [y(1:end-1) u(1:end-1)];
theta = H\y(2:end)
```

Since we did not end the second line with a semicolon, this produces the output

```
theta =

   -0.0567
    0.1875
```

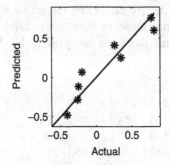

Fig. 2.15 Plot of actual versus predicted values for data in the MATLAB example.

H is a matrix whose columns are the variables to regress. theta(1) is a, and theta(2) is b.

MATLAB has excellent plotting facilities that can aid in system identification. A plot that we employ extensively is the predicted-versus-actual plot with a line of unit slope shown for reference [e.g., Figures 2.12, 2.13, and 2.14(b)]. We can construct such a plot for the sample data in this section using the following commands:

```
yhat = a*y(1:end-1) + b*u(1:end-1);
plot(y(2:end),yhat, ' * ',y,y,' -');
```

The result is displayed in Figure 2.15.

2.8 EXERCISES

1. Identify the busy and idle periods in Figure 2.4.

2. Using the data in Figure 2.1, plot the time evolution of number in system, utilization, and response time in the same manner as Figure 2.4.

3. Draw the time evolution of Figure 2.4 for 2-second averages.

4. Consider the IBM Lotus Domino Server system described in Section 1.6.1. In that description, the administrator seeks to control the RIS for the server. Suppose that a different administrator instead wants to control the CPU utilization of the server. How does this change the control problem?

   (a) What does the target system look like? What happens to the sensor?

   (b) What are the new reference input, control input, system output, and disturbance?

   (c) Which of these are signals? Which are continuous? Which are discrete?

5. We continue with the system of Exercise 4. It is observed that the CPU utilization of the system has significant stochastics. As a result, an experienced control designer suggests that you should use a moving-average filter with

parameter 0.9 on the system output. Further, it is determined that a first-order ARX model should be used to model the IBM Lotus Domino Server.

(a) Draw the new control block diagram.

(b) Write the ARX equations of the IBM Lotus Domino Server, and of the moving-average filter.

(c) What signals do the variables in these equations map to?

(d) What are the parameters that must be identified through experimentation?

(e) You are now asked to design an experiment to identify these parameters. What questions do you need to ask in order to design a proper experiment?

6. Use least-squares regression to estimate the parameter of $y(k+1) = ay(k)$ for $n(k)$ in Figure 2.5. Compute R^2 as well. [Remember that $y(k) = n(k) - \bar{n}$.]

7. Fit a line to Equation (2.1) for $\lambda = 3.8$ over the range $[0, 100]$ and compute the R^2 value. Now fit two curves to the same equation using the ranges $[0, 50]$ and $[51, 100]$. How do the R^2's of the latter fits compare with the R^2 of the first fit?

8. Often, computer systems will give preference to one class of customer over another. One mechanism for doing this is to employ priorities.

(a) Redraw Figure 2.1 under the assumption that requests 22 and 24 have higher priority than the other requests (although they do not preempt lower-priority requests that are being served).

(b) Compare the response times of each request under the priority scheme with those under the scheme without priorities.

(c) How are number in system and utilizations affected by the use of priorities?

9. Consider a queueing system with a waiting area that can accommodate only two customers, in which requests are rejected (and not considered in queueing metrics) if they arrive when the buffer is full. Draw a version of Figure 2.4 for this system assuming that there is no change in either arrival instants or service times. (Remember that at time 0.6 there is a simultaneous arrival and departure.)

(a) How many idle periods are present? How does this compare to the original figure?

(b) How are response times affected? Why?

(c) Where would there be the most benefit if a third server were added?

(d) Return to Figure 2.4 and consider a queueing system whose waiting area is changed from 5 to 2 at time 0.5 so that customers are admitted only if no more than two customers are waiting. Also, assume that no previously admitted customer is discarded. Compare $n(t)$ and $r(t)$ of this system with one that has a fixed buffer size of 2.

10. Write a system of difference equations that describe number in system at departure instants in a first-come, first-serve queueing system with two non-preemptive priority levels.

11. Suppose that

$$y(k + 1) = y^2(k) - y(k)u(k)$$

(a) Find the operating point $\bar{y}$ for $\bar{u} = 2$.

(b) Construct a linear equation about this operating point.

3

Z-Transforms and Transfer Functions

In this chapter we develop the tools for analyzing the statics and dynamics of input–output relationships in discrete, time-invariant, linear systems. Our fundamental tool is the Z-transform, a simple but powerful mathematical technique that is used throughout the remainder of the book. Z-transforms are used to solve difference equations (such as those in Chapter 2), to infer steady-state properties of signals, to assess the stability of systems, and to analyze transient response. We do not assume prior exposure to Z-transforms.

3.1 Z-TRANSFORM BASICS

Control analysis and design frequently involves manipulating signals, especially the following: adding and subtracting signals, shifting signals in time, and observing how signals change after being "operated on" by a system. Thus far, we have described a signal as an ordered sequence, which we refer to as the *time-domain representation*. However, this is not a convenient representation for the kinds of manipulations we need to do.

Z-transforms provide a way to encode signals and to describe systems so that we can easily extract key properties such as the steady-state value of a signal and the settling time of a system. Further, many common ways in which we combine smaller systems into larger systems (e.g., putting elements in series) correspond to simple transformations of the Z-transforms of these systems (e.g., multiplication).

Feedback Control of Computing Systems, by Joseph L. Hellerstein, Yixin Diao, Sujay Parekh, and Dawn M. Tilbury
ISBN 0-471-26637-X   Copyright © 2004 John Wiley & Sons, Inc.

We begin by considering signals. The Z-transform provides a way to express signals as a series of values at specific times. This is accomplished by using the variable z to indicate time delays. Thus, instead of a *list* of values, we end up with a *sum* that is much easier to manipulate mathematically. This representation is much more convenient than the time-domain representation, although the Z-transform is equivalent to the time-domain representation.

To provide some intuition, suppose that we have a signal $\{u(k)\}$ whose first few values are $u(0) = 1$, $u(1) = 0.5$, $u(2) = 0.25$, and $u(3) = 0.125$. The time-domain representation is $\{1, 0.5, 0.25, 0.125, \dots\}$. It turns out that the Z-transform of $\{u(k)\}$ is

$$(1)z^0 + (0.5)z^{-1} + (0.25)z^{-2} + (0.125)z^{-3} + \cdots = \frac{z}{z - 0.5}$$

$z/(z - 0.5)$ is a much more compact notation than the ordered list. Further, it is very easy to manipulate signals using Z-transforms. For example, the Z-transform of the sum of two signals is the sum of their Z-transforms.

Taking our intuition a bit further, consider the signal $\{u(k)\} = \{u(0), u(1), u(2), u(3), u(4), u(5)\} = \{1, 0.8, 0.5, 0.3, 0.2, 0.1\}$, with $u(k) = 0$ for all other values of k. Let $U(z)$ be its Z-transform. Suppose that $\{u(k)\}$ is shifted by one time unit. That is, we have the signal $\{u_{\text{shift}}(k)\} = \{0.8, 0.5, 0.3, 0.2, 0.1\}$, so that $u_{\text{shift}}(k) = u(k + 1)$. Such effects are common in control analysis, but they are cumbersome to express as an ordered set. However, it turns out that the Z-transform of $\{u_{\text{shift}}(k)\}$ is $zU(z)$. This is illustrated in Figure 3.1. Note that for $\{u_{\text{delay}}(k)\} = \{0, 1, 0.8, 0.5, 0.3, 0.2, 0.1\}$, the Z-transform is $z^{-1}U(z)$.

3.1.1 Z-Transform Definition

Z-transforms are defined for discrete-time signals. In this book we make the additional assumption that all signals have a value of 0 for $k < 0$. Consider a discrete-time signal:

$$\{u(k)\} = \{u(0), u(1), u(2), \dots\} \tag{3.1}$$

The *Z-transform* of $\{u(k)\}$ is

$$U(z) = u(0)z^0 + u(1)z^{-1} + u(2)z^{-2} + \cdots = \sum_{k=0}^{\infty} u(k)z^{-k} \tag{3.2}$$

We also refer to the Z-transform of a signal as its *Z-domain representation*. By definition, the sum starts at 0, which is the current time, and goes to ∞. By convention, a capital letter [e.g., $U(z)$] is used to denote the Z-transforms of a signal [e.g., $\{u(k)\}$].

The Z-transform provides an explicit representation of the time-domain signal by encoding the values of the signal as the coefficients of z terms. That is, the value of the signal with Z-transform $U(z)$ at time k is the coefficient of z^{-k}. For example, $u(0)$ is the value of the signal at time $k = 0$, which is indicated by its

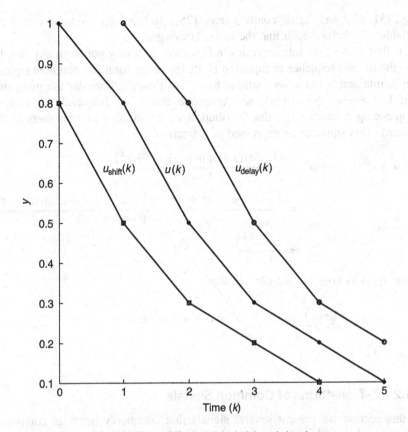

Fig. 3.1 *Time-shifted and time-delayed signals.*

z term having an exponent of 0. $u(1)$ occurs at time $k = 1$, which is indicated by having a z term with an exponent of -1.

To develop this intuition further, consider $\{u(k)\}$ in Figure 3.1. Observe that

$$U(z) = 1 \times z^0 + 0.8 \times z^{-1} + 0.5 \times z^{-2} + 0.3 \times z^{-3} + 0.2 \times z^{-4} + 0.1 \times z^{-5}$$

Now consider the effect of multiplying by z:

$$zU(z) = 1 \times z^1 + 0.8 \times z^0 + 0.5 \times z^{-1} + 0.3 \times z^{-2} + 0.2 \times z^{-3} + 0.1 \times z^{-4}$$

We ignore the coefficient of z^1 since this corresponds to $k = -1$, a term that is not included in the summation in Equation (3.2). Thus, the time-domain representation of $zU(z)$ is $\{0.8, 0.5, 0.3, 0.2, 0.1\}$, which is $\{u_{\text{shift}}(k)\}$. That is, multiplication by z has the effect of shifting the signal to the left (and discarding the $k = 0$ value of the original signal). Similarly, dividing by z has the effect of delaying the original signal by one time unit. This is because $u(k)$ becomes the coefficient of z^{-k-1}, and the coefficient of z^{-k-1} is the value of the signal at time $k + 1$.

The Z-transform is an infinite series. Considerations such as the convergence of the infinite series are discussed in more detail in books on signals and systems (e.g., [51, 69]) and digital controls (e.g., [25]). In this book we assume that the variable z is defined such that the series converges.

At first glance, the infinite series in Equation (3.2) may not seem any simpler than the infinite sequence in Equation (3.1). However, for many common signals, the infinite series has a very simple form. To illustrate, consider the geometric sum $1 + a + a^2 + \cdots + a^k$, an expression that arises frequently in analysis of queueing systems (e.g., the distribution of the number of customers in the system). This sum can be expressed as a fraction:

$$
\begin{aligned}
1 + a + a^2 + \cdots + a^k &= \frac{(1-a)(1 + a + a^2 + \cdots + a^k)}{1-a} \\
&= \frac{1 - a + a - a^2 + a^2 - a^3 + a^3 + \cdots - a^k + a^k - a^{k+1}}{1-a} \\
&= \frac{1 - a^{k+1}}{1-a}
\end{aligned}
$$

In the limit as $k \to \infty$, we can see that

$$
\lim_{k \to \infty} \sum_{i=0}^{k} a^i = \sum_{i=0}^{\infty} a^i = 1 + a + a^2 + \cdots = \frac{1}{1-a}
$$

if $|a| < 1$.

3.1.2 Z-Transforms of Common Signals

In this section we present several signals that commonly occur in computing systems and show how to obtain their Z-transforms. We begin with the *impulse signal*. As depicted in Figure 3.2(a), an impulse models a signal of very short duration. In discrete time, the shortest time unit is one sample time. The unit impulse is defined as $u_{\text{impulse}}(0) = 1$, $u_{\text{impulse}}(k) = 0$ for $k \neq 0$. An impulse signal of any magnitude can be obtained by multiplying $u_{\text{impulse}}(k)$ by an appropriate constant. In computing systems, impulse signals typically result from transients such as a workload surge of short duration. The Z-transform of the unit impulse is

$$
\begin{aligned}
U_{\text{impulse}}(z) &= 1z^0 + 0z^{-1} + 0z^{-2} + \cdots \\
&= 1
\end{aligned}
$$

Next, we consider the *step signal*. As shown in Figure 3.2(b), $\{u_{\text{step}}(k)\} = \{1, 1, 1, 1, \ldots\}$. The name *step* is motivated by the appearance of this signal when it is plotted in continuous time. A step signal occurs in computing systems if, for example, there is a change in workload that occurs in less than one sample time or there is a rapid change in the resources configured (e.g., due to a permanent failure). The Z-transform of the step is

$$
U_{\text{step}}(z) = 1 + z^{-1} + z^{-2} + \cdots = \sum_{k=0}^{\infty} z^{-k} = \frac{1}{1 - z^{-1}} = \frac{z}{z-1} \tag{3.3}
$$

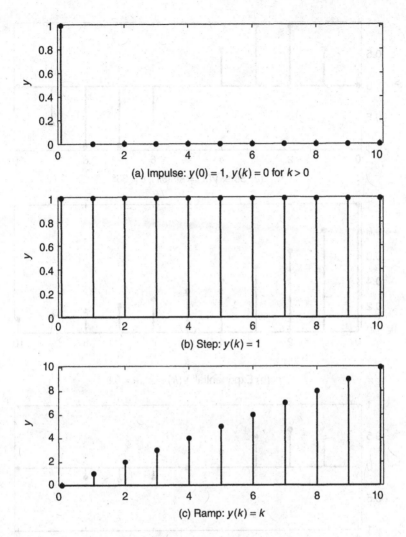

(a) Impulse: $y(0) = 1$, $y(k) = 0$ for $k > 0$

(b) Step: $y(k) = 1$

(c) Ramp: $y(k) = k$

Fig. 3.2 *Common discrete-time signals, part 1.*

The *ramp signal*, $u_{\mathrm{ramp}}(k) = k$, is so-called because when the samples are connected with a straight line, it resembles a ramp as shown in Figure 3.2(c). A ramp can be used to model the gradual buildup of workload in a system or the gradual arrival of end users at the beginning of a workday.

$$U_{\mathrm{ramp}}(z) = 0 + 1z^{-1} + 2z^{-2} + 3z^{-3} + \cdots$$

$$= \sum_{k=0}^{\infty} kz^{-k}$$

$$= \frac{z}{(z-1)^2}$$

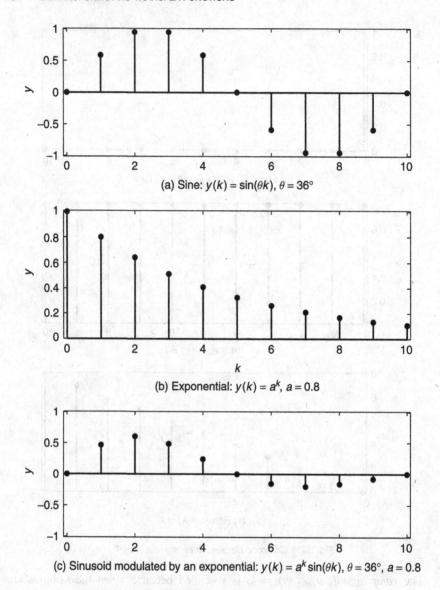

(a) Sine: $y(k) = \sin(\theta k)$, $\theta = 36°$

(b) Exponential: $y(k) = a^k$, $a = 0.8$

(c) Sinusoid modulated by an exponential: $y(k) = a^k \sin(\theta k)$, $\theta = 36°$, $a = 0.8$

Fig. 3.3 *Common discrete-time signals, part 2.*

A discrete sine wave is defined as $u_{\text{sine}}(k) = \sin k\theta$ for a frequency θ. A discrete sine wave is displayed in Figure 3.3(a). Sine waves can be used to model variations in workload due to time of day, day of week, and so on. Another motivation for discussing sine waves is that any periodic signal can be expressed as a combination of sinusoids at different frequencies (using a discrete Fourier expansion).

$$U_{\text{sine}}(z) = 0 + \sin\theta z^{-1} + \sin 2\theta z^{-2} + \sin 3\theta z^{-3} + \cdots$$

$$= \sum_{k=0}^{\infty} \sin(k\theta)z^{-k}$$

$$= \frac{z\sin\theta}{z^2 - (2\cos\theta)z + 1}$$

An exponential or geometric signal is defined as $u_{\text{exp}}(k) = a^k$. If $a > 1$, it grows with time; if $0 < a < 1$, it approaches zero as shown in Figure 3.3(b).

$$U_{\text{exp}}(z) = 1 + az^{-1} + a^2 z^{-2} + a^3 z^{-3} + \cdots$$

$$= \sum_{k=0}^{\infty} a^k z^{-k}$$

$$= \frac{z}{z - a}$$

If $|a| < 1$, we refer to u_{exp} as a *decaying exponential*. If $|a| > 1$, we refer to u_{exp} as a *rising exponential*. If $a = 1$, then $U_{\text{exp}}(z) = z/(z - 1) = U_{\text{step}}(z)$.

The final signal we consider is a sinusoid modulated by an exponential, as displayed in Figure 3.3(c). The time-domain signal is $u_{\text{expsin}}(k) = a^k \sin k\theta$. The Z-transform of this signal is

$$U_{\text{expsin}}(z) = 0 + (a\sin\theta)z^{-1} + (a^2 \sin 2\theta)z^{-2} + (a^3 \sin 3\theta)z^{-3} + \cdots$$

$$= \sum_{k=0}^{\infty} a^k \sin(k\theta)z^{-k}$$

$$= \frac{za\sin\theta}{z^2 - (2a\cos\theta)z + a^2}$$

Both exponential signals and exponentially modulated sinusoids are commonly found in linear systems.

Table 3.1 summarizes the Z-transforms of the common signals just discussed. This table is used extensively in the remainder of the chapter. Note that the Z-transforms in the table (and almost all Z-transforms in the book) are ratios of polynomials of z.

3.1.3 Properties of Z-Transforms

The techniques employed in subsequent chapters combine and otherwise manipulate the Z-transforms of signals to study the time-domain properties of systems. Doing so is facilitated by certain properties of Z-transforms.

TABLE 3.1 Z-Transforms of Common Signals

Signal	Time Domain ($k \geq 0$)	Z-Transform
Impulse	$u(0) = 1$	$U(z) = 1$
Step	$u(k) = 1$	$U(z) = \dfrac{z}{z-1}$
Ramp	$u(k) = k$	$U(z) = \dfrac{z}{(z-1)^2}$
Exponential	$u(k) = a^k$	$U(z) = \dfrac{z}{z-a}$
Sine	$u(k) = \sin k\theta$	$U(z) = \dfrac{z \sin \theta}{z^2 - (2\cos\theta)z + 1}$
Cosine	$u(k) = \cos k\theta$	$U(z) = \dfrac{z(z - \cos\theta)}{z^2 - (2\cos\theta)z + 1}$
ExpSin	$u(k) = a^k \sin k\theta$	$U(z) = \dfrac{za \sin \theta}{z^2 - (2a\cos\theta)z + a^2}$
ExpCos	$u(k) = a^k \cos k\theta$	$U(z) = \dfrac{z(z - a\cos\theta)}{z^2 - (2a\cos\theta)z + a^2}$

First, we note that Z-transforms are linear functions. That is, if a signal $\{u(k)\}$ is multiplied by a constant a in the time domain, to give $y(k) = au(k)$, then its Z-transform is multiplied by the same constant to result in $Y(z) = aU(z)$. Similarly, if two signals $\{u(k)\}$ and $\{v(k)\}$ are added together in the time domain to result in a new signal $y(k) = u(k) + v(k)$, their Z-transforms are added to give $Y(z) = U(z) + V(z)$.

Frequently, our models describe how signals are shifted and delayed. Recall from the discussion at the beginning of Section 3.1 that shifts and delays are easily described in terms of Z-transforms. A delay corresponds to a multiplication by z^{-1}. This can be shown directly from the definition of the Z-transform. Consider $y(k) = u(k-1)$. The Z-transform of $y(k)$ is

$$Y(z) = \sum_{k=0}^{\infty} y(k)z^{-k} = \sum_{k=0}^{\infty} u(k-1)z^{-k} = z^{-1} \sum_{k=0}^{\infty} u(k-1)z^{-(k-1)}$$

$$= z^{-1} \sum_{m=-1}^{\infty} u(j)z^{-m} = z^{-1} \sum_{m=0}^{\infty} u(j)z^{-m}$$

$$= z^{-1}U(z)$$

where we have used the substitution $m = k - 1$ and the fact that $u(-1) = 0$. Similarly, a delay of n sample times is represented as a multiplication by z^{-n}.

TABLE 3.2 Z-Transform Properties[a]

Property	Time Domain	Z-Transform
Scaling	$y(k) = au(k)$	$Y(z) = aU(z)$
Addition	$y(k) = u(k) + v(k)$	$Y(z) = U(z) + V(z)$
Unit delay	$y(k) = u(k-1)$	$Y(z) = z^{-1}U(z)$
n-delay	$y(k) = u(k-n)$	$Y(z) = z^{-n}U(z)$
Unit shift	$y(k) = u(k+1)$	$Y(z) = zU(z) - zu(0)$
n-shift	$y(k) = u(k+n)$	$Y(z) = z^n U(z) - z^n u(0) - \cdots - zu(n-1)$

[a]$u(k), v(k), y(k)$ are discrete-time signals, and $U(z), V(z), Y(z)$ are their corresponding Z-transforms. The numbers a, b, c are constants.

A shift is slightly more complicated because we must consider an initial condition. Let $y(k) = u(k+1)$. Applying the definition of Z-transforms, we have

$$Y(z) = \sum_{k=0}^{\infty} y(k)z^{-k} = \sum_{k=0}^{\infty} u(k+1)z^{-k} = z\sum_{k=0}^{\infty} u(k+1)z^{-(k+1)}$$

$$= z\sum_{m=1}^{\infty} u(j)z^{-m} = z\left[\left(\sum_{m=0}^{\infty} u(m)z^{-m}\right) - u(0)\right]$$

$$= z(U(z) - u(0))$$

The derivation uses the substitution $m = k + 1$ and must include the initial condition $u(0)$. Generalizing, a shift of n sample times is indicated by multiplying by z^n [with some care as to the initial conditions $u(0), u(1), \ldots, u(n-1)$].

The foregoing results are summarized in Table 3.2. An application of these properties is discussed in the following example.

Example 3.1: Measuring RIS in the IBM Lotus Domino Server   In the IBM Lotus Domino Server of Section 1.6.1, every T_s seconds the sensor computes RIS, the number of remote procedure calls (RPCs) in the IBM Lotus Domino Server. The sensor uses the server log, which specifies the time at which each RPC arrived and when it departed. Unfortunately, the log does not contain active RPCs, those that are being processed by the IBM Lotus Domino Server at the time that the log is sampled. Hence, the sensor underestimates the true value of RIS. One way to increase accuracy is to delay one sample time before examining the server log since some of the RPCs that are active at time k will have completed by time $k+1$ and hence have their records recorded in the server log. Indeed, we could delay $n \geq 1$ sample times before reading the log to ensure a still more accurate measurement of RIS.

Introducing delays into a sensor changes its behavior. We use Z-transforms to express this delay. Let $q(k)$ denote the true value of RIS at time k, and let $m(k+n)$ be the measured value of RIS obtained by sampling the server log at time $k+n$. A very simple (and not too accurate) way to model this is to view a delay of one time step as resulting in $m(k) = q(k-1)$. Similarly, a delay of n

time steps is modeled as $m(k) = q(k-n)$. Using this approach, the Z-transform of the output of a sensor with a delay of one time step is $M(z) = z^{-1}Q(z)$. For an n-time-step delay, the Z-transform is $M(z) = z^{-n}Q(z)$.

3.1.4 Inverse Z-Transforms

The time-domain signal $\{u(k)\}$ can be recovered from $U(z)$ in several ways. The simplest is through table look-up. If $U(z)$ can be found directly in Table 3.1, the time-domain signal can be simply read from the table. Even if the desired transform is not a table entry, it may be a combination of entries that allow us to use the properties in Table 3.2 to recover $u(k)$.

For example, consider $U(z) = z/(z-1) + z/(z+0.5)$. We use the entries for step and exponential in Table 3.1 along with the addition property in Table 3.2 to see that $u(k) = 1 + (-0.5)^k$.

A more involved example is $U(z) = 2/(z-1)^2$. This looks similar to the ramp entry $z/(z-1)^2$, but there is a 2 in the numerator and no z. We can make it look like the ramp entry by multiplying by $z^{-1}z = 1$ and factoring out the constant 2:

$$U(z) = 2z^{-1}\frac{z}{(z-1)^2} \tag{3.4}$$

This results in the Z-transform of a ramp multiplied by $2z^{-1}$. Consulting Table 3.2, we see that the multiplication by a scalar (here 2) behaves analogously in the time domain, and the multiplication by z^{-1} corresponds to a unit delay. Thus, the corresponding time domain signal is

$$u(k) = 2(k-1) \tag{3.5}$$

for $k \geq 1$.

Not all Z-transforms can be found in Table 3.1. In fact, there are infinitely many possible time-domain signals, and it would be impossible to compile them all into a table. However, the definition of the Z-transform provides another way to find $\{u(k)\}$. Recall that $U(z)$ is an infinite series in which the coefficient of z^{-k} is $u(k)$. Thus, finding $\{u(k)\}$ is equivalent to determining these coefficients. If $U(z)$ is expressed as a fraction, the $u(k)$ can be found by long division. For example, let $U(z) = 2/(z-1)^2 = 2/(z^2 - 2z + 1)$, as before. We set up the long division:

$$
\begin{array}{r}
2z^{-2} + 4z^{-3} + 6z^{-4} + \cdots \\
z^2 - 2z + 1 \overline{)\, 2 + 0z^{-1} + 0z^{-2} + 0z^{-3} + 0z^{-4} + \cdots} \\
\underline{2 - 4z^{-1} + 2z^{-2}} \\
4z^{-1} - 2z^{-2} \\
\underline{4z^{-1} - 8z^{-2} + 4z^{-3}} \\
6z^{-2} - 4z^{-3} \\
\underline{6z^{-2} - 12z^{-3} + 6z^{-4}} \\
8z^{-3} - 6z^{-4} \\
\vdots
\end{array}
\tag{3.6}
$$

That is, $u(2) = 2$, $u(3) = 4$, and $u(4) = 6$. This is consistent with $u(k) = 2(k-1)$ for $k \geq 1$.

Although long division can always be used to recover the time-domain signal, it can be tedious to perform. An alternative is *partial fraction expansion*, which allows us to express $U(z)$ as a sum of simple components called partial fractions [assuming that $U(z)$ is a ratio of rational polynomials of z]. We can use Table 3.1 to invert the partial fractions and then apply the addition property to construct $\{u(k)\}$.

To illustrate partial fraction expansion, suppose that we have $U(z) = b/(z^2 + a_1 z + a_2)$, and the denominator can be factored as $z^2 + a_1 z + a_2 = (z - p_1)(z - p_2)$, where p_1 and p_2 are both real. Then

$$U(z) = \frac{b}{(z - p_1)(z - p_2)}$$

$$= \frac{c_1}{z - p_1} + \frac{c_2}{z - p_2}$$

where the terms $c_i/(z - p_i)$ are called the partial fractions of $U(z)$. The coefficients of the numerators, c_i, can be found by collecting and matching terms:

$$U(z) = \frac{b}{(z - p_1)(z - p_2)}$$

$$= \frac{c_1}{(z - p_1)} + \frac{c_2}{(z - p_2)}$$

$$= \frac{c_1(z - p_2) + c_2(z - p_1)}{(z - p_1)(z - p_2)}$$

$$= \frac{(c_1 + c_2)z - (c_1 p_2 + c_2 p_1)}{(z - p_1)(z - p_2)}$$

Since the numerators must match for the equality to hold, we have

$$(c_1 + c_2)z = 0z$$

$$-(c_1 p_2 + c_2 p_1) = b$$

which gives us two equations to solve for the two unknowns c_1 and c_2. This simple method works well when there are only two or three terms in the denominator and all of the roots are real and distinct. Although the algebra is more involved for higher-order terms and complex roots, there is a well-developed method for manually finding partial fractions for arbitrary Z-transforms. We omit this presentation here, however, and refer the reader to the MATLAB techniques in Section 3.6 and to [25].

3.1.5   Using Z-Transforms to Solve Difference Equations

As described in Chapter 2, difference equations provide a simple way to model the dynamics of computing systems. It turns out that Z-transforms can be used to solve linear difference equations. By *solve*, we mean expressing the output $y(k+1)$ in terms of the inputs $u(1), \ldots, u(k+1)$ and the initial conditions $y(0)$. Such an expression provides a convenient way to study the control characteristics of systems, such as the effect of changes in the reference input as well as the effects of disturbance and noise inputs.

The following four steps outline the procedure for solving difference equations using Z-transforms:

1. Take the Z-transform of all terms in the difference equation.
2. Solve for the Z-transform of the unknown variable (output).
3. Plug in the Z-transform of the known variable (input).
4. Take the inverse Z-transform to find the output in the time domain.

The last step can sometimes be omitted, since many properties of a signal can be inferred from its Z-transform.

Example 3.2: Discrete integrator A simple example of a linear difference equation is an integrator:

$$y(k + 1) = y(k) + u(k) \tag{3.7}$$

Its Z-transform is found term by term using the properties derived in Section 3.1.3. First, observe that

$$\sum_{k=0}^{\infty} y(k + 1)z^{-k} = zY(z) - zy(0)$$

So

$$zY(z) - zy(0) = Y(z) + U(z) \tag{3.8}$$

We now solve for $Y(z)$ as

$$Y(z) = \frac{.1}{z - 1} \left[U(z) + zy(0) \right] \tag{3.9}$$

This result applies to any input signal and any initial condition $y(0)$. Now assume that $y(0) = 0$ and $U(z) = z/(z - 1)$ (a step function), as shown in the top left plot of Figure 3.4. In this case we have

$$Y(z) = \frac{1}{z - 1} \frac{z}{z - 1} = \frac{z}{(z - 1)^2} \tag{3.10}$$

To find the inverse Z-transform, we consult Table 3.1 and see that $y(k) = k$ is a ramp function. As expected from basic calculus, the integral of a constant is a ramp.

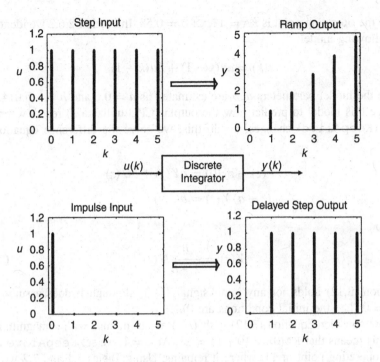

Fig. 3.4 *Inputs and outputs for the discrete integrator. The discrete integral of a step is a ramp, and the discrete integral of an impulse is a delayed step.*

Next, suppose that $u(k)$ is an impulse. Again, we assume that $y(0) = 0$, which results in

$$Y(z) = \frac{1}{z - 1} \cdot 1 = z^{-1} \left(\frac{z}{z - 1} \right) \tag{3.11}$$

This is a *delayed* step in that $y(0) = 0$ and $y(k) = 1$ for $k \geq 1$. Thus, the integral of an impulse is a delayed step. Figure 3.4 summarizes the input–output relationships just discussed.

In general, the integral of a discrete time signal is not the same as its continuous-time counterpart. For example, the discrete integral of a ramp is not a quadratic function, and the discrete integral of a cosine function is not a sine.

Example 3.3: Apache HTTP Server with impulse input Another example of a difference equation is the model of the relationship between KeepAlive and CPU in the Apache HTTP Server. Let $y(k)$ be the offset value of CPU(k) and $u(k)$ be the offset value of KA(k) (KeepAlive). That is,

$$y(k) = \text{CPU}(k) - \overline{\text{CPU}}$$
$$u(k) = \text{KA}(k) - \overline{\text{KA}}$$

where the operating point is $\overline{KA} = 11$, $\overline{CPU} = 0.58$. In Section 2.6.2 we identified the following model:

$$y(k) = ay(k-1) + bu(k-1)$$

where the model parameters a, b are estimated as $a = 0.6$ and $b = -0.014$. We can use this model to predict how the output (CPU utilization) reacts when the input (KeepAlive) changes. To do this, we solve the difference equation to obtain

$$zY(z) - zy(0) = aY(z) + bU(z)$$

$$(z-a)Y(z) = bU(z)$$

and so

$$Y(z) = \frac{b}{z-a}U(z) \tag{3.12}$$

Equation (3.12) holds for any input signal $U(z)$, although it does assume that $y(0) = 0$ (i.e., the initial conditions are 0).

Now consider Equation (3.12) with $U(z)$ as an impulse with a magnitude of 10. This means that $KA(0) = 10 + 11 = 21$. At $k = 1$, we set KeepAlive back to its operating point of 11, where it remains. Using Tables 3.1 and 3.2 we find that $U(z) = 10$, and thus

$$Y(z) = \frac{10b}{z-a} = \frac{-0.14}{z-0.6} = -0.14z^{-1}\frac{z}{z-0.6} \tag{3.13}$$

Again consulting Tables 3.1 and 3.2, we note that multiplying the Z-transform by a constant (-0.14) multiplies the time-domain signal by the same constant. The z^{-1} in front corresponds to a delay of one time step, and the fraction $z/(z-0.6)$ gives a time-domain expression of $(0.6)^k$. Thus, we arrive at the time-domain solution

$$y(k) = -0.14(0.6)^{k-1} \tag{3.14}$$

for $k \geq 1$. That is,

$$CPU(k) = y(k) + \overline{CPU}$$

$$= -0.14(0.6)^{k-1} + 0.58$$

Using this result and assuming that $y(0) = 0$, we have

$$y(k) = \{0, -0.14, -0.084, -0.05, -0.03, -0.018, \ldots\}$$

$$CPU(k) = \{0.58, 0.44, 0.50, 0.53, 0.55, 0.56, \ldots\}$$

A plot of CPU versus time is shown in Figure 3.5. The time evolution of CPU is interpreted as follows. At first, CPU drops by 0.1 due to the increase in

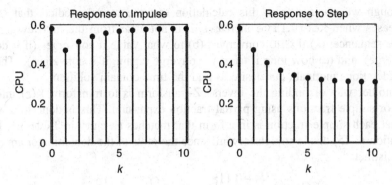

Fig. 3.5 *Predicted response of the Apache HTTP Server output* CPU *utilization to an impulse and step change in the value of* KeepAlive *with a different workload in which $b = -0.11$.*

KeepAlive. However, when KeepAlive returns to its operating point, CPU utilization gradually increases to its operating point. Indeed, as k gets larger, $y(k) \rightarrow 0$ and CPU$(k) \rightarrow 0.58$. After five time steps, CPU is within 1% of 0.58, the operating point for CPU. Note that the speed at which this convergence occurs depends on 0.6, the base of the exponent in Equation (3.14).

Example 3.4: Apache HTTP Server with a step input   Now, consider a step input, $u(k) = 10$ for $k \geq 0$, in which KeepAlive is set to 21 at $k = 0$ and kept there. We use a slight variation on Equation (3.12) in which there is a different workload, so $b = -0.11$.

$$Y(z) = \frac{b}{z-a}\frac{10z}{z-1} = \frac{10bz}{(z-1)(z-a)} = \frac{-0.11z}{z^2 - 1.6z + 0.6} \qquad (3.15)$$

No similar form can be found in Table 3.1. However, we can also compute $y(k)$ directly by long division:

$$
\require{enclose}
\begin{array}{r}
-0.11z^{-1} - 0.18z^{-2} - 0.22z^{-3} + \cdots \\[2pt]
z^2 - 1.6z + 0.6 \enclose{longdiv}{\;-0.11z \quad +0 \quad\;\; +0z^{-1} \quad\;\; +0z^{-2} \quad\;\; +0z^{-3} + \cdots} \\
\end{array}
$$

$$
\begin{aligned}
&- 0.11z + 0.18 - 0.066z^{-1} \\
\hline
&-0.18 + 0.066z^{-1} \\
&-0.18 \;+ 0.29z^{-1} - 0.12z^{-2} \\
\hline
&- 0.22z^{-1} + 0.12z^{-2} \\
&- 0.22z^{-1} + 0.35z^{-2} - 0.13z^{-3} \\
\hline
&- 0.24z^{-2} + 0.13z^{-3}
\end{aligned}
$$

$$(3.16)$$

Thus, we have

$$y(k) = \{0, -0.11, -0.18, -0.22, \dots\}$$
$$\text{CPU}(k) = \{0.58, 0.47, 0.40, \dots\}$$

Although we can see from this calculation that the model predicts that CPU decreases when KeepAlive increases, it is not clear from the first few terms in the sequence: (a) if CPU converges, (b) to what value it converges (if it does converge), and (c) how long it takes to converge (again, if it converges). These considerations motivate our desire to find the time-domain solution.

Another way of finding the inverse Z-transform is to transform $Y(z)$ into a sum of simple fractions using partial fraction expansion. This is done in a way so that each simple fraction is in a form that matches an entry in Table 3.1. For Equation (3.15) this is straightforward since the roots of the denominator are real and distinct:

$$Y(z) = \frac{-0.11z}{(z-1)(z-0.6)} = \frac{c_1}{z-1} + \frac{c_2}{z-0.6} \tag{3.17}$$

We want to solve for the constants c_1 and c_2 such that

$$\frac{-0.11z}{(z-1)(z-0.6)} = \frac{c_1}{z-1} + \frac{c_2}{z-0.6}$$
$$= \frac{c_1(z-0.6) + c_2(z-1)}{(z-1)(z-0.6)}$$
$$= \frac{(c_1+c_2)z - (0.6c_1+c_2)}{(z-1)(z-0.6)}$$

Matching terms in the numerator on the left and right sides of the equation, we get

$$(c_1+c_2)z = -0.11z$$
$$0.6c_1 + c_2 = 0$$

which can be solved to find $c_1 = -0.275$ and $c_2 = 0.165$. Now Table 3.1 can be used to find $y(k)$:

$$Y(z) = \frac{-0.275}{z-1} + \frac{0.165}{z-0.6}$$
$$= -0.275z^{-1}\frac{z}{z-1} + 0.165z^{-1}\frac{z}{z-0.6}$$
$$y(k) = -0.275 + 0.165(0.6)^{k-1} \qquad \text{for } k \geq 1$$

From this we conclude that

$$\text{CPU}(k) = y(k) + \overline{\text{CPU}} \qquad \text{for } k \geq 1$$
$$= 0.305 + 0.165(0.6)^{k-1} \qquad \text{for } k \geq 1$$

This shows that as $k \to \infty$, the term $(0.6)^{k-1}$ approaches zero, and thus $y(k) \to -0.275$ and $\text{CPU}(k) \to 0.305$. A plot of the predicted CPU versus time is shown in Figure 3.5.

3.2 CHARACTERISTICS INFERRED FROM Z-TRANSFORMS

Z-transforms provide insight into the time-domain properties of signals without the need for a time-domain solution. In fact, the most important time-domain properties of signals only require knowledge of the roots of the denominator of the Z-transform. In some cases, these roots are complex numbers. Thus, we begin with a brief review of complex variables.

3.2.1 Review of Complex Variables

Complex variables are often needed to express the roots of polynomials. For example, a first-order polynomial with real coefficients [e.g., $P(z) = az + b$] always has one real root (exactly $z = -b/a$). However, a quadratic or second-order polynomial may have complex roots. The roots of the polynomial $P(z)$ can be found using the well-known quadratic equation

$$P(z) = az^2 + bz + c$$

$$z = \frac{-b \pm \sqrt{b^2 - 4ac}}{2a}$$

If $(b^2 - 4ac) \geq 0$, both roots are real; otherwise, they are complex. We use the imaginary number j to represent the square root of -1. That is, $j = \sqrt{-1}$. (Another convention is $i = \sqrt{-1}$.) The complex roots can then be expressed as

$$z = \frac{-b}{2a} \pm j \frac{\sqrt{4ac - b^2}}{2a} \tag{3.18}$$

where we have factored the -1 out of the square root.

Complex numbers have both a real and an imaginary part. In this example, the real part is $-b/2a$ and the imaginary part is $\pm j\sqrt{4ac - b^2}/2a$. As a numerical example, consider the polynomial $P(z) = z^2 + 2z + 10$, with roots

$$z = \frac{-2 \pm \sqrt{2^2 - 4(1)(10)}}{2(1)}$$

$$= \frac{-2 \pm \sqrt{-36}}{2}$$

$$= -1 \pm j3$$

Thus, we can write $P(z)$ in its factored form as

$$P(z) = (z + 1 + j3)(z + 1 - j3)$$

Using *rectangular coordinates*, complex numbers can be represented graphically. The real part is the coordinate for the horizontal axis, and the imaginary part is the coordinate for the vertical axis. For example, let $z = c + jd$ be a

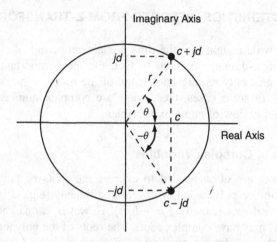

Fig. 3.6 *Summary of the complex plane. For a complex number $c + jd$, the real part (horizontal axis) is c, and the imaginary part (vertical axis) is d. The distance from the origin to (c, d) is $r = \sqrt{c^2 + d^2}$. The angle of the vector to (c, d) is $\theta = \tan^{-1}(d/c)$. $c + jd$ and $c - jd$ are complex conjugates. They have the same distance from the origin. Their angles have opposite signs.*

complex number. This is plotted as shown in Figure 3.6. In addition to rectangular coordinates, z can also be represented as *polar coordinates* consisting of (1) the distance to the origin or the *magnitude of a complex number* z, and (2) the *angle of a complex number* z with respect to the positive real axis. Simple trigonometry gives the distance as $r = \sqrt{c^2 + d^2}$ and the angle as $\theta = \tan^{-1}(d/c)$.

The *complex exponential* is defined as $e^{j\theta} = \cos \theta + j \sin \theta$. Thus, from the definitions of r and θ, we have

$$re^{j\theta} = r (\cos \theta + j \sin \theta)$$

$$= r \frac{c}{\sqrt{c^2 + d^2}} + jr \frac{d}{\sqrt{c^2 + d^2}}$$

$$= c + jd$$

That is,

$$c = r \cos \theta$$

$$d = r \sin \theta$$

(3.19)

We can also use the complex exponential to express sines and cosines. For example, consider

$$e^{j\theta} + e^{-j\theta} = \cos \theta + j \sin \theta + \cos \theta - j \sin \theta = 2 \cos \theta$$

$$e^{j\theta} - e^{-j\theta} = \cos \theta + j \sin \theta - \cos \theta + j \sin \theta = 2j \sin \theta$$

Thus, we have the expressions for sine and cosine in terms of complex exponentials as

$$\cos\theta = \frac{1}{2}(e^{j\theta} + e^{-j\theta})$$

$$\sin\theta = \frac{1}{2j}(e^{j\theta} - e^{-j\theta})$$

Note that these formulas can also be used to obtain the Z-transforms of $\sin k\theta$, $\cos k\theta$ from the Z-transform of the exponential. Since $\sin k\theta = (1/2j)(e^{jk\theta} - e^{-jk\theta}) = (1/2j)[(e^{j\theta})^k - (e^{-j\theta})^k]$, we have that the Z-transform of $\sin k\theta$ is

$$\frac{1}{2j}\left(\frac{z}{z - e^{j\theta}} - \frac{z}{z - e^{-j\theta}}\right) = \frac{1}{2j}\frac{z(z - e^{-j\theta}) - z(z - e^{j\theta})}{(z - e^{j\theta})(z - e^{-j\theta})}$$

$$= \frac{1}{2j}\frac{z\left(e^{j\theta} - e^{-j\theta}\right)}{z^2 - z(e^{j\theta} + e^{-j\theta}) + 1}$$

$$= \frac{z\sin\theta}{z^2 - 2z\cos\theta + 1}$$

3.2.2 Poles and Zeros of a Z-Transform

Many properties of a signal can be inferred from its Z-transform. Consider Equation (3.17). This can be written as

$$Y(z) = \frac{-0.11z}{(z - 1)(z - 0.6)} = \frac{N(z)}{D(z)} \tag{3.20}$$

where $N(z) = -0.11z$ and $D(z) = (z - 1)(z - 0.6)$. That is, $Y(z)$ is a ratio of polynomials in z. It turns out that the denominator polynomial $D(z)$ has special significance. Indeed, it is referred to as the *characteristic polynomial* of the Z-transform. The *characteristic equation* is obtained by setting the characteristic polynomial to 0. Solving for z, we obtain the roots of the characteristic polynomial, which are called the *poles*. One justification for the term pole is that if p is a pole of $Y(z)$, the magnitude of $Y(z)$ increases rapidly as $z \to p$, giving a polelike appearance to the plot of $Y(z)$.

The poles of a Z-transform are important because they determine key properties of $y(k)$, especially stability and settling times. The intuition here is based on the manner in which partial fraction expansion converts a Z-transform into a time-domain expression. In essence, $y(k)$ is expressed as the sum of terms in which a single pole of $Y(z)$ is raised to a power that is some constant plus k. There is one such term for each pole. To illustrate, consider Example 3.4, in which

$$Y(z) = \frac{-0.11z}{(z - 1)(z - 0.6)}$$

The poles are 1 and 0.6, and the time-domain solution is $y(k) = (-0.275)(1)^k + (0.165)(0.6)^{k-1}$. Here, the pole at 1 is raised to the kth power, and the pole at 0.6 is raised to the $(k-1)$th power. Thus, in general, if a pole a is larger than 1, $y(k)$ increases without bound since a^k is unbounded as k increases. If the pole a is negative, $y(k)$ oscillates since a^k is positive if k is even and is negative if k is odd. And if two systems, each with a single pole, are such that $|a_1| < |a_2| < 1$, the system with pole a_1 settles faster than the system with pole a_2 since $|a_1|^k < |a_2|^k$.

Consider the (real-valued) exponential $u(k) = a^k$ that has the Z-transform $U(z) = z/(z-a)$. The denominator polynomial has one root, $z = a$, which is always real. We note that in the limit as $k \to \infty$, the time-domain signal $u(k) = a^k$ approaches zero if the *magnitude* of a is less than 1, whereas it approaches infinity if the magnitude of a is greater than 1. If the magnitude is equal to 1, it stays bounded but does not go to zero (if $a = 1$, we have the step function; if $a = -1$, the signal alternates between ± 1).

Suppose that $|a| < 1$. The speed with which $u(k) \to 0$ depends on the magnitude of a. As shown in Figure 3.7, the convergence is fast if a is close to 0, and becomes slower as a approaches 1. Also note that for $a < 0$, $u(k)$ alternates between positive and negative values.

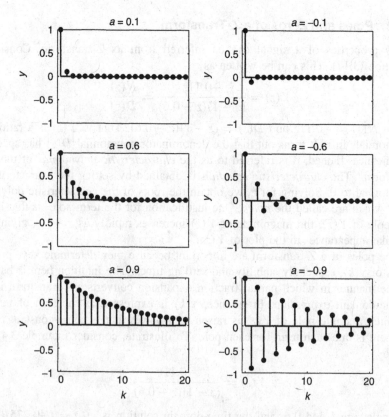

Fig. 3.7 *Effect of pole magnitude on the speed of convergence of an exponentially decaying signal* $y(k) = a^k$.

Theoretically, $u(k)$ never reaches exactly zero. However, a typical rule of thumb is that $u(k) \approx 0$ when it is 2% of $u(0)$. We can find the time (in units of k) to reach this 2% by solving for the value of k when $u(k) = |a|^k = 0.02$ [assuming that $u(0) = 1$].

$$k \log |a| = \log 0.02 = -3.912$$

$$k \approx \frac{-4}{\log |a|}$$

where the logarithm refers to the natural logarithm (base e). If $|a| < 1$, $\log |a|$ is negative, resulting in a positive value for k. To convert k into seconds (or minutes), k must be multiplied by the sample time, T_s.

Now consider the sine function $\sin k\theta$ and its Z-transforms,

$$U(z) = \frac{z \sin \theta}{z^2 - (2 \cos \theta)z + 1}$$

This signal has a quadratic in the denominator, meaning that there are two roots, and thus two poles. We can find them using the quadratic formula as

$$z = \frac{2 \cos \theta \pm \sqrt{4 \cos^2 \theta - 4}}{2}$$

$$= \cos \theta \pm \sqrt{-\sin^2 \theta}$$

$$= \cos \theta \pm j \sin \theta$$

$$= e^{\pm j\theta}$$

Both poles have magnitude 1, and are at an angle of $\pm\theta$ from the positive real axis. Thus, the frequency of oscillation θ is determined by the angle of the roots in the complex plane. Note that since the denominator of the Z-transform of the cosine function is the same as that of the sine function, sine and cosine have the same poles.

Finally, consider the sinusoid modulated by an exponential,

$$U(z) = \frac{za \sin \theta}{z^2 - (2a \cos \theta)z + a^2}$$

Again, there is a quadratic in the denominator, indicating a pair of poles. The quadratic formula gives

$$z = \frac{2a \cos \theta \pm \sqrt{4a^2 \cos^2 \theta - 4a^2}}{2}$$

$$= a \cos \theta \pm \sqrt{-a^2 \sin^2 \theta}$$

$$= a \cos \theta \pm ja \sin \theta$$

$$= ae^{\pm j\theta}$$

The roots have magnitude a and are at an angle of $\pm\theta$ from the real axis. Thus, the rate of decay of the signal (how fast it converges to zero) is determined by a, and the frequency of oscillation is determined by θ.

Our analysis can easily be generalized to handle multiple poles. Recall that using partial fraction expansion, $U(z)$ can be expanded into a sum of simpler terms. It turns out that each term has either a single real pole or a pair of complex poles. We can apply the analysis above to determine the time-domain properties of each term in the partial fraction expansion. Further, due to the addition property of Z-transforms, $u(k)$ is the sum of the time-domain contributions of each term. For example, let

$$U(z) = \frac{z^2 + 5z + 6}{(z-1)(z-0.5)(z^2 - z + 0.5)}$$

$$= \frac{c_1}{z-1} + \frac{c_2}{z-0.5} + \frac{c_3 z + c_4}{z^2 - z + 0.5}$$

$$u(k) = c_1 + c_2(0.5)^k + 0.71^k[d_3 \cos(0.79k) + d_4 \sin(0.79k)]$$

The poles of $U(z)$ are $\{1, 0.5, 0.5 \pm j0.5\}$ or $\{1, 0.5, 0.7e^{\pm j0.79}\}$. For simplicity, we do not compute the coefficients $c_1, c_2, c_3, c_4, d_3, d_4$. However, note that the time-domain properties of u can be determined without knowing the $u(k)$ values exactly. The c_i and d_i terms indicate the relative weight of the contribution of each pole. The pole at 1 contributes a delayed step term, the pole at 0.5 contributes a decaying exponential, and the complex poles at $0.7e^{\pm j0.79}$ contribute a combination of exponentially modulated sine and cosine terms, where the exponential has the base 0.71 and the frequency of the sinusoid is 0.79.

Thus far, we have focused on the denominator of $U(z)$. The roots of the numerator of $U(z)$ are called the *zeros*. That is, if q is a zero of $U(z)$, then $U(q) = 0$. The zeros of $U(z)$ play a role in the time-domain properties of $\{u(k)\}$, although not as central as the poles. In particular, the zeros contribute to the relative weighting of the terms in the partial fraction expansion of $U(z)$ and thus are particularly important in determining the properties of $u(k)$ for small k.

3.2.3 Steady-State Analysis

Often we are interested in what happens to a signal as k becomes very large. In particular, if $\{y(k)\}$ converges, we are interested in the value to which it converges. We refer to this as the *steady-state value* of $y(k)$ and denote it by y_{ss}. One example of where the analysis of steady-state values is of great interest is control error (the difference between the reference value and the output of a feedback system) since we want to know if this signal converges to zero.

There are several ways to find the steady-state value of a signal (assuming that the signal converges). One approach operates directly on the difference equations. To find y_{ss}, we assume that the input is held constant at u_{ss}. If $\{y(k)\}$ converges, we can substitute u_{ss} for u (regardless of the time index) and similarly, substitute

y_{ss} for y. Then we solve for y_{ss}. To illustrate, consider Equation (2.5) as $k \to \infty$:

$$y_{ss} = ay_{ss} + bu_{ss}$$

$$(1 - a)y_{ss} = bu_{ss} \tag{3.21}$$

$$y_{ss} = \frac{b}{1-a}u_{ss}$$

(assuming that $|a| < 1$).

The *final value theorem* provides a second approach to finding y_{ss}. The phrase *final value* originates from the fact that $y_{ss} = y(\infty)$ (assuming that y_{ss} exists).

Theorem 3.1 (Final value theorem). If all the poles of $(z - 1)F(z)$ are inside the unit circle, then

$$\lim_{k \to \infty} f(k) = \lim_{z \to 1}(z - 1)F(z) \tag{3.22}$$

To illustrate the use of the final value theorem, we once again consider Equation (2.5). Taking Z-transforms, we have

$$zY(z) - zy(0) = aY(z) + bU(z)$$

As before, let $u(k) = u_{ss}$, so $U(z) = u_{ss}[z/(z - 1)]$. We can solve for $Y(z)$ as

$$(z - a)Y(z) = zy(0) + b\frac{u_{ss}z}{z - 1}$$

$$Y(z) = \frac{y(0)z}{z - a} + \frac{bu_{ss}z}{(z - a)(z - 1)}$$

Note that $(z - 1)Y(z)$ has one pole at $z = a$. Assuming that $|a| < 1$, the final value theorem can be applied. Thus,

$$\lim_{k \to \infty} y(k) = \lim_{z \to 1}(z - 1)Y(z)$$

$$y_{ss} = \lim_{z \to 1}\left[(z - 1)\frac{y(0)z}{z - a} + (z - 1)\frac{bu_{ss}z}{(z - a)(z - 1)}\right]$$

$$= \frac{b}{1-a}u_{ss}$$

which is the same as Equation (3.21).

We emphasize that care must be taken when applying the final value theorem to ensure that the poles lie within the unit circle. For example, consider $Y(z) = z/(z - 2)$. Blindly applying Equation (3.22) gives

$$\lim_{k \to \infty} y(k) = \lim_{z \to 1}(z - 1)Y(z) = \lim_{z \to 1}(z - 1)\frac{z}{z - 2} = 0 \tag{3.23}$$

However, this result is incorrect because $Y(z)$ has a pole at 2. Indeed, consulting Table 3.1, we see that $y(k) = 2^k$. So $\lim_{k\to\infty} y(k) = \infty$.

Example 3.5: Apache HTTP Server with step input (continued)   Recall the expression for $Y(z)$ from Example 3.4:

$$Y(z) = \frac{-0.11z}{z^2 - 1.6z + 0.6} = \frac{-0.11z}{(z-1)(z-0.6)} \tag{3.15}$$

First, we note that the roots of the denominator of $Y(z)$ are $\{0.6, 1\}$. When we compute $(z-1)Y(z)$, there is a pole at 0.6. This pole is inside the unit circle, so we can apply the final value theorem. We compute

$$\lim_{k\to\infty} y(k) = \lim_{z\to 1}(z-1)Y(z)$$

$$= \lim_{z\to 1}(z-1)\frac{-0.11z}{(z-1)(z-0.6)}$$

$$= \lim_{z\to 1}\frac{-0.11z}{z-0.6}$$

$$= \frac{-0.11}{1-0.6} = \frac{-0.11}{0.4} = -0.275$$

which agrees with our conclusion in Example 3.4. Note that to find the steady-state value, we do not need to compute the time-domain solution. Only the Z-transform $Y(z)$ is needed.

3.2.4 Time Domain versus Z-Domain

An underlying theme in the preceding discussions is that the poles of the Z-transform provide key insights into the time-domain properties of signals. Figure 3.8 shows

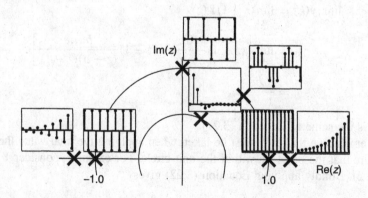

Fig. 3.8 *Relationship between location of the poles of $U(z)$ and the time-domain behavior of $u(k)$.*

the relationship between the location of a pole in the complex plane and the time-domain behavior of a signal with that pole. In particular, we compare this behavior for three partitions of the complex plane: (1) inside versus outside the unit circle, (2) on versus off the positive real axis, and (3) the negative real axis.

First consider the location of poles relative to the unit circle. From the figure, poles that lie outside the unit circle result in unbounded signals, poles that lie on the unit circle result in bounded signals, and poles inside the unit circle result in signals that converge to zero. The rate of convergence depends on the magnitude of the poles: The closer the pole is to the origin, the faster the convergence. When the pole is zero, convergence occurs in one step.

Next, we compare signals with poles that lie on the positive real axis with signals whose poles are not on the positive real axis. (In the complex plane, poles on the negative real axis have an angle of 180 degrees.) Observe that the latter have an oscillatory behavior. The frequency of this oscillation depends on the angle of the pole relative to the origin. As the angle increases, so does the frequency of oscillation. For poles on the unit circle, the oscillation is sustained (as in a sinusoid). For poles inside the unit circle, the oscillation is modulated by a decaying exponential. For poles outside the unit circle, the oscillation is modulated by a rising exponential.

Last, consider poles that lie on the negative real axis. These poles have a negative real part. From Figure 3.8 we see that such poles cause a time-domain oscillation with a period of 2. The reason for this is that the time-domain solution contains a term with the pole raised to the power k, the time index. This term alternates its sign as k changes between even and odd values.

3.3 TRANSFER FUNCTIONS

Thus far, we have used Z-transforms to describe signals. Z-transforms can be used to describe systems as well. Such a description is called a transfer function. A *transfer function* of a system describes how an input $U(z)$ is transformed into the output $Y(z)$. We define the transfer function $G(z)$ as

$$G(z) = \frac{Y(z)}{U(z)} \tag{3.24}$$

Put differently, if we are given the system with transfer function $G(z)$ and the input $U(z)$, we know that the output of the system $Y(z)$ is the product of the transfer function and the input to the system; that is, $Y(z) = G(z)U(z)$.

One interpretation of Equation (3.24) is that it describes the response of a system to a unit impulse (e.g., a short-lived change in request rates). Recall that the Z-transform of the unit impulse is $U_{\text{impulse}}(z) = 1$. Thus, $Y_{\text{impulse}}(z) = G(z)U_{\text{impulse}}(z) = G(z)$. For example, if $G(z) = 10$, the response to a unit impulse is $Y_{\text{impulse}}(z) = 10$ or $y(0) = 10$ and $y(k) = 0$ for $k > 0$. If $G(z) = 10+5z^{-1}+3z^{-2}$, the response to a unit impulse is $Y_{\text{impulse}}(z) = 10+5z^{-1}+3z^{-2}$ or $y(0) = 10$, $y(1) = 5$, $y(2) = 3$, and $y(k) = 0$ for $k > 2$.

To provide more insight, we present some examples of transfer functions. Consider the integrator, a very simple system that is described in Equation (3.9). Here, $Y(z) = [1/(z-1)](U(z) + zy(0))$. A transfer function assumes that initial conditions are zero. That is,

$$Y(z) = \frac{1}{z-1}U(z) \tag{3.25}$$

Thus,

$$G(z) = \frac{Y(z)}{U(z)} = \frac{1}{z-1}$$

A transfer function can be found for any system that can be modeled as a linear difference equation. This is done as follows:

1. Find the difference equation that models the input–output relationship. That is, a difference equation that relates $\{y(k)\}$ to $\{u(k)\}$.
2. Take the Z-transform of all terms in the difference equation (e.g., using the properties outlined in Table 3.2), and *set all initial conditions to zero*.
3. Solve for $Y(z)$ in terms of $U(z)$ by placing all the terms in Y on the left-hand side and all the terms in U on the right-hand side. Every term should be a multiple of either $Y(z)$ or $U(z)$.
4. Collect terms if necessary to find the transfer function $G(z) = Y(z)/U(z)$.

We illustrate the foregoing on the first-order system in Equation (2.5).

1. The difference equation is $y(k+1) = ay(k) + bu(k)$.
2. Taking the Z-transform of both sides of the difference equation yields

$$\sum_{k=0}^{\infty} y(k+1)z^{-k} = \sum_{k=0}^{\infty} ay(k)z^{-k} + \sum_{k=0}^{\infty} bu(k)z^{-k}$$

$$zY(z) - zy(0) = aY(z) + bU(z)$$

Setting initial conditions to 0, we have

$$zY(z) = aY(z) + bU(z)$$

3. Solving for $Y(z)$ in terms of $U(z)$:

$$Y(z) = \frac{bU(z)}{z-a}$$

4. Computing the ratio of $Y(z)$ to $U(z)$ yields

$$G(z) = \frac{Y(z)}{U(z)} = \frac{b}{z-a} \tag{3.26}$$

Consider the following examples.

Example 3.6: Transfer function of the Apache HTTP Server   We start with Equation (2.5). Let $y(k) = \text{CPU}(k) - \overline{\text{CPU}}$ and $u(k) = \text{KA}(k) - \overline{\text{KA}}$. Then $y(k + 1) = 0.6y(k) - 0.014u(k)$. Multiplying both sides by z^{-k} and summing from 0 to ∞, we have

$$z \sum_{k=0}^{\infty} y(k+1)z^{-(k+1)} = 0.6 \sum_{k=0}^{\infty} y(k)z^{-k} - 0.014 \sum_{k=0}^{\infty} u(k)z^{-k}$$

$$zY(z) = 0.6Y(z) - 0.014U(z)$$

$$(z - 0.6)Y(z) = -0.014U(z)$$

$$G(z) = \frac{Y(z)}{U(z)} = \frac{-0.014}{z - 0.6}$$

Example 3.7: Transfer function of the IBM Lotus Domino Server   We start with Example 2.6.1. Let $y(k) = \text{RIS}(k) - \overline{\text{RIS}}$ and $u(k) = \text{MaxUsers}(k) - \overline{\text{MaxUsers}}$. Then $y(k + 1) = 0.43y(k) + 0.47u(k)$. Multiplying both sides by z^{-k} and summing from 0 to ∞, we have

$$z \sum_{k=0}^{\infty} y(k+1)z^{-(k+1)} = 0.43 \sum_{k=0}^{\infty} y(k)z^{-k} + 0.47 \sum_{k=0}^{\infty} u(k)z^{-k}$$

$$zY(z) = 0.43Y(z) + 0.47U(z)$$

$$(z - 0.43)Y(z) = 0.47U(z)$$

$$G(z) = \frac{Y(z)}{U(z)} = \frac{0.47}{z - 0.43}$$

The procedure above can be followed even if the inputs and outputs are vectors. The resulting transfer function $\vec{G}(z)$ is a *matrix*. Details of multiple-input, multiple-output (MIMO) transfer functions are discussed in Chapter 7.

We can follow this procedure for a general difference equation such as Equation (2.7):

$$Y(z) = a_1 z^{-1} Y(z) + \cdots + a_n z^{-n} Y(z)$$
$$+ b_1 z^{-1} U(z) + \cdots + b_m z^{-m} U(z)$$

$$Y(z)\left(1 - a_1 z^{-1} - \cdots - a_n z^{-n}\right) = \left(b_1 z^{-1} + \cdots + b_m z^{-m}\right) U(z)$$

$$Y(z) = \frac{b_1 z^{-1} + \cdots + b_m z^{-m}}{1 - a_1 z^{-1} - \cdots - a_n z^{-n}} U(z)$$

to get the transfer function $G(z)$:

$$G(z) = \frac{Y(z)}{U(z)} = \frac{b_1 z^{-1} + \cdots + b_m z^{-m}}{1 - a_1 z^{-1} - \cdots - a_n z^{-n}}$$

$$= \frac{b_1 z^{n-1} + \cdots + b_m z^{n-m}}{z^n - a_1 z^{n-1} - \cdots - a_n} \tag{3.27}$$

Note that it is very easy to construct a transfer function model if we are given an nth-order difference equation such as Equation (2.7). Specifically, the numerator of the transfer function is the sum of the coefficients of u multiplied by a z term that identifies the time shift for that coefficient. For example, b_1 is the coefficient of $u(k-1)$ in Equation (2.7). It is multiplied by z^{-1} to indicate a shift of one time step. The denominator of the transfer function is 1 minus the sum of the coefficients of y multiplied by a z term in the same manner as for the numerator.

3.3.1   Stability

One of the most important properties of a system is stability. Intuitively, we might think of a system with an unbounded output as unstable. Here, we refine this intuition, focusing on bounded-input, bounded-output (BIBO) stability.[1] Further, we show how BIBO stability can be determined from the transfer function of a system.

Our starting point is to be precise about what it means for a signal to be bounded. A signal $\{u(k)\}$ is a *bounded signal* if there exists a positive constant M such that $|u(k)| \le M$ for all k. If this is not true, the signal is unbounded. For a bounded signal, a pair of horizontal lines at $\pm M$ can be drawn, and the time-domain plot of $u(k)$ never crosses those lines. For an unbounded signal, no matter how far apart the lines are drawn, there exists a k such that the signal crosses the bound. Note that any signal of finite duration is bounded since we can set M to 1 plus the maximum value of $|u(k)|$, which is possible since there are a finite number of signal values. However, in general, we study signals for which $0 \le k \le \infty$. An example of a bounded signal is shown in Figure 3.9(a), and the initial part of an unbounded signal is shown in Figure 3.9(b).

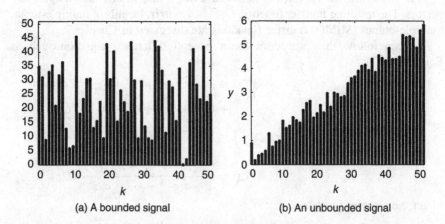

(a) A bounded signal   (b) An unbounded signal

Fig. 3.9 *The first 50 samples of two signals, one bounded and one unbounded. For the bounded signal, $|u(k)|$ is never greater than 50. The unbounded signal has an upward trend; no bound exists.*

[1]There are many definitions of stability. See [64] for more details.

Some examples help to illustrate how this definition can be applied. Suppose that $\{u(k)\}$ is an impulse. That is, $u(k) = 0$ for $k \neq 0$. Now let $M = |u(0)| + 1$. Then, $M > |u(k)|$ for all k, and hence $\{u(k)\}$ is bounded. Using a similar argument, the step signal is bounded as well. Note that the exact magnitude of M does not matter in terms of satisfying the definition of a bounded signal.

Next consider a ramp signal $\{u(k)\}$. Intuitively, we know that $\{u(k)\}$ is not bounded. This can be proved from the definition as follows. If $\{u(k)\}$ were bounded, there would be an M such that $M > |u(k)|$ for all k. Let M' be an integer larger than M. By definition of a ramp, $u(M') = M'$, so $u(M') > M$. This means that $\{u(k)\}$ cannot be bounded. A slightly more complicated case is the exponential signal, $u(k) = a^k$. If $|a| \leq 1$, $\{u(k)\}$ is bounded. But $\{u(k)\}$ is not bounded if $|a| > 1$.

Having defined a bounded signal, we define what is meant by bounded-input, bounded-output stability. A system is *BIBO stable* if for *any* bounded input $\{u(k)\}$, the output $\{y(k)\}$ is bounded. The converse of this definition is often used as well. That is, a system is *not* BIBO stable if there is *at least one bounded input* that produces an *un*bounded output.

Example 3.8: BIBO stability of the integrator   The integrator has a transfer function $G_{\text{Integ}}(z) = 1/(z-1)$. From Example 3.2 we know that the response of an integrator to an impulse is a delayed step, which is bounded. However, the response of an integrator to a step is a ramp, which is unbounded. Since there is one bounded input that produces an unbounded output, the integrator is not BIBO stable.

The Apache HTTP Server example, with transfer function $G_{\text{KA}}(z) = -0.014/(z - 0.6)$, seems stable. With a step input, the output is a combination of a delayed step and a decaying exponential, which is bounded. However, to satisfy the definition, we need to verify that the output remains bounded for *all possible* bounded inputs. Instead of embarking on this tedious search, we cite a theorem that makes it easier to check BIBO stability.

Theorem 3.2 (BIBO stability).   A system represented by a transfer function $G(z)$ is BIBO stable if and only if all the poles of $G(z)$ are inside the unit circle.

(More details can be found in [25].)

We note that this theorem offers a relatively simple test for BIBO stability. Once all the poles (roots of the denominator polynomial) of $G(z)$ have been found, it only remains to check that their magnitudes are all *strictly less than* 1. If one or more poles has a magnitude greater than or equal to 1, the system is not BIBO stable. That is, there exists at least one bounded input signal that results in an unbounded output signal.

This theorem indicates that the integrator is not BIBO stable since it has a pole that is not *inside* the unit circle. This conclusion is consistent with Example 3.8.

Example 3.9: BIBO stability of the Apache HTTP Server   Consider the Apache HTTP Server with transfer function $G_{KA}(z) = -0.014/(z - 0.6)$. This system has one pole at $z = 0.6$. From Theorem 3.2 we conclude that this system is BIBO stable since its one pole is inside the unit circle.

Observe that a system can be BIBO stable even if its output is unbounded. Such situations occur if the input is unbounded as well. As a simple example, consider the system whose transfer function is 1, so $Y(z) = U(z)$. Clearly, this is a stable system. However, if $\{u(k)\}$ is a ramp (which is unbounded), so is $\{y(k)\}$.

There are several examples of unstable computing systems. One is a virtual memory system. Here, the input is the multiprogramming level (MPL), and the output is paging rate. When the multiprogramming level grows beyond a certain level, thrashing results in very large paging rates (e.g., [66]). The paging rates are not truly unbounded since they are limited by disk bandwidth. However, they do increase dramatically. Another example is contention-based communication, such as the slotted-ALOHA network on which Ethernet is based (e.g., [36]). If such networks become overutilized, retransmissions dominate network traffic, causing throughput to degrade dramatically.

Although the definition of stability in this book is BIBO, other definitions of stability are often important in practice. For example, Figure 3.10 shows the effect of increasing the reference value in a system that controls CPU of an Apache HTTP Server. The result is a different kind of instability, one in which CPU alternates between its extreme values, 0 and 1. This system is BIBO stable since the output is bounded. However, the oscillation between extreme values, which is called a *limit cycle*, means that we are no longer able to regulate CPU. In control terminology, outputs with a limited range are called *constrained*. There are constrained inputs as well, such as requiring that MaxClients be positive. Systems with constrained inputs and/or outputs are typically BIBO stable, but they can have limit cycles. Analyzing these systems directly is complicated because they are nonlinear (due to saturation). Instead, we analyze one or more linear approximations for operating regions of interest and ensure BIBO stability for the control systems constructed using these linear approximations. A final consideration related to practice is that the (linear) models we consider are constructed for a specific operating region. As such, stability results apply only within that operating region.

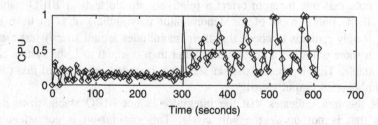

Fig. 3.10   *Example of a limit cycle in* CPU *in an Apache HTTP Server.*

3.3.2 Steady-State Gain

Given a stable system, we would like simple characterizations of its behavior. One such characterization is the steady-state output to a constant input. For example, in the Apache HTTP Server, we would like to know the steady-state value of CPU that is achieved if KeepAlive is constant.

Consider a BIBO stable system and a step input with magnitude u_{ss}. Under these conditions, the output converges. Let y_{ss} denote this final value. The ratio y_{ss}/u_{ss} is called the *steady-state gain* of the system. Sometimes, this is also referred to as *dc gain*. Steady-state gain quantifies the steady-state effect of the input on the output.

Steady-state gain can be computed in a straightforward way. Consider the stable system described by Equation (2.7), which we express as

$$y(k) - a_1 y(k-1) - \cdots - a_n y(k-n) = b_1 u(k-1) + \cdots + b_m u(k-m)$$

Suppose that we apply a step input u_{ss} and then observe y for a long time. Let k be sufficiently large so that we are at steady state and hence $y(k) = \cdots = y(k-n) = y_{ss}$. Clearly, $u(k-1) = \cdots = u(k-m) = u_{ss}$. Then

$$(1 - a_1 - \cdots - a_n)y_{ss} = (b_1 + \cdots + b_m)u_{ss}$$

$$\frac{y_{ss}}{u_{ss}} = \frac{b_1 + \cdots + b_m}{1 - a_1 - \cdots - a_n} \qquad (3.28)$$

More commonly, we compute steady-state gain from the transfer function $G(z)$. This is done as follows. The output to a unit step input is $Y(z) = G(z)[z/(z-1)]$. If $G(z)$ is BIBO stable, all the poles of $(z-1)Y(z)$ are inside the unit circle, and y_{ss} can be found by using the final value theorem,

$$\lim_{k \to \infty} y(k) = \lim_{z \to 1}(z-1)Y(z) = \lim_{z \to 1}(z-1)G(z)\frac{z}{z-1}$$

$$= \lim_{z \to 1} zG(z) = \lim_{z \to 1} G(z) = G(1) \qquad (3.29)$$

Thus, for a unit step input, the steady-state output of the system is $y_{ss} = G(1)$. Let $G(z)$ be defined as in Equation (3.27), which is the transfer function of Equation (2.7). Thus,

$$G(1) = \frac{y_{ss}}{u_{ss}} = \frac{b_1 + \cdots + b_m}{1 - a_1 - \cdots - a_n}$$

Note that this is the same expression for steady-state gain as Equation (3.28).

Thus far, we have assumed that $u_{ss} = 1$. Suppose instead that $U(z)$ is a step of size c. Using the first entry in Table 3.2, we see that the steady-state output of the system is $y_{ss} = cG(1)$.

Example 3.10: Steady-state gain of the Apache HTTP Server Consider once more the Apache HTTP Server example with $G(z) = -0.014/(z - 0.6)$. Its steady-state gain is $G(1) = -0.014/(1-0.6) = -0.014/0.4 = -0.035$. The negative sign in the gain indicates that a positive change in the input (KeepAlive) results in a negative change in the output (CPU), as we have seen in earlier examples.

While steady-state gain offers considerable insight, we must be aware of its limitations as well. Consider again the effect of KeepAlive on CPU, and assume that the steady-state gain is -0.035. Now, suppose that there is a step increase in KeepAlive of 100. Then the linear model predicts that the effect of this increase will be to decrease CPU by 3.5. But this is clearly impossible since the valid range of CPU is between 0 and 1.

Steady-state gain can be used in many ways. For example, since many computing systems have constrained outputs (e.g., utilizations), the steady-state gain can predict the range of inputs that prevents the output from saturating. For example, in the Apache HTTP Server we want to know how much KeepAlive can be decreased before CPU goes to 1. Steady-state gain can be used in an inverse fashion as well, to predict the range of outputs that are achievable given a constrained input variable. A third way in which steady-state gain can be used is to quantify inaccuracies introduced by a measurement sensor. This is discussed further in Section 3.5.2.

3.3.3 System Order

The system order (or model order) for the system with transfer function $G(z)$ is the number of poles (including repeated ones) in the denominator of $G(z)$. For instance, Example 3.9 is a first-order model of the Apache HTTP Server since there is only one (unrepeated) pole.

First-order systems have a limited set of behaviors and are relatively easy to study, even in the time domain. Second- and higher-order systems have more than one pole, some of which may be complex. In Chapter 5 we discuss first-order systems, and in Chapter 6 we address higher-order systems.

We note in passing that the system order is the same as the n in the ARX model of Equation (2.7). This in turn is the same as the number of initial conditions that are needed to solve the difference equation associated with the system.

3.3.4 Dominant Poles and Model Simplification

Typically, the behavior of a system is determined by the poles with the largest magnitude. Figure 3.11 illustrates this for a step response. Eight systems are considered. For each, the transfer function is

$$G_i(z) = \frac{b_i}{(z - p_1) \cdots (z - p_n)}$$

where n is the order of the system. $b_i = (1 - p_1) \cdots (1 - p_n)$ is selected so that the steady-state gain $G_i(1) = 1$. For example, the system with the poles 0.7, 0.1

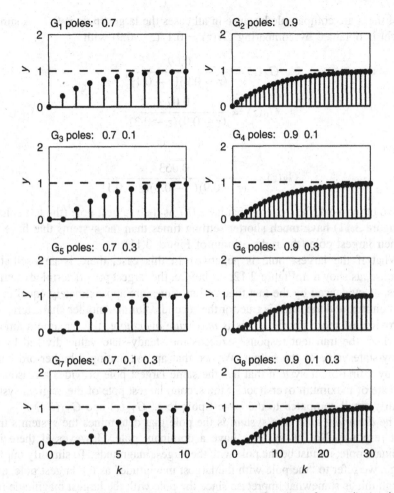

Fig. 3.11 *Influence of the largest magnitude pole on settling times for a unit step input.*
$G_i(z) = \dfrac{b_i}{(z - p_1) \cdots (z - p_n)}$, *where n is the order of the system and b_i is selected to provide a steady-state gain of 1. The dashed line is G(1). Note that the largest pole largely determines settling times [i.e., how quickly y(k) converges to G(1)].*

has the transfer function

$$G_3(z) = \frac{0.27}{(z - 0.7)(z - 0.1)}$$

One property of interest in analyzing systems is *settling time*, the time required for the system to reach its steady-state value (e.g., after a unit step input is applied). Comparing $G_1(z) = 0.3/(z - 0.7)$ with $G_3(z)$, we see that the settling times of these systems are quite similar. [The one time unit of "dead time" in $G_3(z)$ is due to its being a second-order system.] The settling time of the system with poles at 0.7, 0.3 is longer, and that for 0.7, 0.3, 0.1 is longer still. However, all of them are comparable because in all cases the largest pole is 0.7. A similar insight is obtained by comparing $G_2(z) = 0.1/(z - 0.9)$ with

$$G_4(z) = \frac{0.09}{(z - 0.9)(z - 0.1)},$$

$$G_6(z) = \frac{0.07}{(z - 0.9)(z - 0.3)},$$

and

$$G_8(z) = \frac{0.063}{(z - 0.9)(z - 0.3)(z - 0.1)}$$

On the other hand, the systems that have 0.7 as their largest pole (the left column of Figure 3.11) have much shorter settling times than the systems that have 0.9 as their largest pole (the right column of Figure 3.11).

What if the largest pole is negative? In this case, there is an oscillatory response, as shown in Figure 3.12. As before, the largest pole determines settling times, as evidenced by the fact that settling times are approximately equal in the first column, and the same is true for the second column. Another characteristic is approximated more poorly. This is *maximum overshoot*, the maximum amount by which the transient response exceeds the steady-state value divided by the steady-state value of the output. We see that approximating a higher-order system by a first-order system that has the same largest pole provides a reasonable estimate of maximum overshoot if the second largest pole of the original system is fairly small compared to the largest pole [e.g., $G_{12}(z)$ and $G_{13}(z)$].

The *dominant pole* of a system is the pole that determines the system's transient response. Not all systems have a dominant pole. However, if there is a dominant pole, it must be the pole with the largest magnitude. To simplify our language, we refer to "the pole with the largest magnitude" as the largest pole, even though this is somewhat imprecise since the pole with the largest magnitude may be negative. Several factors affect whether the largest pole is a dominant pole. In general, the largest pole should have twice the magnitude of the other poles in order to be a dominant pole. This requirement is evidenced in Figure 3.11. Comparing $G_1(z)$ with

$$G_5(z) = \frac{0.21}{(z - 0.7)(z - 0.3)}$$

we see that the settling time of $G_5(z)$ is approximately the same as that for $G_1(z)$. Other factors affecting the presence of a dominant pole are the absolute value of the largest pole and the order of the system.

The foregoing discussion suggests a way to approximate a high-order transfer function whose largest pole is real. (In Chapter 6 we consider the case where the pole with the largest magnitude is complex.) Consider

$$G(z) = \frac{b(z - q_1) \cdots (z - q_m)}{(z - p_1) \cdots (z - p_n)}$$

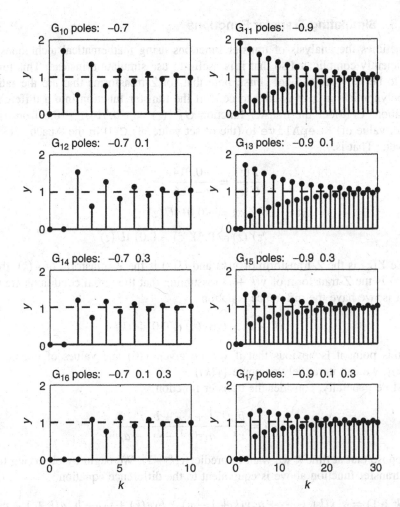

Fig. 3.12 *Influence of a large negative pole on settling times and overshoot for a unit step input.*
$G_i(z) = \dfrac{b_i}{(z - p_1) \cdots (z - p_n)}$, *where n is the order of the system and b_i is selected to provide a steady-state gain of 1. The dashed line is $G(1)$. As in Figure 3.11, the largest-magnitude pole largely determines settling times. The first-order systems [$G_{10}(z)$ and $G_{11}(z)$] provide an accurate approximation of overshoot if the second largest pole is considerably smaller than the largest pole.*

where $m \leq n$. Suppose that p' is the dominant pole. Then $G(z)$ can be approximated by the first-order system $G'(z)$ as

$$G'(z) = \frac{G(1)(1 - p')}{z - p'} \qquad \text{if } p' \text{ is real} \tag{3.30}$$

Note that $G(z)$ and $G'(z)$ have the same steady-state gain $G(1) = G'(1)$, and the settling times of the two systems are approximately the same.

3.3.5 Simulating Transfer Functions

Sometimes the analysis of transfer functions using mathematical techniques is sufficiently complicated so that it is useful to use simulation instead. This turns out to be very easy to do. First, note that for Z-transforms that are the ratios of polynomials in z, it is easy to convert the transfer function into a difference equation. Consider the transfer function $G_{KA}(z) = -0.014/z - 0.6$ from (the offset value of) KeepAlive to (the offset value of) CPU in the Apache HTTP Server. That is,

$$\frac{Y(z)}{U(z)} = \frac{-0.014}{z - 0.6}$$

$$(z - 0.6)Y(z) = -0.014U(z)$$

$$zY(z) = 0.6Y(z) - 0.014U(z)$$

Since $Y(z)$ is the Z-transform of $y(k)$ and $U(z)$ is the Z-transform of $u(k)$, then $zY(z)$ is the Z-transform of $y(k+1)$ (assuming that the initial conditions are 0). That is, we have the difference equation

$$y(k + 1) = 0.6y(k) - 0.014u(k)$$

At this point it is obvious that if we are given $y(0)$ and values of the inputs $\{u(k)\}$, we can iteratively compute $\{y(k)\}$.

More generally, consider the transfer function

$$G(z) = \frac{b_1 z^{n-1} + \cdots + b_m z^{n-m}}{z^n - a_1 z^{n-1} - \cdots - a_n}$$

Suppose that at time k we want to predict $y(k+1)$. We begin by observing that the transfer function above is equivalent to the difference equation

$$y(k + 1) = a_1 y(k) + \cdots + a_n y(k + 1 - n) + b_1 u(k) + \cdots + b_m u(k + 1 - m)$$

Thus, if we know $y(k+1-n), \ldots, y(k)$ and $u(k+1-m), \ldots, u(k)$, we can compute the $y(k+1)$. To compute $y(k+h)$, we use $y(2), \ldots, y(k), u(2), \ldots, u(k+1)$, and the $y(k+1)$ just obtained to compute $y(k+2)$. Continuing in the same way, we can compute $y(k+3), \ldots, y(k+h)$.

Example 3.11: Simulation of the IBM Lotus Domino Server In Section 3.5.2 we discuss the IBM Lotus Domino Server transfer function $S(z)$ from the actual RIS $q(k)$ to the sensor measurement $m(k)$. If there is a one-step delay,

$$S(z) = \frac{0.72z - 0.66}{z^2 - 0.8z}$$

This has the difference equation

$$m(k) = 0.8m(k - 1) + 0.72q(k - 1) - 0.66q(k - 2)$$

TABLE 3.3 Inputs and Outputs in
Simulation Example

k	$q(k)$	$m(k)$
0	1	0
1	1	0
2	1	0.06
3	1	0.11
⋮		
10	1	0.26
⋮		
15	1	0.29
⋮		
20	1	0.30
⋮		
30	1	0.30

Consider a step input in which $q(k) = 1$, $k \geq 0$ with the initial conditions $m(k) = 0$ for $k \in \{0, 1\}$. This can easily be simulated using a spreadsheet. Computations are organized in the manner displayed in Table 3.3. The columns for k and $q(k)$ contain constants. The first two rows of $m(k)$ are constants for initial conditions since this is a second-order system. Formulas are entered starting with row 3 of the $m(k)$ column. For example, the formula for computing $m(3)$ in row four of the table is $0.8m(2) + 0.72q(2) - 0.66q(1) = (0.8)(0.06) + (0.72)(1) - (0.66)(1) = 0.11$.

One way to check the simulation is to compare its steady-state value with that predicted by Equation (3.29). We see that the predicted steady-state value $S(1) = 0.3$ is equal to the simulated value of $m(20) = m(30)$.

Since simulating transfer functions is so easy, why use analytic techniques? There are two reasons. The first is that we gain insights into trade-offs between properties such as settling time and maximum overshoot by seeing how controller parameters and other factors affect the poles of the system. The second reason for employing analytic techniques is that they provide a convenient way to design control systems with specific properties, such as desired settling times and/or steady-state gains. In essence, the analytic techniques allow us to convert a desired settling time into a desired pole value. We can then design a controller that has the desired closed-loop poles.

For a transfer function that is a ratio of polynomials in z (which is the focus in this book), the number of zeros should never be larger than the number of poles.[2] The reason for this is as follows. The number of poles is equal to the order of the polynomial in the denominator of the transfer function, and the number of zeros is equal to the order of polynomial in the numerator. If the numerator polynomial has a higher order than the denominator, the difference equation that

---

[2]We are including repeated poles and zeros in these counts.

corresponds to the transfer function expresses the output $y(k)$ in terms of a *future* input $u(k + h)$ for $h \geq 1$. This violates our notion of causality.

3.4   SUMMARY

1. Z-transforms provide a way to represent a time-domain sequence as polynomial in z. Doing so makes it easy to do operations such as time shifts (multiply by z) and time delays (divide by z).

2. The Z-transform of common signals (e.g., impulse, step, and ramp) can be constructed in a straightforward way and used as a basis for constructing more complicated signals.

3. The inverse of a Z-transform is a time series, which is typically expressed as a difference equation. The difference equation can be computed with the aid of tables included in this chapter. Z-transforms can be used to solve difference equations.

4. A transfer function is a Z-transform that expresses the dynamics of the relationship between inputs and outputs of a system. The results in this book are focused largely on the construction and analysis of transfer functions.

5. Although both signals and transfer functions are expressed as Z-transforms, they are treated very differently. Signals have an inverse Z-transform (e.g., $\{y(k)\}$) as well as properties such as boundedness and a final value (if it exists). None of these apply to transfer functions. On the other hand, transfer functions have properties such as stability, steady-state gain, settling time, and maximum overshoot, none of which make sense for signals.

6. If $G(z)$ is the transfer function of a stable system, $G(1)$ is the steady-state gain [the value achieved by a system in response to a (unit) step input].

7. The order of the system with transfer function $G(z) = N(z)/D(z)$ is the degree of $D(z)$ (the denominator polynomial of z).

8. The poles of a transfer function are the values of z for which the denominator goes to zero. The poles of a system provide valuable information.

    (a) The system is stable (a bounded input produces a bounded output) if the poles lie within the unit circle.

    (b) The settling time of a system is determined largely by the magnitude of its poles. Poles close to 1 result in long settling times. Poles close to 0 have very short settling times.

    (c) Systems with complex poles or real poles that are negative will have an oscillatory response to transients. The frequency of the oscillation depends on the angle of the pole in the complex plane.

9. A dominant pole is a pole whose magnitude is significantly larger than the other poles. Often, it is sufficient to consider the dominant pole when analyzing settling times, oscillations, and overshoot.

10. Given a system with the transfer function $G(z)$, its time-domain response to an input can be simulated without inverting the Z-transform.

3.5 EXTENDED EXAMPLES

The following examples apply Z-transforms to computing systems.

3.5.1 $M/M/1/K$ from System Identification

In Section 2.6.3 we address system identification for $M/M/1/K$. For inputs in the range $[1, 51]$, the system is modeled by the difference equation

$$y(k) = 0.49y(k-1) + 0.033u(k-1)$$

with an operating point for buffer size and response time equal to 26 and 2.7 seconds, respectively. We can convert this to a transfer function as follows:

$$G(z) = \frac{0.033}{z - 0.49}$$

The transfer function has one pole at $z = 0.49$. This is inside the unit circle, and hence the model is BIBO stable. The steady-state gain of the system is $G(1) = 0.065$. The gain is positive, which indicates that if the buffer size is increased by 1, the average response time (in steady state) increases by 65 milliseconds. Recall that this is the linearized response of the system around an operating point, and as such is most accurate near the operating point.

3.5.2 IBM Lotus Domino Server: Sensor Delay

The difference equation for the IBM Lotus Domino Server in Section 2.6.1 can be expressed as a transfer function from MaxUsers to RIS as follows:

$$N(z) = \frac{Q(z)}{U(z)} = \frac{0.47}{z - 0.43}$$

where $q(k) = \text{RIS}(k) - \overline{\text{RIS}}$ and $u(k) = \text{MaxUsers}(k) - \overline{\text{MaxUsers}}$. As indicated in Example 3.1, while RIS can be obtained by postprocessing the server log, it is not obtained through direct measurement for online control. Rather, it is computed by sampling the IBM Lotus Domino Server log periodically. Unfortunately, this log does not contain active RPCs; hence, measured $\text{RIS}(k)$ underestimates the actual $\text{RIS}(k)$.

Let $\text{RIS}(k)$ be the true value of RIS at time k, $\widehat{\text{RIS}}(k)$ be the measured value of RIS reported by the sensor, and $S(z)$ be the transfer function of the sensor. Further, the offset value of measured RIS is denoted by $m(k)$, where $m(k) = \widehat{\text{RIS}}(k) - \overline{\widehat{\text{RIS}}}$ and $\overline{\widehat{\text{RIS}}}$ is the mean value of measured RIS. Note that $m(k)$ depends on $q(k-n)$, where n is the delay due to the sensor. A good way to express this relationship is to look at the difference between $m(k)$ and $m(k-1)$ as compared to $q(k-n)$ and $q(k-1-n)$. This motivates the following difference equation:

$$m(k) - am(k-1) = b_0 q(k-n) + b_1 q(k-1-n)$$

TABLE 3.4   Model Coefficients and Fits for $S(z)$

Delay (n)	R^2	a	b_0	b_1	$S(1)$
0	0.76	0.64	0.17	-0.11	0.16
1	0.84	0.80	0.72	-0.66	0.30
2	0.91	0.92	0.94	-0.91	0.38

To find the transfer function, we compute

$$M(z) - az^{-1}M(z) = b_0 z^{-n} Q(z) + b_1 z^{-1-n} Q(z)$$

$$z^{n+1} M(z) - az^n M(z) = b_0 z Q(z) + b_1 Q(z)$$

$$S(z) = \frac{b_0 z + b_1}{(z - a)z^n}$$

We collected data from a testbed running a product-level IBM Lotus Domino Server with different sensor delays (n). The values of a, b_0, and b_1 are shown in Table 3.4. Note that as n increases from 0 to 2, the fit, indicated by R^2, improves significantly, from 76% to 91%.

We can use steady-state gain to analyze the accuracy of the sensor. The sensor is accurate if measured RIS is equal to actual RIS. That is, we want $S(1) = 1$. From Table 3.4 we see that $S(1)$ increases with n, suggesting that sensor accuracy increases with measurement delay. However, even with a delay of two time units, measured RIS is only 0.38 of the actual value.

3.5.3   Apache HTTP Server: Combining Control Inputs

Example 3.3 contains a difference equation that relates CPU to KeepAlive in the Apache HTTP Server. Below, we repeat this equation with a slightly different notation that qualifies $\{y(k)\}$ and $\{u(k)\}$:

$$y_{CPU}(k) = ay_{CPU}(k-1) + bu_{KA}(k-1)$$

The Apache HTTP Server has another control input that affects CPU: the maximum number of connected clients, MaxClients. In Example 3.3, MaxClients is fixed at its operating point. If MaxClients is varied while keeping KeepAlive fixed at its operating point, we obtain

$$y_{CPU}(k) = cy_{CPU}(k-1) + du_{MC}(k-1)$$

The corresponding transfer function is

$$G_{MC}(z) = \frac{d}{z - c}$$

Since both KeepAlive and MaxClients affect CPU, we would like to know the combined effect of these controls. Assuming that the system is operating in a linear region, the combined effect is obtained by addition:

$$Y_{\text{CPU}}(z) = G_{\text{MC}}Y_{\text{MC}}(z) + G_{\text{KA}}Y_{\text{KA}}(z)$$

Note, however, that this equation assumes that there is *no interaction between the two inputs*. To account for interactions, a MIMO model must be used with MIMO system identification. These considerations are discussed in Chapter 7.

*3.6 Z-TRANSFORMS AND MATLAB

MATLAB represents polynomials as vectors, with the entries in the vector indicating the coefficients of the polynomial. For example, the polynomial $z^2 - z + 0.5$ is represented as

```
[1 -1 0.5]
```

The roots of the polynomial can be extracted as

```
roots([1 -1 0.5])
```

which produces the output

```
ans =

   0.5000 + 0.5000i
   0.5000 - 0.5000i
```

(Note that MATLAB defaults to use i for $\sqrt{-1}$ but it also understands j.) The magnitude and phase angle of a complex number can be found using the commands abs and angle:

```
abs(0.5 + 0.5j)
angle(0.5 + 0.5j)
ans =

   0.7071

ans =

   0.7854
```

Note that the angle is in radians. The real and imaginary parts can be extracted using real and imag:

```
real(exp(j*pi/3))
imag(exp(j*pi/3))
ans =

   0.5000
```

```
ans =
```

```
    0.8660
```

where `pi` represents π.

Polynomials can be multiplied using the `conv` function. For example, we compute $(z^2 - z + 0.5)(z^2 - 1)$

```
conv([1 -1 0.5],[1 0 -1])
```

```
ans =
```

```
    1.0000    -1.0000    -0.5000    1.0000    -0.5000
```

which gives $z^4 - z^3 - 0.5z^2 + z - 0.5$.

The partial fraction expansion of a ratio of polynomials can be found using the `residue` command. For example, if

$$Y(z) = \frac{-0.11z}{z^2 - 1.6z + 0.6}$$

we can get the partial fraction expansion as

```
[r,p,k] = residue([-0.11 0],[1 -1.6 0.6])
```

```
r =
```

```
   -0.2750
    0.1650
```

```
p =
```

```
    1.0000
    0.6000
```

```
k =
```

```
    []
```

Note that the polynomial $-0.11z$ in the numerator is entered as `[-0.11 0]` to indicate that the constant term is zero. The poles are returned in the vector `p` and the numerators are returned in the vector `r`. If the order of the numerator is greater than the order of the denominator, the direct term is returned in `k`. Thus, we have that

$$\frac{-0.11z}{z^2 - 1.6z + 0.6} = \frac{-0.275}{z - 1} + \frac{0.165}{z - 0.6}$$

Using the Control Systems Toolbox, transfer functions can also be entered into MATLAB. For example, the transfer function for an integrator, $G(z) = 1/(z-1)$, is entered using tf by specifying the numerator polynomial, the denominator polynomial, and the sampling time. If the sampling time is set to -1, it is assumed to be unspecified.

```
tf(1,[1 -1],-1)
```

```
Transfer function:
  1
-----
z - 1
```

Sampling time: unspecified

The Apache HTTP Server example with the transfer function $G(z) = -0.014/(z-0.6)$ and a sampling time of 5 seconds is entered as

```
tf(-0.014,[1 -0.6],5)
```

```
Transfer function:
 -0.014
-------
z - 0.6
```

Sampling time: 5

3.7 EXERCISES

1. Find the Z-transform of the following (discrete-time) signals:

    (a) $y(k) = \{0, 0, 3, 3, 3, \ldots\}$
    (b) $y(k) = \{10, 20, 30, 40, \ldots\}$
    (c) $y(k) = \{1, 0.1, 0.01, 0.001, \ldots\}$
    (d) $y(k) = \{0, 0, -0.2, 0.04, -0.008, -0.0016, \ldots\}$

2. Using the answers from Exercise 1, find the Z-transform of the following signals:

    (a) $y(k) = \{0, 0, 9, 9, 9, \ldots\}$
    (b) $y(k) = \{0.01, 0.001, 0.0001, \ldots\}$
    (c) $y(k) = \{10.1, 20.01, 30.001, 40.0001, \ldots\}$

3. Find the time-domain representation of the following signals:

    (a) $U(z) = \dfrac{10z}{z-1}$
    (b) $V(z) = \dfrac{(z-0.5)}{(z^2 - z + 1)}$

(c) $W(z) = \dfrac{2.3}{z(z - 0.3)}$

(d) $Y(z) = z\dfrac{2z - (a + 1)}{(z - 1)(z - a)}$

4. Find $y(1)$, $y(2)$, and $y(3)$ in response to a unit step for

$$F(z) = \frac{K_P 0.47}{z - 0.43 + K_P 0.47}$$

for $K_P \in \{1, 2, 3, 3.5\}$. Assume that all initial conditions are 0. [*Hint:* Translate $F(z)$ into a difference equation and then directly compute the first few terms.]

5. Find the steady-state gain of the transfer function

$$F(z) = \frac{-0.014 K_P}{z - 0.6 - K_P 0.011}$$

for $K_P \in \{1, 100\}$. Do the same for the transfer function

$$F(z) = \frac{K_I(-0.011)}{(z - 0.6)(z - 1) - K_I 0.011}$$

for $K_I \in \{1, 100\}$.

6. For the transfer function $F(z) = -0.014/(z - 0.6)$, plot its step response and determine the settling time.

7. For the following Z-transforms, **(i)** find their poles, **(ii)** plot the poles in the complex plane, and **(iii)** determine the magnitudes and angles of the poles.

(a) $\dfrac{4}{z - 1.5}$

(b) $\dfrac{12}{z^2 - 0.4z - 0.05}$

(c) $\dfrac{1}{z^2 - 0.4z + 0.2}$

(d) $\dfrac{3}{z^3 - 0.2z^2 - 0.03z - 0.36}$

8. For the following transfer functions, **(i)** find the order of the system, **(ii)** compute the poles, and **(iii)** determine if the system is stable.

(a) $\dfrac{2z}{z^2 - 1.4z - 0.45}$

(b) $\dfrac{2z - 1}{z^3 - 1.2z^2 + 0.35z - 0.024}$

(c) $\dfrac{13}{z^4 - z^3 + 0.35z^2 - 0.05z - 0.024}$

(d) $\dfrac{7}{z^4 - 1.31z^3 + 1.21z^2 - 0.287z - 0.0178}$

9. For the following systems, **(i)** determine if the system is stable, **(ii)** predict the final value to a unit step input, **(iii)** determine the settling time (k_s), and **(iv)** simulate a step response.

(a) $\dfrac{0.94}{z - 0.51}$

(b) $\dfrac{7}{z^4 - 1.31z^3 + 1.21z^2 - 0.287z - 0.0178}$

(c) $\dfrac{3z^2 - 1}{z^5 - 0.6z^4 + 0.13z^3 - 0.364z^2 + 0.1416z - 0.288}$

10. Find the response of the systems in Exercise 8 to the signals in Exercises 1–3.

4

System Modeling with Block Diagrams

The key to a successful application of control theory is modeling. In Chapter 2 we described how to model individual components using difference equations, and in Chapter 3, how to analyze these models using Z-transforms. In this chapter we discuss the use of block diagrams to model systems that consist of many components. We discuss the elements of a block diagram and principles for modeling systems using these elements. Also addressed is how to use block diagrams to obtain the transfer function of a system, thereby enabling the analysis of BIBO stability and other properties using the techniques presented in Chapter 3.

4.1 BLOCK DIAGRAMS BASICS

A block diagram specifies the components of a system and the signals that flow between them. The components are themselves systems. This means that block diagrams are often recursive in that components may be expressed as block diagrams of subcomponents, and so on.

A block diagram consists of many interconnected functional blocks. A *functional block*, or simply *block*, represents a component of the system. This is depicted by a rectangle that is usually labeled with the transfer function of the component it represents. A signal is indicated by an arrow and is labeled by the z-domain expression for the signal. Note that the measured output of a block is the result of passing the input through the block's transfer function. If

---

Feedback Control of Computing Systems, by Joseph L. Hellerstein, Yixin Diao, Sujay Parekh, and Dawn M. Tilbury
ISBN 0-471-26637-X   Copyright © 2004 John Wiley & Sons, Inc.

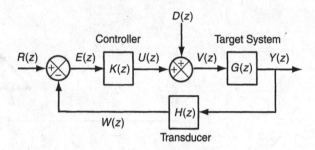

Fig. 4.1 *Block diagram of a closed-loop system.* $R(z)$ *is the reference input,* $E(z)$ *is the control error,* $U(z)$ *is the control input, and* $Y(z)$ *is the system output.*

$V(z)$ is the input, $Y(z)$ is the output, and $G(z)$ is the transfer function, then $Y(z) = G(z)V(z)$. For the most part, each block has one input signal and one output signal.

Figure 4.1 depicts a general form for a feedback control system. There are two inputs to this system, the reference $R(z)$ and the disturbance $D(z)$. The reference specifies the desired value of the output (e.g., response time should be 2 seconds), and the disturbance reflects uncontrolled effects (e.g., execution of administrative tasks). The control error $E(z)$ is the difference between the desired and measured outputs. $E(z)$ is used as input to the *controller*, with transfer function $K(z)$, that produces the control input $U(z)$ (e.g., the setting of MaxClients in the Apache HTTP Server). $U(z)$ is input to the target system $G(z)$ (e.g., the Apache HTTP Server or the IBM Lotus Domino Server), possibly modified by the disturbance $D(z)$, to control the system output. The *transducer* block $H(z)$ models effects such as (1) the conversion between input and output units, (2) sensor delays, and (3) averaging (often referred to as *filtering*).

The simplest block diagrams only include serial connections between blocks in which the output of one block is the input to another block. More complex relationships are possible. In particular, Figure 4.1 includes summation and branching.

The addition of signals is specified by a circle with an "×" through it, as on the left side of Figure 4.1. Such a *summation point* has multiple inputs and one output. A plus or minus sign indicates whether the input signal is added or subtracted. In the figure, the signal $W(z)$ is subtracted from the reference signal $R(z)$ to obtain the error signal $E(z)$.

A *branching point* is the origin of a signal with multiple destinations. For example, $Y(z)$ in Figure 4.1 is used both as the output of the system and as input to the transducer.

Block diagrams provide an effective approach to representing many complex interactions between elements. However, we emphasize that the relationships modeled are only those needed for controller analysis and design. Other relationships, such as sharing common code or having common information models, are not represented in block diagrams. A block need not correspond to an architectural or design element in a software system (e.g., a name server, object, method, or area of shared memory). It could be that a block represents multiple such elements, as may be the case with a transducer block that models measurement delays (which may involve collection and reporting functions present in many architectural elements). A further implication is that the same system could be represented by many different block diagrams.

Example 4.1: Modeling M/M/1/K feedback control Consider the $M/M/1/K$ single-server queue described in Section 2.1 Suppose that we are interested in regulating response time by adjusting the buffer size in the presence of workload variations. Thus, the reference input $R(z)$ to the resulting control system is the desired response time and the output $Y(z)$ is measured response time. Note that although the "real" output of the system is the result of processing requests, for control purposes, the average response time is considered to be the output.

Figure 4.2(a) displays a summation point that computes the control error $E(z)$ from $R(z)$ and $Y(z)$. Figure 4.2(b) shows that the controller $K(z)$ inputs the

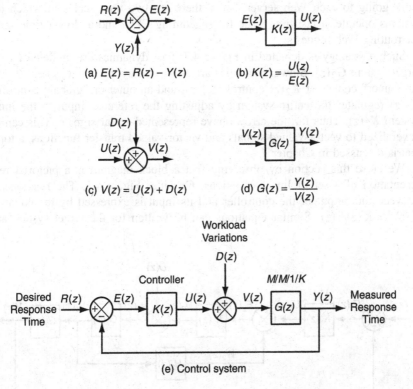

(a) $E(z) = R(z) - Y(z)$

(b) $K(z) = \dfrac{U(z)}{E(z)}$

(c) $V(z) = U(z) + D(z)$

(d) $G(z) = \dfrac{Y(z)}{V(z)}$

(e) Control system

Fig. 4.2 *Components of a control system for regulating the response times of an $M/M/1/K$ queueing system. $R(z)$ is the desired response time, $Y(z)$ is the measured response time that is output from the control system, $E(z)$ is the difference between the desired and measured response time, $K(z)$ is the controller, $U(z)$ is the controller-specified buffer length, $D(z)$ is the disturbance due to workload variations, and $G(z)$ is the $M/M/1/K$ system.*

control error and outputs a control-specified buffer size $U(z)$. Figure 4.2(c) models the actual buffer size $V(z)$ as the sum of $U(z)$ and the disturbance $D(z)$. Figure 4.2(d) displays how the $M/M/1/K$ system takes buffer size as input and outputs the response time of the control system. Figure 4.2(e) contains a block diagram of the entire control system. Note that Figure 4.2(e) is very similar to Figure 4.1, but the latter has a transducer block $H(z)$.

As we show in the next section, one block diagram can be transformed easily into an equivalent diagram using various semantics-preserving operations. These operations allow us to simplify complex diagrams by combining multiple blocks into a single block. Of course, the transfer function of the combined block may be fairly complicated. Alternatively, a block with a complex transfer function can be decomposed into a network of blocks with simpler transfer functions.

A further extension of Figure 4.1 is to consider *cascaded control*, as shown in Figure 4.3. Cascaded control occurs when one controller controls another controller. For example, the operating system of a Web server controls CPU scheduling. However, in clustered environments, a load balancer controls the work going to each Web server. Thus, there are two time scales in which the systems operate: fast time scale for scheduling CPU, and a slower time scale for routing Web requests.

Such a strategy is depicted in Figure 4.3. Fast dynamics are modeled by the target system $G_2(z)$. Slower dynamics are addressed by the target system $G_1(z)$. An "inner" controller $K_2(z)$ controls $G_2(z)$, and an outer or "global" controller $K_1(z)$ regulates the entire system by adjusting the reference input to the inner system $K_2(z)$. Thus far, the arrows have represented scalar signals. This can be generalized to vector-valued signals and vector-valued transfer functions, a topic that is discussed in Chapter 7.

We close this section by observing that a block diagram is a pictorial representation of a set of linear equations. Consider Figure 4.1. The relationship between the output of the controller and its input is expressed by the equation $U(z) = K(z)E(z)$. Similar equations can be written for the target system and

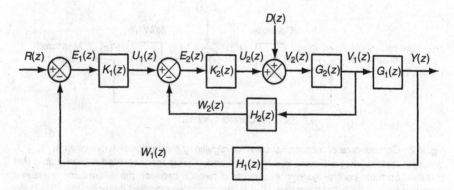

Fig. 4.3 Block diagram of a system using cascaded control.

transducer. Typically, we use a block diagram to find an equation that relates $Y(z)$ to its inputs, such as $D(z)$ and $R(z)$. While the approach is pictorial, we are actually solving a set of equations.

4.2 TRANSFORMING BLOCK DIAGRAMS

In this section we describe how to transform block diagrams using the algebraic rules of Z-transforms. These transformations yield a block diagram that is mathematically equivalent to the original one but is in a more useful form. For example, we can use these transformations to construct the Z-transform of the system or to put the diagram into a more familiar form for which there are known results.

4.2.1 Special Aggregations of Blocks

Figure 4.4 shows combinations of the blocks in Figure 4.1 that have special significance. These combined blocks are used to construct several transfer functions. The first is the *feedforward transfer function*, as specified by the blocks labeled (b) in Figure 4.4(a) and is displayed in Figure 4.4(b). The feedforward transfer function is denoted by $F_{FF}(z)$ and indicates how the control error $E(z)$ is transformed into the output $Y(z)$. Because the controller and target system blocks are in series, the combined transfer function is the product of the component functions. That is, $F_{FF}(z) = G(z)K(z)$. This follows from the definition of transfer functions:

$$F_{FF}(z) = \frac{Y(z)}{E(z)}$$
$$= \frac{U(z)}{E(z)}\frac{Y(z)}{U(z)}$$
$$= K(z)G(z)$$

Note that for the multiplication of scalar transfer functions (our focus here), the order of the transfer functions may be reversed. That is, $G(z)K(z) = K(z)G(z)$. However, this property does not necessarily hold for vector-valued functions (as discussed in Chapter 7).

The feedforward transfer function can be extended to include the transducer, yielding the *loop transfer function*. The loop transfer function is denoted by F_{LP}. Its input is $E(z)$, and its output is $W(z)$. In Figure 4.4(a), the loop transfer function is the block labeled (c) and corresponds to Figure 4.4(c). Since the three blocks are in series, the $F_{LP} = H(z)G(z)K(z)$. This is derived as follows:

$$F_{LP}(z) = \frac{W(z)}{E(z)}$$
$$= \frac{U(z)}{E(z)}\frac{Y(z)}{U(z)}\frac{W(z)}{Y(z)}$$
$$= K(z)G(z)H(z)$$

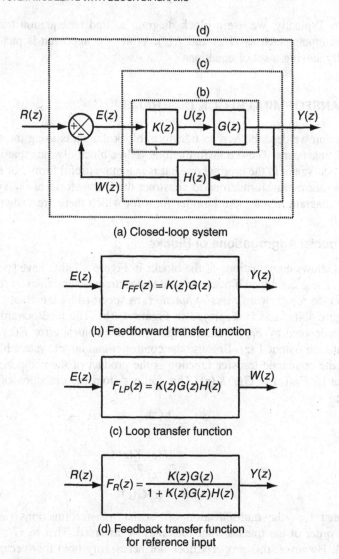

Fig. 4.4 *Transfer functions in closed-loop systems. Dashed lines identify blocks used in several transfer functions in Figure 4.4(a) that are defined in Figure 4.4(b), (c), and (d).*

4.3 TRANSFER FUNCTIONS FOR CONTROL ANALYSIS

In this section we introduce several transfer functions that are used throughout the book to analyze control of computing systems. Figure 4.5 depicts the general form of the block diagram that we use for control analysis. There are three inputs: the reference $R(z)$, disturbance $D(z)$, and noise $N(z)$. Changes in the reference input reflect changes in policy, such as changing a service-level objective. Changes in the disturbance and noise inputs relate to the factors that are uncontrolled. We

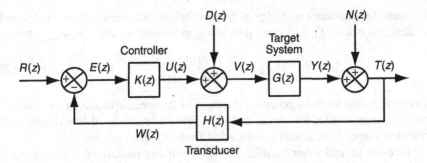

Fig. 4.5 *General form of block diagrams used for control analysis. There are three inputs: the reference $R(z)$, the disturbance $D(z)$, and noise $N(z)$. There are two outputs of interest: the measured output of the system $T(z)$ and the control error $E(z)$.*

are interested in how these changes affect the output of systems. There are two outputs of interest: $T(z)$ and $E(z)$. The measured output (with noise) of the system $T(z)$ is what is being regulated (e.g., CPU utilization, response time). $T(z)$ is the sum of the output of the target system $Y(z)$ and noise $N(z)$. If $N(z) = 0$, then $T(z) = Y(z)$. In these cases, we use $Y(z)$ instead of $T(z)$ as the output of the system. The control error $E(z)$ indicates how close the measured output is to the reference input, where $e(k) = 0$ is the ideal case.

The *reference feedback transfer function* relates the reference input, $R(z)$, to the output, $Y(z)$. Its derivation requires a little algebra. In essence, we solve for $Y(z)/R(z)$ using the set of equations specified by the block diagram. From the definition of a transfer function, only one input is non zero, which in this case is $R(z)$. Thus,

$$W(z) = E(z)K(z)G(z)H(z)$$

$$E(z) = R(z) - W(z)$$

$$= R(z) - E(z)K(z)G(z)H(z)$$

$$[1 + K(z)G(z)H(z)]E(z) = R(z)$$

$$E(z) = \frac{R(z)}{1 + K(z)G(z)H(z)}$$

$$Y(z) = E(z)K(z)G(z)$$

$$= \frac{G(z)K(z)}{1 + H(z)G(z)K(z)}R(z)$$

$$F_R(z) = \frac{Y(z)}{R(z)}$$

$$= \frac{G(z)K(z)}{1 + H(z)G(z)K(z)} \qquad (4.1)$$

Note that the numerator of $F_R(z)$ is the feedforward transfer function $F_{FF}(z)$ and the denominator of $F_R(z)$ is one plus the loop transfer function $F_{LP}(z)$. That is

$$F_R(z) = \frac{F_{FF}(z)}{1 + F_{LP}(z)} \qquad (4.2)$$

This relationship holds in general, regardless of the specific blocks in the feedforward and loop transfer functions, as long as the feedback signal (e.g., transduced measured output with noise) is subtracted from the reference input.

There are several other transfer functions that can be derived from diagrams such as Figure 4.5. The transfer function $F_{RE}(z)$ is from the reference input to the error signal. Here, the feedforward transfer function is 1 and the loop transfer function is as before. Applying Equation (4.2), we have

$$F_{RE}(z) = \frac{E(z)}{R(z)}$$

$$= \frac{1}{1 + K(z)G(z)H(z)} \qquad (4.3)$$

Another transfer function of interest is $F_D(z)$ from the disturbance input to the output in Figure 4.5. Here, the feedforward transfer function is $G(z)$ and the loop transfer function is $K(z)G(z)H(z)$. So

$$F_D(z) = \frac{Y(z)}{D(z)}$$

$$= \frac{G(z)}{1 + K(z)G(z)H(z)} \qquad (4.4)$$

Referring again Figure 4.5, we can assess the effect of a disturbance on control error using the transfer function $F_{DE} = D(z)/E(z)$ [under the assumption that all other inputs are 0, so $R(z) = 0$]. Here, the forward loop for the disturbance to the control error is $-G(z)H(z)$, so

$$F_{DE}(z) = \frac{E(z)}{D(z)}$$

$$= \frac{-G(z)H(z)}{1 + K(z)G(z)H(z)} \qquad (4.5)$$

Last, we consider two transfer functions for which the input is $N(z)$. For these, we use $T(z)$ as the output instead of $Y(z)$. The transfer function from the noise input to the system output $T(z)$ is

$$F_N(z) = \frac{T(z)}{N(z)}$$

$$= \frac{1}{1 + K(z)G(z)H(z)} \qquad (4.6)$$

and the transfer function from the noise input to the control error $E(z)$ is

$$
\begin{aligned}
F_{NE}(z) &= \frac{E(z)}{N(z)} \\
&= \frac{-H(z)}{1 + K(z)G(z)H(z)}
\end{aligned}
\tag{4.7}
$$

4.4 BLOCK DIAGRAM RESTRUCTURING

In some cases, the block diagrams may need to be transformed before it is clear how to apply the simplifications above. These transformations change the appearance of the block diagram, but the underlying equations are equivalent.

Consider the block diagram shown in Figure 4.6(a). There are two feedback loops that are intertwined in a way that makes it difficult to identify the open-loop and closed-loop transfer functions. We can restructure the diagram as follows. First, we move the $K_1(z)$ block to after the summation point, as shown in Figure 4.6(b). To ensure that the input to $K_2(z)$ remains the same, we include a factor of $1/K_1(z)$ in the feedback loop.[1] The next step in Figure 4.7(a)

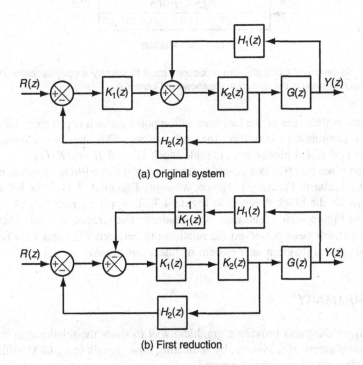

(a) Original system

(b) First reduction

Fig. 4.6 *Sequence of block diagram reductions used to simplify a complex block diagram, part 1. The next steps in the reduction are shown in Figure 4.7.*

[1] We assume that $1/K_1(z)H_1(z)$ is such that the degree of the numerator is no greater than the degree of the denominator.

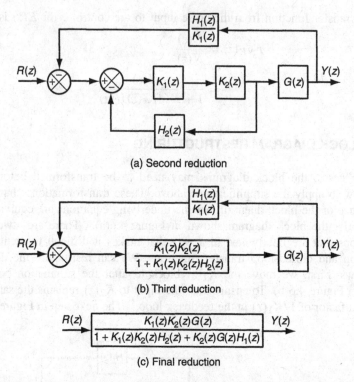

(a) Second reduction

(b) Third reduction

(c) Final reduction

Fig. 4.7 *Sequence of block diagram reductions used to simplify a complex block diagram, part 2. The first steps in the reduction are shown in Figure 4.6.*

interchanges the order of the two summation points, which is possible since addition is a commutative operation for scalar values. This step also combines the $1/K_1(z)$ and $H_1(z)$ blocks into a single block labeled $H_1(z)/K_1(z)$.

We now see that this is a nested structure of two closed-loop systems, each of which is similar to Figure 4.1. Hence, we apply Equation (4.1) to the inner loop, which yields the block diagram in Figure 4.7(b). Applying Equation (4.1) again results in Figure 4.7(c). The interested reader is encouraged to verify that these transformations have preserved the relationship between $R(z)$ and $Y(z)$ (e.g., by expressing each diagram as a system of linear equations).

4.5 SUMMARY

1. Block diagrams provide a graphical way to show the relationship between components of a system by indicating how signals (e.g., CPU utilization, buffer sizes) are communicated.

2. The elements of a block diagram are:

   (a) Blocks, which represent components (which are also systems) and are labeled with their transfer function

(b) Arrows, which indicate the flow of signals and may be annotated by their Z-transform

(c) Summation and branching points, which indicate how signals fan-in and fan-out

3. Complex block diagrams can be transformed into simpler ones by properly manipulating the transfer functions contained in the blocks.

4. There are several transfer functions of interests for feedback control of computing systems. These transfer functions are from the reference, disturbance, or noise input to the measured output or control error.

4.6 EXTENDED EXAMPLES

Block diagrams provide a pictorial representation of relationships between inputs and outputs. In the following, we present several examples of block diagram construction using techniques that we have found to be effective in practice. We also highlight issues that arise during block diagram construction.

4.6.1 IBM Lotus Domino Server

This is a case study of modeling a control system for the IBM Lotus Domino Server. We use this example to demonstrate that block diagram construction is often an iterative process.

Consider the IBM Lotus Domino Server discussed in Section 1.6.1. Requests made by clients to the IBM Lotus Domino Server take the form of remote procedure calls, or RPCs. There are several types of RPCs with different processing requirements. We index these RPCs using the subscripts $1, \ldots, n$.

Based on the foregoing, we propose the model in Figure 4.8(a). The inputs of the IBM Lotus Domino Server are MaxUsers and the rates of the different types of RPCs. The output is RIS, the number of RPCs in the server.

Unfortunately, this model has a flaw. Recall that MaxUsers affects how many users access the system. Hence, MaxUsers and the RPC rates are not independent!

This problem arises in part because we model complex relationships at a high level of abstraction. One way to resolve this is to develop a more detailed model. In particular, we introduce the concept of a transaction, which we define as end-user actions such as "read mail" and "send mail." These actions generate a sequence of RPCs that accomplish a set of related functions on the IBM Lotus Domino Server (e.g., open a database, retrieve a view, retrieve the messages in the view). Depending on the specific RPCs in the transaction, there may be multiple checks for admission to the IBM Lotus Domino Server. Thus, the rate at which transactions arrive is, in general, larger than the rate at which transactions are accepted by the IBM Lotus Domino Server. This is modeled by the components labeled *Admit*. There is one such component for each of the m types of transactions. Next, we must convert from units of transaction rates

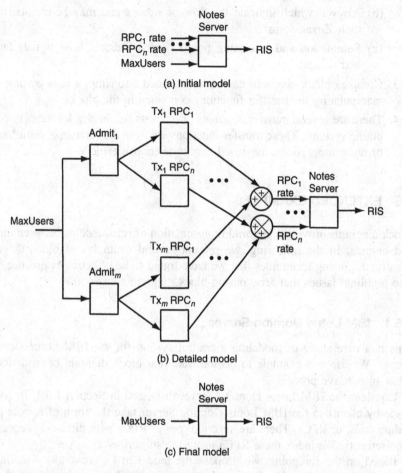

Fig. 4.8 *Evolution of models of the IBM Lotus Domino Server. Figure 4.8(b) and (c) assume that the load offered exceeds* MaxUsers.

to RPC rates. There is one such conversion function for each combination of transaction type and RPC type. This is modeled by the "Tx RPC" blocks.

The effect of MaxUsers is essentially a *min* operation. That is, *Active users* = min{MaxUsers, *All users*}. We focus on the region where MaxUsers<*All users* because this represents the region where the system is overloaded and most in need of control. In this case, *Active users*=MaxUsers. We now have a complete mapping from MaxUsers to RPC rates, as shown in Figure 4.8(b), where MaxUsers is an input to a set of *m* "admit" blocks, each of which is essentially a scaling factor that determines the rate at which each of the *m* transaction types is generated. Each transaction results in zero or more RPCs of each type RPC$_1$ $\cdots$ RPC$_n$. The IBM Lotus Domino Server model then maps the rate of the *n* RPCs into RIS. Observe that this model eliminates MaxUsers as an input to the IBM Lotus Domino Server.

The revised model clearly describes the dependencies within the admission scheme and indicates the role of MaxUsers in determining RIS. However, this is a complex model. If there are m transaction types and n RPC types, we must model $m + nm + 1$ transfer functions!

We simplify the model by taking a higher-level view. In particular, we redefine the block for the IBM Lotus Domino Server so that it encompasses all of the blocks in Figure 4.8(b). Now the diagram simplifies to the one shown in Figure 4.8(c).

4.6.2 Apache HTTP Server with Control Loops

This example is a case study of controlling CPU and memory utilizations (hereafter denoted by CPU and MEM) in the Apache HTTP Server as described in Section 1.6.3. The situation considered involves two control inputs and two outputs.

The control inputs are MaxClients and KeepAlive. Some background is needed to understand how these controls work. In the Apache HTTP Server, clients (e.g., a user at a Web browser) connect to the server before they can make requests. In version 1 of the Apache HTTP Server, each connection is associated with a process on the Web server. MaxClients controls the number of these processes and hence the number of clients that can be connected concurrently. In addition, version 1.1 of the hypertext transfer protocol (HTTP) allows connections to persist between requests. Persistent connections have the advantage of decreasing delays for clients that interact frequently by reducing server overheads for connection buildup and tear-down. However, a disadvantage of persistent connections is that throughput can be reduced. This occurs if the number of connections equals MaxClients (which occurs under heavy loads) and one or more workers is idle (e.g., as a result of long user "think times"). To address this situation, the Apache HTTP Server includes the parameter KeepAlive that controls how long a connection may remain idle before it is closed.

A simple way to model control of the Apache HTTP Server is to address MaxClients and KeepAlive separately as two single-input, single-output (SISO) models. Observe that increasing KeepAlive forces server processes to wait longer for their connected (but idle) clients and hence decreases CPU. Increasing MaxClients increases the number of server processes, which in turn increases both MEM (due to the larger memory footprint) and CPU (since a larger pool of processes means more contention for execution resources). Since KeepAlive affects only CPU, one SISO loop is KeepAlive-CPU. MaxClients affects both CPU and MEM. Since we already have a SISO loop for CPU, the second loop must be MaxClients-MEM. This is displayed in Figure 4.9(a).

Although simple, the SISO approach fails to capture the combined effects of KeepAlive and MaxClients. Thus, we consider a second approach that is depicted in Figure 4.9(b), in which both control inputs can potentially affect both outputs. Such multiple-input, multiple-output (MIMO) models are addressed in Chapter 7.

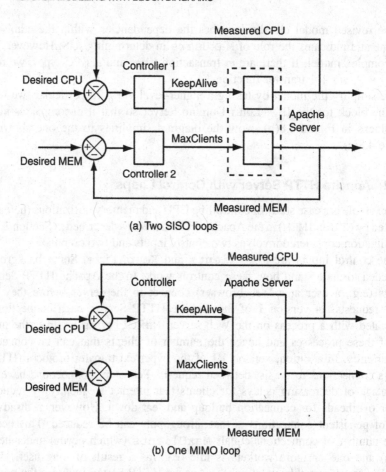

Fig. 4.9 *Block diagrams for alternative models for controlling the Apache HTTP Server.*

We close by noting that the choice between SISO and MIMO models often depends on the specifics of the control system. For example, increasing Max-Clients increases both MEM and CPU. The latter is potentially a problem if it causes the control error in the CPU SISO loop to become more negative. But when this happens, KeepAlive increases to compensate for the larger CPU. We note that if KeepAlive affected both CPU and MEM, the feedback mechanism may not have been able to compensate for the modeling inaccuracies of the multiple SISO model.

4.6.3 Streaming

Streaming is widely used in the Internet to deliver audio and video content. Providing a high-quality streaming service requires ensuring that end-to-end response times do not exceed user-perceivable values. End-to-end response times are managed by controlling the response times of each resource traversed by the streaming requests. Examples of such resources are the CPUs and network interfaces of the systems traversed in the path between server and client.

In the streaming example of Section 1.6.6, there is a controller at each resource that determines how much nonstreaming traffic is accepted. The latter are often referred to as best-efforts requests. Examples of best-efforts requests are packets in file transfers and e-mails since end users rarely notice modest variations in the response times of such requests. Best-efforts requests may be discarded (and later retransmitted by the sender) if there are excessive delays for streaming requests.

There are several ways to architect a streaming system. One approach is to centralize control decisions. Such an architecture is displayed in Figure 4.10(a) for a system consisting of two resources whose transfer functions are denoted by $G_1(z)$ and $G_2(z)$. The input to these resources is the probability of discarding a best-efforts request, and the output is the average response time of streaming

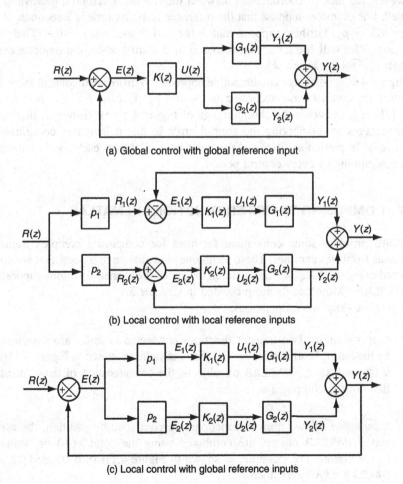

(a) Global control with global reference input

(b) Local control with local reference inputs

(c) Local control with global reference inputs

Fig. 4.10 *Block diagrams for streaming media. The diagrams are distinguished based on whether control is local or global and how the reference input is obtained.*

requests $Y(z)$. There is one controller $K(z)$ that determines the discard probability for both $G_1(z)$ and $G_2(z)$. The reference response time is $R(z)$. The control error $E(z)$ is $R(z) - Y(z)$.

In a streaming system, it is common for resources to be distributed, which makes it problematic to have a single global controller. Further, it may be undesirable to have the same discard probability for all resources. Rather, it is preferable to have a higher discard probability for resources that are traversed earlier to reduce the consumption of resources by requests that are subsequently discarded. These considerations motivate a second architecture. Here, we partition the reference response time into components for each resource. As shown in Figure 4.10(b), there are two SISO control loops. The reference input for loop 1 is $p_1 R(z)$, and the reference input for loop 2 is $p_2 R(z)$. Of course, $p_1 + p_2 = 1$.

The second architecture allows resources to work independent of each other. However, the lack of coordination between the resources can be a disadvantage as well. For example, suppose that the reference response time is 2 seconds, with $p_1 = 0.5 = p_2$. Further, suppose that $y_1(k) = 1.5$ and $y_2(k) = 0.4$. Then the first controller will force the first resource to discard best-efforts requests even though $y_1(k) + y_2(k) < r(k)$.

Figure 4.10(c) displays an alternative approach to distributed control. Here we partition the *control error* according to p_1 and p_2. That is, $E_i(z) = p_i[R(z) - Y(z)]$. Doing so avoids the shortcomings of Figure 4.10(b). However, there are disadvantages to distributing the control error in that it increases coordination overheads. In particular, $R(z) - Y(z)$ must be available to each local controller at the beginning of every control period.

*4.7   COMPOSING TRANSFER FUNCTIONS IN MATLAB

MATLAB provides some convenient facilities for composing complex transfer functions from simpler ones. These techniques are applied to objects that are constructed using the MATLAB tf function or any of the related functions supported by MATLAB. (More details are presented in Chapter 3.)

There are three main operations:

1. *Concatenation.* Two transfer functions connected in series are represented by the multiplication operator (*). For example, as shown in Figure 4.11(a), if G1 and G2 are MATLAB tf objects, the concatenation of these transfer functions is computed as

    ```
    G = G1 * G2
    ```

2. *Summation.* If two transfer functions are combined by addition, the associated MATLAB objects are combined using the "plus" (+) or "minus" (−) operators. For example, as shown in Figure 4.11(b), if G1 and G2 are MATLAB tf objects, then

    ```
    G = G1 + G2
    ```

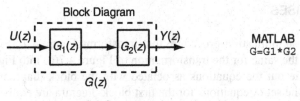

(a) Concatenation composition

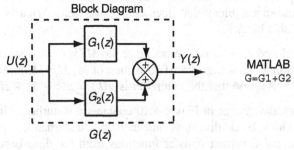

(b) Summation composition

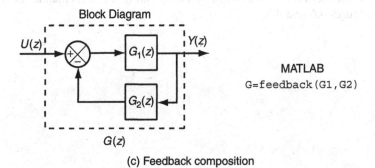

(c) Feedback composition

Fig. 4.11 *Composing transfer functions with* MATLAB. G1 *is the* MATLAB *object that corresponds to* $G_1(z)$, *and* G2 *is the* MATLAB *object that corresponds to* $G_2(z)$. *The figures show how to obtain* G, *the* MATLAB *object that corresponds to* $G(z)$.

3. *Feedback loop.* Finally, MATLAB provides a convenient way to describe closed-loop systems. For example, as shown in Figure 4.11(c), if G1 and G2 are MATLAB tf objects, the transfer function for the feedback loop $G(z)$ is

```
G=feedback(G1,G2)
```

Here, the first argument is the feedforward transfer function and the second argument is the transducer on the feedback path. Note that negative feedback is assumed.

4.8 EXERCISES

1. Verify the simplification procedure that transforms Figure 4.7(a) into Figure 4.7(b). Do the same for the transformation of Figure 4.7(b) into Figure 4.7(c). (*Hint:* Write out the equations associated with the block diagrams and then show that the set of equations for the first block diagram are equivalent to the set of equations for the second block diagram.)

2. Suppose in Figure 4.2(e) that $r(k)$ is in milliseconds and $y(k)$ is in seconds. Include a transducer block that does unit conversions. What is the transfer function of this block?

3. Derive the closed-loop transfer function of the $M/M/1/K$ control block diagram in Example 4.1 using a transfer function of $M/M/1/K$ that is described in Chapter 2. Assume that the controller is $u(k) = u(k-1) + e(k-1)$.

4. Suppose that the system in Figure 4.10 contains a disturbance input for the resources. Draw block diagrams that include a disturbance input for each architecture and construct transfer functions from the disturbance inputs to the outputs.

5. Show the steps required to simplify Figure 4.3 in the same manner as is done in Figures 4.6 and 4.7.

5

First-Order Systems

In this chapter we present techniques for analyzing first-order systems. First-order systems are of interest for several reasons: (1) many real-world systems (e.g., the IBM Lotus Domino Server and the Apache HTTP Server) can be modeled as first-order systems; (2) several approximations used in control design are based on first-order systems; and (3) first-order systems are simple and hence have pedagogical value. In the chapter we address both the statics and dynamics of first-order systems, with particular emphasis on dynamics. We specifically consider the response to initial conditions as well as to different types of input signals, especially the impulse, step, ramp, and sinusoid. The properties studied are stability, steady-state output, settling time, and maximum overshoot. Where possible, simple formulas are used to communicate the underlying theory. Various examples are used to demonstrate application of the theory to computing systems.

5.1 FIRST-ORDER MODEL

The first-order system model we use is specified in Equation (2.5):

$$y(k + 1) = ay(k) + bu(k)$$

Feedback Control of Computing Systems, by Joseph L. Hellerstein, Yixin Diao, Sujay Parekh, and Dawn M. Tilbury
ISBN 0-471-26637-X   Copyright © 2004 John Wiley & Sons, Inc.

where u is the offset of the input and y is the offset of the output. The transfer function of the first-order model is

$$G(z) = \frac{b}{z - a}$$

Note that a is the pole of this system.

Although simple, first-order models are very useful for control analysis and design of computing systems. For example, our model of the IBM Lotus Domino Server in Equation (2.29) and the Apache HTTP Server in Equation (2.30) are in the form of Equation (2.5).

The first-order model can be interpreted in an intuitive way. We begin with the parameter a that specifies how the next value of the output depends on the current value of the output. This is related to the lag 1 autocorrelation of the sequence of output values. For the most part, $a > 0$ in computing systems since there tends to be a positive correlation between metric values such as response time and number in system in queueing systems. For example, a is positive in our models of the IBM Lotus Domino Server, the Apache HTTP Server, and $M/M/1/K$.

Sometimes, negative feedback within the target system can cause $a < 0$. An example of such feedback is window-size adjustments in TCP/IP. Let $v(k)$ be the window size at time k. Consider a model for the *change* in window size $y(k) = v(k) - v(k - 1)$. Suppose that traffic is heavy but stationary. If $y(k) > 0$ (the window size increased), network congestion may well occur, causing round-trip times to increase. As a result, $v(k+1) < v(k)$ and so $y(k+1) < 0$. However, if $y(k) < 0$, contention is reduced, round-trip time decreases, so $y(k + 1) > 0$. Such effects can cause negative autocorrelations and hence result in $a < 0$.

A third possibility is that $a = 0$, or at least $|a|$ is very small. Typically, this indicates that there is little dynamics, possibly as a result of long sampling times.

The parameter b describes the functional relationship between the input and the output. If $b > 0$, a positive change in the input causes a positive change in the output. If $b < 0$, the output changes in the opposite direction as the input. For example, in the Apache HTTP Server, as the input MaxClients increases, so does the output CPU since concurrently processing more requests increases CPU. However, as the input KeepAlive increases, the output CPU *decreases*. This is because a larger KeepAlive value results in more idle workers, so CPU utilization declines.

Equation (2.5) is a deterministic model. That is, if $y(k)$ and $u(k)$ are known, Equation (2.5) predicts $y(k+1)$ exactly. Most computing systems have a significant stochastic component. Thus, we use Equation (2.5) only as an approximation to the true behavior of the system, and recognize the limits of its predictive ability. Even so, we have found Equation (2.5) to be very useful in practice. We note in passing that Section 5.7 provides an analysis of transient response in the presence of stochastics.

Before continuing, we underscore a point made repeatedly in this book. Linear models are constructed around an operating point and are valid only within the operating region for which they were developed. As such, the analysis that follows is predicated on the assumption that changes to initial conditions and/or inputs do not place the system outside its operating region.

5.2 SYSTEM RESPONSE

The system response describes how the output y behaves over time. The output can change for many reasons. During startup, there may be a "warm-up" period during which buffers fill and processes complete their initializations. During operation, there may be a transient fault in the system, or the workload may change. All of these behaviors can be described by the system's time-domain response. If the system is adequately modeled by a difference equation such as Equation (2.5), the output can be described by the solution to that equation with the appropriate $\{u(k)\}$ and initial conditions.

5.2.1 Steady-State and Transient Responses

The system response in the time domain can be divided into two parts: the steady-state or long-term response (in the limit as time goes to infinity), and the transient or short-term response. Although in theory the transient response is infinitely long, in practice, a finite duration that captures the interesting behavior is considered.

For example, consider the Apache HTTP Server operating with a constant arrival rate of page requests. Memory and CPU utilizations will be more or less constant over time. If the arrival rates change, memory and CPU utilizations will also change; however, they may take some amount of time to reach their new operating values. The time before the new operating condition is reached is called the *transient response*, and after the new operating condition is reached the system is said to be in steady state.

Figure 1.3 illustrates the steady-state and transient responses to a step change in the reference input. The *steady-state output* of a system is the output that results as time goes to infinity. From Chapter 3, we know that the system must be BIBO stable to ensure convergence for bounded signals. We emphasize that since our models are constructed within an operating region, BIBO stable really means BIBO stable within the operating region of the model.

The output of a BIBO stable system may converge to a single value, called y_{ss}, defined as $y_{ss} = \lim_{k \to \infty} y(k)$; or it may converge to another signal. For the latter, we use the notation $y_{ss}(k)$ to denote that the output has reached steady state but is not a constant. We note here that the response of a BIBO stable system always converges to a steady-state output that has the same form as the input signal. That is, a step input gives a constant steady-state output, a ramp input gives a steady-state ramp output, a sinusoid input gives a steady-state sinusoid output, and so forth. This property is explored in more detail later in this chapter.

The settling time of the system is the time required before steady state is reached (to a reasonable degree of accuracy). In this book, we use a 2% criterion to define the settling time. (The precise definition depends on the input signal.) The *transient response* of a system is defined as the output during its settling time.

The maximum overshoot is the maximum amount that the transient system output overshoots its steady-state value, divided by its steady-state value. The maximum overshoot is often expressed as a percentage. Other characteristics of the transient response include the peak time (the time to reach the maximum overshoot point) and the delay time (the elapsed time before output starts to react to input signal). These characteristics are usually not used as commonly as are the settling time and maximum overshoot.

Example 5.1: Transient response in the Apache HTTP Server   Figure 5.1 shows the transient response of the Apache HTTP Server controlled by a feedback controller. The desired value of CPU utilization changes from 0.3 to 0.8 at 900 seconds. The feedback controller acts to achieve this goal by adjusting MaxClients. This results in CPU utilization changing as shown in Figure 5.1. The output reflects both the control action and the effects of stochastics. A similar plot is shown for memory utilization. Here, there are fewer stochastics, so the transient response is clear.

Figure 5.2 shows the transient response of the Apache HTTP Server controlled by a more "aggressive" feedback controller. A too-aggressive controller can cause more system oscillation and larger overshoot.

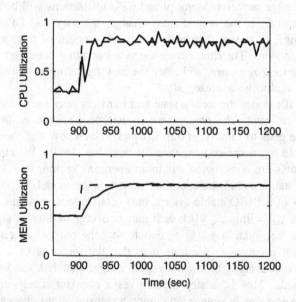

Fig. 5.1 *Transient response of the Apache HTTP Server under control of a less aggressive controller. The solid lines indicate the measured values. The dashed lines indicate the desired values.*

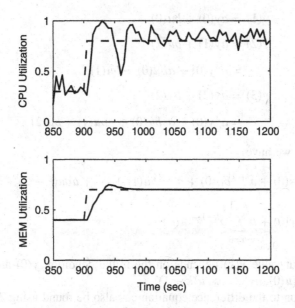

Fig. 5.2 *Transient response of the Apache HTTP Server under control of a more aggressive controller. The solid lines indicate the measured values. The dashed lines indicate the desired values.*

5.2.2 Input Signal Model

To find the solution of Equation (2.5), the input signal must be known. From Figure 4.5, we know that there are three kinds of inputs: the reference input, disturbance input, and noise input. For example, in computing systems the disturbance input can be used to model a change in the workload, a change in the system parameters, or a fault condition. Indeed, the response to a disturbance input is one of the more useful analyses for computing systems. A transient fault of very short duration can be modeled as an impulse; that is, the signal is zero for all time except for $k = 0$. A sudden jump in arrival rates can be modeled as a step, followed by a negative step when the workload returns to its previous level. A gradual increase or decrease in workload, such as at the start of a workday, can be modeled as a ramp signal. Periodic variations in workload (e.g., to reflect daily cycles or as a surrogate for variability) can be modeled with a sine wave or combination of sine waves.

5.2.3 Time-Domain Solution

Both the transient and steady-state responses of a first-order system can be found by solving Equation (2.5). This can be done either directly in the time domain or by using Z-transforms as in Chapter 3.

For the solution in the time domain, we proceed by iteratively solving the difference equation, using the initial condition $y(0)$ and the input signal $\{u(k)\}$:

$$y(1) = ay(0) + bu(0)$$

$$y(2) = ay(1) + bu(1)$$

$$= a^2 y(0) + abu(0) + bu(1)$$

$$y(3) = ay(2) + bu(2)$$

$$= a^3 y(0) + a^2 bu(0) + abu(1) + bu(2)$$

Generalizing, we have

$$y(k) = a^k y(0) + a^{k-1} bu(0) + a^{k-2} bu(1) + \cdots + abu(k-2) + bu(k-1)$$

$$= a^k y(0) + b \sum_{n=0}^{k-1} a^{k-1-n} u(n) \tag{5.1}$$

The kth output value $y(k)$ depends on the initial condition $y(0)$ and the first k input values $\{u(0), u(1), \dots, u(k-1)\}$.

The solution to the difference equation can also be found using Z-transforms. First, we take the Z-transform of Equation (2.5) to get

$$zY(z) - zy(0) = aY(z) + bU(z)$$

$$(z - a)Y(z) = zy(0) + bU(z)$$

$$Y(z) = \frac{z}{z-a} y(0) + \frac{b}{z-a} U(z) \tag{5.2}$$

When the inverse Z-transform is taken, there will be two terms: one including the initial condition $y(0)$ and one including the input $U(z)$. Once the input $U(z)$ is known, $Y(z)$ can be found directly, and $y(k)$ can be determined using the inverse Z-transform.

Equation (5.1) decomposes the factors affecting the output into the initial condition $y(0)$ and the input signal $\{u(k)\}$. Let $y_{\text{initial}}(k) = a^k y(0)$ be the effects due to initial conditions and $y_{\text{input}}(k) = b \sum_{n=0}^{k-1} a^{k-1-n} u(n)$ be the effects due to the input signal. Clearly,

$$y(k) = y_{\text{initial}}(k) + y_{\text{input}}(k)$$

This is an example of the *superposition property*, which allows us to analyze $y_{\text{initial}}(k)$ and $y_{\text{input}}(k)$ separately and then combine the results. That is, initial conditions are studied with $u(k) = 0$, and the input signal is studied with $y(0) = 0$. The superposition property also applies to combinations of inputs. So, if u is a sum of a step and a sine, the response of the system to the two different input components can be found separately and then added together.

In the remainder of this chapter we study the response of first-order systems to initial conditions (with zero input) and to several different types of input signals (with zero initial conditions).

5.3 INITIAL CONDITION RESPONSE

Consider the first-order system represented by Equation (2.5) with $u(k) = 0$ for all k. Under these conditions, the response of the system depends only on the initial condition $y(0)$ and on the system parameter a, which is the pole of the transfer function. This is called the *initial condition response*. From Equation (5.1) we see that

$$y(k) = a^k y(0) \qquad (5.3)$$

Figure 5.3 evaluates the effect on the output of different values of the parameter a. For simplicity, we assume that the initial condition is $y(0) = 1$ since the magnitude of the initial conditions affects only the scaling of the output. The four plots on the top of Figure 5.3 have $a < 0$, and the four on the bottom have $a > 0$. Note that negative values of a result in an oscillatory output (the output flip-flops between positive and negative), while positive values of a result in an output that is always the same sign as the initial condition [here positive, but if $y(0) < 0$, the output would always be negative].

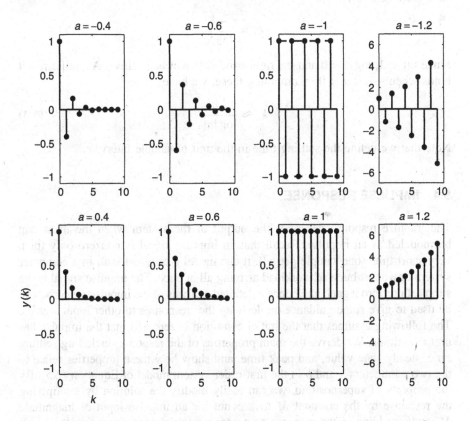

Fig. 5.3 *Response to initial conditions of a first-order system with $y(0) = 1$ and various values of a. The dashed line indicates y_{ss}, the steady-state signal, if it exists.*

The four plots on the left side of Figure 5.3 have $|a| < 1$, and hence correspond to stable systems. In all of these stable systems, the output converges to zero. Recall that in the system model, a zero output corresponds to the operating point. This means that if for some reason the system starts operating away from its normal operating condition (such as due to execution of administrative tasks), it will converge if it is stable. However, if the system is not stable, such as those shown in the two plots on the right-hand side of Figure 5.3, the output does not converge, and the response to a nonzero initial condition is unbounded. If $|a| = 1$, the output is bounded but does not converge to the operating point.

For a stable system, we define its settling time to initial conditions as the time until the output is within 2% of its largest magnitude value. From Equation (5.3), we see that the largest magnitude is achieved at $|y(0)|$. Noting that for convergence we must have $|a| < 1$, we find k_s such that

$$|a^{k_s}| = \frac{|y(k_s)|}{|y(0)|} < 0.02$$

Taking the natural logarithm of both sides, and noting that $\log 0.02 \approx -4$, we have for $0 < a < 1$,

$$k_s \approx \frac{-4}{\log a}$$

Since $|a| < 1$, $\log a < 0$ and the right-hand side will be positive. A similar result holds when $-1 < a < 0$. Combining these, we have

$$k_s \approx \frac{-4}{\log |a|} \tag{5.4}$$

Note that we define the settling time in the unit of sample intervals.

5.4 IMPULSE RESPONSE

The impulse response describes the output of the system when the input can be modeled as an impulse. Recall that an impulse signal is nonzero only for a very short time (one sample period). It can model a transient fault in a computer system or a short burst of workload arriving all at once. The impulse signal is the simplest nonzero signal, and hence a detailed analysis of the impulse response can be used to give some guidance on deriving the responses to other input signals. The following assumes that the initial condition is zero and that the impulse has unit magnitude. We derive the main properties of the response, including settling time, steady-state value, and peak time, and show how these properties relate to the two parameters a and b in the first-order system model of Equation (2.5). By the property of superposition, we can easily modify the solution by multiplying the response by the constant M to account for an impulse input of magnitude M, and/or adding in the response to a nonzero initial condition using the result of Equation (5.3).

Consider the first-order system in Equation (2.5) with zero initial condition, that is, $y(0) = 0$, and a unit impulse input, that is, $\{u(k)\} = \{1, 0, 0, \ldots\}$. From Equation (5.1) we can see that the output $y(k)$ has the form

$$y(k) = b \sum_{n=0}^{k-1} a^{k-1-n} u(n)$$

$$= ba^{k-1} \qquad \text{for } k \geq 1 \qquad (5.5)$$

This result can also be derived using Z-transforms. First, we take the Z-transform of Equation (2.5):

$$zY(z) - zy(0) = aY(z) + bU(z)$$

Then, setting the initial condition $y(0)$ to 0 and noting that the Z-transform of an impulse input is $U(z) = 1$, we solve for $Y(z)$ to get

$$(z - a)Y(z) = bU(z) = b \cdot 1$$

$$Y(z) = \frac{b}{z - a} = bz^{-1} \frac{z}{z - a}$$

and finally, consulting Table 3.1, we find the time-domain expression for $y(k)$ as

$$y(k) = ba^{k-1}$$

which agrees exactly with Equation (5.5), as expected.

The impulse response differs from the initial conditions response in Equation (5.3) in two important ways: (1) the response is delayed by one time step [$y(0) = 0$], and (2) the output is multiplied by b.

Paralleling Figure 5.3, the impulse responses of different systems (for eight different values of a) are plotted in Figure 5.4. Systems with a negative pole $a < 0$ are on the top row, and those with a positive pole $a > 0$ are on the bottom row. The oscillatory response of systems with a negative pole is also seen in the impulse responses. As expected, the output converges to 0 for those systems whose pole lies within the unit circle. The two systems with $|a| = 1$ do not converge, but they do not diverge either. When $|a| > 1$, the output increases without bound.

For all bounded impulse responses (those with $|a| \leq 1$), the peak time occurs at $k = 1$, when $y(1) = y_{\text{max}} = b$ [from Equation (5.5)]. The settling time k_s is such that $y(k_s)$ is 2% of y_{max}. Clearly, for an impulse, $y_{\text{max}} = b$. Thus,

$$|y(k_s)| \approx |ba^{k_s-1}| = 0.02|b|$$

$$(k_s - 1) \log |a| \approx \log 0.02 \approx -4$$

$$k_s \approx \frac{-4}{\log |a|} + 1 \qquad (5.6)$$

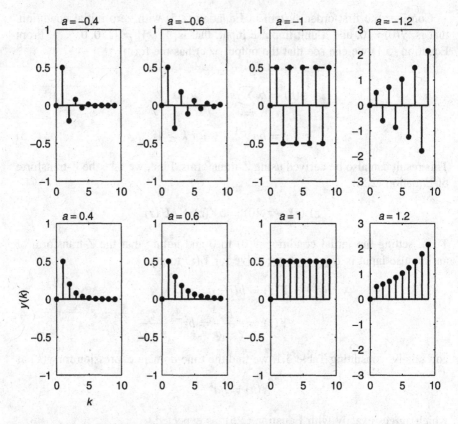

Fig. 5.4 *Impulse response of a first-order system, with zero initial condition, $y(0) = 0$. The parameter a is varied, and $b = 0.5$ for all responses. The dashed line indicates y_{ss}, the steady-state value, if it exists.*

For simplicity, we will often further approximate the settling time as

$$k_s \approx \frac{-4}{\log |a|} \qquad (5.7)$$

As a simple numerical example, consider the first-order systems with poles $|a_1| = 0.4$ and $|a_2| = 0.6$. The settling times of these systems are

$$k_{s_1} \approx \frac{-4}{\log(0.4)} \approx 5$$

$$k_{s_2} \approx \frac{-4}{\log(0.6)} \approx 8$$

(where we have rounded the settling times up to the next-highest integer). This means that for the system with $|a_1| = 0.4$, $|y(5)| < 0.02|y_{max}| = 0.01$. When $|a_2| = 0.6$, after eight sample times the output is less than 0.01. It can be seen from these equations and from Figure 5.4 that settling time increases with the magnitude of the pole a. As $a \to 0$, the settling time decreases, until at $a = 0$ the settling time is exactly one sample time.

Example 5.2: Impulse response in the IBM Lotus Domino Server Consider the IBM Lotus Domino Server from Section 2.6.1, which is described as

$$y(k + 1) = 0.43y(k) + 0.47u(k)$$

This model is constructed around the operating point $\overline{\text{MaxUsers}} = 165$, $\overline{\text{RIS}} = 135$. Thus, the value of y and u in the model are the offset between the actual values of MaxUsers and RIS and their operating points:

$$y(k) = \text{RIS}(k) - \overline{\text{RIS}}$$

$$u(k) = \text{MaxUsers}(k) - \overline{\text{MaxUsers}}$$

Suppose that there are administrative tasks of short duration whose effect can be modeled as a change in the MaxUsers value seen by the IBM Lotus Domino Server. Thus, MaxUsers(k) refers to the value of MaxUsers that is specified through the IBM Lotus Domino Server command console or through appropriate programming interfaces. Consider a situation in which multiple administrative tasks are initiated at the same time. We refer to this as an *administrative job*. The execution of administrative tasks is an example of a disturbance. Let $d(k)$ denote the effect of these tasks on the effective value of MaxUsers at time k. Then we have the following dynamics:

$$y(k + 1) = 0.43y(k) + 0.47[u(k) + d(k)] \tag{5.8}$$

Figure 5.5 displays a block diagram of the system just described.

If the administrative job runs for a short time, we model it as an impulse signal (whose magnitude depends on the RPCs in the job). We consider a disturbance of magnitude $M = 40$ (i.e., MaxUsers is increased by 40). Further, we assume that the system was running at its operating point before the disturbance occurred, thus MaxUsers(k) = $\overline{\text{MaxUsers}}$, so $u(k) = 0$. The time-domain solution for y can be obtained from Equation (5.5). Noting that we must multiply this by the magnitude of the input to get the correct response, we obtain

$$y(k) = ba^{k-1}M = (0.47)(0.43)^{k-1}(40) = 18.8(0.43)^{k-1}$$

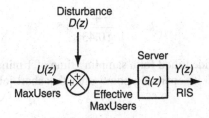

Fig. 5.5 *IBM Lotus Domino Server with a disturbance input that is modeled as a change in* MaxUsers *as seen by the server.*

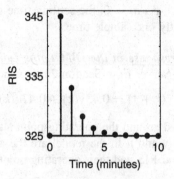

Fig. 5.6 *Prediction of offset RIS in the IBM Lotus Domino Server as a result of the execution of a short administrative job that is modeled as an impulse.*

We can also use Z-transforms to find the impulse response y. We let the initial condition $y(0) = 0$; this implies that at time $k = 0$, the system was originally at its operating point. Also, for an impulse response of magnitude 40 at time $k = 0$, we have $D(z) = 40$.

$$zY(z) - zy(0) = 0.43Y(z) + 0.47D(z)$$

$$(z - 0.43)Y(z) = 0.47(40) = 18.8$$

$$Y(z) = \frac{18.8}{z - 0.43} = 18.8z^{-1}\frac{z}{z - 0.43}$$

$$y(k) = 18.8(0.43)^{k-1}$$

As expected, both derivations give the same result for y. Note that the pole of this system is 0.43.

The impulse response of Figure 5.6 shows the behavior of RIS in the IBM Lotus Domino Server predicted by the model after the short-term job runs on the server. The RIS initially increases by 18.8 (for a total RIS of $135 + 18.8$), and then gradually decreases to its operating point ($y_{ss} = 0$, or RIS = 135). The time taken to reach the steady state (within 2% of the final value of the output) is the settling time. Using Equation (5.6), we compute

$$k_s \approx \frac{-4}{\log 0.43} \approx 5$$

Since the model was identified for a sampling time of 1 minute, this system takes 5 minutes to return to its operating point after this short job has been processed on the server.

Another example of an impulse response in a real system is given in Example 3.3, Apache Web Server with impulse input.

5.5 STEP RESPONSE

The step response describes the output of the system to a sustained change in input that can be modeled as a step. A unit step is a signal that is zero for all time $k < 0$, and one for all times $k \geq 0$. It is called a step because when the points are connected in the time domain, it resembles a step. Steps are frequently used to model discontinuous changes in workload or parameter settings. We assume in this section that the initial condition is $y(0) = 0$; if the initial condition is nonzero, we can find the total response by superposition of the initial condition response and the step response.

5.5.1 Numerical Example

Before deriving the general form of the step response of a first-order system, we consider some numerical results for solving the first-order system in Equation (2.5) with zero initial conditions and a unit step input. The results for eight different values of a are shown in Figure 5.7; in all cases, the parameter $b = 0.5$. Several observations can be made from this figure. For stable systems, those with a pole inside the unit circle ($|a| < 0$), the step response converges to a constant, nonzero value. For systems with poles outside the unit circle ($|a| > 1$), the output is unbounded. When the poles are on the unit circle, the figure is inconclusive. Although systems with $|a| = 1$ are not BIBO stable, there may still be some bounded inputs that result in bounded outputs, such as when $a = -1$. However, a bounded input may also result in an unbounded output, such as the step response with $a = 1$. The figure also shows that the time taken for the step response to converge (the settling time) is shorter for smaller values of a. Finally, similar to the impulse response, a negative value of a results in oscillations in the output.

5.5.2 Time-Domain Solution

Consider the time-domain solution from Equation (5.1), and let the input be a unit step ($u(k) = 1$ for all $k \geq 0$) and the initial condition be zero [$y(0) = 0$]:

$$y(k) = b \sum_{n=0}^{k-1} a^{k-1-n} = b \sum_{n=0}^{k-1} a^n$$

Recall from Chapter 3 that this geometric series can be expressed as

$$y(k) = b \frac{1 - a^k}{1 - a} \tag{5.9}$$

The step response can also be computed using Z-transforms. For this, we use Equation (5.2) and set the initial condition equal to zero to get

$$Y(z) = \frac{b}{z - a} U(z)$$

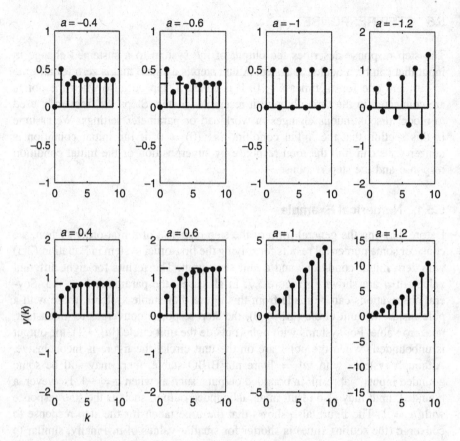

Fig. 5.7 Step response of a first-order system. $y(0) = 0$, $b = 0.5$. The dashed line indicates y_{ss}, the steady-state value, if it exists.

Recall that the transfer function $G(z)$ is defined as

$$G(z) = \frac{Y(z)}{U(z)} = \frac{b}{z - a}$$

Thus, to find the output, we multiply the transfer function by the Z-transform of the input, $Y(z) = G(z)U(z)$. From Table 3.1, the Z-transform of a unit step is $U(z) = z/(z - 1)$, and thus

$$Y(z) = G(z)U(z) = \frac{b}{z - a}\frac{z}{z - 1} \tag{5.10}$$

For completeness, we solve for the inverse Z-transform, although many properties can be determined simply from the form of $Y(z)$.

In order to find $y(k)$ from $Y(z)$, we need to match the form of one or more entries in Table 3.1. We do this through a partial fraction expansion, using one term for each pole in the denominator of $Y(z)$:

$$Y(z) = \frac{b}{z-a}\frac{z}{z-1} = \frac{c_1}{z-a} + \frac{c_2}{z-1}$$

$$= \frac{c_1(z-1) + c_2(z-a)}{(z-1)(z-a)}$$

$$= \frac{(c_1 + c_2)z - (c_1 + c_2 a)}{(z-1)(z-a)}$$

Solving for the constants c_1 and c_2, we get

$$(c_1 + c_2) = b$$

$$(c_1 + c_2 a) = 0$$

$$c_1 = \frac{-ab}{1-a}$$

$$c_2 = \frac{b}{1-a}$$

and thus, we have the form of $Y(z)$ and can use Table 3.1 to find $y(k)$:

$$Y(z) = \frac{c_1}{z-a} + \frac{c_2}{z-1}$$

$$= \frac{-ab/(1-a)}{z-a} + \frac{b/(1-a)}{z-1}$$

$$= z^{-1}\frac{-ab}{1-a}\frac{z}{z-a} + z^{-1}\frac{b}{1-a}\frac{z}{z-1}$$

$$y(k) = \frac{-ab}{1-a}a^{k-1} + \frac{b}{1-a}$$

$$y(k) = \frac{b(1-a^k)}{1-a} \tag{5.11}$$

Although this agrees with the time-domain solution of Equation (5.9), it clearly shows that there are two contributions to the response: one from the pole (the exponential term with a) and the other from the step input. For any system, the output dynamics are a combination of the input signal dynamics and the internal dynamics of the system due to its pole(s).

5.5.3 Steady-State Response

From Theorem 3.2 we know that the first-order system is BIBO stable if and only if $|a| < 1$. A step is a bounded input, and hence, the step response of a stable first-order system is bounded. In fact, if the system is stable, the step response is not only bounded, but converges to a final value. This steady-state value, y_{ss}, can be found either as the limit as $k \to \infty$ of $y(k)$ or from the final value theorem applied to $Y(z)$. Both approaches to finding y_{ss} are considered here.

From Equation (5.9) we have

$$y_{ss} = \lim_{k \to \infty} y(k) = \lim_{k \to \infty} b \frac{1 - a^k}{1 - a} = \frac{b}{1 - a}$$

The limit exists if $|a| < 1$. Alternatively, we can use the final value theorem applied to the expression $Y(z)$ from Equation (5.10):

$$y_{ss} = \lim_{z \to 1} (z - 1) Y(z) = \lim_{z \to 1} (z - 1) \frac{b}{z - a} \frac{z}{z - 1} = \lim_{z \to 1} \frac{b}{z - a} = \frac{b}{1 - a}$$

The final value theorem can be applied only if all the poles of $(z - 1)Y(z)$ are inside the unit circle: in this case, if $|a| < 1$.

Although the same answer can be found either from the time-domain solution or from the final value theorem applied to $Y(z)$, we note that to apply the final value theorem, the exact form of the time-domain response is not needed. Thus, if only the final value is desired, there is no need to find the time-domain response. We also note that, by definition, the final value of the system output to a unit step input is exactly the *steady-state gain* of the system:

$$G(1) = \frac{b}{1 - a}$$

5.5.4 Transient Response

The transient response is how the response behaves before it reaches steady state. The expression for y in Equation (5.11) allows the transient and steady-state responses to be separated easily. We have

$$y(k) = \frac{-ab}{1 - a} a^{k-1} + \frac{b}{1 - a}$$

$$= y_{tr}(k) + y_{ss}$$

The transient part of the step response is thus

$$y_{tr}(k) = \frac{-ab}{1 - a} a^{k-1} = -\frac{b}{1 - a} a^k$$

The settling time k_s for a step input is such that $y(k_s)$ is within 2% of the steady-state value y_{ss}. That is,

$$\left| \frac{y(k_s^*) - y_{ss}}{y_{ss}} \right| = \left| \frac{y_{tr}(k_s^*)}{y_{ss}} \right| = \left| \frac{[b/(1 - a)]a^{k_s}}{b/(1 - a)} \right| \approx 0.02$$

$$\left| a^{k_s} \right| \approx 0.02$$

$$k_s \log |a| \approx -4$$

$$k_s \approx \frac{-4}{\log |a|} \tag{5.12}$$

Recall that since $|a| < 1$, $\log |a|$ will be negative. Note that the settling time for the step response is the same as the settling time for the initial condition response from Equation (5.4), but one less than the settling time for the impulse response from Equation (5.6). This is because the settling time is defined with regard to 2% of the maximum deviation. For the initial condition response and the step response, the maximum deviation occurs at $k = 0$. However, for impulse response, the maximum deviation occurs at $k = 1$.

Another important property of the transient response is the peak value, y_{max}. This can be important in the case that the output is saturated and cannot reach the predicted peak value. In that case, the system would no longer be operating in its linear region, and the linear model would not be a good predictor of its behavior. In other cases, too large an output response could cause problems in the system, even though the steady-state value would be acceptable. Thus, the peak value should be considered.

From Figure 5.7, consider the four stable responses (those on the left-hand side of the figure). When the pole a is positive, the peak value is the steady-state value, and it is reached after the settling time. However, when the pole a is negative, there are oscillations in the response, and the peak value is reached at $k = 1$. This can also be seen from the time-domain response of Equation (5.9). Since $y(k) = b(1 + a + a^2 + a^3 + \cdots)$, if $a > 0$, then $y(k)$ is uniformly increasing and there is no peak value. However, if $-1 < a < 0$, then $y(k)$ alternately increases and decreases, but by a diminishing difference at each step. Thus, the maximum value is taken when $y(1) = b$. The peak time is $k_p = 1$.

In practice, the peak value depends not only on the system parameter b but also on the magnitude of the step input. For example, if a step input of 10 units is applied, the maximum value is $10b$. Also, the peak value has units that must be accounted for (such as response time, number in system, etc). A more intrinsic description of the peak value is the *maximum overshoot*, denoted M_p, which is defined as the fraction (often expressed as a percentage) by which the response exceeds its steady-state value.

$$M_p = \frac{y_{max} - y_{ss}}{y_{ss}}$$

The overshoot for the first-order system with a negative pole ($a < 0$) is

$$M_p = \frac{y_{max} - y_{ss}}{y_{ss}} = \frac{b - [b/(1 - a)]}{b/(1 - a)} = -a \qquad (5.13)$$

Since this relationship is valid only for a stable system, we have that $|a| < 1$, and hence this can easily be interpreted as the fractional or percentage overshoot. For a stable system with positive pole ($a > 0$), as $y_{max} = y_{ss}$, we have $M_p = 0$.

Example 5.3: Step response in the IBM Lotus Domino Server Consider again the IBM Lotus Domino Server in Example 5.2 with a long-running administrative job. This is modeled as a step with magnitude $M = 40$. If the system is initially at its operating point, the initial condition is zero, and we can use the transfer function $G(z)$ to study the response of the system.

We use the transfer function $G(z) = 0.47/(z-0.43)$. The output can be found by multiplying the transfer function by the input. Treating the administrative jobs as a disturbance with Z-transform $D(z) = 40z/(z-1)$, we have

$$Y(z) = G(z)D(z) = \frac{0.47}{z-0.43} \frac{40z}{z-1} = \frac{18.8z}{(z-0.43)(z-1)}$$

Instead of finding the inverse Z-transform of $Y(z)$, we determine some important properties of y directly from its Z-transform. First, note that $Y(z)$ has two poles, and hence its time-domain solution has two terms. One corresponds to the pole at $z = 1$ and the other corresponds to the pole at $z = 0.43$. The final value theorem can be applied because all the poles of $(z-1)Y(z)$ are within the unit circle. Hence, we compute

$$y_{ss} = \lim_{k\to\infty} y(k) = \lim_{z\to1}(z-1)Y(z)$$

$$= \lim_{z\to1}(z-1)\frac{18.8z}{(z-0.43)(z-1)} = \frac{18.8\cdot1}{1-0.43} = 33$$

This means that in steady state, after the transient response has died down, the RIS (output) will be 33 more than the operating point (or $135 + 33 = 168$).

The settling time, or the time required to reach this new steady-state value, can also be determined from the poles of $Y(z)$. The pole at 0.43 will contribute a term such as $c_1(0.43)^k$ to the time response. When this term has decreased to 2% of its maximum value, the transient response can be considered to be approximately zero. Applying Equation (5.12), we compute that the settling time as

$$k_s \approx \frac{-4}{\log 0.43} \approx 5$$

If the new job finishes some time later, this can be modeled as a negative step; the initial condition must also be taken into account to solve for this response. A simulation of the step response for the IBM Lotus Domino Server is shown in Figure 5.8.

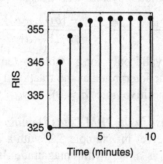

Fig. 5.8 Predicted RIS in the IBM Lotus Domino Server after a long job (modeled as a step) runs. The time scale is in minutes.

For another example of a step response, see Example 3.4, Apache Web Server with step input.

5.6 TRANSIENT RESPONSE TO OTHER SIGNALS

The response of a first-order system to any input u can be found either from the time domain expression of Equation (5.1) or from the Z-transform expression of Equation (5.2). Although the impulse and step are the two most common input signals encountered in computing systems, in this section we also consider the response of a first-order system to a ramp input and to a sinusoidal input.

5.6.1 Ramp Response

The ramp response describes the output of a system to a unit ramp, a signal that increases linearly for $k \geq 0$, $u(k) = k$. It is called a *ramp* because when the points are connected in the time domain, it resembles a ramp. Ramps can be used to model workload that arrives gradually, such as at the start of a working day. A ramp signal is unbounded and thus is never seen in practice; however, a section of a ramp is often an appropriate signal to use for modeling.

We assume in this section that the initial condition is $y(0) = 0$. If the initial condition of the system is not zero, the total response can be found by superposition of the initial condition response (as derived in Section 5.3) and the ramp response.

Before delving into the ramp response in detail, consider the numerical experiments presented in Figure 5.9. Note that the output is unbounded for all different values of a. Even if the system is BIBO stable (when $|a| < 1$), the output is unbounded because the ramp input is unbounded. When the system is BIBO stable, however, the steady-state output is also a ramp.

Now, consider the time-domain solution in detail. From Equation (5.1) we set $u(n) = n$ and simplify the sums.

$$y(k) = b \sum_{n=0}^{k-1} na^{k-n-1}$$

$$= \frac{b(k + a^k - 1 - ak)}{(1-a)^2}$$

$$= \left[\frac{b}{1-a}k - \frac{b}{(1-a)^2} \right] + \left[\frac{b}{(1-a)^2} \right] a^k \qquad (5.14)$$

$$= y_{ss}(k) + y_{tr}(k)$$

It can be seen that the ramp response has three terms: a ramp, a constant, and a decaying geometric term. If the system is BIBO stable (i.e., if $|a| < 1$), we can see that the first two terms, the ramp plus the constant, constitute the steady-state

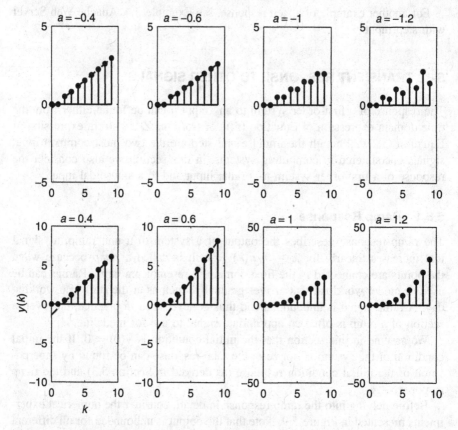

Fig. 5.9 Ramp response of a first-order system. $y(0) = 0$, $b = 0.5$. The dashed line indicates the steady-state signal $y_{ss}(k)$, if it exists.

response. The last term, the decaying geometric, constitutes the transient part of the response since it goes to zero as $k \to \infty$. Note that the slope of the ramp input is 1, and the slope of the steady-state ramp output is $b/(1 - a)$. This is exactly the steady-state gain of the system $G(1)$.

The time-domain solution can also be determined using Z-transforms. From Table 3.1, the Z-transform of a unit ramp input is $U(z) = z/(z - 1)^2$. Thus, we have

$$Y(z) = G(z)U(z) = \frac{b}{z - a} \frac{z}{(z - 1)^2} = \frac{d_1}{z - a} + \frac{d_2}{z - 1} + \frac{d_3}{(z - 1)^2}$$

Since the denominator for $Y(z)$ is third order, three terms are needed in the partial fraction expansion. Since one of the poles ($z = 1$) is repeated, it contributes two terms: one with $(z - 1)$ in the denominator and one with $(z - 1)^2$ in the denominator. The constants d_1, d_2, d_3 can be found by putting the right-hand side over a common denominator and equating coefficients to solve:

$$\frac{bz}{(z-a)(z-1)^2} = \frac{d_1(z-1)^2 + d_2(z-a)(z-1) + d_3(z-a)}{(z-a)(z-1)^2}$$

$$0z^2 + bz + 0 = d_1(z^2 - 2z + 1) + d_2(z^2 - z - az + a) + d_3(z-a)$$

$$= (d_1 + d_2)z^2 + (-2d_1 - d_2 - ad_2 + d_3)z + (d_1 + ad_2 - ad_3)$$

The three equations that need to be solved for the three unknowns are

$$0 = d_1 + d_2$$

$$b = -2d_1 - d_2 - ad_2 + d_3$$

$$0 = d_1 + ad_2 - ad_3$$

The first equation gives $d_1 = -d_2$, and then there remain two equations to solve for two unknowns. A bit of algebra reveals that

$$d_1 = \frac{ab}{(1-a)^2}$$

$$d_2 = \frac{-ab}{(1-a)^2}$$

$$d_3 = \frac{b}{1-a}$$

and thus the Z-transform of the ramp response is given by

$$Y(z) = \frac{d_1}{z-a} + \frac{d_2}{z-1} + \frac{d_3}{(z-1)^2}$$

$$= \frac{ab}{(1-a)^2}z^{-1}\frac{z}{z-a} + \frac{-ab}{(1-a)^2}z^{-1}\frac{z}{z-1} + \frac{b}{1-a}z^{-1}\frac{z}{(z-1)^2}$$

$$y(k) = \frac{ab}{(1-a)^2}a^{k-1} + \left[\frac{-ab}{(1-a)^2} + \frac{b}{1-a}(k-1)\right] \quad \text{for } k \geq 1 \quad (5.15)$$

$$= y_{tr}(k) + y_{ss}(k)$$

Although the form is not exactly the same as Equation (5.14), the two expressions can be shown to be identical after some further algebraic manipulation. The delay in the response is shown clearly in Equation (5.15).

The transient part of the response is given by $y_{tr}(k) = c_3 a^k = d_1 a^{k-1} = [b/(1-a)^2]a^k$. The transient reaches its maximum value at $k = 1$ (since there is a one time unit delay in the first-order system we consider). The 2% settling time is when the value of the transient part of the response is less than 2% of the maximum value of the transient part, equivalently, when $a^{k-1} < 0.02$. Following the settling time derivation from the impulse response, we see that the settling time will be

$$k \approx 1 + \frac{-4}{\log|a|}$$

For simplicity, we can further approximate this as

$$k_s \approx \frac{-4}{\log |a|} \tag{5.16}$$

Note that the settling time for the ramp response is the same as the settling time for the impulse response from Equation (5.6). This is because the maximum deviation occurs at $k = 1$ for both cases. We also note that the transient part of the response is oscillatory if $a < 0$.

5.6.2 Frequency Response

Another type of input signal that is often seen in computing systems is a sinusoidal signal. Cyclic patterns in user traffic due to time of day or day of the week can often be modeled as sinusoids. In general, any periodic signal can be expressed as a sum of sinusoids using a Fourier series [51]. By the principle of superposition, the response of a linear system to a sum of sinusoids is simply the sum of the responses to each sinusoid individually.

Figure 5.10 shows the output of several first-order systems to a sinusoidal input $u(k) = \sin(0.5k)$. Note that if the system is BIBO stable ($|a| < 1$), the

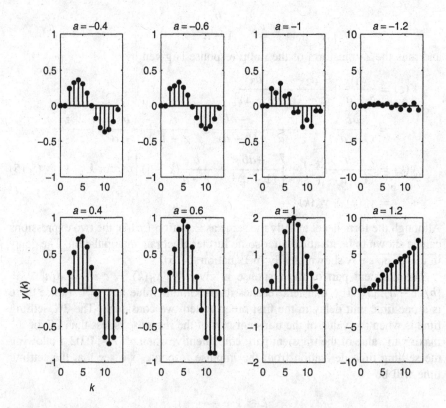

Fig. 5.10 First-order system responses to a sine wave. Different values of a are indicated in the plot; $b = 0.5$. The sine wave input is $u(k) = \sin(0.5k)$.

output is also a sinusoid with the same frequency as that of the input. However, the magnitude of the output is different from that of the input. In addition, the output is not in phase with the input; it reaches its maximum and zero values at different times.

The time-domain solution of Equation (5.1) is difficult to find with a sinusoidal input, so we focus on the Z-transform solution. From Table 3.1, the Z-transform of a sinusoidal input $u(k) = \sin(\theta k)$ is

$$U(z) = \frac{z \sin \theta}{z^2 - (2 \cos \theta)z + 1}$$

Thus, the Z-transform of the output can be found from

$$Y(z) = G(z)U(z) = \frac{b}{z - a} \frac{z \sin \theta}{z^2 - (2 \cos \theta)z + 1}$$

To find the time-domain solution from the Z-transform, we need to perform a partial fraction expansion. Since the denominator of $Y(z)$ is third order, we need three terms in the expansion. One term will have in the denominator the factor $(z - a)$, and the other two terms will be associated with the complex poles from the sinusoid: $(z - e^{j\theta})$ and $(z - e^{-j\theta})$ (as discussed in Chapter 3):

$$\frac{b}{z - a} \frac{z \sin \theta}{z^2 - (2 \cos \theta)z + 1} = \frac{c_1}{z - a} + \frac{c_2}{z - e^{j\theta}} + \frac{c_3}{z - e^{-j\theta}}$$

Although the algebra required to find the constants c_1, c_2, c_3 is straightforward, it is tedious and requires the manipulation of complex numbers. We omit it here. However, it can be seen from the form of the solution for $Y(z)$ that the only terms that can be present in the time domain $y(k)$ are the decaying exponential (due to the pole at $z = a$) and sinusoidal terms due to the complex poles at $z = e^{\pm j\theta}$:

$$y(k) = d_1 a^k + d_2 \sin(\theta k + \phi)$$

If the system is BIBO stable, then in steady state only the sinusoidal term is present. Noting that $\max_k |\sin(\theta k + \phi)| = 1$ and assuming that $d_1 \leq d_2$, we have

$$k_s \approx \frac{-4}{\log |a|} \tag{5.17}$$

The output of the system is a sinusoid with the same frequency as the input. The magnitude of the output and the phase shift will depend on frequency of the input and on the system properties [50]. In particular, we have

$$d_2 = \frac{b}{\sqrt{a^2 - 2a \cos \theta + 1}}$$

$$\phi = \tan^{-1} \left(\frac{\sin \theta}{a - \cos \theta} \right)$$

5.7 EFFECT OF STOCHASTICS

The models discussed thus far in this chapter are deterministic. That is, if the current value of the output and the current value of the input are known, the next value of the output can be predicted exactly. Most computing systems are not deterministic but contain a significant stochastic component. These stochastics arise from many sources, such as the distribution of user "think times" when browsing Web pages and changes in data requirements. A stochastic component may even be built into a system such as in the random wait time to resend after a collision in the Ethernet protocol [36].

When studying the behavior of a computing system, the significance of the transient response compared to the stochastics of the system must be understood. If the stochastic component is large, the first-order system model may not predict the system behavior very well. To explore this issue, we use simulations of the $M/M/1/K$ queueing system. Figure 5.11 shows the results for four separate runs of an $M/M/1/K$ simulation with different mean service times s; the arrival rate is held constant at 1 request per second throughout the experiment. The

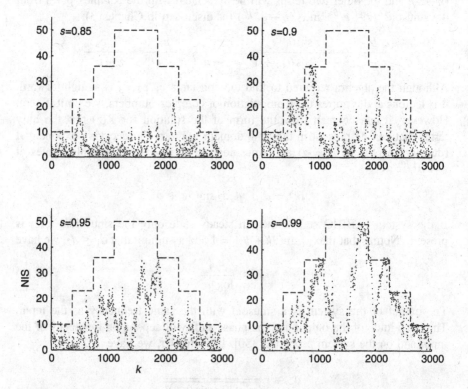

Fig. 5.11 The dots in each figure show the output (average number of jobs in service) for a single simulation of an $M/M/1/K$ system. The input is the buffer size K (indicated by the dashed lines), the arrival rate is fixed at 1 request per second, and the mean service time s is indicated in each figure.

input signal is the buffer size K and is shown in the figures by dashed lines. Each dot indicates the number of requests in system averaged over a 1-second interval. Considerable variability can be observed in the measurements; in fact, it is difficult to discriminate between the transient response due to changes in buffer size and the natural stochastic behavior of the system at a fixed buffer size.

To reduce the variability of the measurements, we repeated the same set of experiments 250 times and averaged the output signal over all 250 replications. The results are shown in Figure 5.12. In this figure, the two sets of dots for each time instant show the 95% confidence bounds (plus and minus two standard deviations from the average) for the measured number of jobs in the system; the average and standard deviation are computed over the 250 replications. Instead of showing the buffer size K (which is the same as in Figure 5.11), each figure also includes the predicted steady-state number in system from Equation (2.1). By replicating the simulation experiments and averaging, variability is reduced and transient characteristics are seen more clearly.

The width of the confidence bounds quantifies the effect of variability on the measurements. The confidence interval curves of Figure 5.12 give us much more insight into effect of buffer size and allow us to better detect the presence and

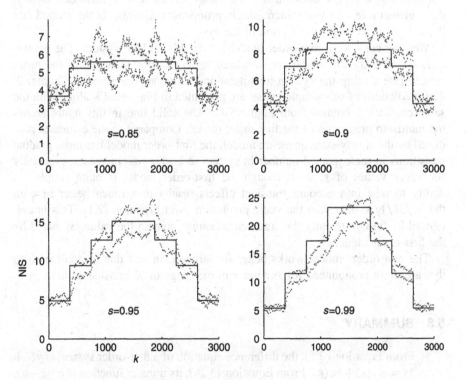

Fig. 5.12 *Assessment of transients in $M/M/1/K$ as buffer size is changed. The inputs are varied as in Figure 5.11. The dotted lines are plus and minus two standard deviations around the mean value of number in system measured over 250 replications. The solid line is the expected steady-state value of number in system from queueing theory.*

magnitude of transient effects. If there were no transient effect, the confidence bounds should include the mean steady-state value of the system as shown by the solid lines in Figure 5.12. However, the mean value does not always lie within the confidence bounds, especially just after the buffer length K has changed.

Consider first the plot where the mean service time is $s = 0.85$. For the most part, the prediction indicated by the solid line lies within the confidence interval shown by the dotted lines. Where this occurs, it suggests that the measurements are varying around their steady-state values, so there is no transient effect due to changes in K. However, there are some exceptions. Right after the first change in buffer size (at $T = 500$), the confidence bounds are below the expected steady-state value. Although the duration of this effect is short, its presence suggests a transient. Also note that in the last stepdown of the downward ramp, the confidence bounds are above the expected steady-state value, suggesting another transient effect.

As the mean service rate s increases to 0.9, the transient effect becomes more pronounced in that the solid line is farther away from the confidence bounds for one or more of the steps in buffer size. Also, the time needed before the confidence bounds contain the steady-state value is longer, suggesting that the transient has a longer duration. As the mean service time s increases further, the transient effect becomes increasingly pronounced and affects the second and third steps of the input in addition to the first.

We now consider a first-order model for the $M/M/1/K$ system. The parameters a and b for the model are estimated for each different value of the mean service rate s using the system identification techniques described in Chapter 2. The predictions of this simple model are presented in Figure 5.13, along with the same confidence bounds from Figure 5.12. The solid line in this figure shows the multistep prediction of the first-order model. Compared to the estimates produced by the steady-state queueing model, the first-order model has more gradual transitions in the expected number in system as buffer size increases, especially for larger values of s. Even though the first-order model is quite simple, its ability to take into account transient effects results in a much better fit with the $M/M/1/K$ data than the static prediction from Equation (2.1). This is evidenced by how frequently the confidence bounds contain the value estimated by the first-order model.

The first-order model works better for larger s, in part due to nonlinearities that are more pronounced for smaller s in the range of K considered here.

5.8 SUMMARY

1. From Equation (2.5), the difference equation of a first-order system is $y(k+1) = ay(k) + bu(k)$. From Equation (3.26), its transfer function is $b/(z-a)$.
2. The system response consists of the steady-state response and the transient response. The transient response is the time from the change in the initial conditions or the input signal until the steady state is reached.

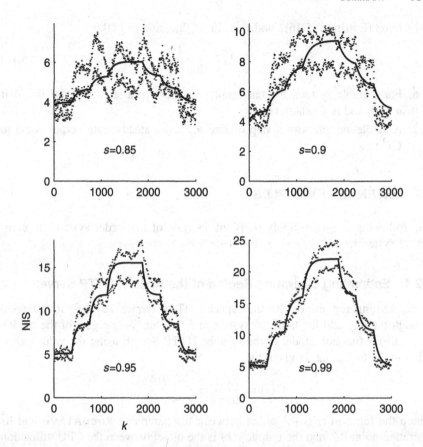

Fig. 5.13 *Assessment of first-order model for explaining transient response in an $M/M/1/K$ queueing system. Arrival rate is 1 request per second. Mean service time, s, is indicated in each figure. The dotted lines are plus and minus two standard deviations around the mean value of number in system measured over 250 replications. The solid line is the estimated number in system from multiple-step prediction for a first-order model.*

3. Transient analysis can be divided into two parts: response to initial conditions and response to the input signal. These two effects can be combined using the superposition property.

4. Transient response is determined largely by the pole a of the first-order system. The response is:

   (a) Unstable if $|a| > 1$

   (b) Oscillatory if the $a < 0$

   (c) Converges quickly if $|a|$ is close to 0

   (d) Converges slowly if $|a|$ is close to 1 (but not outside the unit circle)

5. For a stable system, settling time k_s is the time required to get sufficiently close to the steady-state value. Using the 2% criterion, the settling time for initial conditions [Equation (5.4)], impulse [Equation (5.7)], step [Equation (5.12)],

ramp [Equation (5.16)], and sine wave [Equation (5.17)] is

$$k_s \approx \frac{-4}{\log |a|} \tag{5.18}$$

6. For a stable system, the maximum overshoot to a step response is $-a$ if $a < 0$, and is 0 otherwise.

7. A stable system with a step of size u_{ss} has a steady-state output equal to $G(1)u_{ss}$.

5.9 EXTENDED EXAMPLES

The following examples apply transient analysis of first-order systems to computing systems.

5.9.1 Estimating Operating Region of the Apache HTTP Server

The operating regions of the the Apache HTTP Server can be investigated through the physical limits of the system and the steady-state gain of the model. The transfer function model of the Apache HTTP Server, using the values identified in Section 2.6.2, is given by

$$G(z) = \frac{Y(z)}{U(z)} = \frac{-0.014}{z - 0.59}$$

where the input $u(k)$ is the offset between the parameter KeepAlive and its operating point $\overline{\text{KA}}$, and the output $y(k)$ is the offset between the CPU utilization and its operating point $\overline{\text{CPU}}$:

$$u(k) = \text{KeepAlive}(k) - \overline{\text{KA}} = \text{KeepAlive}(k) - 11$$

$$y(k) = \text{CPU}(k) - \overline{\text{CPU}} = \text{CPU}(k) - 0.58$$

We can use this model to predict the operating region over which this linear model can be used.

First, we find the steady-state gain of the system model, as in Section 5.5.3, and we compute that

$$G(1) = \frac{-0.014}{1 - 0.59} = -0.034$$

The steady-state gain is negative, indicating that if KeepAlive increases by 1 (second), then CPU decreases by 0.034 (or 3.4%).

Suppose we conjecture that a reasonable operating region for KeepAlive is [1, 30] (i.e., KeepAlive has a minimum value of 1 and a maximum value of 30). To use the linear model, we need to compute the offsets from the operating point. Thus, the limits are

$$u_1 = 1 - \overline{\text{KeepAlive}} = -10 \qquad u_2 = 30 - \overline{\text{KeepAlive}} = 19$$

The steady-state outputs associated with these inputs can be found using the steady-state gain, $y_{ss} = G(1)u_{ss}$:

$$y_1 = (-0.034)(-10) = 0.34 \qquad y_2 = (-0.034)(19) = -0.65$$

and using the operating point again, we compute that

$$CPU_1 = y_1 + \overline{CPU} = 0.92 \qquad CPU_2 = y_2 + \overline{CPU} = -0.069$$

However, since CPU cannot be negative, KeepAlive $\in [1, 30]$ is not a reasonable operating region. We can compute the maximum operating region starting from the physical limits on CPU (between 0 and 1). Thus, let

$$y_3 = 0 - \overline{CPU} = -0.58 \qquad y_4 = 1 - \overline{CPU} = 0.42$$

We use the inverse of the steady-state gain to find the corresponding input offsets, $u_{ss} = y_{ss}/G(1)$:

$$u_3 = \frac{-0.58}{-0.034} = 17 \qquad u_4 = \frac{0.42}{-0.034} = -12$$

and then we find the KeepAlive values as

$$KeepAlive_3 = u_3 + \overline{KeepAlive} = 28$$

$$KeepAlive_4 = u_4 + \overline{KeepAlive} = -1$$

This gives a negative value of KeepAlive, which is also unreasonable. We will assume that the minimum value of KeepAlive is 1, and thus, the maximum operating region over which the linear model can be used is

$$KeepAlive \in [1, 28] \qquad CPU \in [0, 0.92]$$

Of course, CPU can never be exactly zero, so a smaller limit on KeepAlive might be warranted. We recall, however, that the linear model (identified from experimental data) is most accurate near the operating point, and that such a model can only approximate the system's response. These limits computed from the steady-state gain can be useful as an initial assessment of the potential operating region of the system.

5.9.2 IBM Lotus Domino Server with a Disturbance

In this example we study further the effects of a disturbance in the IBM Lotus Domino Server. It also motivates the next example on feedback control. In this example an administrative job executes on the IBM Lotus Domino Server. The job has the effect of distorting MaxUsers so that its effective value is $MaxUsers(k) + d(k)$, where $d(k)$ is the disturbance.

Figure 5.5 displays a block diagram of the system we study using the transfer function of the IBM Lotus Domino Server that is identified in Section 2.6.1,

$$G(z) = \frac{Y(z)}{V(z)} = \frac{0.47}{z - 0.43}$$

In the time domain, this is the first-order difference equation

$$y(k + 1) = 0.43y(k) + 0.47[u(k) + d(k)]$$

The output $y(k)$ is the offset value of the number of RPCs in system (RIS), and $u(k)$ is the offset value of MaxUsers(k). That is,

$$u(k) = \text{MaxUsers}(k) - \overline{\text{MaxUsers}} = \text{MaxUsers}(k) - 165$$

$$y(k) = \text{RIS}(k) - \overline{\text{RIS}} = \text{RIS}(k) - 135$$

The system is initially at its operating point. A step disturbance of magnitude 100 occurs at time $k = 0$. The steady-state value of the output of the system is $d_{ss}G(1)$, where d_{ss} is the magnitude of the disturbance step. Note that $G(1) = (0.47)(1 - 0.43) = 0.82$. Hence, $y_{ss} = 82$, or RIS increases by 82. The steady-state value of RIS is then

$$\text{RIS}_{ss} = 82 + \overline{\text{RIS}} = 217$$

The time-domain response can be computed with MATLAB and is shown in Figure 5.14.

This increased RIS will result in longer response times, and hence is undesirable. If the administrator knew the magnitude and timing of the disturbance, MaxUsers could be adjusted to compensate for the disturbance. Of course, such information is rarely available in practice.

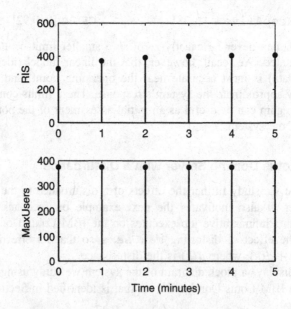

Fig. 5.14 Time response of the output RIS for the IBM Lotus Domino Server when a step disturbance of magnitude 100 occurs at time $k = 0$.

5.9.3 Feedback Control of the IBM Lotus Domino Server

This is a continuation of the last example, in which there is an administrative job that introduces a step disturbance of 100 RPCs. We assume that administrators have no prior knowledge of the administrative job and so cannot adjust MaxUsers to compensate for their presence. We propose a solution based on feedback control, as depicted in Figure 5.15. We assume that the controller is able to measure the current RIS. The feedback controller adjusts the value of MaxUsers automatically to account for the extra administrative tasks (the disturbance). The value K of the controller is called the *controller gain*.

We find the output $Y(z)$ as a function of the disturbance input $D(z)$ using a Z-domain analysis.

$$Y(z) = \frac{0.47}{z - 0.43}[U(z) + D(z)]$$

$$U(z) = -KY(z)$$

$$(z - 0.43)Y(z) = 0.47[-KY(z) + D(z)]$$

$$(z - 0.43 + 0.47K)Y(z) = 0.47D(z)$$

$$Y(z) = \frac{0.47}{z - (0.43 - 0.47K)}D(z) \qquad (5.19)$$

This can be done in the time domain as well:

$$y(k+1) = 0.43y(k) + 0.47[u(k) + d(k)]$$

$$u(k) = -Ky(k)$$

$$y(k+1) = 0.43y(k) + 0.47[-Ky(k) + d(k)]$$

$$= (0.43 - 0.47K)y(k) + 0.47d(k)$$

Note that the pole of the closed-loop system has changed—instead of being at 0.43, it is now at $(0.43 - 0.47K)$, and hence, depends on the value of K. In Chapter 8 we present methods for choosing an appropriate value of K; here, we

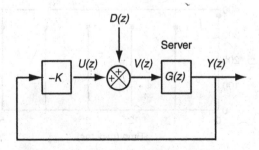

Fig. 5.15 *Feedback control of the IBM Lotus Domino Server with a disturbance input modeled as increasing the effective number of users on the system.*

just consider several possible values of K and see how they affect the pole location and system response.

Consider $K = 1$. We see that the closed-loop pole is $0.43 - 0.47K = -0.04$. To illustrate the operation of the system, suppose that $10 = y(k) = \text{RIS}(k) - 135$. Then $u(k) = -10K = -10$, so $\texttt{MaxUsers}(k) = -10 + 165 = 155$.

Figure 5.16 displays the step response of the $K = 1$ system to a disturbance of magnitude 100. We see that the steady-state value of the output is 180. To understand why, we proceed as follows. From Equation (5.19), the steady-state gain of the closed-loop system is $0.47/(1 + 0.04) = 0.45$. So the steady-state value of the output to an input of magnitude 100 is $(100)(0.45) + 135 = 180$. This is certainly an improvement compared with the open-loop system in Figure 5.14 in that the feedback controller has a steady-state error of $180 - 135 = 45$ as opposed to $217 - 135 = 82$ for the open-loop system.

While $K = 1$ decreases the steady-state error, it is not eliminated. To improve matters, we try a larger gain, such as $K = 3.5$. This causes the system to react more strongly to the measured error in the RIS. The closed-loop pole is predicted to be at $0.43 - 0.47(3.5) = -1.215$. Since the pole is outside the unit circle, the closed-loop system is unstable. The predicted response, along with the input $\texttt{MaxUsers}$, is shown in Figure 5.17. In effect, the large control gain causes an overreaction to a change in the measured RIS. For example, at $k = 1$, RIS is too large, so $\texttt{MaxUsers}$ is decreased almost to zero. Then, at $k = 2$, RIS is too small, so $\texttt{MaxUsers}$ is increased, and so on. At $k = 3$, $\texttt{MaxUsers}$ becomes negative, which is meaningless in practice, so the prediction of the linear model

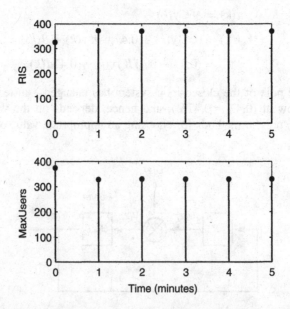

Fig. 5.16 Time response of the output RIS for the IBM Lotus Domino Server with a feedback controller. The gain $K = 1$, and the step magnitude 100 occurs at time $k = 0$.

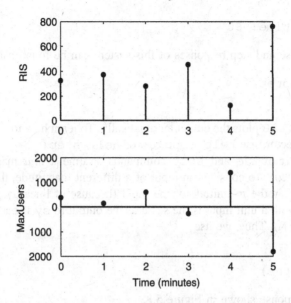

Fig. 5.17 *Time response of the output RIS for the Notes server in closed-loop with a gain $K = 5$ (unstable) when a step disturbance of magnitude 100 occurs at time $k = 0$.*

after $k = 3$ cannot be used. However, the instability that is predicted can be observed in the physical system.

It should be noted that the behavior of the IBM Lotus Domino Server has not changed with feedback control. The IBM Lotus Domino Server remains a stable first-order system with a pole at 0.43. What has been changed is the behavior of the closed-loop system with the transfer function $Y(z)/D(z)$.

This example underscores the need to design feedback loops in a systematic way. In Chapters 8 to 11 we address this topic in detail.

*5.10 ANALYZING TRANSIENT RESPONSE WITH MATLAB

Using the Control Systems Toolbox, transfer functions can be entered into MAT-LAB as described in Section *3.6. Once the transfer function has been entered, the impulse and step response can be computed directly using the commands step and impulse. For example, the IBM Lotus Domino Server considered in this chapter with transfer function $G(z) = 0.47/(z - 0.43)$ and a sampling time of 60 seconds is entered as

```
notes = tf(0.47,[1 -0.43],60)

Transfer function:
  0.47
-------
z - 0.43
```

```
Sampling time: 60
```

The impulse and step responses of this system can be found using

```
impulse(notes)
step(notes)
```

Note that MATLAB plots the output automatically. To learn how to save the output values in a vector, use help impulse or help step.

Both the impulse and step commands assume a *unit* magnitude input (impulse or step). To consider an input of a different magnitude, the system can be multiplied by the magnitude of the input (because of linearity, the output to M*system with a unit input is the same as the output to system with an input of magnitude M). Thus, we use

```
M = 40
step(M*notes)
```

to get the response shown in Figure 5.8.

To find the output of a system to a different input, the function lsim can be used to simulate any linear system. In addition to the transfer function, a vector of input signals and a time vector are needed. The time vector must have the same sampling time as the system, and the input vector must have a one-to-one correspondence with the time vector. To simulate the output of the Notes example to a ramp input for 10 sample times (600 seconds), we use the following commands:

```
time = 0:60:600;
ramp = 0:1:10;
lsim(notes,ramp,time)
```

5.11 EXERCISES

1. For the following first-order system, (i) find their poles, (ii) determine if they are stable, (iii) compute the steady-state gains for the stable systems, and (iv) plot the step response curve.

   (a) $\dfrac{4}{z - 1.5}$

   (b) $\dfrac{12}{z - 0.05}$

   (c) $\dfrac{-1}{z + 0.2}$

   (d) $\dfrac{3}{z - 0.36}$

2. Compute the constants c_1, c_2, c_3, d_1, d_2, and ϕ in Section 5.6.2. Note that c_2 and c_3 have conjugate complex values.

3. Consider the warm-up period of the IBM Lotus Domino Server. The initial condition is $RIS(0) = 0$, and the input is $MaxUsers = \overline{MaxUsers} = 165$. Use the linear model of Section 2.6.1, and note that the initial condition is $y(0) = RIS(0) - \overline{RIS} = -135$. Find and plot $RIS(k)$. What is the final value? How long does the system take to reach its final value?

4. Repeat Exercise 3 for the Apache HTTP Server. The initial condition is $CPU(0) = 0$, and the input is $KeepAlive = \overline{KA} = 11$. Use the linear model of Section 2.6.2. Find and plot $CPU(k)$. What is the final value? How long does the system take to reach its final value?

5. Follow the examples in Section 5.9.3 to compute the closed-loop pole and plot the time response of RIS for the IBM Lotus Domino Server in closed-loop for $K = 2$, $K = 3$, and $K = 4$.

6. Consider the models of $M/M/1/K$ for different operating regions as detailed in Section 2.6.3.

   (a) Find the transfer function and poles for each. Find their steady-state gains and settling times.

   (b) Construct feedback loops as in Section 5.9.3 for the three systems in part (a). Find the transfer functions, poles, steady-state gains, and settling times of closed-loop systems.

7. Determine a value for controller gain K in Section 5.9.3 such that settling time is 10. (*Hint:* Express the closed-loop pole in terms of K and solve for k_s.) What is the steady value of the output in response to a disturbance input of 100? Repeat this for a settling time of 5.

8. Figure 5.18 contains an open-loop system in which the Apache HTTP Server is subjected to a disturbance that can be modeled as a change in KeepAlive. Suppose the disturbance can be modeled as an impulse of magnitude 5 at time $k = 0$. Find the response CPU(k).

9. Considering again Figure 5.18, suppose the disturbance can be modeled as a step of magnitude 10. Find the response CPU(k).

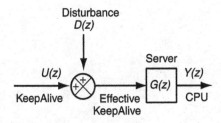

Fig. 5.18 *Apache HTTP Server with a disturbance input that is modeled as a change in* KeepAlive *as seen by the server.*

10. Consider again Figure 5.18, and suppose that the disturbance can be modeled such that $d(k) = 10$ for $k \in [0, 2)$, $d(k) = -4$ for $k \in [2, 5)$, and $d(k) = 2$ for $k \in [5, \infty)$.

   (a) Use a time-domain analysis to find $\text{CPU}(k)$.

   (b) Find $D(z)$ and use a Z-domain analysis to find $\text{CPU}(k)$.

   (c) For part (b), how can the superposition property be used?

   (Use the operating point specified in Section 5.9.1.)

6

Higher-Order Systems

In this chapter we extend the analysis in Chapter 5 to systems with two or more poles and one or more zeros. Such systems are commonly referred to as *higher-order systems*. In computing systems, higher-order systems often result from having many first-order components connected in series.

The presence of multiple poles and zeros makes it more difficult to estimate settling times and maximum overshoot. Thus, we develop simple approximations for both. For example, the approximation for settling time is based on a dominant pole analysis that uses the results for first-order systems. Another complication in higher-order systems is that poles may be complex, a situation that indicates a oscillatory response to common inputs such as the impulse and step. Although we address complex poles, we first discuss systems with real poles and zeros so that readers less interested in mathematical details need only skim the material on complex poles.

6.1 MOTIVATION AND DEFINITIONS

The order of the system reflects the extent to which previous inputs and outputs affect the current output. For example, the current output of a first-order system is determined by its input and output at the last sample time. In contrast, the current output of a second-order system is affected by its previous two inputs

---

Feedback Control of Computing Systems, by Joseph L. Hellerstein, Yixin Diao, Sujay Parekh, and Dawn M. Tilbury
ISBN 0-471-26637-X   Copyright © 2004 John Wiley & Sons, Inc.

and outputs. More formally, a system is of order n if

$$y(k) = a_1 y(k-1) + \cdots + a_n y(k-n) + b_1 u(k-1) + \cdots + b_m u(k-m)$$
(6.1)

where $1 \leq m \leq n$. That is, $y(k)$ depends on the previous n outputs and the previous m inputs. These relationships are depicted in Figure 6.1, in which the solid circles indicate variables and there is a line between $y(k)$ and each variable that affects $y(k)$. In some systems, it is possible that the current output can be affected by the current input, in which case we permit $m = 0$. However, $m < 0$ violates the principle of casuality in that the current output is affected by a future input.

The transfer function of a higher-order system can be obtained in a straightforward way. First, we shift forward n time units, which yields

$$y(n+k) = a_1 y(n+k-1) + \cdots + a_n y(k)$$
$$+ b_1 u(n+k-1) + \cdots + b_m (n+k-m)$$

Taking the Z-transforms of both sides and assuming that all initial conditions are 0, we have

$$z^n Y(z) = a_1 z^{n-1} Y(z) + \cdots + a_n Y(z)$$
$$+ b_1 z^{n-1} U(z) + \cdots + b_m z^{n-m} U(z)$$
$$Y(z)(z^n - a_1 z^{n-1} - \cdots - a_n) = U(z)(b_1 z^{n-1} + \cdots + b_m z^{n-m})$$
$$G(z) = \frac{(b_1 z^{m-1} + \cdots + b_m) z^{n-m}}{z^n - a_1 z^{n-1} - \cdots - a_n}$$
(6.2)

where $G(z) = Y(z)/U(z)$ is the transfer function of the system.

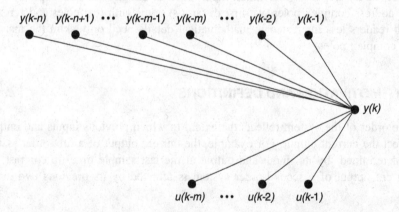

Fig. 6.1 *Relationship between the current output and previous inputs and outputs in a model of order n. $y(k)$ depends on the previous outputs $y(k-1), \ldots, y(k-n)$ and the previous inputs $u(k-1), \ldots, u(k-m)$.*

Higher-order systems arise frequently as a result of combining lower-order systems, as illustrated in the following example.

Example 6.1: IBM Lotus Domino Server with sensor delay The transfer functions for the IBM Lotus Domino Server $N(z)$ and its sensor $S(z)$ are

$$N(z) = \frac{Q(z)}{U(z)} = \frac{0.47}{z - 0.43}$$

$$S(z) = \frac{M(z)}{Q(z)} = \frac{0.17z - 0.11}{z - 0.64}$$

[$N(z)$ is derived in Example 3.7 and $S(z)$ in Section 3.5.2.] Figure 6.2 displays a system in which the output of the IBM Lotus Domino Server is input into the sensor as a result of the way in which measurements are collected. Thus, the transfer function for this system is $N(z)S(z)$, which is

$$\frac{M(z)}{U(z)} = \frac{0.08z - 0.052}{z^2 - 1.07z + 0.28} \tag{6.3}$$

This is a second-order system. Equation (6.3) can be rewritten as a difference equation in the same form as Equation (6.1):

$$m(k + 2) = 1.07m(k + 1) - 0.28m(k) + 0.08u(k + 1) - 0.052u(k)$$

Here $n = 2 = m$.

We can rewrite Equation (6.2) by factoring the numerator and denominator:

$$G(z) = \frac{b(z - q_1) \cdots (z - q_m)z^{n-m}}{(z - p_1) \cdots (z - p_n)} \tag{6.4}$$

For example, Equation (6.3) can be rewritten as

$$\frac{M(z)}{U(z)} = \frac{0.08(z - 0.65)}{(z - 0.43)(z - 0.64)}$$

Here, $b = 0.08$, $q_1 = 0.65$, $p_1 = 0.43$, and $p_2 = 0.64$. Put in this form, there is much we can already say about higher-order systems. From Chapter 3 we know that the q_i are the zeros of $G(z)$ and the p_i are its poles. Note that because there are multiple poles, we use the notation p_i instead of the a used in Chapter 5.

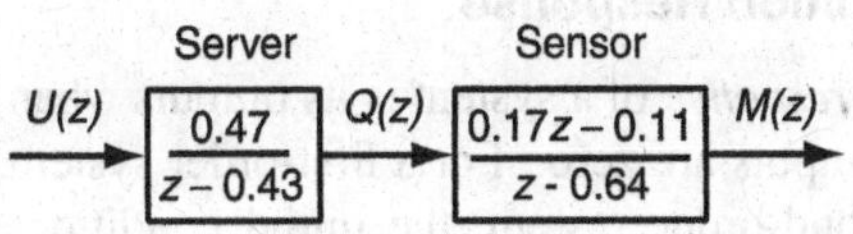

Fig. 6.2 Block diagram of the IBM Lotus Domino Server whose measured output is provided by a sensor.

From Theorem 3.2 we know that a system is stable if, and only if, $|p_i| < 1$. Further, the steady-state gain of $G(z)$ is $G(1)$, regardless of the order of $G(z)$.

From Chapter 5 we know that the poles of a first-order system determine its settling time and maximum overshoot. Not surprisingly, the poles of a higher-order system play a fundamental role in its transient response as well. However, the analysis of higher-order systems is more complicated in that the combined effects of multiple poles must be considered. Also, transient response is affected by zeros as well as poles. Further, there may be complex poles (those with a nonzero imaginary part), a situation that cannot occur in a first-order system (since it has only one pole and the difference equations have real-valued coefficients).

We can use *dominant pole analysis* to approximate the behavior of higher-order systems. This approach approximates the original system with a first-order system whose pole is the largest pole of the original system. In the sequel we assume that the largest pole is truly a *dominant pole* in the sense that it determines the settling time and maximum overshoot of the system.

We have structured the discussion of higher-order systems into two parts. The first focuses on systems with two or more *real* poles and the effects of zeros. The second addresses complex poles. The first part includes less mathematical detail than the latter part. Doing so should provide the reader with considerable intuition about higher-order systems even if the discussion of complex poles is only skimmed.

6.2 REAL POLES

In this section we analyze higher-order systems in which the poles are real. The analysis also applies to systems with complex poles that have a real dominant pole. Our analysis is based on the dominant pole approximation in Equation (3.30) in which the transfer function $G(z)$ is approximated by

$$G(z) \approx G'(z) = \frac{G(1)(1 - p')}{z - p'}$$

where $p' = \max_i\{|p_i|\}$.

In the remainder of this section we use the $G'(z)$ approximation to study settling times and maximum overshoot. For the most part, we compare systems with a steady-state gain of 1 so as to make it easier to compare transient responses. We proceed in the same manner as in Chapter 5 by studying the transient response to initial conditions and to various signals. Then we consider the effect of zeros.

6.2.1 Initial Condition Response

The *initial condition response* of a system is its outputs when the initial conditions are nonzero and the inputs are zero. For a first-order system, the initial condition is $\{y(0)\}$. For a second-order system, the initial conditions are $\{y(0), y(1)\}$. In general, a system of order n has n initial conditions. The initial conditions may well differ from the system's steady-state value.

Consider the following second-order system

$$G(z) = \frac{b}{(z - p_1)(z - p_2)} \qquad (6.5)$$

where b is such that $G(1) = 1$. If p_2 is the dominant pole, we have the first-order approximation

$$G'(z) = \frac{G(1)(1 - p_2)}{z - p_2} \qquad (6.6)$$

$$= \frac{b}{(1 - p_1)(z - p_2)} \qquad (6.7)$$

Clearly, $G'(1) = G(1) = 1$. From Equation (5.4), the initial condition response of $G'(z)$ has settling time $k_s \approx -4/\log|p_2|$.

Figure 6.3 plots the response to initial conditions for several first- and second-order systems. For the first-order systems, $y(0) = 1$, and for the second-order

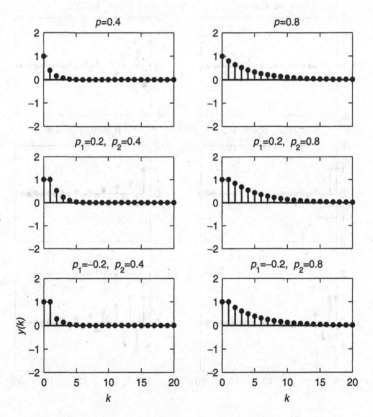

Fig. 6.3 *Initial condition response of first- and second-order systems whose dominant pole is positive. Initial conditions are set to 1. Note that systems have similar settling times if they have the same dominant pole.*

systems, $y(0) = 1 = y(1)$ with $|p_2| > |p_1|$. We see that settling time is largely determined by the dominant pole p_2. Specifically, in the left column of the figure, where $p_2 = 0.4$, the systems have similar settling times; systems in the right column of the figure, where $p_2 = 0.8$, have similar settling times. However, the systems in the left column have a much shorter settling time than those in the right column because the dominant pole of the former is smaller than the latter.

Figure 6.4 displays the effect of having the dominant pole be negative. As discussed in Chapter 5, there is an oscillating response. While the magnitude of the oscillations and the settling times of the systems depend on the particular poles, the systems whose dominant pole is the same tend to have a similar settling time.

In the sequel we set initial conditions to 0, so that $y(0) = 0$ in the first-order systems and $y(0) = 0 = y(1)$ in the second-order systems. Doing so does not limit our analysis since the effect of initial conditions can be incorporated by applying the superposition property.

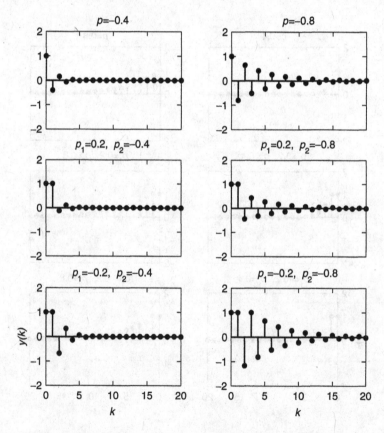

Fig. 6.4 *Initial condition response of first- and second-order systems whose dominant pole is negative. Initial conditions are set to 1. Note that systems have similar settling times if they have the same dominant pole.*

6.2.2   Impulse Response

The impulse input is defined as $u(0) = 1$ and $u(k) = 0$ for $k \neq 0$. In computing systems, such inputs arise if there is a workload spike. Once again, we use $G(z)$ as defined in Equation (6.5) and the approximation $G'(z)$ as specified in Equation (6.7). Applying Equation (5.6), the impulse response of $G'(z)$ has settling time $k_s \approx -4/\log|p'|$. For example, if $|p'| = 0.4$, then $k_s \approx 4$. And if $|p'| = 0.8$, then $k_s \approx 18$.

Figure 6.5 plots the impulse response for the same first- and second-order systems as in Figure 6.3. As with the response to initial conditions, the dominant pole largely determines settling time. For example, the settling time of systems in the first column is between 3 and 6, and the settling time of systems in the second column is between 15 and 20. Both results are consistent with the estimates constructed above.

Figure 6.6 displays the impulse response of systems whose dominant pole is negative. As with initial condition response, substantial oscillations are apparent.

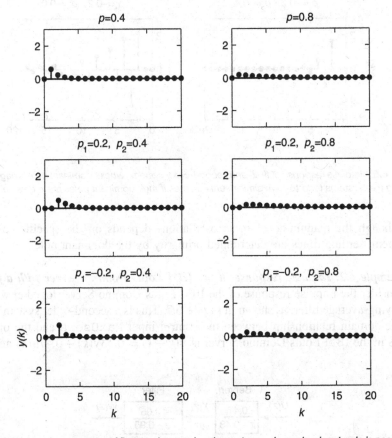

Fig. 6.5 *Impulse response of first- and second-order systems whose dominant pole is positive. Note that systems tend to have similar settling times if their dominant pole is the same.*

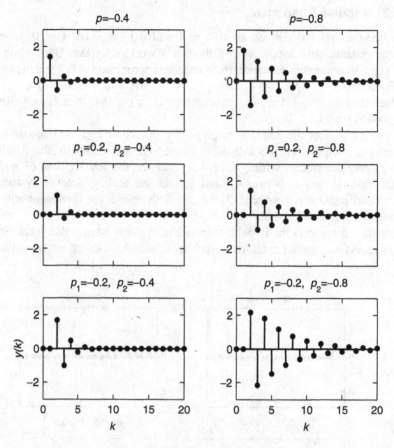

Fig. 6.6 *Impulse response of first- and second-order systems whose dominant pole is negative. Note that systems tend to have similar settling times if their dominant poles are the same.*

Although the magnitude of these oscillations depends on the specifics of the system, settling times are determined primarily by the dominant pole.

Example 6.2: Impulse response in the IBM Lotus Domino Server with a filter
Consider the impulse response of the IBM Lotus Domino Server together with a moving-average filter, as shown in Figure 6.7. This is a second-order system. The time-domain relationship between the control input MaxUsers and the output RIS in the IBM Lotus Domino Server is $y(k + 1) = 0.43y(k) + 0.47u(k)$ and its

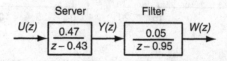

Fig. 6.7 *Block diagram of the IBM Lotus Domino Server with a filter.*

transfer function is

$$G(z) = \frac{Y(z)}{U(z)} = \frac{0.47}{z - 0.43}$$

The model is constructed around the operating point $\overline{\text{MaxUsers}} = 375$, $\overline{\text{RIS}} = 325$. Thus, the values of y and u in the model are the offsets between the actual values of MaxUsers and RIS and their operating points:

$$y(k) = \text{RIS}(k) - \overline{\text{RIS}}$$

$$u(k) = \text{MaxUsers}(k) - \overline{\text{MaxUsers}}$$

We add a moving-average filter with the time-domain input–output relationship $w(k+1) = 0.95w(k) + 0.05y(k)$, where $w(k)$ is the filter (smoothed) output. This filter has the transfer function

$$H(z) = \frac{W(z)}{Y(z)} = \frac{0.05}{z - 0.95}$$

Note that the steady-state gain of $H(z)$ is 1 [i.e., $H(1) = 1$].

Placing the two systems above in series yields a system $F(z)$ that smoothes the output of the IBM Lotus Domino Server. The transfer function from $U(z)$ to $W(z)$ is

$$F(z) = \frac{W(z)}{U(z)} = G(z)H(z) = \frac{0.024}{(z - 0.43)(z - 0.95)}$$

$F(z)$ is a second-order system with two real poles. Its poles lie within the unit circle, so $F(z)$ is stable. Also, since $H(1) = 1$, the steady-state value of $F(z)$ is the same as $G(z)$.

Now consider a situation in which several short-running RPCs are placed into the queue for the IBM Lotus Domino Server. The resulting output can be viewed as the response to an impulse. Figure 6.8 plots this response for an

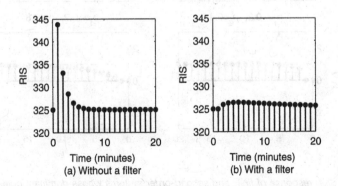

Fig. 6.8 *Response of the IBM Lotus Domino Server to an impulse of magnitude 40. Including a filter smoothes the response, but it also increases the settling time.*

impulse of magnitude 40 for two cases: $G(z)$, the system without a filter, and $F(z)$, the system with a filter. We see that the magnitude of the response of the system without a filter, Figure 6.8(a), is much larger than the system with a filter, Figure 6.8(b). On the other hand, the filter increases settling times.

6.2.3 Step Response

The step input is defined as $u(k) = 1$ for $k \geq 0$. One way in which step inputs arise in computing systems is if there is a change in configuration parameters, such as changing MaxClients in the Apache HTTP Server.

We use $G(z)$ and $G'(z)$ as defined in Equations (6.5) and (6.7), respectively. Applying Equation (5.12), we know that the step response of $G'(z)$ has a settling time of $k_s \approx -4/\log|p'|$.

Figure 6.9 plots the step response of the same first- and second-order systems as in Figure 6.3. Once again, the dominant pole largely determines settling time.

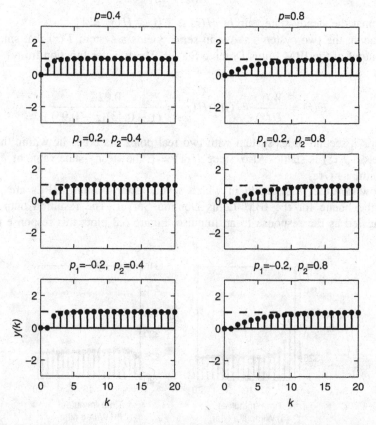

Fig. 6.9 Step response of first- and second-order systems whose dominant pole is positive. The dashed line indicates the steady-state value of the output. Note that systems tend to have similar settling times if their dominant poles are the same. Also, there is no overshoot.

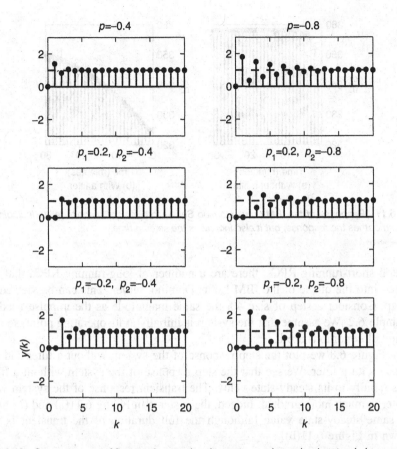

Fig. 6.10 Step response of first- and second-order systems whose dominant pole is negative. The dashed line indicates the steady-state value of the output. Note that systems tend similar settling times if their dominant pole is the same. The negative pole introduces overshoot.

Figure 6.10 displays the step response in systems whose dominant pole is negative. Note that settling times are comparable to when the dominant pole is positive.

Having a negative pole causes the system to overshoot its steady-state value. This is quantified by M_P, the maximum percent by which a step response exceeds its steady-state value. From Equation (5.13), we know that for a first-order system with a pole $p < 0$, $M_P = -p$. This is a rough approximation to the simulation results in Figure 6.10. However, we do observe that systems with a larger (magnitude) dominant pole generally have greater overshoot. We see that the second-order systems differ from this estimate of M_P as follows. If the second pole is positive, the actual overshoot is less than that for the first order. If the second pole is negative, the overshoot is larger.

Example 6.3: Step response in the IBM Lotus Domino Server with a filter
Consider again the IBM Lotus Domino Server in Example 6.2. Now, instead of

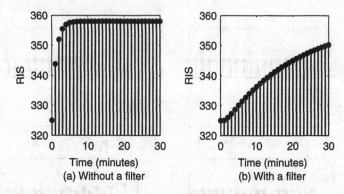

Fig. 6.11 *Response of the IBM Lotus Domino Server to a step of magnitude* 40. *Including a filter smoothes the response, but it also increases the settling time.*

several short-running RPCs, there are a number of long-running RPCs that are placed into the queue of the IBM Lotus Domino Server. This can be viewed as a step. Consider a step of size 40, the same magnitude as the impulse used in Example 6.2. We assume that the system is initially at its operating point, so that all initial conditions are 0.

In Figure 6.8 we plot the step response of the system without a filter and the system with a filter. We see that the step response of the system without a filter rises rapidly to its steady-state value. The transient response of the system with a filter is much more gradual. Indeed, the systems in Figure 6.11(a) and (b) have the same steady-state value [although the full duration of the transient is not shown in Figure 6.11(b)].

6.2.4   Other Signals

There is a wide range of input signals of interest in computing systems. The response of higher-order systems to these signals can be studied analytically or using simulation. Here, we consider briefly two other signals of interest: ramps and sine waves. Ramps typically arise as a result of human behavior, especially staggered starts to a workday. Sine waves can be used to study the effects of cyclic patterns in user traffic, such as due to time of day, and they also provide a way to study the effects of variability.

Figure 6.12 plots the ramp response of first- and second-order systems in which the dominant pole is negative. The input signal is defined as $u(k) = k$ for $k \geq 0$. The solid line indicates the output signal to which the system converges. We see that as with a step response, the presence of a negative pole causes the system to overshoot.

Next, we examine the response to the sinusoidal input $u(k) = \sin(k/1.5)$. Figure 6.13 considers the case in which the dominant pole is positive. Once again we see that the dominant pole largely determines the response. Figure 6.14 studies the case in which the dominant pole is negative. We see a combination

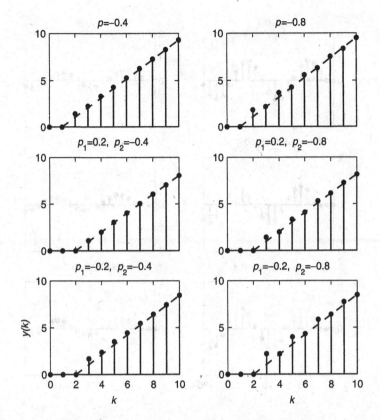

Fig. 6.12 *Ramp response of first- and second-order systems whose dominant pole is negative. Note that systems tend to have similar settling times if their dominant poles are the same. The negative pole introduces overshoot.*

of two sources of oscillation—the sinusoidal input and the negative pole. Thus, it is clear that both the magnitude and sign of the dominant pole must be considered in order to predict the response to a sinusoidal input.

6.2.5 Effect of Zeros

The effect of a zero q on a pole p depends on the difference $|p - q|$. To see this, consider the second-order system

$$G(z) = \frac{b(z - q_1)}{(z - p_1)(z - p_2)} \tag{6.8}$$

which has the poles p_1, p_2 and the zero q_1. If $q_1 = p_1$, these two terms cancel and we have the first-order system $G(z) = b/(z - p_2)$. This reduction in the order of a system is called *pole–zero cancellation*.

Figure 6.15 studies the effect of zeros on the step response of several second-order systems that have the same steady-state gain (10). There are six plots.

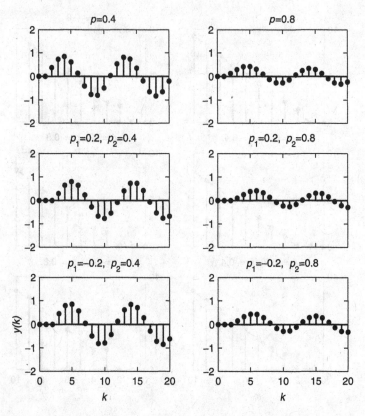

Fig. 6.13 *Sinusoid response of first- and second-order systems whose dominant pole is positive. $u(k) = \sin(k/1.5)$. Note that systems have a similar settling time if their dominant pole is the same.*

Figure 6.15(a) and (b) display the step response of first-order systems with a pole at 0.5 and 0.8, respectively. Figure 6.15(c) through (f) do the same for second-order systems, three of which have a zero. We see that Figure 6.15(c), the second-order system without a zero, has a transient response very much like Figure 6.15(b), the first-order system with $p_1 = 0.8$. This is consistent with dominant pole analysis. Further, observe that the transient response of Figure 6.15(d) is very close to that of Figure 6.15(c). This is because the zero in Figure 6.15(d) is quite distant from its dominant pole. On the other hand, Figure 6.15(e), a second-order system with $q_1 = 0.8$, is almost identical to Figure 6.15(a). This is a result of pole–zero cancellation.

One final comment on Figure 6.15. Observe that Figure 6.15(f) has a zero that is outside the unit circle. The step response depicted in the figure is characteristic of such systems—initially, the system moves in the direction *opposite* to the steady-state value. Systems with a zero outside the unit circle are called *non-minimum-phase systems*. In general, non-minimum-phase systems are undesirable since initially, they respond in the opposite way from that desired.

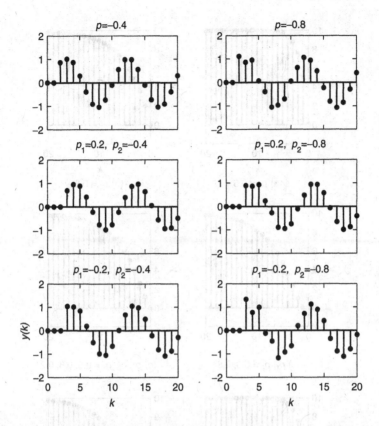

Fig. 6.14 Sinusoid response of first- and second-order systems whose dominant pole is negative. Note that systems tend to have similar settling times if their dominant poles are the same. The negative pole introduces overshoot.

6.3 COMPLEX POLES

In this section we study the effect of complex poles in high-order systems. The intuition is that complex poles result in an oscillatory response to both impulse and step inputs. However, going beyond this intuition involves some mathematical details. As such, readers may prefer to skim this section on their first reading of the chapter, and study it in more detail later.

6.3.1 Second-Order System

Our analysis focuses on second-order systems. The time-domain equation for a second-order system is

$$y(k) = a_1 y(k-1) + a_2 y(k-2) + b_1 u(k-1) + b_2 u(k-2) \qquad (6.9)$$

The equation says that the current value of the output $y(k)$ depends on the value of the output at two previous instances $y(k-1)$ and $y(k-2)$, and the value of

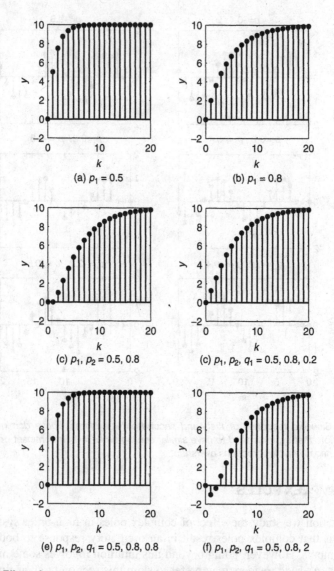

Fig. 6.15 Effect of zeros on step response for systems with a steady-state gain of 10. p_i are the poles, and q_1 is the zero. Pole–zero cancelation in Figure 6.15(e) causes it to behave like Figure 6.15(a) rather than Figure 6.15(b). Having $q_1 = 2 > 1$ in Figure 6.15(f) causes the system initially to move in the opposite direction of the steady-state value.

the input at two previous instance $u(k-1)$ and $u(k-2)$. The constants a_1, a_2, b_1, and b_2 define the system model.

The transfer function of the second-order system in Equation (6.9) is

$$G(z) = \frac{Y(z)}{U(z)} = \frac{b_1 z + b_2}{z^2 - a_1 z - a_2} \tag{6.10}$$

The zero of this system is the value of z for which the numerator is zero. The poles are the roots of the quadratic in the denominator. There are two cases for the poles:

1. If $a_1^2 \geq -4a_2$, the second-order system has two real poles:

$$\{p_1, p_2\} = \frac{a_1 \pm \sqrt{a_1^2 + 4a_2}}{2}$$

In this case, we can rewrite Equation (6.10) as

$$G(z) = \frac{b_1 z + b_2}{z^2 - a_1 z - a_2} = \frac{b_1 z + b_2}{(z - p_1)(z - p_2)}$$

In particular, if $a_1^2 = -4a_2$, the system has two identical real poles at $a_1/2$.

2. If $a_1^2 < -4a_2$, the system has a pair of complex poles

$$\{p_1, p_2\} = \frac{a_1}{2} \pm j \frac{\sqrt{-4a_2 - a_1^2}}{2} = re^{\pm j\theta}$$

where $r = \sqrt{-a_2}$ and $\theta = \cos^{-1}(a_1/2\sqrt{-a_2})$. (Note that $a_2 < 0$ as $a_1^2 < -4a_2$.) In this case, we typically rewrite Equation (6.10) as

$$G(z) = \frac{b_1 z + b_2}{z^2 - a_1 z - a_2} = \frac{b_1 z + b_2}{z^2 - 2r \cos\theta z + r^2}$$

6.3.2 Impulse Response

We determine the time-domain impulse response by computing the inverse of the Z-transform of the output of $G(z)$ when the input is an impulse. If $\{u(k)\}$ is an impulse, then $U(z) = 1$. So if $G(z)$ has two real poles p_1 and p_2,

$$Y(z) = G(z)U(z) = \frac{b_1 z + b_2}{(z - p_1)(z - p_2)} \times 1$$

$$= \frac{c_1}{z - p_1} + \frac{c_2}{z - p_2}$$

$$= c_1 \frac{z}{z - p_1} z^{-1} + c_2 \frac{z}{z - p_2} z^{-1}$$

where

$$c_1 = \frac{b_1 p_1 + b_2}{p_1 - p_2} \quad \text{and} \quad c_2 = -\frac{b_1 p_2 + b_2}{p_1 - p_2}$$

Using Table 3.1, we see that the inverse Z-transform of this system is

$$y(k) = c_1 p_1^{k-1} + c_2 p_2^{k-1} \tag{6.11}$$

For a stable system (i.e., $|p_i| < 1$), the impulse response is a linear combination of decaying exponentials. In this form, it is apparent why this system would be unstable if either $|p_i| > 1$, since we would have one term that grows without bound. It is also clear why the dominant pole approximation works well since if $|p_2| > |p_1|$, then $|p_2|^k \gg |p_1|^k$ for moderate to large k.

For second-order systems with complex poles at $re^{\pm j\theta}$, we have

$$Y(z) = \frac{b_1 z + b_2}{z^2 - 2r\cos\theta z + r^2}$$

$$= \frac{b_1 z}{z^2 - (2r\cos\theta)z + r^2} + \frac{b_2}{z^2 - (2r\cos\theta)z + r^2}$$

$$= \frac{b_1}{r\sin\theta}\frac{r\sin\theta z}{z^2 - (2r\cos\theta)z + r^2} + \frac{b_2}{r\sin\theta}\frac{r\sin\theta z}{z^2 - (2r\cos\theta)z + r^2}z^{-1}$$

This yields the time-domain solution

$$y(k) = \frac{r^{k-1}}{\sin\theta}\left\{b_1\sin k\theta + \frac{b_2}{r}\sin[(k-1)\theta]\right\} \qquad (6.12)$$

Thus, the response is a sum of sinusoids of frequency θ modulated by an exponential. If $|r| < 1$ (i.e., the system is stable), the response decays exponentially with time.

Consider the impulse response of a second-order system with poles p_1, p_2 such that

$$y(k) = (p_1 + p_2)y(k-1) - p_1 p_2 y(k-2) + bu(k-2)$$

or

$$Y(z) = \frac{b}{(z - p_1)(z - p_2)}U(z)$$

Figure 6.16 shows the impulse responses of several such systems with initial conditions set to zero. The systems in the top row have positive real poles, whereas those in the bottom row have complex poles. None of the systems has a zero.

We see that the presence of complex poles leads to oscillatory system response. Note that all of the complex poles in Figure 6.16 have the same magnitude, which is $\sqrt{0.8^2 + 0.4^2} = 0.89$ (although the angles are different). Since the magnitude of these complex poles (0.89) is larger than the dominant real poles in the top row, we see that the settling time for these systems is longer.

The settling time of the complex poles is determined by the decaying exponential r^{k-1} of Equation (6.12). Observe that the sum of sinusoids term is at most $(b_1 + b_2/r)$, hence the maximum value of $|y(k)|$ is $c = (1/\sin\theta)(b_1 + b_2/r)$. Further, defining the settling time as the output being within 2% of its steady-state value, we have

$$k_s \approx \frac{-4}{\log(r)} \qquad (6.13)$$

For the examples with complex poles, we have $r = 0.89$, which gives

$$k_s \approx \frac{-4}{\log(0.89)} \approx 35$$

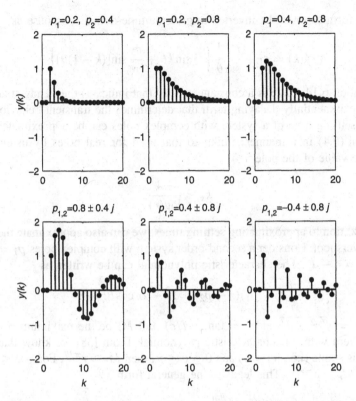

Fig. 6.16 *Impulse responses of second-order systems with different poles ($b = 1$).*

6.3.3 Step Response

For second-order systems with complex poles, we compute the step response as
follows:

$$
Y(z) = \frac{b_1 z + b_2}{z^2 - 2r \cos\theta\, z + r^2} \frac{z}{z - 1}
$$

$$
= \frac{c_1}{z - 1} + \frac{c_2 z + c_3}{z^2 - 2r \cos\theta\, z + r^2}
$$

$$
= \frac{c_1}{z - 1} + \frac{c_2}{r \sin\theta} \frac{r \sin\theta\, z}{z^2 - 2r \cos\theta\, z + r^2}
$$

$$
+ \frac{c_3}{r \sin\theta} \frac{r \sin\theta\, z}{z^2 - 2r \cos\theta\, z + r^2} z^{-1}
$$

where we solve for c_1, c_2, and c_3 as

$$
c_1 = \frac{b_1 + b_2}{1 - 2r \cos\theta + r^2}, \qquad c_2 = b_1 - \frac{b_1 + b_2}{1 - 2r \cos\theta + r^2},
$$

$$
c_3 = r^2 \frac{b_1 + b_2}{1 - 2r \cos\theta + r^2}
$$

This form can now be inverted to give the time-domain response as

$$y(k) = c_1 + \frac{r^{k-1}}{\sin\theta}\left\{c_2 \sin k\theta + \frac{c_3}{r}\sin[(k-1)\theta]\right\} \tag{6.14}$$

In Equation 6.14 there is a constant term c_1 that indicates the steady-state value and an exponentially decaying term that determines the transient behavior.

The settling time of a system with complex poles can be approximated using Equation (5.4) in a manner similar to that used for real poles by using r, the absolute value of the pole

$$k_s \approx \frac{-4}{\log(r)} \tag{6.15}$$

In addition to approximating settling times, we can also approximate the maximum overshoot. Consider a second-order system with complex poles $p_1 = c+dj$ and $p_2 = c - dj$. The characteristic polynomial can be written as

$$(z - p_1)(z - p_2) = z^2 - 2r\cos\theta z + r^2$$

where $r = \sqrt{c^2 + d^2}$ and $\theta = \tan^{-1}(d/c)$. Let M_p be the maximum overshoot of a system with this characteristic polynomial. From [38] we know that if the system is stable (i.e., $|r| < 1$) and $0 \le \theta \le \pi$, then $M_p \approx r^{\pi/\theta}$. For $-\pi \le \theta < 0$, we use $M_p \approx r^{-\pi/\theta}$. This leads to the general form

$$M_p \approx r^{\pi/|\theta|} \qquad \text{for } -\pi \le \theta \le \pi \tag{6.16}$$

To gain some intuition into this approximation, suppose that $\theta = 0$ and hence p_1, p_2 are positive and real. This situation can be interpreted as having two first-order systems in series, both of which have a positive pole. Here, $M_p = r^{\pi/0} = r^\infty = 0$. That is, there is no overshoot, which is what we expect if there is a positive real pole in a first-order system. Now suppose that $\theta = \pi$. Here, p_1, p_2 are negative and real, which can be interpreted as having two first-order systems in series, both of which have a negative real pole. Let $r = \max\{|p_1|, |p_2|\}$. Note that $M_p = r^1 = r$, which is the maximum overshoot of a first-order system with a negative pole at r.

We use Equation (6.16) to predict the maximum overshoot of several systems whose step response is in Figure 6.17. Consider the systems with the complex poles $\{p_1, p_2\} = 0.8 \pm 0.4j$:

$$r = \sqrt{0.8^2 + 0.4^2} = 0.89$$

$$\theta = \tan^{-1}\left(\frac{0.4}{0.8}\right) = 0.46$$

so that the maximum overshoot is

$$M_p = 0.89^{\pi/0.46} = 45\%$$

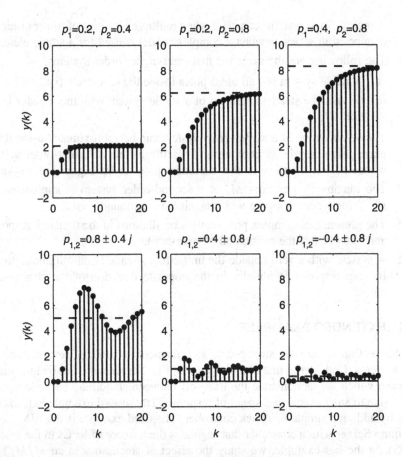

Fig. 6.17 *Step responses of second-order systems with real and complex poles. All of the systems with complex poles have oscillations and overshoot. The second-order systems evidence different m_p because their poles have different angles.*

From Figure 6.17, the steady-state value $y_{ss} = 5$. So the peak value y_{max} is

$$y_{ss}(1 + M_P) = 5 \times 1.45 = 7.25$$

which is close to the simulation result of ≈ 7.8 in Figure 6.17.

We note that the approximation in Equation (6.16) works well for second-order systems without zeros. It remains a good approximation for higher-order systems if the largest pole is a dominant pole and if the zeros do not contribute much to transient response.

6.4 SUMMARY

1. Higher-order systems have transfer functions with multiple poles and may have multiple zeros as well. Further, some of the poles and zeros may be

complex. Such systems can arise when multiple elements of lower order are connected in series or when a complex model is used for a single element.

2. The following are the same for first- and higher-order systems:

   (a) A stable system has all of its poles inside the unit circle (i.e., $|p_i| < 1$).

   (b) $G(1)$ is the steady-state gain of a stable system with the transfer function $G(z)$.

3. The settling time of a higher-order system can be approximated using dominant pole analysis by computing the settling time of a first-order system whose pole is the same as the dominant pole of the higher-order system.

4. The maximum overshoot M_P of a second-order system is approximately $r^{\pi/|\theta|}$ for a complex pole with magnitude r and angle $\pm\theta$.

5. The presence of complex poles causes oscillations in the transient response and complicates the estimation of overshoot.

6. A system with a zero outside the unit circle is called non-minimum-phase. Its step response is initially in the opposite direction of the steady-state output.

6.5 EXTENDED EXAMPLES

In this section we analyze steady-state and transient behavior of several computing systems. Considered first is the Apache HTTP Server with a moving-average filter in which we demonstrate the trade-off between smoothing variable signals (e.g., due to stochastics) and speed of response. The second example extends the first by adding a simple feedback controller. The third example is the IBM Lotus Domino Server with a controller that regulates the number of RPCs in the system (RIS). In the last example, we study the effect of stochastics in an $M/M/1/K$ queue with a moving-average filter and a controller.

6.5.1 Apache HTTP Server with a Filter

The stochastic nature of computing systems often necessitates that signals be smoothed to reduce noise. Consider the Apache HTTP Server. In practice, workload stochastics make it difficult to discern the effect of control inputs such as KeepAlive on measured outputs such as CPU. Figure 6.18 displays a block diagram of a system that uses a moving-average filter to reduce the effects of random fluctuations. In the diagram, the input to the Apache HTTP Server is KeepAlive, and the output is sampled CPU; the latter is in turn input to the filter, and its output is smoothed CPU.

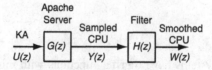

Fig. 6.18 Apache server with a filter.

To obtain the transfer function for the Apache HTTP Server, we return to Chapter 2, in which statistical techniques characterized this system's input–output relationships in terms of the difference equation $y(k+1) = 0.59y(k) - 0.014u(k)$. From this, we obtain the transfer function for $G(z)$:

$$G(z) = \frac{Y(z)}{U(z)} = \frac{-0.014}{z - 0.59} \qquad (6.17)$$

where $U(z)$ and $Y(z)$ are defined relative to the operating point:

$$u(k) = KA(k) - \overline{KA} = KA(k) - 11$$

$$y(k) = CPU(k) - \overline{CPU} = CPU(k) - 0.58$$

We structure the filter as follows. Let $\{y(k)\}$ be the input to the filter and $\{w(k)\}$ be its output. Then

$$w(k+1) = cw(k) + (1-c)y(k) \qquad (6.18)$$

where $0 \le c < 1$ is chosen to provide a desired level of smoothing. If c is very small, the filtered signal looks like the input. If c is very large, new inputs have little effect on the filtered output. Taking the Z-transform of both sides of Equation (6.18) (and assuming that initial conditions are zero), we have $zW(z) = cW(z) + (1-c)Y(z)$. So

$$H(z) = \frac{W(z)}{Y(z)} = \frac{1-c}{z-c} \qquad (6.19)$$

Note that $H(1) = 1$ so that the filter does not affect the steady-state gain of a system into which it is incorporated.

Consider the transfer function $F(z)$ from the input KeepAlive to the output smoothed CPU. From Figure 6.18,

$$F(z) = \frac{W(z)}{U(z)}$$

$$= \frac{Y(z)}{U(z)} \frac{W(z)}{Y(z)}$$

$$= G(z)H(z)$$

$$= \frac{-0.014(1-c)}{(z-0.59)(z-c)}$$

$F(z)$ is a second-order system with two real poles. Since $0 \le c < 1$, the poles are within the unit circle, and hence the system is stable.

How should c be chosen? To answer this question, we consider two input signals. The first is a sinusoid, which is used as a surrogate for stochastics. Figure 6.19 displays the sinusoidal transient response of Figure 6.18 for four values of c. In all cases, there is a sinusoidal output. However, the variability of the output is much smaller if c is larger.

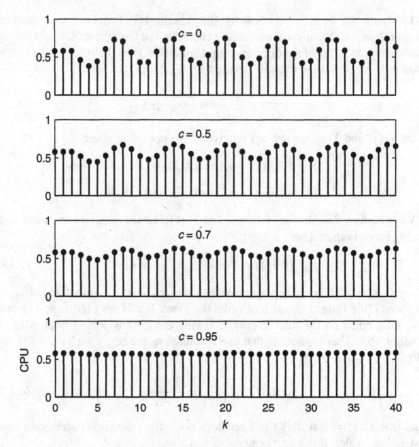

Fig. 6.19 *Sinusoidal response of the Apache HTTP Server for different filter coefficients c.* $u(k) = \sin(k)$. *A larger c provides more smoothing.*

Figure 6.20 displays the transient response to a step in which KeepAlive increases from 11 (the operating point) to 21. The steady-state output of the system is $(21 - 11)F(1) + \overline{CPU}$, which is approximately 0.24. First, note that the settling time for $c = 0$ is the same as for $c = 0.5$. This is because in both systems the largest pole is 0.59. As c becomes larger than 0.59, settling times increase. For example, if $c = 0.95$ in $F(z)$, then $k_s \approx -4/\log(0.95) = 78$, which is a substantial increase from $k_s = 8$ for $c = 0$. Long settling times can be problematic since characteristics of computing systems (e.g., workloads) can change quickly.

The foregoing illustrates a common trade-off in the use of filters. A high level of filtering (e.g., $c = 0.95$) typically makes the system slow to respond to changes. On the other hand, a filter that allows for a fast response (e.g., $c = 0.5$) does a poor job of smoothing stochastics. A good compromise is to choose c equal to the magnitude of the dominant pole without the filter since this is the largest value of c for which there is little effect on settling times.

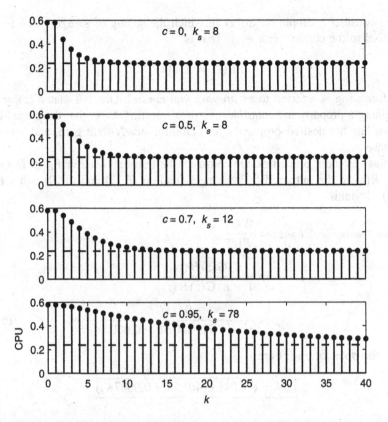

Fig. 6.20 *Step response of the Apache HTTP Server for different filter coefficients c. Step size is* 10. *When c is larger, settling times are longer.*

6.5.2 Apache HTTP Server with a Filter and Controller

This example extends the preceding example to include feedback control. The system considered is shown in Figure 6.21. $R(z)$ is the reference input. The smoothed output, $W(z)$, is subtracted from $R(z)$ to produce the control error $E(z)$. The controller takes this signal as input and produces as output $U(z)$, the new setting of KeepAlive.

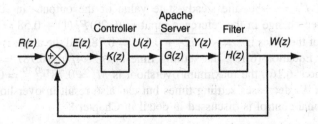

Fig. 6.21 *Apache server with a filter and a controller.*

We consider a simple controller in which the setting of KeepAlive is proportional to the control error $e(k)$. That is,

$$u(k) = K_P e(k)$$

The foregoing is referred to as *proportional control*. Observe that $K(z) = K_P$. Designing a proportional controller requires selecting K_P so that the closed-loop system has the desired properties for stability, steady-state gain, and transient response.

To assess these properties, we construct the transfer function $F_R(z)$ from the input $R(z)$ to the output $W(z)$. Using Equations (6.17) and (6.19) and setting $c = 0.95$ yields

$$
\begin{aligned}
F_R(z) &= \frac{W(z)}{R(z)} \\[2mm]
&= \frac{K_P G(z) H(z)}{1 + K_P G(z) H(z)} \\[2mm]
&= \frac{-0.0007 K_P}{z^2 - 1.54z + 0.56 - 0.0007 K_P}
\end{aligned}
\tag{6.20}
$$

Thus, the poles of $F_R(z)$ are

$$\frac{1.54 \pm \sqrt{1.54^2 - 4(0.56 - 0.0007 K_P)}}{2}$$

The poles are complex if $K_P < -47$; otherwise, the poles are real. For example, if $K_P = -80$, the closed-loop transfer function is

$$\frac{0.056}{z^2 - 1.54z + 0.616}$$

which has the complex poles $0.77 \pm 0.15j$. This means that there will be some oscillation in the system output. On the other hand, if $K_P = -20$, the poles are 0.91 and 0.63.

Figure 6.22 plots the step response of $F_R(z)$ to an increase of 0.20 in the reference value for several values of K_P. We can apply our analysis techniques to predict the steady-state value, settling time, and maximum overshoot. For example, if $K_P = -80$, the steady-state value of the output in response to to a 0.20 step change in the reference input is $(0.20) F_R(1) + 0.58 = 0.73$. The magnitude of the poles is $r = \sqrt{0.77^2 + 0.15^2} = 0.78$, and the angle is $\theta = 0.19$. Thus, from Equation (6.15), the settling time $k_s \approx -4/\log(0.78) = 16$. Also, from Equation (6.16), the maximum overshoot is $M_P = 0.78^{\pi/0.19} = 0.02$. Note that a larger K_P decreases settling times but can also result in overshoot.

Proportional control is discussed in detail in Chapter 8.

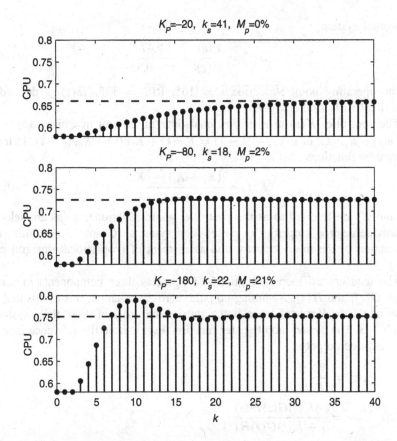

Fig. 6.22 *Step response of the closed-loop system Equation (6.20) as k_p is varied. The step size is 0.2.*

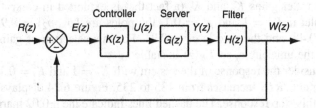

Fig. 6.23 *The IBM Lotus Domino Server with a filter and a controller. The reference input $R(z)$ and the output $W(z)$ are in units of RIS. The control input $U(z)$ is in units of MaxUsers.*

6.5.3 IBM Lotus Domino Server with a Filter and Controller

In this example we study the IBM Lotus Domino Server with a proportional–integral controller and a moving-average filter. Figure 6.23 displays the closed-loop system we analyze. The IBM Lotus Domino Server is modeled by a first-order system

$$G(z) = \frac{Y(z)}{U(z)} = \frac{0.47}{z - 0.43}$$

at the operating point $\overline{\text{MaxUsers}} = 165$, $\overline{\text{RIS}} = 135$. $H(z)$ is defined in Equation (6.19) with $c = 0.95$.

The controller $K(z)$ uses proportional–integral control in which $u(k) = K_I \sum_i^k e(i) + K_P e(k)$, or $u(k) - u(k-1) = K_I e(k) + K_P e(k) - K_P e(k-1)$. In terms of transfer functions, this is

$$K(z) = \frac{(K_P + K_I)z - K_P}{z - 1} \tag{6.21}$$

K_P and K_I are referred to as the controller gains. Controller gains are selected to provide desired properties of closed-loop systems. (Chapter 9 provides more description of the motivation for and assessment of proportional–integral control.)

The feedforward loop of Figure 6.23 connects three components in series: $K(z)$, $G(z)$, and $H(z)$. Assuming no pole–zero cancellation, this means that the order of the feedforward loops is the sum of the order of these three systems, which is 3. The closed-loop transfer function $F_R(z)$ from the reference input to the measured output is

$$
\begin{aligned}
F_R(z) &= \frac{W(z)}{R(z)} \\
&= \frac{K(z)G(z)H(z)}{1 + K(z)G(z)H(z)} \\
&= \frac{0.026(K_P + K_I)z - 0.024K_P}{z^3 - 2.4z^2 + [1.8 + 0.024(K_P + K_I)]z - 0.024K_P - 0.41}
\end{aligned}
$$

$F_R(z)$ has three poles and one zero. The locations of poles and zeros are affected by the controller gains K_P and K_I (a fact that is exploited in controller design). For example, if $K_P = 1$ and $K_I = 0.1$, the poles are $\{p_1, p_2\} = 0.95 \pm 0.047j$ and $p_3 = 0.48$, and the zero is $q_1 = 0.91$. For this selection of gains, all poles are within the unit circle, so $F_R(z)$ is stable.

Now consider the response of the system with $K_P = 1$ and $K_I = 0.1$, where the reference input RIS increases from 135 to 235. Figure 6.24 displays simulation results for this step response. The dashed lines indicate the ± 0.02 margins around 235. The predicted steady-state value of this system is $\overline{\text{RIS}} + (235 - 135)F_R(1) = 235$, which is consistent with the simulation results. Since the dominant poles are $\{p_1, p_2\}$, we predict a settling time of $k_s \approx -4/\log(r) = 78$, where $r = |p_1| = |p_2| = \sqrt{0.95^2 + 0.047^2} = 0.95$. We see that the prediction is fairly accurate.

6.5.4 $M/M/1/K$ with a Filter and Controller

In this section we use the $M/M/1/K$ queueing system to study the effects of stochastics on the accuracy of the analysis techniques that we have developed.

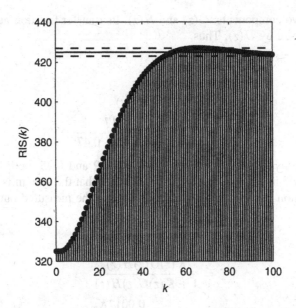

Fig. 6.24 *Step response of the closed-loop system in Figure 6.23 for the IBM Lotus Domino Server with a proportional–integral controller. Step size is* 100; $k_p = 1$; $K_I = 0.1$. *The long settling time is a result of having a pair dominant closed-loop poles with a magnitude of 0.95.*

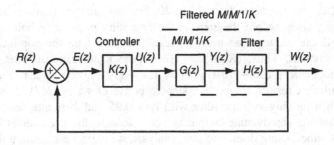

Fig. 6.25 $M/M/1/K$ *with a filter and a controller. The dashed line indicates the feedforward loop.*

Figure 6.25 displays the system that we study. $G(z)$ is the transfer function from the buffer size $U(z)$ to the response time $Y(z)$ of an $M/M/1/K$ system as obtained in the system identification studies summarized in Table 2.3. We use the operating point $(\overline{K}, \overline{R}) = (26, 2.7)$, for which the transfer function is $G(z) = 0.033/(z - 0.49)$. $H(z)$ is the moving-average filter defined in Equation (6.18), with $c = 0.95$. The controller $K(z)$ regulates response times by adjusting the buffer length used by the $M/M/1/K$ system $G(z)$. We use $K(z) = K_P$, which is proportional control.

Our starting point is Figure 6.25. We consider two transfer functions: (1) the filtered $M/M/1/K$ transfer function [from $U(z)$ to $W(z)$], and (2) the closed-loop transfer function (from $R(z)$ to $W(z)$). The filtered $M/M/1/K$ system

$G_F(z)$ has two components: $G(z)$ and $H(z)$. Its transfer function quantifies how $W(z)$ is affected by $U(z)$. Thus,

$$G_F(z) = \frac{W(z)}{U(z)} \tag{6.22}$$

$$= G(z)H(z)$$

$$= \frac{0.0017}{z^2 - 1.42 + 0.47}$$

This is a second-order system with poles at 0.49 and 0.95, both of which are real and lie within the unit circle (which indicates that the system is stable). The transfer function from the reference input $R(z)$ to the measured output $W(z)$ is

$$F_{RW}(z) = \frac{W(z)}{R(z)} \tag{6.23}$$

$$= \frac{K(z)G(z)H(z)}{1 + K(z)G(z)H(z)}$$

$$= \frac{0.0017K_P}{z^2 - 1.42 + 0.47 + 0.0017K_P}$$

The poles of $F_{RW}(z)$ depend on the choice of K_P.

First, we study $G_F(z)$. Consider the response of this system to a step input in which buffer size increases from 10 to 20. For this analysis (and in the sequel), we use the values before the step as the operating point, a technique that we have found can reduce inaccuracies resulting from the the nonlinearities of queueing systems. Thus, $(\overline{K}, \overline{R}) = (10, 1.4)$. So the response time after the step should be $\overline{R} + (20 - 10)G_F(1) = 1.4 + (10)(0.065) = 2.1$. Figure 6.26 plots simulation results for such a step response of an $M/M/1/K$ system in series with a moving-average filter with $c = 0.95$ and 1-minute sample times. We see that the steady-state output is very close to the predictions from our analysis. Further, using dominant pole analysis, we expect the settling time to be $k_s \approx -4/\log(0.95) = 78$ samples, or 1.3 hours. This matches reasonably well with the simulation results.

Now consider the closed-loop system $F_R(z)$. This, too, is a second-order system, but the location of its poles depends on the choice of K_P. In particular, the p_i are the set of all z that satisfy the characteristic equation $z^2 - 1.4 + 0.47 + 0.0017K_P = 0$. The poles are complex if $K_P > 33$, and are real otherwise.

Suppose that $K_P = 80$. Then,

$$F_R(z) = \frac{0.13}{z^2 - 1.4 + 6.0}$$

and the poles are $0.72 \pm 0.28j$. These poles correspond to $k_s = 15$ and $M_p = 11\%$. To assess this prediction, Figure 6.27 we plot in the response of Figure 6.25 with $K_P = 80$ to a step increase from 1 to 2.5. The estimated settling time is consistent with the simulation results. Although the estimated maximum

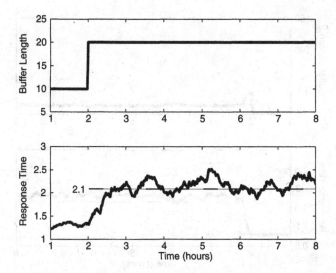

Fig. 6.26 *Open-loop response of $M/M/1/K$. The response time is filtered. The operating point used for prediction is the lower step, $(\overline{K}, \overline{R}) = (10, 1.4)$. The dashed line is predicted response time using a linear model.*

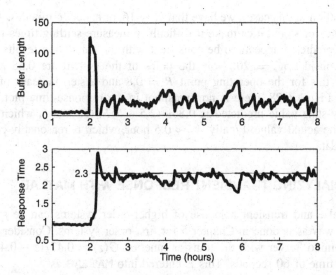

Fig. 6.27 *Step response of Figure 6.25 for $k_p = 80$. The dashed line is the predicted steady-state response. Note that there is considerable overshoot.*

overshoot is smaller than what is obtained in the simulations, the estimate seems reasonable given that $M/M/1/K$ is a stochastic system. Also, the predicted steady-state values are close to those reported by the simulations. If $\overline{R} = 1$, the predicted response time is $1 + (2.5 - 1)F_R(1) = 2.3$, which is consistent with the values observed. Further, using dominant pole analysis (which is a considerable

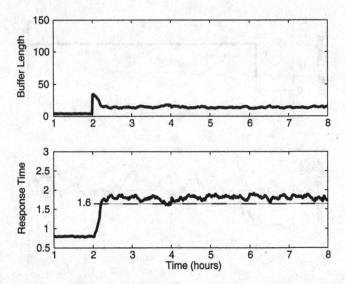

Fig. 6.28 *Step response of Figure 6.25 for $k_p = 20$. The dashed line is the predicted steady-state response. Note that there is little overshoot.*

approximation in this case), we have that $k_s \approx 16$, or about 16 minutes. Although the presence of stochastics make it difficult to measure settling times precisely, the value predicted appears to be consistent with the simulation results.

Last, consider $K_P = 20$. Now the poles of the system are 0.58 and 0.86. We study this for the operating point $\overline{R} = 0.8$ and a step increase of 1.5. As shown in Figure 6.28, there is no overshoot in the response-time plot. Further, the steady-state value predicted is $0.8 + (2.5 - 1)F_R(1) = 1.6$, which is fairly close to the actual value. Finally, $k_s \approx 0.5$ hour, which is reasonably consistent with the data.

*6.6 ANALYZING TRANSIENT RESPONSE WITH MATLAB

The impulse and transient response of higher-order systems can be studied in the same way as is done in Chapter 5 for first-order systems. Consider the IBM Lotus Domino Server with the transfer function $G(z) = 0.47/(z - 0.43)$ and a sampling time of 60 seconds. This is entered into MATLAB as

```
notes = tf(0.47,[1 -0.43],60)

Transfer function:
 0.47
-------
z - 0.43

Sampling time: 60
```

Similarly, the moving-average filer with transfer function $G(z) = 0.05/(z - 0.95)$ and a sampling time of 60 seconds is entered as

```
filter = tf(0.05,[1 -0.95],60)
```

```
Transfer function:
 0.05
-------
z - 0.95
```

Sampling time: 60

The open-loop system model consists of these two systems connected in series. It is computed in MATLAB as

```
open = notes*filter
```

```
Transfer function:
 0.0235
---------------------
z^2 - 1.38 z + 0.4085
```

Sampling time: 60

The steady-state gain is computed as follows:

```
dcgain(open)
```

```
ans =
```

```
 0.8246
```

The impulse and step responses of this system can be found using

```
impulse(open)
```

```
step(open)
```

6.7 EXERCISES

1. Write the difference equation for $G(z) = Y(z)/U(z)$, where

$$G(z) = \frac{b_1 z^{m-1} + \cdots + b_m}{z^n - a_1 z^{n-1} - \cdots - a_n}$$

and $1 \leq m \leq n$. Draw a picture similar to Figure 6.1 that depicts the relationship between the current output and previous inputs and outputs. How does this differ from Figure 6.1?

2. Estimate M_P for the second-order systems with poles $0.4 \pm 0.8j$ and $-0.4 \pm 0.8j$. How do these estimates compare with the simulation results in Figure 6.17?

3. For the following second-order systems, (i) find the pole locations, (ii) plot them in the complex plane, (iii) determine if they are stable, (iv) compute the steady-state gains for the stable systems, (v) plot the step response curve, and (vi) estimate the settling time to step input.

   (a) $\dfrac{4}{(z - 1.5)(z - 0.5)}$

   (b) $\dfrac{12}{(z - 0.05)(z - 0.85)}$

   (c) $\dfrac{-1}{(z + 0.2)(z - 0.2)}$

4. Repeat Exercise 3 for the following systems:

   (a) $\dfrac{3}{(z - 0.36)(z - 0.36)}$

   (b) $\dfrac{3z - 1.56}{(z - 0.52)(z - 0.36)}$

   (c) $\dfrac{0.3}{z^2 - 0.2z + 0.6}$

5. Consider the IBM Lotus Domino Server with a moving average filter as presented in Example 6.2. Find the "warm-up" response of the system using an initial condition of $RIS(0) = 0$. Compare with the results from Exercise 3 in Chapter 5.

6. Consider the IBM Lotus Domino Server example in Section 6.5.3.

   (a) For $K_I = 0.1$, find the largest K_P such that the system is still stable.
   (b) For $K_P = 1$, find the largest K_I such that the system is still stable.
   (c) Plot the pole locations as K_I, K_P are varied between their values in Section 6.5.3 and these maximum values. At what point does the system become unstable?

7. Figure 6.29 extends the system in Section 6.5.1 by adding a sensor between the Apache HTTP Server and the filter. Suppose that the transfer function of the sensor is

$$S(z) = \frac{0.17z - 0.11}{z - 0.64}$$

   (a) What is the order of the feedforward transfer function from $E(z)$ to $W(z)$? How many zeros does it have? What is the order and the number of zeros of the closed-loop transfer function from $R(z)$ to $W(z)$?

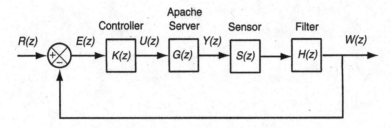

Fig. 6.29   *Apache HTTP Server with a filter, controller, and a sensor.*

(b) List the poles and zeros of the feedforward transfer function. How do the zero(s) affect the pole(s)?

(c) What is the closed-loop transfer function?

(d) For what values of K_p will the closed-loop system be stable? When will the poles be complex?

(e) What is the smallest settling time (and the associated K_p) that the system can achieve? Will there be overshoot with this settling time?

8. Consider the the Apache HTTP Server example in Section 6.5.1, and let the filter pole be the same as the system pole, $c = 0.59$. Compute the sinusoidal response and the step response and compare your result with the other values of c shown in Figures 6.19 and 6.20. How does the step response compare to that of the Apache HTTP Server without a filter?

9. Consider the the Apache HTTP Server example in Section 6.5.1. Find a value of K_p for which the steady-state gain is 0.99. For this K_p, what are the estimated settling time and maximum overshoot?

10. Consider a system modeled by a fourth-order transfer function

$$H(z) = \frac{Y(z)}{U(z)} = \frac{1}{z^4 + 0.9z^3 + 0.06z^2 + 0.74z + 0.18}$$

(a) Find the dominant pole(s).

(b) Estimate the settling time k_s and the maximum overshoot using the dominant pole approximation.

(c) Compute the response to a unit step input. Compare the actual overshoot and settling time to the approximations in part (c).

7

State-Space Models

In this chapter we introduce state-space models for describing system dynamics, an alternative to the transfer function models presented in Chapter 5 and 6. The idea of state space is to characterize how the system operates in terms of one or more variables. Such state variables need not be measured outputs. Indeed, they may not even be directly measurable. However, the state variables must be able to express the dynamics of the system. State-space models provide a scalable approach to modeling systems with a large number of inputs and outputs. It turns out that many of the techniques and results for transfer functions, such as dominant pole analysis, apply to state space as well.

7.1 STATE VARIABLES

It is sometimes convenient to describe system dynamics in terms of variables other than the control input and the measured output. These auxiliary variables are referred to as *state variables*. We motivate their use with an example.

Example 7.1: Modeling a tandem queue This example is motivated by complex systems such as multitiered e-commerce environments in which there are multiple interconnected components. A common way to model such systems is as a network of queueing systems.

Feedback Control of Computing Systems, by Joseph L. Hellerstein, Yixin Diao, Sujay Parekh, and Dawn M. Tilbury
ISBN 0-471-26637-X   Copyright © 2004 John Wiley & Sons, Inc.

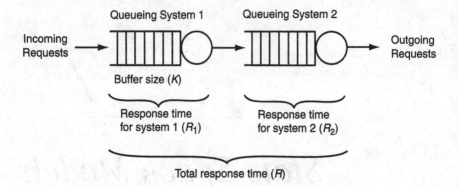

Fig. 7.1   Architecture diagram of a tandem queue.

One of the simplest queueing networks is a tandem queue. As depicted in Figure 7.1, the tandem queue consists of two queueing systems in series. Incoming requests arrive at system 1. If the server is idle, the request begins service immediately. Otherwise, the request waits in buffer 1 until the server becomes available. If buffer 1 is full, the request is discarded (e.g., as in packet-switching networks).[1] Departures from the first system become arrivals at the second system. The second queueing system handles incoming requests in the same manner as the first system. Departures from the second system are outgoing requests.

For the purposes of this example, we assume that buffer 2 is sufficiently large so that departures from queue 1 are never discarded. We seek to control the end-to-end response time of the tandem queue, which is the sum of the response times of the two queues. Thus, the size of buffer 1 $K(k)$ is the control input, and end-to-end response time $R(k)$ is the measured output.

Although this is a SISO system, it is natural to model it differently. Let $R_1(k)$ be the average response time during the kth interval of requests entering the first queueing system, and let $R_2(k)$ be the same metric for the second queueing system. It is natural to construct separate models for the dynamics of $R_1(k)$ and $R_2(k)$ since each queueing system can be modeled using a first-order ARX model. However, neither of these variables is being controlled. We only want to control their sum, $R(k)$.

In the example, $R_1(k)$ and $R_2(k)$ are examples of state variables. Neither is a measured output (although it is also possible for a state variable to be a measured output). However, state variables are sufficient to express the dynamics of the tandem queue system. In general, state variables may not even be measured.

Often, multiple state variables may be required to characterize system operation. As such, it is natural to use a vector representation of state. Let $x_1(k), \ldots, x_n(k)$ be the values of the n state variables that describe system state at

---

[1]We assume that requests consume one unit of space in the buffer.

time k. The vector representation of these variables is $\mathbf{x}(k) = \begin{bmatrix} x_1(k) \\ \vdots \\ x_n(k) \end{bmatrix}$. (Vectors are denoted by boldface lowercase letters.) It is not required that state variables be unrelated to one another. For example, one state variable may be a time-delayed value of another state variable.

Example 7.2: Vector representation of state variables for a tandem queue
Continuing Example 7.1, a vector representation of the state is

$$\mathbf{x}(k) = \begin{bmatrix} x_1(k) \\ x_2(k) \end{bmatrix}$$

$$= \begin{bmatrix} R_1(k) - \overline{R}_1 \\ R_2(k) - \overline{R}_2 \end{bmatrix}$$

where $\overline{R}_i$ is the operating point of queue i. The offset value $x_i(k) = R_i(k) - \overline{R}_i$. The control input $K(k)$ has the offset value

$$u(k) = K(k) - \overline{K}$$

The Apache HTTP Server provides another example of a state-space model.

Example 7.3: State description of the Apache HTTP Server   As discussed in Section 1.6.3, the Apache HTTP Server has control inputs KeepAlive (KA) and MaxClients (MC) and the measured outputs CPU and MEM. The offset values are $u_1(k) = \text{KA}(k) - \overline{\text{KA}}$, $u_2(k) = \text{MC}(k) - \overline{\text{MC}}$, $y_1(k) = \text{CPU}(k) - \overline{\text{CPU}}$, and $y_2(k) = \text{MEM}(k) - \overline{\text{MEM}}$. The operating point is $\overline{\text{CPU}} = 0.58$, $\overline{\text{KA}} = 11$, $\overline{\text{MEM}} = 0.55$, and $\overline{\text{MC}} = 600$. Figure 7.2(a) displays the relationship between these scalar inputs and outputs.

A vector representation can be constructed as well. Define

$$\mathbf{u}(k) = \begin{bmatrix} u_1(k) \\ u_2(k) \end{bmatrix}$$

$$\mathbf{y}(k) = \begin{bmatrix} y_1(k) \\ y_2(k) \end{bmatrix}$$

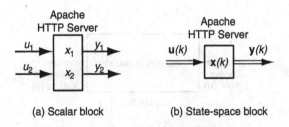

(a) Scalar block   (b) State-space block

Fig. 7.2 *Scalar and state-space block diagrams of the Apache HTTP Server with* $\mathbf{x}(k) = \mathbf{y}(k)$.

Further, for this example, it is convenient to have the output variables also be the state variables. Thus, $\mathbf{x}(k) = \mathbf{y}(k)$. Figure 7.2(b) displays the block diagram using the vector representation. Note that the double lines in this figure indicate vector-valued variables.

7.2 STATE-SPACE MODELS

State-space models use state variables in two ways. The first is to describe dynamics by showing how $\mathbf{x}(k + 1)$ evolves from $\mathbf{x}(k)$. The second is to obtain the measured output $\mathbf{y}(k)$ from the state $\mathbf{x}(k)$. Figure 7.3 depicts how input, output, and state variables relate to the system.

Example 7.4: State-space model of a tandem queue Continuing with Example 7.1, assume that each queue is an $M/M/1/K$ queueing system. Requests arrive at the system at a rate of 3.8 per second, and the service rate is 4 requests per second. Thus, the utilization $\rho = 0.95$. The sampling time is $T_s = 60$ seconds. The second queueing system has service rate 3.7 and a fixed buffer size that is large enough so that no incoming request is dropped. Further, the operating point is $\overline{R}_1 = 2.5$, $\overline{R}_2 = 6.5$, so $\overline{R} = \overline{R}_1 + \overline{R}_2 = 9$. $\overline{K} = 25$ is such that $\overline{R}$ is achieved with the arrival and service rates for the queueing systems.

We start by modeling the first queueing system. A first-order ARX model

$$x_1(k + 1) = a_{11}x_1(k) + bu(k)$$

is used to represent the dynamics between buffer size and response time of the first queueing system. Using system identification techniques, the model parameters are $a_{11} = 0.13$ and $b = 0.069$.

The dynamics of the second queueing system are affected by those of the first system. In particular, long response times in the first queueing system often indicate the presence of many requests, all of which will eventually enter the second queueing system. This observation motivates the following model of the dynamics of the second queueing system:

$$x_2(k + 1) = a_{22}x_2(k) + a_{21}x_1(k).$$

Using system identification techniques, we obtain $a_{21} = 0.46$ and $a_{22} = 0.63$.

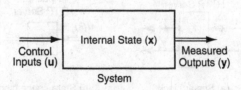

Fig. 7.3 *Representation of variable used in state-space models. The bold letters and double lines indicate vector values instead of scalars.*

To summarize, the state-space dynamics are

$$x_1(k + 1) = 0.13x_1(k) + 0.069u(k)$$
$$x_2(k + 1) = 0.46x_1(k) + 0.63x_2(k)$$

$$(7.1)$$

and we know that

$$y(k) = x_1(k) + x_2(k) \qquad (7.2)$$

It is often more convenient to write state models in matrix notation. We use the following:

$$\mathbf{x}(k + 1) = \mathbf{A}\mathbf{x}(k) + \mathbf{B}u(k) \qquad (7.3)$$

$$y(k) = \mathbf{C}\mathbf{x}(k) \qquad (7.4)$$

where $\mathbf{x}(k)$ is an $n \times 1$ vector of state variables, $\mathbf{A}$ is an $n \times n$ matrix, $\mathbf{B}$ is an $n \times m_I$ matrix, $\mathbf{u}(k)$ is an $m_I \times 1$ vector of inputs, $\mathbf{y}$ is an $m_O \times 1$ vector of outputs, and $\mathbf{C}$ is an $m_O \times n$ matrix. (The subscripts I and O indicate input and output.) Note that matrices are denoted by boldface uppercase letters. Two exceptions to this are that $\mathbf{B}$ and $\mathbf{C}$ are always uppercase even though $\mathbf{B}$ is a vector if $m_I = 1$ and $\mathbf{C}$ is a vector if $m_O = 1$.

Example 7.5: Matrix representation of state model of a tandem queue   From Equation (7.4) we see that the number of states n in the tandem queue is 2, and $m_I = 1 = m_O$. Thus,

$$\mathbf{x}(k + 1) = \mathbf{A}\mathbf{x}(k) + \mathbf{B}u(k)$$

where

$$\mathbf{A} = \begin{bmatrix} 0.13 & 0 \\ 0.46 & 0.63 \end{bmatrix}$$

$$\mathbf{B} = \begin{bmatrix} 0.069 \\ 0 \end{bmatrix}$$

and

$$y(k) = \mathbf{C}\mathbf{x}(k)$$

where

$$\mathbf{C} = \begin{bmatrix} 1 & 1 \end{bmatrix}$$

Figure 7.4 depicts block diagrams for the scalar and matrix representation of the state-space model of the tandem queue.

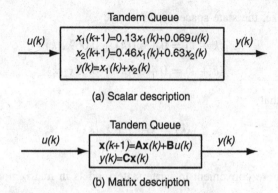

Fig. 7.4 Scalar and matrix descriptions of the state-space model of the tandem queue.

The same approach can be used with the Apache HTTP Server example.

Example 7.6: State-space model of the Apache HTTP Server   Consider Example 7.3. Suppose that the following state dynamics hold:

$$x_1(k+1) = 0.54x_1(k) - 0.11x_2(k) - 0.0085u_1(k) + 0.00044u_2(k) \quad (7.5)$$

$$x_2(k+1) = -0.026x_1(k) + 0.63x_2(k) - 0.00025u_1(k) + 0.00028u_2(k) \quad (7.6)$$

Then

$$\mathbf{x}(k+1) = \mathbf{A}\mathbf{x}(k) + \mathbf{B}\mathbf{u}(k)$$
$$\mathbf{y} = \mathbf{C}\mathbf{x}(k) \quad (7.7)$$

where

$$\mathbf{A} = \begin{bmatrix} 0.54 & -0.11 \\ -0.026 & 0.63 \end{bmatrix}$$

$$\mathbf{B} = \begin{bmatrix} -0.0085 & 0.00044 \\ -0.00025 & 0.00028 \end{bmatrix}$$

$$\mathbf{C} = \begin{bmatrix} 1 & 0 \\ 0 & 1 \end{bmatrix}$$

Note that $n = 2 = m_I = m_O$. Figure 7.5 depicts scalar and matrix descriptions of a block for the state-space model of the Apache HTTP Server.

Note that the matrix representation of the state-space model of the tandem queue in Figure 7.4(b) has the same form as the matrix representation of the state-space model of the Apache HTTP Server in Figure 7.5(b). In fact, the only difference is that we have different values for **A**, **B**, and **C**. Thus, to better describe the state-space models, we sometimes use scalar representations in block diagrams.

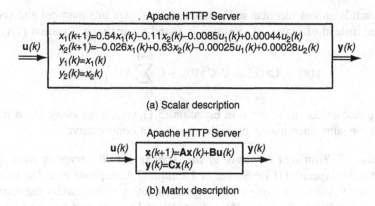

(a) Scalar description

(b) Matrix description

Fig. 7.5 *Scalar and matrix descriptions of the state-space model of the Apache HTTP Server.*

To summarize, state-space models provide a concise expression of the relationships between inputs and outputs in MIMO systems. A system with m_I inputs and m_O outputs has $m_I \times m_O$ transfer functions. However, there are just two state-space equations: Equations (7.3) and (7.4).

7.3 SOLVING DIFFERENCE EQUATIONS IN STATE SPACE

In this section we address how to solve the difference equation for state dynamics specified in Equations (7.3) and (7.4) based on the inputs $\mathbf{u}(0), \dots , \mathbf{u}(k)$ and the initial conditions $\mathbf{x}(0)$. The result is an explicit solution that provides a convenient way to assess properties of state-space models such as steady-state gain, settling time, and maximum overshoot.

We begin by focusing on state dynamics: $\mathbf{x}(k + 1) = \mathbf{Ax}(k) + \mathbf{Bu}(k)$. The solution to this set of equations requires knowledge of the initial condition, $\mathbf{x}(0)$, and the input signal $\{\mathbf{u}(0), \dots , \mathbf{u}(k)\}$. Proceeding as in Section 5.2.3, we have

$$\mathbf{x}(1) = \mathbf{Ax}(0) + \mathbf{Bu}(0)$$

$$\mathbf{x}(2) = \mathbf{Ax}(1) + \mathbf{Bu}(1)$$

$$= \mathbf{A}^2\mathbf{x}(0) + \mathbf{ABu}(0) + \mathbf{Bu}(1)$$

$$\mathbf{x}(3) = \mathbf{Ax}(2) + \mathbf{Bu}(2)$$

$$= \mathbf{A}^3\mathbf{x}(0) + \mathbf{A}^2\mathbf{Bu}(0) + \mathbf{ABu}(1) + \mathbf{Bu}(2)$$

Generalizing, we see that

$$\mathbf{x}(k) = \mathbf{A}^k\mathbf{x}(0) + \mathbf{A}^{k-1}\mathbf{Bu}(0) + \mathbf{A}^{k-2}\mathbf{Bu}(1) + \cdots + \mathbf{ABu}(k-2) + \mathbf{Bu}(k-1)$$

$$= \mathbf{A}^k\mathbf{x}(0) + \sum_{i=0}^{k-1} \mathbf{A}^{k-1-i}\mathbf{Bu}(i) \qquad (7.8)$$

This result is almost identical to Equation (5.1), except that matrices and vectors are used instead of scalars. The output is found by applying Equation (7.4):

$$\mathbf{y}(k) = \mathbf{Cx}(k) = \mathbf{CA}^k\mathbf{x}(0) + \mathbf{C}\sum_{i=0}^{k-1}\mathbf{A}^{k-1-i}\mathbf{Bu}(i)$$

Note that unlike the scalar b in Equation (5.1), we cannot move the $\mathbf{B}$ matrix outside the sum since matrix multiplication is not commutative.

Example 7.7: Transient response of the Apache HTTP Server in state space
Consider the Apache HTTP Server of Example 7.3. Suppose that due to background work, MEM is no longer at its operating point. We consider the response to initial conditions. That is, $\mathbf{u}(k) = 0$, or MaxClients and KeepAlive are kept at their operating points.

Equation (7.7) provides a way to predict the evolution of the system output. Suppose that the initial MEM value is 0.75, or 0.2 larger than its operating point. The initial condition is thus

$$\mathbf{x}(0) = \left[\begin{array}{c} 0 \\ 0.2 \end{array}\right]$$

We solve for $\mathbf{x}(k)$ as

$$\mathbf{x}(1) = \mathbf{Ax}(0) = \left[\begin{array}{cc} 0.54 & -0.11 \\ -0.026 & 0.63 \end{array}\right]\left[\begin{array}{c} 0 \\ 0.2 \end{array}\right]$$

$$= \left[\begin{array}{c} -0.022 \\ 0.126 \end{array}\right] \tag{7.9}$$

$$\mathbf{x}(2) = \mathbf{Ax}(1) = \left[\begin{array}{c} -0.026 \\ 0.08 \end{array}\right]$$

Note that even though CPU starts at its operating point, the model predicts that CPU decreases during the transient phase (although only by a small amount). Figure 7.6 displays the model predictions for $\mathbf{x}(k)$. Observe that eventually, $\mathbf{x}(k) = 0$. That is, the state returns to its operating point.

The solution to the difference Equation (7.3) can also be found using Z-transforms. Although the algebra for solving a difference equation using Z-transforms is similar to that in Chapter 3, some care must be taken since matrix multiplication is not commutative. We begin by taking the Z-transform of Equation (7.3):

$$z\mathbf{X}(z) - z\mathbf{x}(0) = \mathbf{AX}(z) + \mathbf{BU}(z) \tag{7.10}$$

From this we deduce that

$$(z\mathbf{I} - \mathbf{A})\mathbf{X}(z) = z\mathbf{x}(0) + \mathbf{BU}(z)$$

$$\mathbf{X}(z) = (z\mathbf{I} - \mathbf{A})^{-1}(z\mathbf{x}(0) + \mathbf{BU}(z)) \tag{7.11}$$

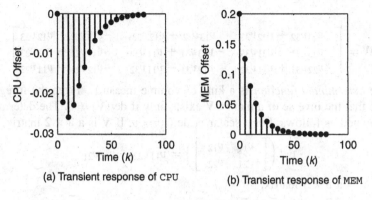

(a) Transient response of CPU   (b) Transient response of MEM

Fig. 7.6 *Response to initial conditions of the Apache HTTP Server.*

$$\mathbf{Y}(z) = \mathbf{C}\mathbf{X}(z)$$

$$= \mathbf{C}(z\mathbf{I} - \mathbf{A})^{-1}(z\mathbf{x}(0) + \mathbf{B}\mathbf{U}(z)) \tag{7.12}$$

The superscript of -1 indicates that a matrix inverse is taken. Not all matrices are invertible. A matrix that has an inverse is called a *nonsingular matrix*. The matrix $\mathbf{I}$ is the identity matrix, where

$$\mathbf{I} = \begin{bmatrix} 1 & 0 & \cdots & 0 \\ 0 & 1 & \cdots & 0 \\ \vdots & \vdots & & \vdots \\ 0 & 0 & \cdots & 1 \end{bmatrix}$$

Typically, the dimension of the $\mathbf{I}$ is implicit, usually $n \times n$ (where n is the number of state variables). Note that if $\mathbf{V}$ is invertible, then $\mathbf{V}\mathbf{V}^{-1} = \mathbf{V}^{-1}\mathbf{V} = \mathbf{I}$.

The inverse of a matrix can be found in a straightforward way. Let $\mathbf{V}$ be a nonsingular 2×2 matrix,

$$\mathbf{V}^{-1} = \begin{bmatrix} v_{11} & v_{12} \\ v_{21} & v_{22} \end{bmatrix}^{-1}$$

$$= \frac{1}{\det(\mathbf{V})} \begin{bmatrix} v_{22} & -v_{12} \\ -v_{21} & v_{11} \end{bmatrix} \tag{7.13}$$

where det is the determinant function, which is described shortly. If $\mathbf{V}$ is a nonsingular 3×3 matrix,

$$\mathbf{V}^{-1} = \begin{bmatrix} v_{11} & v_{12} & v_{13} \\ v_{21} & v_{22} & v_{23} \\ v_{31} & v_{32} & v_{33} \end{bmatrix}^{-1} \tag{7.14}$$

$$= \frac{1}{\det(\mathbf{V})}\mathbf{W} \tag{7.15}$$

where

$$\mathbf{W} = \begin{bmatrix} -v_{23}v_{32} + v_{22}v_{33} & v_{13}v_{32} - v_{12}v_{33}, & -v_{13}v_{22} + v_{12}v_{23} \\ v_{23}v_{31} - v_{21}v_{33} & -v_{13}v_{31} + v_{11}v_{33} & v_{13}v_{21} - v_{11}v_{23} \\ -v_{22}v_{31} + v_{21}v_{32} & v_{12}v_{31} - v_{11}v_{32} & -v_{12}v_{21} + v_{11}v_{22} \end{bmatrix}$$

The *determinant function* is a kind of volume measure. From the foregoing, we see that the inverse of a matrix $\mathbf{V}$ exists only if $\det(\mathbf{V}) \neq 0$. The determinant is computed as follows. For a scalar v, $\det(v) = v$. If $\mathbf{V}$ is a 2×2 matrix, then

$$\det\left(\begin{bmatrix} v_{11} & v_{12} \\ v_{21} & v_{22} \end{bmatrix} \right) = v_{11}v_{22} - v_{12}v_{21} \tag{7.16}$$

and if $\mathbf{V}$ is a 3×3 matrix,

$$\det\left(\begin{bmatrix} v_{11} & v_{12} & v_{13} \\ v_{21} & v_{22} & v_{23} \\ v_{31} & v_{32} & v_{33} \end{bmatrix} \right) = v_{11}v_{22}v_{33} - v_{12}v_{21}v_{33} - v_{11}v_{23}v_{32}$$

$$+ v_{13}v_{21}v_{32} + v_{12}v_{23}v_{31} - v_{13}v_{22}v_{31} \tag{7.17}$$

Appendix D contains formulas for computing the determinant of matrices of larger dimensions as well as more background on linear algebra.

Now we return to the discussion of using Z-transforms to solve difference equations for state-space models. This is done using the following steps:

1. Substitute into Equation (7.12) the values for $\mathbf{A}$, $\mathbf{B}$, $\mathbf{C}$, $\mathbf{x}(0)$, and $\mathbf{U}(z)$.
2. Do the necessary matrix addition and multiplication operations. The result should be an $m_O \times 1$ vector of Z-transforms.
3. Invert each of these Z-transforms in the same manner as discussed in Chapter 3.

Example 7.8: Time-domain solution for the Apache HTTP Server MIMO model
We extend Example 7.7 to show how the time-domain solution can be obtained using Z-transforms. The initial conditions are $\mathbf{x}(0) = \begin{bmatrix} 0 \\ 0.2 \end{bmatrix}$, the control input is $\mathbf{U}(z) = 0$, and

$$\mathbf{A} = \begin{bmatrix} 0.54 & -0.11 \\ -0.026 & 0.63 \end{bmatrix}$$

$$\mathbf{B} = \begin{bmatrix} -0.0085 & 0.00044 \\ -0.00025 & 0.00028 \end{bmatrix}$$

$$\mathbf{C} = \begin{bmatrix} 1 & 0 \\ 0 & 1 \end{bmatrix}$$

Applying Equation (7.12), we have

$$\mathbf{Y}(z) = \mathbf{C}(z\mathbf{I} - \mathbf{A})^{-1}[z\mathbf{x}(0) + \mathbf{B}\mathbf{U}(z)]$$

$$\begin{bmatrix} Y_1(z) \\ Y_2(z) \end{bmatrix} = \begin{bmatrix} 1 & 0 \\ 0 & 1 \end{bmatrix} \left(z\mathbf{I} - \begin{bmatrix} 0.54 & -0.11 \\ -0.026 & 0.63 \end{bmatrix} \right)^{-1} z \begin{bmatrix} 0 \\ 0.2 \end{bmatrix}$$

Observe that

$$zI - A = \begin{bmatrix} z - 0.54 & 0.11 \\ 0.026 & z - 0.63 \end{bmatrix}$$

Applying Equation (7.13) yields

$$(zI - A)^{-1} = \frac{1}{\det(zI - A)} \begin{bmatrix} z - 0.63 & -0.11 \\ -0.026 & z - 0.54 \end{bmatrix}$$

where $\det(zI - A) = (z - 0.54)(z - 0.63) - (0.11)(0.026) = z^2 - 1.17z + 0.34$. Hence,

$$\begin{bmatrix} Y_1(z) \\ Y_2(z) \end{bmatrix} = \begin{bmatrix} 1 & 0 \\ 0 & 1 \end{bmatrix} \begin{bmatrix} \dfrac{z - 0.63}{z^2 - 1.17z + 0.34} & \dfrac{-0.11}{z^2 - 1.17z + 0.34} \\ \dfrac{-0.026}{z^2 - 1.17z + 0.34} & \dfrac{z - 0.54}{z^2 - 1.17z + 0.34} \end{bmatrix} z \begin{bmatrix} 0 \\ 0.2 \end{bmatrix}$$

$$= \begin{bmatrix} \dfrac{z^2 - 0.63z}{z^2 - 1.17z + 0.34} & \dfrac{-0.11z}{z^2 - 1.17z + 0.34} \\ \dfrac{-0.026z}{z^2 - 1.17z + 0.34} & \dfrac{z^2 - 0.54z}{z^2 - 1.17z + 0.34} \end{bmatrix} \begin{bmatrix} 0 \\ 0.2 \end{bmatrix}$$

$$= \begin{bmatrix} \dfrac{-0.022z}{z^2 - 1.17z + 0.34} \\ \dfrac{0.2z^2 - 0.108z}{z^2 - 1.17z + 0.34} \end{bmatrix}$$

The inverse Z-transform of $Y_1(z)$ is $y_1(k) = (0.125)0.54^{k-1} - (0.147)0.63^{k-1}$, $k \geq 1$. The inverse Z-transform of $Y_2(z)$ is $y_2(k) = (0.2)0.63^k$, $k \geq 0$.

7.4 CONVERTING BETWEEN TRANSFER FUNCTION MODELS AND STATE-SPACE MODELS

Sometimes a model is more natural to express as a transfer function, but it is easier to solve in state space. Fortunately, any system represented by difference equations can also be easily expressed as a state-space model. In this section we describe how this can be accomplished.

Consider the second-order ARX scalar model

$$y(k) = a_1 y(k - 1) + a_2 y(k - 2) + b_1 u(k - 1) \tag{7.18}$$

To convert this model to state space, we start by specifying the state variables. The state variables must provide sufficient "context" to determine the next output of the system if the input is known. Since two previous values of the output are needed to compute $y(k + 1)$, we "store" these values as the state vector:

$$x(k) = \begin{bmatrix} y(k - 1) \\ y(k) \end{bmatrix}$$

Observe that this implies that

$$\mathbf{x}(k+1) = \begin{bmatrix} y(k) \\ y(k+1) \end{bmatrix}$$

To model the dynamics of the system, we express $\mathbf{x}(k+1)$ in terms of $\mathbf{x}(k)$ and the control input.

Reordering the terms and shifting time in Equation (7.18), we have the following two equations, one for each state variable:

$$\begin{bmatrix} y(k) = 0y(k-1) + 1y(k) + 0u(k) \\ y(k+1) = a_2 y(k-1) + a_1 y(k) + b_1 u(k) \end{bmatrix} \tag{7.19}$$

The first equations simply says that $y(k) = y(k)$. The second equation is a time-shifted version of Equation (7.18). Putting this into matrix form, we have

$$\begin{bmatrix} y(k) \\ y(k+1) \end{bmatrix} = \begin{bmatrix} 0 & 1 \\ a_2 & a_1 \end{bmatrix} \begin{bmatrix} y(k-1) \\ y(k) \end{bmatrix} + \begin{bmatrix} 0 \\ b_1 \end{bmatrix} u(k) \tag{7.20}$$

$$y(k) = \begin{bmatrix} 0 & 1 \end{bmatrix} \begin{bmatrix} y(k-1) \\ y(k) \end{bmatrix} \tag{7.21}$$

Equation (7.20) is actually the same as Equation (7.19); Equation (7.21) is a restatement of $y(k) = y(k)$. Now, define the matrices $\mathbf{A}, \mathbf{B}, \mathbf{C}$ as

$$\mathbf{A} = \begin{bmatrix} 0 & 1 \\ a_2 & a_1 \end{bmatrix} \qquad \mathbf{B} = \begin{bmatrix} 0 \\ b \end{bmatrix} \qquad \mathbf{C} = \begin{bmatrix} 0 & 1 \end{bmatrix}$$

Note that $\mathbf{x}(k+1) = \mathbf{A}\mathbf{x}(k) + \mathbf{B}u(k)$ and $y(k) = \mathbf{C}\mathbf{x}(k)$. These equations are special cases of Equations (7.3) and (7.4), where the input and output are scalars instead of vectors.

The foregoing can be generalized to an nth-order ARX model that has the form

$$y(k) = a_1 y(k-1) + a_2 y(k-2) + \cdots + a_n y(k-n) + b_1 u(k-1) \tag{7.22}$$

Here the state is

$$\mathbf{x}(k) = \begin{bmatrix} x_1(k) \\ x_2(k) \\ \vdots \\ x_{n-1}(k) \\ x_n(k) \end{bmatrix} = \begin{bmatrix} y(k-n+1) \\ y(k-n+2) \\ \vdots \\ y(k-1) \\ y(k) \end{bmatrix}$$

Proceeding as before, we have

$$\begin{bmatrix} x_1(k+1) \\ x_2(k+1) \\ \vdots \\ x_{n-1}(k+1) \\ x_n(k+1) \end{bmatrix} = \begin{bmatrix} 0 & 1 & \cdots & 0 & 0 \\ 0 & 0 & \cdots & 0 & 0 \\ \vdots & \vdots & & \vdots & \vdots \\ 0 & 0 & \cdots & 0 & 1 \\ a_n & a_{n-1} & \cdots & a_2 & a_1 \end{bmatrix} \begin{bmatrix} x_1(k) \\ x_2(k) \\ \vdots \\ x_{n-1}(k) \\ x_n(k) \end{bmatrix} + \begin{bmatrix} 0 \\ 0 \\ \vdots \\ 0 \\ b_1 \end{bmatrix} u(k)$$

(7.23)

$$y(k) = \begin{bmatrix} 0 & \cdots & 1 \end{bmatrix} \begin{bmatrix} x_1(k) \\ \vdots \\ x_n(k) \end{bmatrix}$$

(7.24)

or, equivalently,

$$\mathbf{x}(k+1) = \mathbf{A}\mathbf{x}(k) + \mathbf{B}u(k)$$
$$y(k) = \mathbf{C}\mathbf{x}(k)$$

where

$$\mathbf{A} = \begin{bmatrix} 0 & 1 & \cdots & 0 & 0 \\ \vdots & \vdots & & \vdots & \vdots \\ 0 & 0 & \cdots & 0 & 1 \\ a_n & a_{n-1} & \cdots & a_2 & a_1 \end{bmatrix}$$

$$\mathbf{B} = \begin{bmatrix} 0 \\ 0 \\ \vdots \\ 0 \\ b_1 \end{bmatrix}$$

$$\mathbf{C} = \begin{bmatrix} 0 & \cdots & 1 \end{bmatrix}$$

Equations (7.23) and (7.24) provide a way to structure state-space models that makes it easy to see the effect of control inputs. A further appeal of control canonical form is that the states $x_i(k)$ are delayed values of the output $y(k)$, so all of the states can easily be measured.

Example 7.9: Converting the IBM Lotus Domino Server with a sensor into a state-space model Consider the IBM Lotus Domino Server with a sensor, as described in Section 3.5.2. The input to the IBM Lotus Domino Server is MaxUsers, and its output is RIS. The latter is input to the sensor, and the sensor output is measured RIS. The difference equations for these two systems are expressed in terms of the offsets: $u(k)$ is the difference between MaxUsers(k) and its operating point $\overline{\text{MaxUsers}}$, $v(k)$ is the difference between RIS and its operating point $\overline{\text{RIS}}$, and $y(k)$ is the difference between measured RIS and its operating point.

First, we convert the transfer functions to difference equations. Adapting the notation of Section 3.5.2 to this chapter, we have

$$G(z) = \frac{V(z)}{U(z)} = \frac{0.47}{z - 0.43}$$

In a straightforward way, we see that this is equivalent to

$$v(k + 1) = 0.43v(k) + 0.47u(k) \tag{7.25}$$

Similarly, for the sensor (with no delay), we have

$$S(z) = \frac{Y(z)}{V(z)} = \frac{0.17z - 0.11}{z - 0.64} \tag{7.26}$$

$$y(k + 1) = 0.64y(k) + 0.17v(k + 1) - 0.11v(k)$$

The transfer function from MaxUsers to the sensor output is

$$H(z) = G(z)S(z) = \frac{0.08z - 0.52}{(z - 0.43)(z - 0.64)} \tag{7.27}$$

To put Equations (7.25) and (7.26) into state-space form, we first need to specify the state vector. Since there are two equations, each including one delay, the state vector must be two-dimensional. We choose

$$\mathbf{x}(k) = \begin{bmatrix} x_1(k) \\ x_2(k) \end{bmatrix} = \begin{bmatrix} v(k) \\ y(k) \end{bmatrix}$$

The state-space equation thus has the form

$$\mathbf{x}(k + 1) = \begin{bmatrix} v(k + 1) \\ y(k + 1) \end{bmatrix} = \begin{bmatrix} 0.43 & 0 \\ a_{21} & a_{22} \end{bmatrix} \begin{bmatrix} v(k) \\ y(k) \end{bmatrix} + \begin{bmatrix} 0.47 \\ b_2 \end{bmatrix} u(k)$$

$$y(k) = \begin{bmatrix} 0 & 1 \end{bmatrix} \begin{bmatrix} v(k) \\ y(k) \end{bmatrix}$$

Note that in this case

$$\mathbf{A} = \begin{bmatrix} 0.43 & 0 \\ a_{21} & a_{22} \end{bmatrix}$$

$$\mathbf{B} = \begin{bmatrix} 0.47 \\ b_2 \end{bmatrix}$$

$$\mathbf{C} = \begin{bmatrix} 0 & 1 \end{bmatrix}$$

The first row of the $\mathbf{A}$ and $\mathbf{B}$ matrices are obtained from Equation (7.25). The missing values a_{21}, a_{22} in the second row must come from Equation (7.26), which can be computed by substituting Equation (7.25) into Equation (7.26):

$$y(k+1) = 0.64y(k) + 0.17[0.43v(k) + 0.47u(k)] - 0.11v(k)$$

$$= 0.64y(k) + (0.17)(0.43)v(k) + (0.17)(0.47)u(k) - 0.11v(k)$$

$$= 0.64y(k) + 0.73v(k) - 0.11v(k) + 0.08u(k)$$

$$y(k+1) = -0.037v(k) + 0.64y(k) + 0.08u(k)$$

and now we can fill in the rest of the $\mathbf{A}$ and $\mathbf{B}$ matrices easily.

$$\mathbf{x}(k+1) = \begin{bmatrix} v(k+1) \\ y(k+1) \end{bmatrix} = \begin{bmatrix} 0.43 & 0 \\ -0.037 & 0.64 \end{bmatrix} \begin{bmatrix} v(k) \\ y(k) \end{bmatrix} + \begin{bmatrix} 0.47 \\ 0.08 \end{bmatrix} u(k) \tag{7.28}$$

and

$$y(k) = \begin{bmatrix} 0 & 1 \end{bmatrix} \mathbf{x}(k)$$

In a MIMO system, there are multiple transfer functions that model potentially complex interrelationships between inputs and outputs. If the operating points for the different models are different, it may not make sense to combine them into a MIMO state-space model. If it makes sense for the application, however, it is usually possible to construct a state-space model from the multiple transfer functions.

Now we consider going from a state-space model to a transfer function model for SISO systems. Recall that in the definition of a transfer function, all initial conditions are assumed to be zero. Thus, we take the general solution of a state-space equation, Equation (7.8), and set the initial conditions to zero, to get

$$\mathbf{Y}(z) = \mathbf{C}(z\mathbf{I} - \mathbf{A})^{-1}\mathbf{B}U(z) \tag{7.29}$$

In the SISO case, when $Y(z)$ and $U(z)$ are scalars, it follows directly that the transfer function is

$$G(z) = \frac{Y(z)}{U(z)} = \mathbf{C}(z\mathbf{I} - \mathbf{A})^{-1}\mathbf{B} \tag{7.29a}$$

Example 7.10: Converting from a state-space model to a transfer function for the IBM Lotus Domino Server with a sensor   For the state-space representation in Example 7.9, we have

$$\mathbf{A} = \begin{bmatrix} 0.43 & 0 \\ -0.037 & 0.64 \end{bmatrix}$$

$$\mathbf{B} = \begin{bmatrix} 0.47 \\ 0.08 \end{bmatrix}$$

$$\mathbf{C} = \begin{bmatrix} 0 & 1 \end{bmatrix}$$

We use Equation (7.29) to convert this to a transfer function.

Note that

$$zI - A = \begin{bmatrix} z - 0.43 & 0 \\ 0.037 & z - 0.64 \end{bmatrix}$$

From Equation (7.13) we have

$$[zI - A]^{-1} = \frac{1}{(z - 0.64)(z - 0.43)} \begin{bmatrix} z - 0.64 & 0 \\ -0.037 & z - 0.43 \end{bmatrix}$$

Applying Equation (7.29a) gives us

$$G(z) = C[zI - A]^{-1} B$$

$$= [0 \quad 1] \frac{1}{(z - 0.64)(z - 0.43)} \begin{bmatrix} z - 0.64 & 0 \\ -0.037 & z - 0.43 \end{bmatrix} \begin{bmatrix} 0.47 \\ 0.08 \end{bmatrix}$$

$$= \frac{0.08z - 0.52}{(z - 0.64)(z - 0.43)}$$

Note that this is the same as the original transfer function in Equation (7.27).

7.5 ANALYSIS OF STATE-SPACE MODELS

In this section we develop results for the stability, steady-state gain, settling time, and maximum overshoot of state-space systems.

7.5.1 Stability Analysis of State-Space Models

We use the BIBO (bounded input, bounded output) criterion for stability that is described in Chapter 3. That is, a system is stable if all bounded inputs produce bounded outputs. It turns out that the analysis of BIBO stability for state space can be done using Theorem 3.2 in much the same way as for transfer function models. But doing so requires that we generalize the definition of a transfer function.

Consider the expression for $Y(z)$ in Equation (7.12). To study the transfer function from $U(z)$ to $Y(z)$, we first set the initial conditions $x(0) = 0$.[2] This yields

$$Y(z) = C(zI - A)^{-1}BU(z) \tag{7.30}$$

We define the *transfer function matrix* as

$$G(z) = C(zI - A)^{-1}B \tag{7.31}$$

so

$$Y(z) = G(z)U(z)$$

[2]The effects of the initial condition may be added in later using the principle of superposition.

$G(z)$ has as many rows as there are outputs and as many columns as there are inputs. The (i, j)th entry g_{ij} represents the effect of the jth input u_j on the ith output y_i. Note that unless there is just one input and one output, we cannot write $G(z) = Y(z)/U(z)$ because the division operation is not defined for vectors.

The *poles of a state-space model* with the transfer function matrix $G(z)$ are the solutions to

$$\det(z\mathbf{I} - \mathbf{A}) = 0 \qquad (7.32)$$

$\det(z\mathbf{I} - \mathbf{A})$ is called the *characteristic polynomial* of the state-space system, and Equation (7.32) is the *characteristic equation*. The values of z that satisfy the characteristic equation are also referred to as the *eigenvalues* of $\mathbf{A}$. Below is a simple example of computing the poles of a state-space model.

Example 7.11: Open-loop poles of the IBM Lotus Domino Server   Recall from Example 7.9 that for the state-space model of the IBM Lotus Domino Server

$$\mathbf{A} = \begin{bmatrix} 0.43 & 0 \\ -0.037 & 0.64 \end{bmatrix}$$

The characteristic polynomial is $\det(z\mathbf{I}-\mathbf{A}) = (z-0.43)(z-0.64)-(0)(-0.037) = (z - 0.43)(z - 0.64)$. Thus, the poles are 0.43 and 0.64 since these are the values of z for which the characteristic equation is 0.

The BIBO stability criterion of Theorem 3.2 state that for a system to be stable, its poles must lie within the unit circle (have magnitude less than 1). Thus, *if one or more of the eigenvalues of $\mathbf{A}$ are on or outside the unit circle, the system is unstable.*

Example 7.12: Stability of the Apache HTTP Server   Recall from Example 7.6 that the $\mathbf{A}$ matrix for the Apache HTTP Server is given as

$$\mathbf{A} = \begin{bmatrix} 0.54 & -0.11 \\ -0.026 & 0.63 \end{bmatrix}$$

The stability of the Apache HTTP Server is determined by the eigenvalues of $\mathbf{A}$, which are also the roots of the characteristic polynomial $\det(z\mathbf{I} - \mathbf{A})$.

We compute the characteristic polynomial of $\mathbf{A}$ as

$$\det(z\mathbf{I} - \mathbf{A}) = \det\left(\begin{bmatrix} z & 0 \\ 0 & z \end{bmatrix} - \begin{bmatrix} 0.54 & -0.11 \\ -0.026 & 0.63 \end{bmatrix} \right)$$

$$= \det \begin{bmatrix} z - 0.54 & 0.11 \\ 0.026 & z - 0.63 \end{bmatrix}$$

$$= (z - 0.54)(z - 0.63) - (0.11)(0.026)$$

$$= z^2 - 1.17z + 0.337$$
$$= (z - 0.65)(z - 0.52)$$

Thus, the eigenvalues of the Apache HTTP Server are 0.65 and 0.52. Since both eigenvalues are inside the unit circle (have magnitude less than 1), the Apache HTTP Server is stable.

7.5.2 Steady-State Analysis of State-Space Models

The steady-state analysis of state-space models is done in the same way as for transfer function models.

Consider the steady-state value in response to a unit step input. The unit step in vector form is

$$\mathbf{u}(k) = \begin{bmatrix} 1 \\ \vdots \\ 1 \end{bmatrix}, \qquad k \geq 0$$

which has the Z-transform

$$\mathbf{U}(z) = \begin{bmatrix} 1 \\ \vdots \\ 1 \end{bmatrix} \frac{z}{z - 1}$$

From Equation (7.12) and assuming that all initial conditions are 0,

$$\mathbf{Y}(z) = \mathbf{C}(z\mathbf{I} - \mathbf{A})^{-1}\mathbf{B}\mathbf{U}(z)$$

$$= \mathbf{G}(z) \begin{bmatrix} 1 \\ \vdots \\ 1 \end{bmatrix} \frac{z}{z - 1}$$

From Equation (3.22), we know that the steady-state value of $\mathbf{Y}(z)$ is $\lim_{z \to 1}(z - 1)\mathbf{Y}(z)$ if the poles of $(z - 1)\mathbf{Y}(z)$ are within the unit circle. Thus, for a step input, the steady-state value of $\mathbf{y}(k)$ is $\lim_{z \to 1}(z - 1)\mathbf{G}(z)\mathbf{U}(z)$ if the poles of $\mathbf{Y}(z)$ are within the unit circle. If we generalize to non-unit-step inputs $\mathbf{u}_{ss} = \begin{bmatrix} u_{ss}^1 \\ \vdots \\ u_{ss}^{m_I} \end{bmatrix}$,

$$\mathbf{y}_{ss} = \lim_{z \to 1}(z - 1)\mathbf{Y}(z)$$

$$= \lim_{z \to 1}(z - 1)\mathbf{C}(z\mathbf{I} - \mathbf{A})^{-1}\mathbf{B}\mathbf{U}(z)$$

$$= \mathbf{C}(\mathbf{I} - \mathbf{A})^{-1}\mathbf{B}\mathbf{u}_{ss}$$

$$= \mathbf{G}(1)\mathbf{u}_{ss} \qquad (7.33)$$

The *steady-state gain for state-space models* is

$$G(1) = C(I - A)^{-1}B \tag{7.34}$$

This gain is a matrix whose (i, j)th entry describes the steady-state effect on the ith output y_i due to the jth input u_j. This turns out to be very useful in predicting the operating regions of MIMO systems.

Example 7.13: Steady-state analysis of the Apache HTTP Server Consider the Apache HTTP Server as described in Equation (7.7). This system model has two inputs (KeepAlive and MaxClients) and two outputs (CPU and MEM). We have already seen in Example 7.12 that the system model is stable. Thus, the steady-state gain is

$$G(1) = C(I - A)^{-1}B$$

$$= \begin{bmatrix} -0.019 & 0.00079 \\ 0.00063 & 0.00070 \end{bmatrix}$$

The $G(1)$ matrix provides some intuition. Element $g_{11} = -0.019$. This is the steady-state change in CPU resulting from a unit magnitude change in Keep-Alive. As we have seen in Example 3.10, this gain is negative. That is, increasing KeepAlive decreases CPU (in particular increasing KeepAlive by 1 second decreases CPU by 0.019 or approximately 2%). Element $g_{12} = 0.0079$ is the increase in CPU due to a unit change in MaxClients. The positive sign shows that CPU increases as MaxClients increases. The smaller absolute value of g_{12} compared with g_{11} reflects both differences in the value ranges of KeepAlive versus MaxClients as well as the magnitude of the effect of MaxClients on CPU.

Steady-state gain can be used to predict the steady-state output to a step input. Suppose that we increase KeepAlive from its operating point of 11 to 30 and we increase MaxClients from its operating point of 600 to 800. Computing the offsets from the operating point, we find that the steady-state input is

$$u_{ss} = \begin{bmatrix} 19 \\ 200 \end{bmatrix}$$

The steady-state output is predicted as follows:

$$y_{ss} = G(1)u_{ss} = \begin{bmatrix} -0.019 & 0.00079 \\ 0.00063 & 0.00070 \end{bmatrix} \begin{bmatrix} 19 \\ 200 \end{bmatrix}$$

$$= \begin{bmatrix} -0.20 \\ 0.15 \end{bmatrix}$$

Thus, we predict that CPU will decrease by 0.2 from its operating point and MEM will increase by 0.15. That is, the final values of CPU $= 0.32$, MEM $= 0.68$.

Steady-state gain can be used in another way as well—to predict the inputs needed to achieve desired outputs. Suppose that the desired utilizations are CPU = 0.8, MEM = 0.4. This translates into a desired steady-state output of

$$\mathbf{y}_{ss} = \begin{bmatrix} 0.28 \\ -0.13 \end{bmatrix}$$

We invert the steady-state gain to get

$$\mathbf{u}_{ss} = \mathbf{G}(1)^{-1}\mathbf{y}_{ss} = \begin{bmatrix} -52 & 58 \\ 47 & 1400 \end{bmatrix}\begin{bmatrix} 0.28 \\ -0.13 \end{bmatrix}$$

$$= \begin{bmatrix} -22 \\ -170 \end{bmatrix}$$

Now, adding the offsets to these steady-state inputs, we see that we must set KeepAlive = −11, MaxClients = 430. Since a negative KeepAlive is impossible, the model predicts that it is not feasible to achieve these desired utilizations. The infeasibility of this reference point has also been observed experimentally by Diao et al. [17].

7.5.3 Transient Analysis of State-Space Models

The transient analysis of state-space models is very similar to that for transfer function models. Consider the state-space model $\mathbf{x}(k + 1) = \mathbf{A}\mathbf{x}(k) + \mathbf{B}u(k)$. We know that the poles are the eigenvalues of $\mathbf{A}$. That is, we must find the z such that $\det(z\mathbf{I} - \mathbf{A}) = 0$. If these eigenvalues lie within the unit circle, the system is stable.

Once the poles are identified, we proceed as in Chapter 6 by using dominant pole analysis. Let $p = re^{j\theta}$ be the dominant pole (where $\theta = 0$ if there is a single real pole). Then, from Equation (5.4), we know that $k_s \approx -4/\log|r|$. From Equation (6.16) we know that the maximum overshoot $M_P \approx r^{\pi/|\theta|}$.

Example 7.14: Settling time of the Apache HTTP Server Consider Example 7.6, in which Equation (7.7) is a state-space model of the Apache HTTP Server with

$$\mathbf{A} = \begin{bmatrix} 0.54 & -0.11 \\ -0.026 & 0.63 \end{bmatrix}$$

From Example 7.12 we know that the poles of this system are 0.52 and 0.65. Treating 0.65 as the dominant pole, the settling time is $-4/\log 0.65 = 9$ (rounding to the nearest whole number). Figure 7.7 plots the step response predicted by Equation (7.7) to the inputs $\begin{bmatrix} 19 \\ 200 \end{bmatrix}$. We see that approximate settling time computed by dominant pole analysis is very close to the settling time predicted by Equation (7.7).

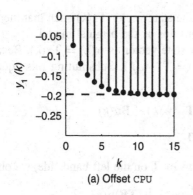
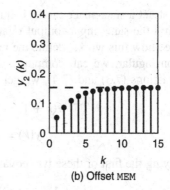

(a) Offset CPU   (b) Offset MEM

Fig. 7.7 *Transient response of the offset values of CPU and MEM in the Apache HTTP Server. The dashed line is the steady-state value.*

7.6 SPECIAL CONSIDERATIONS IN STATE-SPACE MODELS

State-space models provide a concise way to describe systems with a large number of inputs and outputs, something that is very difficult to do with transfer function models. However, state-space models introduce some considerations that are not present in transfer function models. One such consideration is the selection of state variables. Another is controllability, whether we can drive the system to an arbitrary state if the control inputs are properly selected. A third consideration is observability, if it is possible to determine the state $\mathbf{x}(k)$ based on the measured output $\mathbf{y}(k)$.

7.6.1 Equivalence of State Variables

The choice of state variables is not unique. That is, for the inputs $\mathbf{u}$, there are many choices for the state variables $\mathbf{x}$ that produce the same outputs $\mathbf{y}$. Of course, with different state variables there are different state-space models, as specified by $\mathbf{A}$, $\mathbf{B}$, and $\mathbf{C}$.

Sometimes it is desirable to transform the state variables such that the state-space model has a particular form, such as the control canonical form described earlier. Consider the tandem queue example, in which the state variables are the response times of the queueing systems. In practice, response-time measurements are difficult to obtain since probes must be inserted in multiple places. Thus, it may be more convenient to measure the number in the system (which can be sampled by a single probe) and estimate response times using Little's result [35] (although this approach works well only if arrival rates do not change much). Of course, with different state variables, there are typically different values for $\mathbf{A}$, $\mathbf{B}$, and $\mathbf{C}$.

It turns out that if the new state variables can be expressed as a linear combination of the old state variables, there is a straightforward way to determine $\mathbf{A}$, $\mathbf{B}$, and $\mathbf{C}$ for the new model. Let $\mathbf{T}$ be a $n \times n$ nonsingular matrix. Then we can construct a state-space model using the state vector $\mathbf{Tx}(k)$ such that the new model has the same input–output relationships as the original model.

To see how this works, define the new state vector as $\mathbf{w}(k) = \mathbf{Tx}(k)$. Because $\mathbf{T}$ is nonsingular, we can compute $\mathbf{x}(k) = \mathbf{T}^{-1}\mathbf{w}(k)$. Substituting this equality into Equations (7.3) and (7.4), we get

$$\mathbf{T}^{-1}\mathbf{w}(k+1) = \mathbf{AT}^{-1}\mathbf{w}(k) + \mathbf{Bu}(k)$$

$$\mathbf{y}(k) = \mathbf{CT}^{-1}\mathbf{w}(k)$$

Multiplying the first of these two equations by $\mathbf{T}$ on the left-hand side, we obtain

$$\mathbf{w}(k+1) = (\mathbf{TAT}^{-1})\mathbf{w}(k) + (\mathbf{TB})\mathbf{u}(k)$$

$$\mathbf{y}(k) = (\mathbf{CT}^{-1})\mathbf{w}(k)$$

The $\mathbf{A}, \mathbf{B}, \mathbf{C}$ matrices have been replaced by $(\mathbf{TAT}^{-1})$, $(\mathbf{TB})$, $(\mathbf{CT}^{-1})$, respectively. The input $\mathbf{u}$ and output $\mathbf{y}$ are the same as in the original model. Only the choice of state variables has changed.

7.6.2 Controllability

In state-space models, we are sometimes concerned about the relationship between the input $\mathbf{u}(k)$ and the state vector $\mathbf{x}(k)$. For example, in the tandem queue it may be desirable to have the inputs drive the system into a specific state as characterized by the response times of the individual queueing systems. The term *controllability* means that for any achievable final state $\mathbf{x}_d$, there exists some sequence of input values $\{\mathbf{u}(0), \mathbf{u}(1), \dots, \mathbf{u}(M-1)\}$ that will drive the system to $\mathbf{x}(M) = \mathbf{x}_d$.

Consider a system with a single input so that $u(k)$ is a scalar. Without loss of generality, we assume a zero initial condition $\mathbf{x}(0) = \mathbf{0}$. Substituting into Equation (7.8), we see that

$$\mathbf{x}(k) = \mathbf{A}^{k-1}\mathbf{B}u(0) + \mathbf{A}^{k-2}\mathbf{B}u(1) + \cdots + \mathbf{AB}u(k-2) + \mathbf{B}u(k-1) \quad (7.35)$$

Since $\mathbf{A}^j$ is an $n \times n$ matrix and $\mathbf{B}$ is $n \times 1$, $\mathbf{A}^j\mathbf{B}$ is $n \times 1$. Further, the inputs $u(i)$ are scalars. Thus, $\mathbf{x}(k)$ is a linear combination of the vectors $\{\mathbf{A}^{k-1}\mathbf{B}, \mathbf{A}^{k-2}\mathbf{B}, \dots, \mathbf{AB}, \mathbf{B}\}$. It turns out that if $\mathbf{A}$ is $n \times n$ and $k \geq n$, the space spanned by these vectors (i.e., all linear combinations of the vectors) can be expressed as a linear combination of the n vectors $\{\mathbf{A}^{n-1}\mathbf{B}, \mathbf{A}^{n-2}\mathbf{B}, \dots, \mathbf{AB}, \mathbf{B}\}$. (For more details, see the discussion of the Cayley–Hamilton theorem in [37].) The *controllability matrix* $\mathcal{C}$ is the matrix whose columns are these vectors. That is,

$$\mathcal{C} = \begin{bmatrix} \mathbf{A}^{n-1}\mathbf{B} & \mathbf{A}^{n-2}\mathbf{B} & \cdots & \mathbf{AB} & \mathbf{B} \end{bmatrix} \quad (7.36)$$

where n is the number of states in the system (i.e., length of $\mathbf{x}$). *A linear time-invariant system is controllable if and only if $\mathcal{C}$ is invertible.*

If a single-input system is controllable, it is straightforward to find the inputs needed to drive the system to a desired state. To see this, rewrite Equation (7.35) for $k = n$ and put the inputs into a vector:

$$\mathbf{x}(n) = \mathbf{A}^{n-1}\mathbf{B}u(0) + \mathbf{A}^{n-2}\mathbf{B}u(1) + \cdots + \mathbf{B}u(n-1)$$

$$= \begin{bmatrix} \mathbf{A}^{n-1}\mathbf{B} & \mathbf{A}^{n-2}\mathbf{B} & \cdots & \mathbf{B} \end{bmatrix} \begin{bmatrix} u(0) \\ u(1) \\ \vdots \\ u(n-1) \end{bmatrix}$$

$$= \mathcal{C} \begin{bmatrix} u(0) \\ u(1) \\ \vdots \\ u(n-1) \end{bmatrix}$$

and then multiply both sides of the equation by the inverse of the controllability matrix:

$$\mathcal{C}^{-1}\mathbf{x}(n) = \begin{bmatrix} u(0) \\ u(1) \\ \vdots \\ u(n-1) \end{bmatrix} \tag{7.37}$$

Example 7.15: Controllability of a tandem queue In the tandem queue example,

$$\mathbf{A} = \begin{bmatrix} 0.13 & 0 \\ 0.46 & 0.63 \end{bmatrix}$$

$$\mathbf{B} = \begin{bmatrix} 0.069 \\ 0 \end{bmatrix}$$

So the controllability matrix is computed as

$$\mathcal{C} = \begin{bmatrix} AB & B \end{bmatrix}$$

$$= \begin{bmatrix} 0.009 & 0.069 \\ 0.032 & 0 \end{bmatrix}$$

$\det(\mathcal{C}) = -0.022 \neq 0$, so $\mathcal{C}$ is nonsingular. Hence, the system is controllable.

The following example considers the inputs needed to drive the IBM Lotus Domino Server into a specific state.

Example 7.16: Controllability of the IBM Lotus Domino Server with a sensor
The state-space dynamics of the IBM Lotus Domino Server with a sensor are given in Equation (7.28) as

$$\mathbf{x}(k+1) = \begin{bmatrix} 0.43 & 0 \\ -0.037 & 0.64 \end{bmatrix} \mathbf{x}(k) + \begin{bmatrix} 0.47 \\ 0.080 \end{bmatrix} u(k)$$

To determine controllability, we first compute $\mathbf{AB}$:

$$\mathbf{AB} = \begin{bmatrix} 0.43 & 0 \\ -0.037 & 0.64 \end{bmatrix} \begin{bmatrix} 0.47 \\ 0.080 \end{bmatrix} = \begin{bmatrix} 0.20 \\ 0.034 \end{bmatrix}$$

and then form the controllability matrix

$$\mathcal{C} = \begin{bmatrix} AB & B \end{bmatrix} = \begin{bmatrix} 0.20 & 0.47 \\ 0.034 & 0.080 \end{bmatrix}$$

Since $\mathcal{C}$ is a 2×2 matrix, its determinant is easy to compute:

$$\det(\mathcal{C}) = \det \left(\begin{bmatrix} 0.20 & 0.47 \\ 0.034 & 0.080 \end{bmatrix} \right) = (0.20)(0.08) - (0.47)(0.034) = 0.000027$$

Since the determinant is nonzero, $\mathcal{C}$ is nonsingular and hence the system is controllable.

Now, suppose that we want to drive the system to the state

$$\mathbf{x}(2) = \begin{bmatrix} 1 \\ 1 \end{bmatrix}$$

This corresponds to an increase in both $v(k)$ and $y(k)$ of 1. The inverse of $\mathcal{C}$ is

$$\mathcal{C}^{-1} = \frac{1}{0.000027} \begin{bmatrix} 0.080 & -0.47 \\ -0.034 & 0.20 \end{bmatrix} = \begin{bmatrix} 300 & -1800 \\ -130 & 760 \end{bmatrix}$$

We compute the inputs that would be required as

$$\begin{bmatrix} u(0) \\ u(1) \end{bmatrix} = \mathcal{C}^{-1} \begin{bmatrix} 1 \\ 1 \end{bmatrix} = \begin{bmatrix} -1500 \\ 630 \end{bmatrix}$$

While we have in theory computed the inputs needed to drive the system to $\mathbf{x}(2)$, these inputs are not achievable in practice. To see why, consider $k = 1$. MaxUsers should be decreased from its operating point by 1500, and then at $k = 2$, MaxUsers should be increased by 630 over its operating point by 630. Since the operating point of MaxUsers is only 375, and the user pool is not likely to change that fast, it is unreasonable to expect that this sort of change could be achieved in practice.

The underlying issue here is that $\mathcal{C}$ is nearly singular, which is apparent by $\det(\mathcal{C})$ being so small. Because of this, large changes in the input are required to effect the desired change in state.

It is worthwhile to note that a system constructed from a SISO ARX model such as Equation (7.22) using the control canonical form of Equation (7.23) is always controllable. This is easily seen from the controllability matrix. Consider Equation (7.23) with $n = 3$. The controllability matrix is

$$\mathcal{C} = \begin{bmatrix} A^2B & AB & B \end{bmatrix} = b_1 \begin{bmatrix} 1 & 0 & 0 \\ a_1 & 1 & 0 \\ a_2 + a_1^2 & a_1 & 1 \end{bmatrix}$$

since

$$\mathbf{AB} = \begin{bmatrix} 0 & 1 & 0 \\ 0 & 0 & 1 \\ a_3 & a_2 & a_1 \end{bmatrix} \begin{bmatrix} 0 \\ 0 \\ b_1 \end{bmatrix} = b_1 \begin{bmatrix} 0 \\ 1 \\ a_1 \end{bmatrix}$$

$$\mathbf{A(AB)} = \begin{bmatrix} 0 & 1 & 0 \\ 0 & 0 & 1 \\ a_3 & a_2 & a_1 \end{bmatrix} b_1 \begin{bmatrix} 0 \\ 1 \\ a_1 \end{bmatrix} = b_1 \begin{bmatrix} 1 \\ a_1 \\ a_2 + a_1^2 \end{bmatrix}$$

Note that the diagonal entries in the controllability matrix $\mathcal{C}$ are all b_1, and the entries above the diagonal are all zeros. This means that $\det(\mathcal{C}) = b_1^3$. So the controllability matrix is invertible, and the system is controllable. This makes intuitive sense as well in that $b_1 \neq 0$ means that the control input has an effect on the measured output.

The foregoing analysis can be generalized to consider $m_I > 1$ inputs. If $\mathbf{u}(k)$ is $m_I \times 1$, then $\mathbf{B}$ is an $n \times m_I$ matrix, which means that $\mathcal{C}$ has dimensions $n \times nm_I$. Thus, the criteria for controllability is that $\text{rank}(\mathcal{C}) = n$. (See [50] for more details.)

7.6.3 Observability

State-space models express dynamics in terms of state variables. Thus, system identification and prediction require measured values of state variables or ways to infer these values. A system is *observable* if all states of the system can be deduced by observing the measured outputs. Consider the tandem queue in Example 7.1. The states are the individual response times of the two queueing systems, and the measured output is the end-to-end response time. If the system is observable, we can infer the components of response time from the end-to-end response time. Doing so would allow us to isolate the bottleneck queueing system, an important consideration in problem determination and tuning.

We begin by considering a system with n states and 1 output. Without loss of generality, assume that the input is zero since nonzero inputs can be handled using the principle of superposition. Thus, observability means that the following holds: Given the system model specified by $\mathbf{A}$, $\mathbf{B}$, $\mathbf{C}$ and the outputs $y(0), \ldots, y(k)$, we can determine the state $\mathbf{x}(k)$.

First, note that if we know $\mathbf{x}(0)$, then $y(k)$ is readily determined. To see this, note that by applying Equation (7.3) repeatedly, $y(k) = \mathbf{Cx}(k) = \mathbf{CA}^k\mathbf{x}(0)$. After n sample times, we have

$$\begin{bmatrix} y(n-1) \\ y(n-2) \\ \vdots \\ y(1) \\ y(0) \end{bmatrix} = \begin{bmatrix} \mathbf{CA}^{n-1}\mathbf{x}(0) \\ \mathbf{CA}^{n-2}\mathbf{x}(0) \\ \vdots \\ \mathbf{CAx}(0) \\ \mathbf{Cx}(0) \end{bmatrix} = \begin{bmatrix} \mathbf{CA}^{n-1} \\ \mathbf{CA}^{n-2} \\ \vdots \\ \mathbf{CA} \\ \mathbf{C} \end{bmatrix} \mathbf{x}(0)$$

Now consider the *observability matrix* $\mathcal{O}$, which relates the initial condition to the output.

$$\mathcal{O} = \begin{bmatrix} CA^{n-1} \\ CA^{n-2} \\ \vdots \\ CA \\ C \end{bmatrix} \tag{7.38}$$

If $\mathcal{O}$ is invertible, we can readily compute $x(0)$ from the output sequence. That is,

$$x(0) = \mathcal{O}^{-1} \begin{bmatrix} y(n-1) \\ y(n-2) \\ \vdots \\ y(1) \\ y(0) \end{bmatrix}$$

A linear time-invariant system is observable if and only if $\mathcal{O}$ is invertible.

Example 7.17: Inferring components of end-to-end response times in a tandem queue Consider the state description of the tandem queue in Example 7.5 for which

$$x(k+1) = \begin{bmatrix} 0.13 & 0 \\ 0.46 & 0.63 \end{bmatrix} x(k) + \begin{bmatrix} 0.069 \\ 0 \end{bmatrix} u(k)$$

$$y(k+1) = \begin{bmatrix} 1 & 1 \end{bmatrix} x(k)$$

That is, $A = \begin{bmatrix} 0.13 & 0 \\ 0.46 & 0.63 \end{bmatrix}$ and $C = \begin{bmatrix} 1 & 1 \end{bmatrix}$. So $\mathcal{O} = \begin{bmatrix} 1 & 1 \\ 0.59 & 0.63 \end{bmatrix}$. Note that $\det(\mathcal{O}) = (1)(0.63) - (1)(0.59) \neq 0$. So the observability matrix is invertible and hence the system is observable.

Since the tandem queue is observable, we can recover state information from the output. Suppose that the tandem queue has the initial conditions $x(0) = \begin{bmatrix} 1 \\ 1 \end{bmatrix}$, which means that the response time for queueing system 1 is $\overline{R}_1 + 1 = 3.5$, and the response time for queueing system 2 is $\overline{R}_2 + 1 = 7.5$. Assuming that $u(k) = 0$, the output of the system is $y(0) = Cx(0) = 2$, $y(1) = CAx(0) = 1.22$.

Now suppose that we are given $\mathcal{O}$, $y(0)$, and $y(1)$, but we cannot directly measure the response times of the individual queueing systems. Since the system is observable, we can determine $x(0)$ as follows:

$$x(0) = \mathcal{O}^{-1} \begin{bmatrix} y(1) \\ y(0) \end{bmatrix}$$

$$= \begin{bmatrix} 15.75 & -25 \\ -14.75 & 25 \end{bmatrix} \begin{bmatrix} 2 \\ 1.22 \end{bmatrix}$$

$$= \begin{bmatrix} 1 \\ 1 \end{bmatrix}$$

While the foregoing is an interesting example, it has practical limitations in that a modest level of noise in the output can make it difficult to estimate internal state. A more reliable approach to inferring the values of state variables is to use online observers. More details on this topic can be found in [9].

The following is a more elaborate example of checking for observability.

Example 7.18: Observability of a third-order ARX model   Consider a third-order ARX model

$$y(k) = a_1 y(k-1) + a_2 y(k-2) + a_3 y(k-3) + b_1 u(k-1)$$

which we time shift to

$$y(k+1) = a_1 y(k) + a_2 y(k-1) + a_3 y(k-2) + b_1 u(k) \qquad (7.39)$$

As described in Section 7.4, this can be expressed as a state-space model:

$$\begin{bmatrix} y(k-1) \\ y(k) \\ y(k+1) \end{bmatrix} = \begin{bmatrix} 0 & 1 & 0 \\ 0 & 0 & 1 \\ a_3 & a_2 & a_1 \end{bmatrix} \begin{bmatrix} y(k-2) \\ y(k-1) \\ y(k) \end{bmatrix} + \begin{bmatrix} 0 \\ 0 \\ b_1 \end{bmatrix} u(k)$$

$$y(k) = \begin{bmatrix} 0 & 0 & 1 \end{bmatrix} \begin{bmatrix} y(k-2) \\ y(k-1) \\ y(k) \end{bmatrix}$$

The $\mathbf{A}, \mathbf{C}$ matrices are given by

$$\mathbf{A} = \begin{bmatrix} 0 & 1 & 0 \\ 0 & 0 & 1 \\ a_3 & a_2 & a_1 \end{bmatrix} \qquad \mathbf{C} = \begin{bmatrix} 0 & 0 & 1 \end{bmatrix}$$

To find the observability matrix, we need to compute $\mathbf{CA}$ and $\mathbf{CA}^2$. First, we compute $\mathbf{CA}$:

$$\mathbf{CA} = \begin{bmatrix} 0 & 0 & 1 \end{bmatrix} \begin{bmatrix} 0 & 1 & 0 \\ 0 & 0 & 1 \\ a_3 & a_2 & a_1 \end{bmatrix}$$

$$= \begin{bmatrix} a_3 & a_2 & a_1 \end{bmatrix}$$

and then $\mathbf{CA}^2$:

$$\mathbf{CA}^2 = \mathbf{CA(A)} = \begin{bmatrix} a_3 & a_2 & a_1 \end{bmatrix} \begin{bmatrix} 0 & 1 & 0 \\ 0 & 0 & 1 \\ a_3 & a_2 & a_1 \end{bmatrix}$$

$$= \begin{bmatrix} a_1 a_3 & a_1 a_2 + a_3 & a_1^2 + a_2 \end{bmatrix}$$

Now, we form the observability matrix:

$$\mathcal{O} = \begin{bmatrix} \mathbf{CA}^2 \\ \mathbf{CA} \\ \mathbf{C} \end{bmatrix} = \begin{bmatrix} a_1 a_3 & a_1 a_2 + a_3 & a_1^2 + a_2 \\ a_3 & a_2 & a_1 \\ 0 & 0 & 1 \end{bmatrix}$$

To determine if $\mathcal{O}$ is invertible, we compute its determinant using Equation (7.17). With a little computation, we discover that $\det(\mathcal{O}) = -a_3^2$. So the system is observability as long as $a_3 \neq 0$. We note in passing that if $a_3 = 0$, we would have a second-order rather than a third-order system.

What should be done if a system is not observable? First, we note that although observability is often desirable, it is not essential. (In contrast, stability is essential.) If observability is a requirement and $\mathcal{O}$ is singular, the most common approach is to include additional variables in the measured outputs that can be predicted by the $\mathbf{x}(k)$. Indeed, even if the system is theoretically observable, it may be that the observability matrix $\mathcal{O}$ is nearly singular and so in practice it may be difficult to reconstruct all of the state variables, particularly if there is noise in the output (a common situation in computing systems). Such systems may also require additional measured outputs.

7.7 SUMMARY

1. Transfer function models are effective at modeling SISO systems, those with a single input and a single output. State-space models provide a scalable approach to modeling MIMO systems, those with a multiple inputs and outputs. Specifically, if there are m_I inputs and m_O outputs, then there are $m_I \times m_O$ transfer functions but only two state-space equations.

2. The set of variables used in a state-space model is called the state vector or just state. The value of the state vector at time k is denoted by $\mathbf{x}(k)$.

3. A state-space model consists of two equations. The first, $\mathbf{x}(k+1) = \mathbf{A}\mathbf{x}(k) + \mathbf{B}\mathbf{u}(k)$, describes the dynamics of the state variables. The second, $\mathbf{y}(k) = \mathbf{C}\mathbf{x}(k)$, specifies how state affects the measured outputs.

4. A system represented by an nth-order difference equation can be converted into a state-space model in a straightforward way.

5. A state-space model can be viewed as a first-order difference equation. This can be solved either directly by recursion or indirectly with Z-transforms.

6. The poles of a state-space system are the eigenvalues of the $\mathbf{A}$ matrix.

7. Using the bounded-input, bounded-output (BIBO) criterion of Theorem 3.2, a system is stable if the eigenvalues of $\mathbf{A}$ are inside the unit circle.

8. The settling time and maximum overshoot of a stable state-space model are computed from its poles in the same way as is done with transfer function models.

TABLE 7.1   Key Differences between State-Space and Transfer Function Frameworks

Property	Transfer Function	State Space
Domain	z	Time
Poles	Roots of denominator polynomial	Eigenvalues of the $\mathbf{A}$ matrix
Uniqueness	Unique	Many equivalent representations
Suited for	SISO	MIMO and SISO

9. State-space models have a transfer function matrix $\mathbf{G}(z)$ that relates inputs to outputs, where $\mathbf{G}(z) = \mathbf{C}(z\mathbf{I} - \mathbf{A})^{-1}\mathbf{B}$. That is, $\mathbf{Y}(z) = \mathbf{G}(z)\mathbf{U}(z)$.

10. The steady-state gain for state-space models is $\mathbf{G}(1) = \mathbf{C}(\mathbf{I} - \mathbf{A})^{-1}\mathbf{B}$ if the system is stable. The steady-state values of a state-space model can be found using the final value theorem.

11. A system is controllable if it can be driven to an arbitrary state by properly choosing a sequence of inputs. This condition holds if and only if its controllability matrix $\mathcal{C}$ has full rank.

12. A system is observable if its state can be inferred from its outputs. This condition holds if and only if the observability matrix $\mathcal{O}$ has full rank.

13. Table 7.1 compares transfer function and state-space models. In practice, the choice between transfer function and state-space models depends on the structure of the problem at hand.

7.8   EXTENDED EXAMPLES

We begin with a case study of MIMO system identification, a key challenge in constructing MIMO models of computing systems. Considered next is a state-space model of the IBM Lotus Domino Server with a sensor delay.

7.8.1   MIMO System Identification of the Apache HTTP Server

In this section we use the Apache HTTP Server to describe an approach to system identification for MIMO models and demonstrates the value of using a MIMO model instead of multiple SISO models.

In the Apache HTTP Server, the inputs are MaxClients (MC) and Keep-Alive (KA); the outputs are CPU and MEM. We consider the operating point $\overline{\text{KA}} = 11$, $\overline{\text{MC}} = 600$, $\overline{\text{CPU}} = 0.58$, and $\overline{\text{MEM}} = 0.55$. Hence,

$$u_1(k) = \text{KA}(k) - \overline{\text{KA}} = \text{KA}(k) - 11$$

$$u_2(k) = \text{MC}(k) - \overline{\text{MC}} = \text{MC}(k) - 600$$

$$y_1(k) = \text{CPU}(k) - \overline{\text{CPU}} = \text{CPU}(k) - 0.58$$

$$y_2(k) = \text{MEM}(k) - \overline{\text{MEM}} = \text{MEM}(k) - 0.55$$

Further,

$$\mathbf{u}(k) = \begin{bmatrix} u_1(k) \\ u_2(k) \end{bmatrix}$$

$$\mathbf{x}(k) = \mathbf{y}(k) = \begin{bmatrix} y_1(k) \\ y_2(k) \end{bmatrix}$$

The goal of system identification is to construct a model that relates inputs to outputs. Doing so requires having data that vary the inputs over a range that is representative of what will occur in practice. Our approach varies MaxClients and KeepAlive using discrete sine waves based on the following principles:

- The operating point of each input is chosen to be its mean value over the run.
- The amplitude of the sine wave is selected to cover the range of possible values of the input.
- For MIMO system identification, the periods of the two sine waves are relatively prime (i.e., not a multiple of one another). By so doing, we obtain a more uniform coverage of the input space.

Applying these principles, the MaxClients sine wave has a mean of 600, an amplitude of 500, and a period of 500 seconds. The KeepAlive sine wave has a mean of 11, an amplitude of 10, and a period of 1200 seconds. Figure 7.8 shows both input signals plotted over time as well as a scatter plot of KeepAlive versus MaxClients. Note that a fairly uniform coverage of the input space is achieved.

We consider two approaches to modeling the Apache HTTP Server: multiple SISO models and a single MIMO model. The multiple SISO approach is depicted in Figure 7.9(a). One SISO model captures the relationship between KeepAlive and CPU; the other SISO model quantifies the relationship between

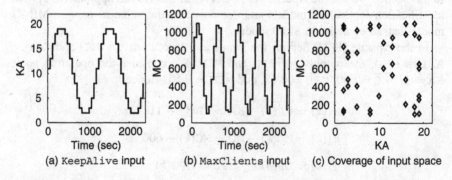

(a) KeepAlive input   (b) MaxClients input   (c) Coverage of input space

Fig. 7.8 *Inputs used for system identification, and the coverage of the input space.*

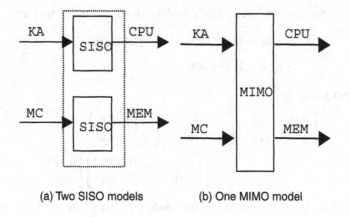

Fig. 7.9 *Architectures for the Apache HTTP Server with two inputs and two outputs.*

MaxClients and MEM. The second approach is depicted in Figure 7.9(b), where a single MIMO model captures the relationship between the inputs and the outputs.

The two approaches to modeling the Apache HTTP Server result in slightly different considerations for system identification. For the multiple SISO approach, separate system identification is done for the two SISO models as described in Section 2.4.2. The one additional consideration made here is to choose the value of KeepAlive (MaxClients) when MaxClients (KeepAlive) is varied. We use KeepAlive = 11 (MaxClients = 600), which is its mean value. MIMO system identification varies the inputs simultaneously. Note that in general more data are required for MIMO system identification than for SISO in order to obtain uniform coverage of the input space (especially if there are more than two inputs).

Figure 7.10 plots the input data used and the outputs from system identification experiments. Model parameters are estimated using least-squares regression, as

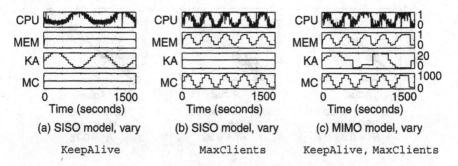

Fig. 7.10 *Results of system identification experiments for the Apache HTTP Server. In the SISO models, only one input is varied; the other is set to its mean value. In the MIMO model, both inputs are varied simultaneously. All three plots have the same scale.*

described in Section 2.4.3. The SISO models identified in this way are

$$y_1(k+1) = 0.60y_1(k) - 0.014u_1(k) \tag{7.40}$$

$$y_2(k+1) = 0.49y_2(k) + 0.00036u_2(k) \tag{7.41}$$

The MIMO model is

$$
\begin{bmatrix} y_1(k+1) \\ y_2(k+1) \end{bmatrix} = \begin{bmatrix} 0.54 & -0.11 \\ -0.026 & 0.63 \end{bmatrix} \begin{bmatrix} y_1(k) \\ y_2(k) \end{bmatrix}
$$
$$
+ \begin{bmatrix} -0.0085 & 0.00044 \\ -0.00025 & 0.00028 \end{bmatrix} \begin{bmatrix} u_1(k) \\ u_2(k) \end{bmatrix} \tag{7.42}
$$

Next, we evaluate the quality of the models produced by the multiple SISO and MIMO approaches. The first evaluation employs one-step prediction (as described in Section 2.4.4), in which the predicted output at $k+1$ is compared with the observed value $y(k+1)$. We focus on CPU since MEM is relatively easy to predict. Figure 7.11 plots predicted versus measured values of CPU. A perfect model has all observations (the diamonds) on the line of unit slope. Figure 7.11(a) plots the SISO results using the SISO data. The fit is quite good; $R^2 = 0.93$. Figure 7.11(b) plots the results for the MIMO model using the MIMO data (both inputs are varied). The fit here is also quite good, $R^2 = 0.92$.

At first glance, it may seem that the predictions of the SISO model are as accurate as those of the MIMO model. However, this is not the case. The issue is that SISO identification does not vary MaxClients, so it tells us much less than the MIMO model. Indeed, if we use the SISO model on the MIMO data, in which both KeepAlive and MaxClients vary, the SISO model does considerably worse. This is shown in Figure 7.11(c), where $R^2 = 0.78$.

Our second evaluation employs multiple step predictions. For this, we use data collected from a real Apache HTTP Server. Figure 7.12 compares the predictions obtained from the SISO and MIMO models with the Apache HTTP Server. It is clear that the SISO model is much less accurate than the MIMO model in

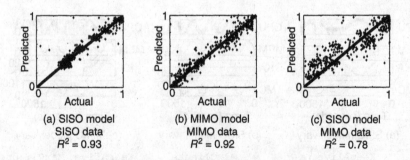

Fig. 7.11 Results of one-step-ahead predictions for the CPU utilization. In each plot, the horizontal axis is the actual value and the vertical axis is the predicted value. The line indicates when the actual value equals the predicted value, which occurs when the model is perfect.

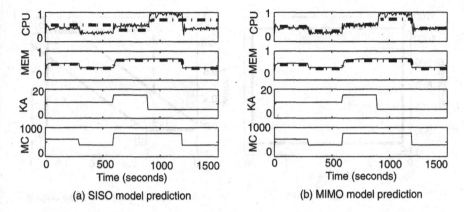

(a) SISO model prediction (b) MIMO model prediction

Fig. 7.12 *Results of multiple step prediction. In each plot, the solid line is the experimental data and the dashed line is the model prediction. Both tuning parameters are varied in the experiment.*

terms of predicting the effect of MaxClients on CPU. However, there are regions in which the accuracy of the MIMO model degrades, especially when KeepAlive = 6 and MaxClients = 800. These regions reflect limitations of the linear model. In particular, the linear model is most accurate near the center of the operating region (KeepAlive = 11 and MaxClients = 600) and less accurate farther from the center of the operating region.

Once we have a system model, it can be used in many ways. For example, the system model can be used to determine regions of feasible outputs. Consider the SISO system models in Equations (7.40) and (7.41) and the MIMO model in Equation (7.42). These models can be used to determine steady-state values of CPU and MEM based on the ranges of the inputs KeepAlive and Max-Clients. This is illustrated in Figure 7.13. Figure 7.13(a) displays the range of KeepAlive and MaxClients used. The corners that define the boundaries of this range are labeled a, b, c, and d. Figure 7.13(b) displays four candidate values of (CPU, MEM), as depicted by the bold x's. The dashed rectangle is the feasible region of MEM and CPU predicted by the SISO models based on the inputs in Figure 7.13(a). Each corner is labeled with a letter enclosed in a dashed box to indicate the point in the input space that produces that output. The solid parallelogram is the feasible region predicted by the MIMO model, and its visible corners are labeled by letters enclosed in a solid box. The x's indicate four combinations of MEM and CPU. Note that all four x's fall within the rectangle that the SISO models predict as being feasible, while only two of the x's are predicted as being feasible by the MIMO model.

Consider (CPU = 0.3, MEM = 0.7), a point that the MIMO model predicts as infeasible for the input range but that the SISO model predicts is feasible. Inverting the MIMO model, we determine that the inputs needed to realize these outputs are (KA = 30, MC = 800), a combination that does not lie within Figure 7.13(a). Our experimental results using a testbed with a production Apache HTTP Server

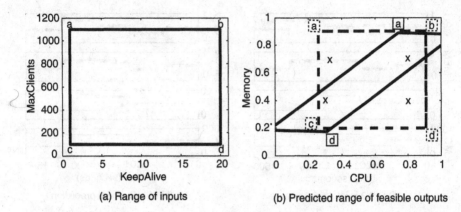

Fig. 7.13 *Determining feasible regions for steady-state values of outputs. Part (a) shows the range of* KeepAlive *and* MaxClients *considered. The corners of this region are labeled a, b, c, d. Part (b) displays the regions into which the inputs are mapped. The SISO predictions are indicated by the dashed rectangle, with corners labeled with letters enclosed in dashed squares in correspondence to the input range. The MIMO model prediction is enclosed by the solid line (parallelogram) with visible corners labeled with solid squares in correspondence with its associated input. Candidate outputs are denoted by an "×".*

confirm this conclusion. The second point that the MIMO model predicts is infeasible is (CPU = 0.8, MEM = 0.4). Again inverting the MIMO model, we determine that (KA = −10, MC = 450), a setting that cannot be achieved since KeepAlive cannot be negative. Once again, our experimental results confirm the results of the MIMO model.

7.8.2 State-Space Model of the IBM Lotus Domino Server with Sensor Delay

In this section we study the IBM Lotus Domino Server with a sensor delay of one time unit, which is an extension of Example 7.9. The difference equation for the IBM Lotus Domino Server is given by Equation (7.25): $v(k + 1) = 0.43v(k) + 0.47u(k)$. From Section 3.5.2 we know that the transfer function of the sensor is

$$H(z) = \frac{Y(z)}{V(z)} = \frac{b_0 z + b_1}{z(z - a)}$$

Putting this into the form of a difference equation and including the values of the constants obtained from system identification as reported in Section 3.5.2, we have

$$y(k + 2) = 0.80y(k + 1) + 0.72v(k + 1) - 0.66v(k) \qquad (7.43)$$

To construct a state-space representation of this system, we start with the state vector. There are two equations (one for the IBM Lotus Domino Server and one for the sensor), but in total, there are three delays. Thus, the state vector must be three-dimensional. We choose

$$\mathbf{x}(k) = \begin{bmatrix} x_1(k) \\ x_2(k) \\ x_3(k) \end{bmatrix} = \begin{bmatrix} v(k) \\ y(k) \\ y(k+1) \end{bmatrix}$$

So the state-space equation can be expressed as

$$\mathbf{x}(k+1) = \begin{bmatrix} v(k+1) \\ y(k+1) \\ y(k+2) \end{bmatrix} = \begin{bmatrix} 0.43 & 0 & 0 \\ 0 & 0 & 1 \\ a_{31} & a_{32} & a_{33} \end{bmatrix} \begin{bmatrix} v(k) \\ y(k) \\ y(k+1) \end{bmatrix} + \begin{bmatrix} 0.47 \\ 0 \\ b_3 \end{bmatrix} u(k)$$

$$y(k) = \begin{bmatrix} 0 & 1 & 0 \end{bmatrix} \begin{bmatrix} v(k) \\ y(k) \\ y(k+1) \end{bmatrix} = \mathbf{C}\mathbf{x}(k)$$

The first row of the **A** and **B** matrices is obtained in from Equation (7.25). The second row is just the equality $y(k+1) = y(k+1)$. The third row has four unknowns: a_{31}, a_{32}, a_{33}, and b_3. To determine the values of these constants, we use Equation (7.25) and substitute for $v(k)$ in Equation (7.43).

$$y(k+2) = 0.80y(k+1) + 0.72\,(0.43v(k) + 0.47u(k)) - 0.66v(k)$$

$$= -0.35v(k) + 0y(k) + 0.8y(k+1) + 0.34u(k)$$

That is, $a_{31} = -0.35$, $a_{32} = 0$, $a_{33} = 0.8$, and $b_3 = 0.34$. In matrix form, this is

$$\mathbf{x}(k+1) = \begin{bmatrix} v(k+1) \\ y(k+1) \\ y(k+2) \end{bmatrix} = \begin{bmatrix} 0.43 & 0 & 0 \\ 0 & 0 & 1 \\ -0.35 & 0 & 0.80 \end{bmatrix} \begin{bmatrix} v(k) \\ y(k) \\ y(k+1) \end{bmatrix} + \begin{bmatrix} 0.47 \\ 0 \\ 0.34 \end{bmatrix} u(k)$$

This is in the form of Equation (7.3) with

$$\mathbf{A} = \begin{bmatrix} 0.43 & 0 & 0 \\ 0 & 0 & 1 \\ -0.35 & 0 & 0.80 \end{bmatrix}$$

$$\mathbf{B} = \begin{bmatrix} 0.47 \\ 0 \\ 0.34 \end{bmatrix}$$

We now illustrate the operation of this system in terms of the state-space equation. Suppose that the system starts at its operating point. That is, $\mathbf{x}(0) = \mathbf{0}$ or $v(0) = y(0) = y(1) = 0$). Now, consider a step input of magnitude 20 which is applied at time $k = 1$. This means that the value of MaxUsers is increased to 20 more than its operating point (or to a value of 395). We can solve for the state vector as a function of time using the state-space equations.

$$\mathbf{x}(0) = \begin{bmatrix} 0 \\ 0 \\ 0 \end{bmatrix}$$

$$\mathbf{x}(1) = \mathbf{A}\mathbf{x}(0) + \mathbf{B}u(0) = \begin{bmatrix} 9.4 \\ 0 \\ 6.8 \end{bmatrix}$$

$$\mathbf{x}(2) = \mathbf{A}\mathbf{x}(1) + \mathbf{B}u(1) = \begin{bmatrix} 13.4 \\ 6.8 \\ 8.9 \end{bmatrix}$$

$$\mathbf{x}(3) = \mathbf{A}\mathbf{x}(2) + \mathbf{B}u(2) = \begin{bmatrix} 15.2 \\ 8.9 \\ 9.2 \end{bmatrix}$$

Figure 7.14 displays the step response of the three state variables. The steady-state values of the states can be found using an analysis similar to Equation (7.34) by observing that

$$\mathbf{x}(z) = (z\mathbf{I} - \mathbf{A})^{-1}\mathbf{U}(z)$$

Thus, we have the steady-state values of the states expressed as

$$
\begin{aligned}
\mathbf{x}_{ss} &= (\mathbf{I} - \mathbf{A})^{-1}\mathbf{B}u_{ss} \\
&= \begin{bmatrix} 0.57 & 0 & 0 \\ 0 & 1 & -1 \\ 0.35 & 0 & 0.20 \end{bmatrix}^{-1} \begin{bmatrix} 0.47 \\ 0 \\ 0.34 \end{bmatrix} \quad (20) \\
&= \begin{bmatrix} 16.5 \\ 4.9 \\ 4.9 \end{bmatrix}
\end{aligned}
$$

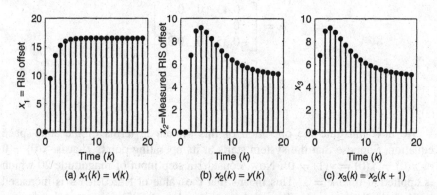

(a) $x_1(k) = v(k)$ (b) $x_2(k) = y(k)$ (c) $x_3(k) = x_2(k+1)$

Fig. 7.14 Step response of the IBM Lotus Domino Server.

*7.9 CONSTRUCTING STATE-SPACE MODELS IN MATLAB

In this section we use Equation (7.7) to demonstrate the construction and analysis of state-space models in MATLAB. We begin by entering the matrices that define the state-space model:

```
>>A = [0.54 -0.11; -0.026 0.63]

A =

    0.5400   -0.1100
   -0.0260    0.6300

>>B = [-0.0085 0.00044; -0.00025 0.00028]

B =

   -0.0085    0.0004
   -0.0003    0.0003

>>C = [1 0; 0 1]

C =

    1    0
    0    1
```

Next, we use the MATLAB ss command to construct the state-space model:

```
>>sys = ss(A,B,C,0,-1)

a =

              x1          x2
    x1       0.54       -0.11
    x2      -0.026       0.63


b =

              u1          u2
    x1     -0.0085      0.00044
    x2     -0.00025     0.00028


c =

              x1          x2
    y1        1           0
    y2        0           1
```

```
d =
                    u1              u2
        y1          0               0
        y2          0               0
```

Sampling time: unspecified
Discrete-time model.

The MATLAB ss function generalizes the state-space model in two ways. First, Equation (7.4) is generalized to $y(k) = Cx(k) + Du(k)$. D is the fourth argument of ss, so we set it to 0. Second, ss can specify both continuous- and discrete-time models. The latter can be indicated by having -1 as the fifth argument of ss.

The poles of the model can be found by computing the eigenvalues of A using the eig function:

```
>>eig(A)

ans =

    0.5151
    0.6549
```

We can also find the poles directly from the model object sys:

```
>>pole(sys)

ans = -

    0.5151
    0.6549
```

Further, the model object sys can be used to compute steady-state gain:

```
>>DCG = dcgain(sys)

DCG =

    -0.0186      0.0008
     0.0006      0.0007
```

The four outputs represent the steady-state gain of each of the two inputs for each of the two outputs. The response to a step input can be obtained using

```
>>y=step(sys,1:10)

y(:,:,1) =

    -0.0085    -0.0003
    -0.0131    -0.0002
    -0.0155    -0.0000
    -0.0169     0.0001
    -0.0176     0.0003
    -0.0181     0.0004
    -0.0183     0.0005
    -0.0184     0.0005
    -0.0185     0.0006
    -0.0186     0.0006


y(:,:,2) =

   1.0e-003 *

     0.4400     0.2800
     0.6468     0.4450
     0.7403     0.5435
     0.7800     0.6032
     0.7948     0.6397
     0.7988     0.6624
     0.7985     0.6765
     0.7968     0.6854
     0.7949     0.6911
     0.7932     0.6947
```

The rows indicate the time k. The first two columns, y (:,:,1), are the responses of the first output to the inputs. The second two columns are the responses of the second output to the inputs. Note that the transient response converges to the steady-state gain.

7.10 EXERCISES

1. Using the Apache HTTP Server model of Equation (7.7), predict the final values of CPU and MEM for settings of MaxClients = 400 and KeepAlive = 15. What is predicted to occur if KeepAlive = 1 and MaxClients = 1000? Is this realistic? Why or why not? What does the result tell you about the model?

2. Consider the state-space model in which

$$A = \begin{bmatrix} a_{11} & a_{12} \\ a_{21} & a_{22} \end{bmatrix} = \begin{bmatrix} 0.54 & -0.11 \\ -0.26 & 0.63 \end{bmatrix}$$

What is the settling time of this system if a_{11} is 10% larger? How about 10% smaller? How much would settling times change if there could be a maximum of a 10% error in estimating any of the a_{ij}?

3. For the IBM Lotus Domino Server with a sensor that has no delay, predict the steady-state values of all of the states for a step input of 20 (i.e., MaxUsers is 20 over its operating point). How do the steady-state values of the state variables in the no-delay system compare with the steady-state values of the system in Section 7.8.2?

4. Check the observability of the IBM Lotus Domino Server and sensor model both with and without delay in the sensor. Explain the answers you obtained.

5. For the IBM Lotus Domino Server with a sensor and a delay of two time units,

   (a) How many states will be needed?
   (b) Put the equations into state-space form.
   (c) Check the stability of the system. What are the poles?
   (d) Construct the observability matrix $\mathcal{O}$ and determine whether or not the system is observable.
   (e) Construct the controllability matrix $\mathcal{C}$ and determine whether or not the system is controllable.
   (f) Predict the steady-state values of all the states to a step input of 10 (MaxUsers is 10 over its operating point).
   (g) Find and plot the step response (only the output).

6. Using the state-space model of the tandem queue in Example 7.5,

   (a) Study the response to initial condition

$$x(0) = \begin{bmatrix} 1 \\ 1 \end{bmatrix}$$

   (b) Predict the end-to-end response time when the size of buffer 1 is 30.

7. Convert the following state-space models into transfer function models:

   (a) $\quad A = \begin{bmatrix} 10 & 10 \\ 3 & 5 \end{bmatrix}, B = \begin{bmatrix} 3 \\ 0 \end{bmatrix}, C = \begin{bmatrix} 3 & 1 \end{bmatrix}$

   (b) $\quad A = \begin{bmatrix} 1 & 1 \\ 0.5 & 0.5 \end{bmatrix}, B = \begin{bmatrix} 1 \\ 1 \end{bmatrix}, C = \begin{bmatrix} 1 & 0 \end{bmatrix}$

(c) $$A = \begin{bmatrix} 10 & 27 & 5 \\ 12 & 5 & 22 \\ 3 & 16 & 22 \end{bmatrix}, B = \begin{bmatrix} 2 & 2 \\ 3 & 0 \\ 10 & 0 \end{bmatrix}, C = \begin{bmatrix} 1 & 1 & 0 \end{bmatrix}$$

8. Convert the following ARX models into state-space models:

   (a) $y(k) = 0.2y(k-1) + 0.3y(k-2) + u(k-1)$
   (b) $y(k) = 0.1y(k-1) - 0.4y(k-2) + y(k-3) + 0.5u(k-1)$
   (c) $y(k) = y(k-2) + 0.3y(k-4) + u(k-2)$

9. Analyze the stability and steady state gains of the following state-space models:

   (a) $$A = \begin{bmatrix} 0.25 & 10 \\ 5 & 0.5 \end{bmatrix}, B = \begin{bmatrix} 1 \\ 0 \end{bmatrix}, C = \begin{bmatrix} 1 & 1 \end{bmatrix}$$

   (b) $$A = \begin{bmatrix} 1 & 1 \\ 1 & 0.5 \end{bmatrix}, B = \begin{bmatrix} 0 \\ 1 \end{bmatrix}, C = \begin{bmatrix} 0 & 1 \end{bmatrix}$$

   (c) $$A = \begin{bmatrix} 1 & 7 & 5 \\ 2 & 5 & 2 \\ 1 & 6 & 8 \end{bmatrix}, B = \begin{bmatrix} 1 \\ 1 \\ 0 \end{bmatrix}, C = \begin{bmatrix} 1 & 1 & 1 \end{bmatrix}$$

10. Analyze the controllability and observability of the following state-space models:

    (a) $$A = \begin{bmatrix} 0 & 2 \\ 5 & 0 \end{bmatrix}, B = \begin{bmatrix} 1 \\ 0 \end{bmatrix}, C = \begin{bmatrix} 1 & 0 \end{bmatrix}$$

    (b) $$A = \begin{bmatrix} 1 & 1 & 2 \\ 1 & 0 & 1 \\ 2 & 3 & 4 \end{bmatrix}, B = \begin{bmatrix} 0 \\ 1 \\ 2 \end{bmatrix}, C = \begin{bmatrix} 0 & 1 & 1 \end{bmatrix}$$

    (c) $$A = \begin{bmatrix} 1 & 4 & 2 & 3 \\ 1 & 2 & 2 & 10 \\ 1 & 9 & 8 & 7 \\ 1 & 2 & 1 & 9 \end{bmatrix}, B = \begin{bmatrix} 1 & 9 \\ 1 & 0 \\ 0 & 8 \\ 2 & 7 \end{bmatrix}, C = \begin{bmatrix} 1 & 0 & 1 & 0 \end{bmatrix}$$

Part III

Control Analysis and Design

8

Proportional Control

In this chapter we describe proportional control and analyze its characteristics
in computing systems. We use the simplicity of proportional control as a way to
provide insights into feedback control systems, including detailed examples with
step-by-step simulations. We introduce the concept of pole placement design, a
technique that views control design as constructing systems with desired closed-
loop poles. Other topics covered in this chapter include assessing controller
quality, controlling a first-order system with measurement delays and a moving-
average filter, and root locus analysis.

8.1 CONTROL LAWS AND CONTROLLER OPERATION

In this section we provide a detailed description of the operation of a feedback
control system. The intent is to familiarize the reader with the inputs, outputs,
and components of feedback systems and to gain insights into important properties. Consider the IBM Lotus Domino Server. We want to use MaxUsers to
control the number of RPCs being processed in the server (which is roughly
equal to the number of active users). Figure 8.1 puts this into a general framework. The IBM Lotus Domino Server is the target system. Its control input is
MaxUsers, and the output is RIS, the number of RPCs in the Notes Server.
The operating point of the IBM Lotus Domino Server is $(\overline{\text{MaxUsers}}, \overline{\text{RIS}})$. In
our case, $(\overline{\text{MaxUsers}}, \overline{\text{RIS}}) = (375, 325)$. The kth offset value of the input is

Feedback Control of Computing Systems, by Joseph L. Hellerstein, Yixin Diao, Sujay Parekh, and
Dawn M. Tilbury
ISBN 0-471-26637-X   Copyright © 2004 John Wiley & Sons, Inc.

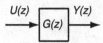

Fig. 8.1 *Open-loop control. Administrator specifies the control input U(z) needed to achieve the output desired.*

$u(k) = \text{MaxUsers}(k) - \overline{\text{MaxUsers}}$, and for the output it is $y(k) = \text{RIS}(k) - \overline{\text{RIS}}$. For the purposes of this example, we want the steady-state value of the output to be 335. That is, $y_{\text{ss}} = 10$.

Our first observation is that the control input and output are in different units. The control input, MaxUsers, refers to the number of *connected* users, whereas the output is in units of *active* users. The relationship between the units of the input and output is described by the transfer function of the target system. We use $G(z)$ to denote the transfer function, where $G(z) = Y(z)/U(z)$. From the system identification studies of the IBM Lotus Domino Server in Chapter 2,

$$G(z) = \frac{Y(z)}{U(z)} = \frac{0.47}{z - 0.43}$$

In the time domain, this is $y(k+1) = (0.43)y(k) + (0.47)u(k)$. Further, we know from Chapter 3 that the steady-state gain is $G(1) = y_{\text{ss}}/u_{\text{ss}}$. Thus, the value of MaxUsers needed so that $y_{\text{ss}} = 10$ is $u_{ss} = y_{\text{ss}}/G(1) = 10/0.82 = 12$.

Figure 8.2 displays the results of simulating the system in Figure 8.1 using the time-domain form of $G(z)$ for the IBM Lotus Domino Server. We assume that $y(0) = 0$. Thus, $y(1) = (0.43)y(0) + (0.47)u(0) = (0.47)(12) = 5.7$; and $y(2) = (0.43)y(1) + (0.47)u(1) = (0.43)(0.57) + (0.47)(12) = 8.1$. Note that by $k = 5$, we have $y(k) = 9.9$. Thus, by having the administrator specify the proper input $u(k)$, we are able to achieve the desired output $y(k)$.

Now consider administrative tasks that occasionally execute in the background. Such tasks can affect the way that MaxUsers operates. In general, these effects are referred to as *disturbances*. Other examples of disturbances are changes in workload and transient failures of hardware and software.

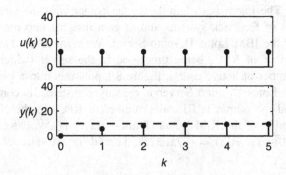

Fig. 8.2 *Simulation of the open-loop system in Figure 8.1 with $a = 0.43$ and $b = 0.47$. To achieve $y(k) = 10$, we must set $u(k) = 12$.*

Figure 8.3 shows a block diagram in which open-loop control is done in the presence of a disturbance. The disturbance signal is denoted by $D(z)$. The effect of the disturbance is modeled by adding $d(k)$ to the value specified by the administrator.

Figure 8.4 extends the simulation in Figure 8.2 to consider the disturbance in Figure 8.3. In the first five time units, $d(k) = 0$, so we are able to achieve

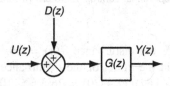

Fig. 8.3 *Open-loop control in the presence of a disturbance. Administrator specifies the control input $U(z)$ needed to achieve the desired output $Y(z)$, but the effect of the control is modified by the disturbance.*

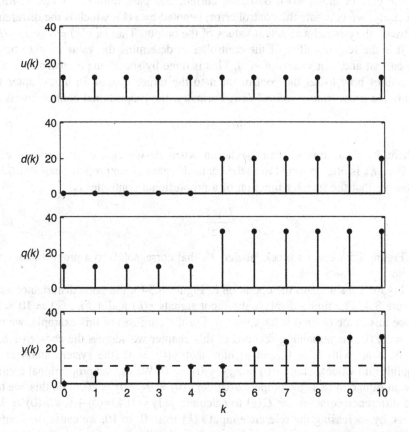

Fig. 8.4 *Simulation of the open-loop system in Figure 8.3 with $G(z) = \frac{Y(z)}{U(z)} = \frac{0.47}{z-0.43}$, and $d(k) = 20$ for $k \geq 5$. The output differs greatly from the desired value of 10 once $d(k) \neq 0$.*

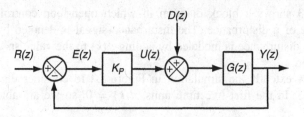

Fig. 8.5 *Feedback using proportional control. There are two inputs: the reference $R(z)$ and the disturbance $D(z)$.*

$y(k) = 10$. When $k = 5$, the disturbance $d(k) = 20$. To find the new steady-state output, we must add the effect of the disturbance to the control input, so $y_{ss} = G(1)(u_{ss} + d_{ss}) = (0.82)(12 + 20) = 26.3 >> 10$.

Compensating for disturbances requires a more complex system, as displayed in Figure 8.5. First, we must explicitly specify the desired output value. This is called the *reference signal* and is denoted by $r(k)$. Second, we compute settings of the control input, $u(k)$, based on current and past values of y and r. More precisely, we compute the control error, denoted by $e(k)$, which is the difference between the desired and actual values of the output. That is, $e(k) = r(k) - y(k)$.

It is the responsibility of the controller to determine the value of $u(k)$ based on current and past values of $e(k)$. This is done by specifying a *control law* that quantifies how to set the control input to the target system. In this chapter we study the *proportional control law*. Formally, the proportional control law is

$$u(k) = K_P e(k) \tag{8.1}$$

where K_P is a constant that is chosen when designing the proportional controller. K_P is often referred to as the controller gain of the proportional controller. Observe that the transfer function of a proportional controller is

$$\frac{U(z)}{E(z)} = K_P \tag{8.2}$$

In Figure 8.5 we see a block labeled K_P that corresponds to a proportional controller.

Figure 8.6 simulates the operation of Figure 8.5 for the same disturbance as in Figure 8.4. The figure displays the input signals $r(k)$ and $d(k)$. $r(k) = 10 = r_{ss}$ since this is the desired value for $y(k)$. For the purposes of this example, we use $K_P = 2$. (In the remaining sections of this chapter we address the choice of K_P.)

We start with $k = 0$, and assume that $y(0) = 0$ (the system starts at its equilibrium value). Thus, $e(0) = r_{ss} - y(0) = 10$. We use the proportional control law in Equation (8.1) to compute $u(0)$. So $u(0) = K_P e(0) = 20$. With this, we use the difference equation for $G(z)$ to calculate $y(1) = 0.43y(0) + 0.47u(0) = 9.4$. Thus, by increasing the reference input $r(k)$ from 0 to 10, we cause the control error to increase, which in turn increases u thereby increasing y. This happens because $K_P > 0$ and $b = 0.47 > 0$. (Clearly, if $b < 0$, we want $K_P < 0$.) To

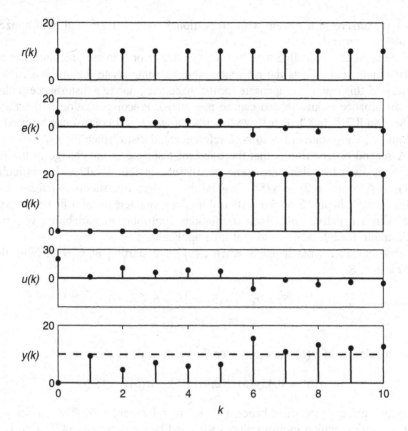

Fig. 8.6 *Simulation of a proportional controller for a step response in the presence of a disturbance. Initial conditions are zero. The target system has the transfer function $G(z) = 0.47/(z - 0.43)$, and $K_P = 2$. The dashed line shows the reference value for $y(k)$.*

summarize the calculations:

$$e(0) = r(0) - y(0) = 10 - 0 = 10$$

$$u(0) = K_P e(0) = (2)(10) = 20$$

$$y(1) = 0.43y(0) + 0.47u(0) = 9.4$$

Now, we begin the feedback sequence again with $k = 1$. Note that k advances as we traverse $G(z)$ because this block includes a time lag. Had there been other blocks with time lags, more time may have elapsed in traversing the feedback loop.

Moving ahead to $k = 4$, observe that $y(k)$ converges to a value that is *less than* the reference value. Thus, the steady-state error e_{ss} is greater than zero since $e_{ss} = r_{ss} - y_{ss}$. Put differently, the controller is inaccurate in that its output differs from what is desired. With proportional control, if the control error $e(k)$ is zero, the control input $u(k)$ is also zero. Thus, if the reference and/or the disturbance input is nonzero in a system with proportional control, there will be a nonzero steady-state error.

One approach to dealing with this steady-state error is to use precompensation, a technique that adjusts the reference input to compensate for this inaccuracy. Of course, this cannot compensate for the inaccuracy due to a disturbance (unless the disturbance is known and can be measured). Precompensation is illustrated in Section 8.7.2. In Chapter 9 we describe how integral control can be used to eliminate steady-state errors to both reference and disturbance inputs.

A second observation is that the transient response to the change in the reference is such that there are some oscillations in the y values. In particular, $y(1) > y(5)$ and $y(2) < y(5)$. That is, this system overshoots its steady-state value. From Chapter 5 we know that this is a characteristic of a first-order system with a negative pole. Such oscillations contribute to variability, which is undesirable for interactive and real-time applications.

Now consider what happens when $d(k) > 0$ starting at $k = 5$. Note that $y(5) = 6.4$. So

$$e(5) = r_{ss} - y(5) = 10 - 6.4 = 3.6$$

$$u(5) = K_p e(5) = (2)(3.6) = 7.2$$

The calculation of $y(6)$ must consider $d(5)$ since this is nonzero.

$$y(6) = 0.43y(5) + 0.47[u(5) + d(5)] = 15.5$$

Thus, the effect of the disturbance at $k = 5$ is to increase $y(6)$. This causes $e(6)$ to be negative, which in turn reduces $u(6)$ and hence decreases $y(7)$. That is,

$$e(6) = r_{ss} - y(6) = 10 - 15.5 = -5.5$$

$$u(6) = K_p e(6) = 2(-5.5) = -11$$

$$y(7) = 0.43y(6) + 0.47[u(6) + d(6)] = 10.9$$

These simple computations illustrate how the feedback controller compensates for a disturbance. The disturbance causes the output to increase, the control error then increases, and the feedback mechanism adjusts the control input to reduce the error.

Moving ahead to $k = 10$, we see that $y(k)$ again converges to a new steady-state value. Thus, in some sense the controller is able to reject the effects of the disturbance. Even so, observe that $y(10) \neq 10 = r_{ss}$, which is the value we hope to achieve. Further, $y(10) = 12.7 > 6.4 = y(5)$. Thus, although the system converges around $k = 10$, the disturbance has altered the output of the system.

Thus far, we have dealt with disturbances that are perturbations in the operation of the target system. Next we consider what happens if the *measurements* of the target system are noisy. For example, it may be that under heavy load, certain events are not captured (e.g., if the measurement collection process is low priority).

Figure 8.7 shows how measurement noise is incorporated into the block diagram. There is an additional input $N(z)$ that models the noise process. This signal is added to the output $Y(z)$ to produce $T(z)$.

Figure 8.8 displays the results of simulating the system in Figure 8.7 for the same inputs as in Figure 8.6 and a noise input $n(k) = 5$, $k \geq 10$. The presence

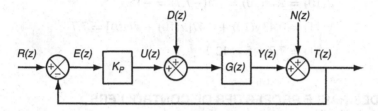

Fig. 8.7 Feedback using proportional control in the presence of measurement noise. There are three inputs: the reference $R(z)$, the disturbance $D(z)$, and measurement noise $N(z)$.

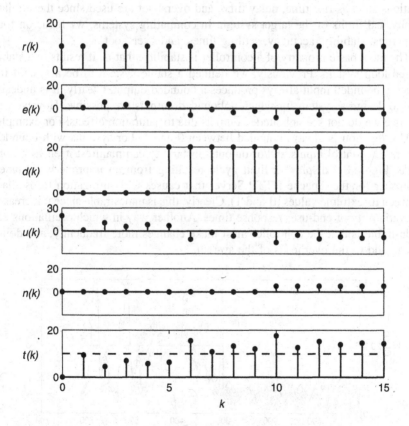

Fig. 8.8 Simulation of a proportional controller for a step response in the presence of a disturbance and noise. Initial conditions are zero. The target system has the transfer function $G(z) = 0.47/(z − 0.43)$, and $K_P = 2$. The dashed line shows the reference value for $y(k)$. $n(k) = 5$ for $k \geq 10$.

of noise changes the output values seen by the controller by adding $n(k)$. Thus, we have

$$t(10) = y(10) + n(10) = 12.7 + 5 = 17.7$$

$$e(10) = r_{ss} - [y(10) + n(10)] = 10 - 17.7 = -7.7$$

$$u(10) = K_p e(10) = (2)(-7.7) = -15.4$$

$$y(11) = 0.43y(10) + 0.47[u(10) + d(10)] = 7.7$$

$$t(11) = 7.7 + 5 = 12.7$$

8.2 DESIRABLE PROPERTIES OF CONTROLLERS

Designing feedback systems requires having clear criteria for what makes one controller preferable to another. In mechanical and electrical engineering, specifications such as rise time, delay time, and overshoot are used since these relate to physical limits of the target system. In computing systems, we focus on four properties: stability, accuracy, settling times, and overshoot.

The most basic property of a controller is stability; that is, it results in a stable closed-loop system. Previously, we defined a stable system to be a system for which a bounded input always produces a bounded output. Clearly, it is undesirable to design a system for which unbounded outputs are possible. However, in practice we do not see unbounded outputs due to saturation effects. For example, CPU utilization is always bounded between 0 and 1. For systems with bounded (saturated) control inputs and/or outputs, instability can manifest itself as a *limit cycle*. Figure 8.9 displays a limit cycle resulting from an improperly designed controller for the Apache HTTP Server that causes CPU utilization to oscillate between its extreme values (0 and 1). Clearly, this is undesirable since it increases the variability of end-user response times. Another way in which oscillations are undesirable is that the controller must make changes more frequently, and doing so can add to the overheads of the system.

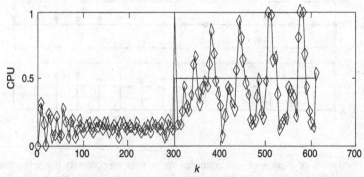

Fig. 8.9 *Example of instability in controlling CPU utilization of the Apache HTTP Server. Note that after the reference changes at $k = 300$, the utilization begins to oscillate between its extreme values of 0 and 1.*

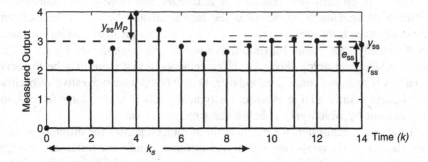

Fig. 8.10 *SASO properties in the step response of a closed-loop system (which is a repetition of Figure 1.3). Stability is consistent with having a bounded output. Accuracy is quantified by the steady-state error e_{ss}, where a larger magnitude indicates greater inaccuracy. Settling time is indicated by K_s. Overshoot is quantified by M_P, the maximum overshoot.*

A second property that we desire in a controller is that it be accurate. We quantify the accuracy of a closed loop in terms of steady-state error. From Figure 8.10, we see that $e_{ss} = r_{ss} - y_{ss}$. An accurate controller is one for which $e_{ss} = 0$, so that the control objective is achieved. For example, poor accuracy is evident in Figure 8.6, in that $r_{ss} = 10 \neq y_{ss}$.

Why is accuracy important? To answer this question, consider a subscription-based e-commerce site that provides different levels of service quality depending on the fees that a customer pays. Suppose that the response-time goals are 2 seconds for "gold customers," 5 seconds for "silver customers," and best efforts (no goal) for "bronze customers." An inaccurate controller might cause one of the following to occur:

1. The response times of silver and/or gold customers might be much smaller than their goals as a result of refusing to serve more bronze customers than could have been served, thereby causing a potential loss of revenue to the service provider. In this situation, $e_{ss} > 0$.

2. The response times of silver and/or gold customers might exceed their goals as a result of serving too many bronze customers, thereby resulting in financial penalties to the service provider. Here, $e_{ss} < 0$.

Although much of the theory we present is concerned only with the magnitude of e_{ss} and not its sign, in practice there are different costs associated with positive and negative errors.

A third property of interest is the *settling time* of the system, the time for the output to reach a new steady-state value after a change in one of the inputs. As shown in Figure 8.10, we use k_s to denote the settling time. Typically, we consider settling time in response to a step input, and we consider the output to have settled when it is within 2% of its steady-state value. Since changes in reference inputs are infrequent, we are particularly interested in the settling time for disturbance inputs (e.g., transient failures and changes in workloads).

The final property we consider is *maximum overshoot*. As indicated in Figure 8.10, maximum overshoot is the largest amount by which the transient response exceeds the steady-state value as a result of a change in an input, scaled by the steady-state value. Maximum overshoot, which we denote by M_P, is of concern when enforcing service-level agreements in that there may be financial penalties if response times are too large. Overshoot is also suggestive of oscillatory behavior since a large overshoot is typically followed by a large undershoot [the amount by which $y(k)$ is below the steady-state value].

To assess a controller, we evaluate these four properties for different parameter choices in the controller design and different conditions (reference change, disturbance, noise, etc.) For example, we commonly consider a step change in the inputs since we can compose arbitrary signals by a sequence of steps. Another consideration is the robustness of the controller to errors in estimating the parameters of the target system. By robustness, we mean the effect on stability as a result of under- or overestimated open-loop poles and/or zeros. For example, in a first-order system such as $G(z) = b/(z - a)$, we might want to know if the closed-loop poles lie within the unit circle if a and b are underestimated by 25%.

8.3 FRAMEWORK FOR ANALYZING PROPORTIONAL CONTROL

In this section we develop a general framework for analyzing the properties of stability, accuracy, settling time, and maximum overshoot. Our analysis framework assumes that there is a transfer function that describes the target system over a desired operating range. Obtaining such a transfer function may require system identification (as described in Chapter 2) and/or the techniques developed in Chapters 4 through 6. This accomplished, we analyze the following properties:

- *S*tability is assessed by determining if the poles of the closed-loop transfer function have a magnitude less than 1.
- *A*ccuracy is quantified by the magnitude of the steady-state control error e_{ss}. We can assess the accuracy of a closed-loop system by computing the steady-state gain of its transfer function from the reference input to the measured output. There is a zero steady-state error if and only if this steady-state gain is 1.
- *S*ettling time is a function of the closed-loop poles and is estimated using Equation (5.18) by employing the dominant pole approximation.
- *O*vershoot is a property of the response to a step change in the reference input. Overshoot occurs if one or more poles with a nonzero angle in the complex plane (although the magnitude of the overshoot involves other factors as well).

We refer to these as the *SASO* properties. The purpose of control analysis is to ascertain the SASO properties of the closed-loop system. The purpose of control design is to construct a closed-loop system with the desired SASO properties.

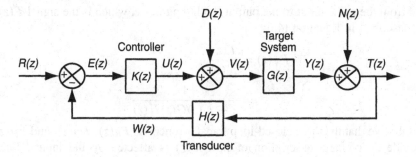

Fig. 8.11 *Block diagram of a closed-loop system (repeated from Figure 4.5).* $R(z)$ *is the reference input,* $D(z)$ *is the disturbance input,* $N(z)$ *is the noise input,* $E(z)$ *is the control error,* $U(z)$ *is the control input, and* $Y(z)$ *is the system output.*

We begin by taking a broader perspective of the system under study by including a measurement transducer (e.g., to describe measurement delays or a moving-average filter). This is shown in Figure 8.11. The inputs are the reference $R(z)$, disturbance $D(z)$, and noise $N(z)$. The processing blocks are the proportional controller K_P, target system $G(z)$, and measurement transducer $H(z)$.

8.3.1 Closed-Loop Transfer Functions

The analysis of the SASO properties requires studying multiple transfer functions. We do this by separately considering the reference, disturbance, and noise inputs. That is, when analyzing one input, the others are set to zero. (Of course, the combined effect of multiple inputs can be obtained easily using the superposition property.)

Recall from Chapter 4 that we denote transfer functions by a subscript that indicates the nonzero input signal and, in some cases, the output signal. From Figure 8.11 the transfer function from the reference input to the measured output is detailed in Equation (4.1):

$$F_R(z) = \frac{Y(z)}{R(z)}$$
$$= \frac{G(z)K(z)}{1 + K(z)G(z)H(z)}$$

the transfer function from the disturbance input to the measured output is specified in Equation (4.4):

$$F_D(z) = \frac{Y(z)}{D(z)}$$
$$= \frac{G(z)}{1 + K(z)G(z)H(z)}$$

and from the noise input to the output [including noise, which is the signal $T(z)$] is described in Equation (4.6):

$$F_N(z) = \frac{T(z)}{N(z)}$$

$$= \frac{1}{1 + K(z)G(z)H(z)}$$

Observe that the three closed-loop transfer functions $F_R(z)$, $F_D(z)$, and $F_N(z)$ provide a complete description of how $Y(z)$ is affected by the inputs. Each of these transfer functions assumes that only one input is nonzero. Using the principle of superposition, the output can be expressed as a sum of the effect of each input. That is,

$$T(z) = F_R(z)R(z) + F_D(z)D(z) + F_N(z)N(z)$$

Thus, we can analyze each transfer function in isolation and greatly simplify the analysis.

Example 8.1: Apache with proportional control   Consider the open-loop transfer function for the Apache HTTP Server from KeepAlive to CPU. The operating point is $(\overline{KA}, \overline{CPU}) = (11, 0.58)$, as described in Chapter 2. Thus, $u(k) = KA(k) - \overline{KA}$, and $y(k) = CPU(k) - \overline{CPU}$.

$$G(z) = \frac{Y(z)}{U(z)} = \frac{-0.014}{z - 0.59}$$

We use the foregoing to obtain the closed-loop transfer functions under proportional control. Substituting into Equation (4.1) and simplifying, we have

$$F_R(z) = \frac{Y(z)}{R(z)} = \frac{K_P(-0.014)}{z - 0.59 + K_P(-0.014)}$$

From Equation (4.4), we have

$$F_D(z) = \frac{Y(z)}{D(z)} = \frac{-0.014}{z - 0.59 + K_P(-0.014)}$$

and from Equation (4.6), we have

$$F_N(z) = \frac{T(z)}{N(z)} = \frac{z - 0.59}{z - 0.59 + K_P(-0.014)}$$

Note that $H(z) = 1$ in all of the foregoing.

Observe that *the three transfer functions have the same poles*, the values of z for which $1 + K_P G(z)H(z) = 0$. Thus, we only need to analyze one set of poles to assess stability, settling time, and maximum overshoot. The analysis of the pole-related properties of the system of Figure 8.11 requires studying specific plant and transducer transfer functions $G(z)$ and $H(z)$, although a first- or second-order approximation of the closed-loop characteristic polynomial can be useful for estimating these properties.

8.3.2 Stability

The stability of the closed-loop system is determined by the closed-loop poles. From the foregoing, we see that all of the transfer functions we consider have the same poles, which are the solutions to the characteristic equation

$$1 + K_P G(z) H(z) = 0 \tag{8.3}$$

The values of the closed-loop poles depend not only on the plant and transducer transfer functions $G(z)$ and $H(z)$, but also on the value of the proportional gain K_P. The system is stable in closed loop if all of the poles have magnitude less than 1.

One method for visualizing how the closed-loop poles depend on K_P is to plot the *root locus* of the system. This graphical approach is used to plot all possible locations of the solutions of Equation (8.3) as K_P varies from 0 to ∞. For simplicity in the following, assume that $H(z) = 1$ and that

$$G(z) = \frac{b_1 z^{-1} + \cdots + b_m z^{-m}}{1 - a_1 z^{-1} - \cdots - a_n z^{-n}}$$

In this case, Equation (8.3) becomes

$$1 + K_P G(z) = 0 \tag{8.4}$$

Note that there are always n solutions to Equation (8.4), the same number as the number of poles in $G(z)$ (for any physical system, $n \geq m$). Consider first the limit as $K_P \to 0$. We can rewrite Equation (8.4) as

$$\frac{1}{G(z)} + K_P = 0$$

Since $G(z)$ is inverted, in the limit as $K_P \to 0$, the solutions to Equation (8.4) are the *poles* of $G(z)$. To consider the limit as $K_P \to \infty$, we rewrite Equation (8.4) as

$$\frac{1}{K_P} + G(z) = 0$$

Hence, in the limit as $K_P \to \infty$, the solutions to Equation (8.4) are the *zeros* of $G(z)$. If $G(z)$ has m finite zeros and n poles, it is considered that $G(z)$ has $n - m$ zeros at infinity. Note that if $m < n$, $\lim_{z \to \infty} G(z) = 0$. The solutions to Equation (8.4) are also continuous; that is, a small change in K_P gives only a small change in the solutions.

The root locus is, as its name implies, the locations of all possible roots of Equation (8.4) as K_P varies from 0 to ∞. There are n branches in the root locus, one for each pole of $G(z)$. Each branch starts at a pole of $G(z)$ and ends at a zero (either finite or at infinity). Note that any system that has at least one zero at infinity will always become unstable in closed loop for a large enough value of K_P. Thus, stability is an important property to verify. A number of rules have been developed to facilitate drawing the root locus [25], or a computer program such as MATLAB can be used. In the case when $H(z) \neq 1$, $G(z)$ in Equation (8.4) can be replaced by $G(z)H(z)$ and the same procedure is followed. The closed-loop system has as many poles as the combined number of poles in $G(z)H(z)$, and each branch of the root locus starts at one of the poles of $G(z)$ or $H(z)$ and ends at one of the zeros (finite or at infinity).

Example 8.2: Root locus of the IBM Lotus Domino Server with measurement delay   Consider the IBM Lotus Domino Server, a first-order system with $a = 0.43$, $b = 0.47$ with a two-time-unit measurement delay. The system transfer functions are

$$G(z) = \frac{Y(z)}{U(z)} = \frac{0.47}{z - 0.43}$$

$$H(z) = \frac{Y(z)}{V(z)} = \frac{1}{z^2}$$

There are three open-loop poles; two at 0 and one at 0.43. There are no finite zeros; thus, all three zeros are at infinity. The root locus of this system is shown in Figure 8.12. The branches of the root locus, indicating the locations of the closed-loop poles, start at the open-loop poles (indicated by "×") and move to the zeros at infinity as K_p increases. Since there are two open-loop poles at $z = 0$ (corresponding to the two-time-unit measurement delay), there are two branches of the root locus that start at the origin (the third branch starts at the pole $z = 0.43$). The unit circle is also shown as a dotted line in the root locus plot. The closed-loop system becomes unstable at the smallest value of K_p such that one of the poles is outside the unit circle, in this case, at $K_p = 1.7$.

8.3.3 Accuracy

The accuracy of a proportional controller can be analyzed in a very general way, since it is independent of the pole locations (as long as they are all inside the

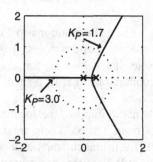

Fig. 8.12   *Root locus plot for the IBM Lotus Domino Server with a measurement delay of two time units. The solid lines indicate the closed-loop poles that occur as K_P varies from 0 to ∞; the dotted line is the unit circle. The values of K_P when the branches cross the unit circle are indicated on the plot.*

unit circle). Let $F_R(z) = Y(z)/R(z)$ be the transfer function from the reference input to the output of a stable feedback control system. Let $r(k)$ be the reference input with steady-state value r_{ss}. We claim that this system has $e_{ss} = 0$ if, and only if, $F_R(1) = 1$. To see this, note that

$$e_{ss} = \lim_{k \to \infty} r(k) - y(k) = r_{ss} - y_{ss}$$

Recall that $F_R(1) = y_{ss}/r_{ss}$ is the steady-state gain. Thus,

$$e_{ss} = r_{ss}[1 - F_R(1)] \tag{8.5}$$

So $e_{ss} = 0$ if, and only if, $F_R(1) = 1$.
Thus, we want

$$1 = \frac{K_P G(1)}{1 + H(1) K_P G(1)}.$$

so $e_{ss} = 0$ only if

$$K_P = \frac{1}{G(1)(1 - H(1))}.$$

Clearly, if $H(1) = 1$, then K_P must be infinite. Unfortunately, $H(1) = 1$ is very common. For example, $H(1) = 1$ if there is an n-time-unit delay or if the output is filtered using a moving average to reduce noise. *If $H(1) = 1$, then proportional control results in $|e_{ss}| > 0$; steady-state control error can be reduced by using a larger K_P.*
We are also interested in the steady-state gain of $F_D(z)$ and $F_N(z)$. Here, however, we want the steady-state gains to be 0 so that we can eliminate constant disturbances and noise. For the disturbance input,

$$F_D(1) = 0$$
$$= \frac{G(1)}{1 + K_P G(1) H(1)}$$

and the steady-state error to a constant disturbance input d_{ss} is

$$e_{ss} = d_{ss} F_D(1) \tag{8.6}$$

This means that we are more effective at rejecting disturbances if K_P is large.
The situation for noise proceeds as with the disturbance. We want $F_N(1) = 0$. That is,

$$F_N(1) = 0$$
$$= \frac{1}{1 + K_P G(1) H(1)}$$

Thus, we want a larger K_P in order to eliminate noise. Note that a smaller K_P means a larger e_{ss} and less effective elimination of disturbances. This type of steady-state analysis of noise and disturbances is only useful for constant values of n and d. Although disturbances are often constant, noise is usually time varying, and hence a thorough treatment of noise requires a frequency-domain analysis, which is beyond the scope of this book.

8.3.4   Settling Time

The settling time of a system depends on the magnitude of the largest closed-loop pole. The closer the pole is to the unit circle, the longer the system takes to settle. As noted in Chapters 5 and 6, a system that has a pole with magnitude r contributes a term of the form r^k to the transient response. This term is less than 2% of its maximum value when $k > -4/\log r$.

Using the dominant pole approximation, we estimate settling time from Equation (5.18):

$$k_s \approx \frac{-4}{\log r} \tag{8.7}$$

where $r = \max_i |p_i|$ is the magnitude of the largest closed-loop pole.

8.3.5   Maximum Overshoot

The *maximum overshoot* is the absolute value of the largest difference between the output signal and its steady-state value, divided by the steady-state value. We use M_P to denote the maximum overshoot to a unit step input. Let $y_{\max}$ be the maximum value of $y(k)$ in response to a step. If $y_{\max} \leq y_{ss}$, then $M_P = 0$. Otherwise, $M_P = |y_{\max} - y_{ss}|/|y_{ss}|$. M_P is defined only for a change in the reference input.

We can estimate M_P from the transfer function $G(z)$ using the first- and second-order transfer functions of Chapters 5 and 6. First, consider a stable system with transfer function $G(z)$, and suppose that p_1 is the dominant pole. If p_1 is real, we can use Equation (3.30) to approximate $G(z)$ by a first-order system $G'(z)$ with a pole at p_1 and the same steady-state gain as $G(z)$:

$$G'(z) = \frac{(1 - p_1)G(1)}{z - p_1}$$

This is an accurate approximation if p_1 is a dominant pole. If $p_1 > 0$, our estimate is that $M_P = 0$. Otherwise, from Equation (5.13), our estimate is that $M_P = |p_1|$.

If p_1 is complex, there are a pair of complex poles, $p_1, p_2 = re^{\pm j\theta}$, with magnitude r and angle θ. We approximate $G(z)$ by a second-order system $G'(z)$

with poles at p_1, p_2 and the same steady-state gain as $G(z)$:

$$G'(z) = \frac{K'}{(z - p_1)(z - p_2)} = \frac{K'}{z^2 - (2r \cos\theta)z + r^2}$$

where $K' = (1 - 2r \cos\theta + r^2)G(1)$. From Equation (6.16), a conservative estimate of the maximum overshoot of the second-order system is given by $M_p = r^{\pi/|\theta|}$. In summary, we have

$$M_p \approx \begin{cases} 0 & \text{real dominant pole } p_1 \geq 0 \\ |p_1| & \text{real dominant pole } p_1 < 0 \\ r^{\pi/|\theta|} & \text{dominant poles } p_1, p_2 = re^{\pm j\theta} \end{cases} \quad (8.8)$$

Zeros in the transfer function can substantially increase the overshoot. If there are finite zeros (other than at 0), more detailed analysis or simulation should be used to find the maximum overshoot.

8.4 P-CONTROL: ROBUSTNESS, DELAYS, AND FILTERS

In this section we analyze three systems: a first-order target system, a first-order system with measurement delay, and a first-order system with measurement delay and a moving-average filter.

8.4.1 First-Order Target System

In this subsection we study the pole-related properties of proportional control of a first-order target system. Studying a first-order system is in part motivated by simplicity. It is also motivated by our experience that a first-order model provides a fairly accurate description of the control characteristics of many real-world systems, including the Apache HTTP Server and the IBM Lotus Domino Server.

Figure 8.13 displays a block diagram of the control system we consider. This is a special case of Figure 8.11 in which $G(z) = b/(z - a)$ and $H(z) = 1$. Since we focus on the poles and all the closed-loop transfer functions have the same

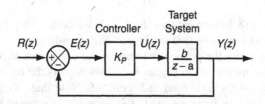

Fig. 8.13 Proportional control of a first-order system.

poles, it suffices to consider $F_R(z)$. Substituting into Equation (4.1), we obtain

$$F_R(z) = \frac{Y(z)}{R(z)} = \frac{K_p b}{z - a + K_p b} \tag{8.9}$$

The poles are the roots of $z - a + K_p b$. That is,

$$p = a - K_p b \tag{8.10}$$

and hence from Equation (8.7), the settling time is

$$k_s = \frac{-4}{\log(a - K_p b)} \tag{8.11}$$

This result provides insights into Figure 8.6. We see that $p = a - K_p b = 0.43 - (2)(0.47) = -0.51$. Since the pole lies within the unit circle, the closed-loop system is stable. Using Equation (3.29), we conclude that the steady-state response to a unit step is $K_p b/(1 - a - K_p b) = 0.62$, which is consistent with $y(5)$. Also, note that the pole is less than 0. This explains both the oscillations and the overshoot in the output $y(k)$.

$F_R(z)$ is a first-order system with input $R(z)$ and output $Y(z)$. Its time-domain solution can be found using Equation (5.1):

$$y(k) = (a - K_p b)^k y(0) + K_p b \sum_{n=0}^{k-1} (a - K_p b)^{k-1} r(n)$$

For a unit step input and zero initial conditions, we have

$$y(k) = K_p b \frac{1 - (a - K_p b)^k}{1 - a + K_p b} \tag{8.12}$$

Using a, b, and K_p as in Figure 8.6, we obtain

$$y(k) = (0.94)\frac{1 - (-0.51)^k}{1.51}, \qquad k \geq 0$$

For example,

$$y(1) = (0.94)\frac{1 - (-0.51)^1}{1.51} = (0.94)\frac{1.51}{1.51} = 0.94$$

From Equation (8.10) we see how K_p affects the closed-loop poles. A small K_p results in a closed-loop pole that is close to the open-loop pole. However, larger values of K_p can cause the poles to be outside the unit circle, thereby resulting in instability. This is quantified in Figure 8.14, which plots the relationship between K_p and the pole for the a, b used in Figure 8.6. Note that $K_p > 0$ because we must increase $u(k)$ to increase $y(k)$. For example, we know that MaxUsers must be increased to increase the number of active users in the IBM Lotus

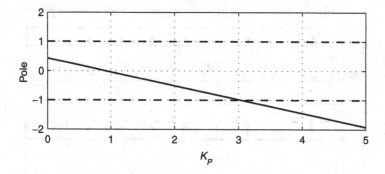

Fig. 8.14 *Effect of K_P on the closed-loop pole of a first-order target system with $a = 0.43$ and $b = 0.47$.*

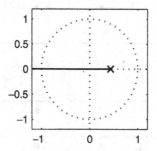

Fig. 8.15 *Effect of K_P on the closed-loop pole of a first-order target system $G(z) = 0.47/(z - 0.43)$. The $\times$ shows the location of the pole when $K_P = 0$. The unit circle is shown to indicate the stability boundary.*

Domino Server. Also, it makes little sense to have $K_P = 0$ since this means that there is no feedback control. Indeed, $K_P = 0$ results in $F_R(z) = 0$.

Another way to visualize the effect of K_P on the closed-loop system is to plot the root locus, the location of the pole as K_P is varied. The location of the closed-loop pole in the complex plane varies with K_P . This is shown in Figure 8.15. At $K_P = 0$, the pole is at a. As K_P increases, the pole gets smaller and then becomes negative. When the pole goes outside the unit circle, the closed-loop system becomes unstable.

The time-domain effects of K_P are illustrated in Figure 8.16. With $K_P = 1$, the convergence to steady state occurs within one time step. To see why, note that Figure 8.14 shows that the closed-loop pole is approximately 0 if $K_P = 1$. Not surprisingly, with a small K_P, $|e_{ss}|$ is large (as seen in Figure 8.16). For $K_P = 2$, in Figure 8.16, we see overshoot and oscillations. This is also explained in Figure 8.14 by the fact that the pole is $-0.5 < 0$. For $K_P = 3$, the pole is -1 and $y(k)$ oscillates between two values. At $K_P = 3.5$, the pole is -1.25 and the system is unstable.

It is straightforward to construct a bound for a and b so as to ensure the stability of the closed-loop system. The closed-loop system is stable if its poles

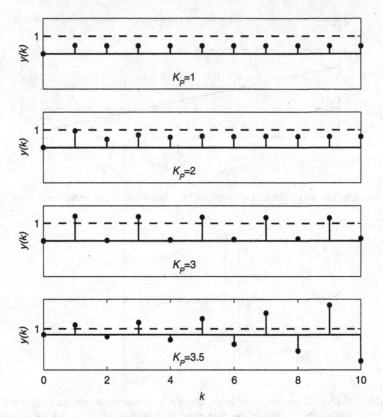

Fig. 8.16 *Time-domain, unit step response for proportional control of a first-order target system with a = 0.43 and b = 0.47. Larger values of K_P improve accuracy but can lead to instability.*

lie within the unit circle. That is, $|a - K_p b| < 1$. Assuming that $0 < a \le 1$ (which has been the case in our studies), we have

$$\frac{a-1}{b} < K_P < \frac{1+a}{b}$$

If $b > 0$, this simplifies to

$$0 \le K_P < \frac{1+a}{b}$$

Often, we are unable to estimate accurately the parameters of the target system, such as a, b in a first-order system. Thus, an important consideration in choosing K_p is robustness. A controller is *robust* if its behavior does not change much if there are errors in estimating the parameters of the target system.

Figure 8.17 shows how the closed-loop pole changes if a and b are over- or under-estimated. In both plots, the true values of a and b are 0.43 and 0.47, respectively. Consider the bottom plot, which addresses the effect of errors in estimating b. If the true value of b is 0.47, the middle (solid) line expresses the

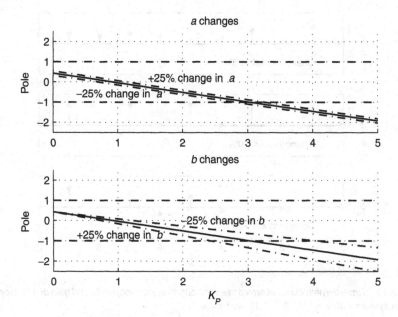

Fig. 8.17 *Robustness of proportional control to errors in estimating the open-loop pole and gain of a first-order target system with $a = 0.43$, $b = 0.47$. The top plot shows how the closed-loop pole changes with errors in estimating the open-loop pole. The bottom plot shows how the closed-loop pole is affected by errors in estimating b. The solid line is with no change; it is the same line as in Figure 8.14.*

relationship between K_p and the closed-loop pole (this is the same line as in Figure 8.14). Now consider the case in which the estimated value of b is 25% smaller than its true value. That is, we estimate $b = 0.35$ instead of $b = 0.47$. The lower dashed-dotted line shows how this error in estimating b changes the predicted effect of K_p on the closed-loop pole. In particular, we predict smaller-magnitude closed-loop poles. As a result, we predict that the system becomes unstable at $K_p \approx 4$. In fact, the system goes unstable at $K_p = 3$. Thus, by underestimating b we might mistakenly choose K_p that causes the system to go unstable.

Now consider the case where the estimated b is 25% greater than its true value; that is, we use $b = 0.59$ instead of $b = 0.47$. Here, the predicted closed-loop poles are larger than the true closed-loop poles. This leads to a more conservative selection of the control gain K_p.

The top plot in Figure 8.17 studies the effect of errors in estimating a, the open-loop pole. First, observe that the effect is much less pronounced than for b in that the three lines lie very close together. Also note that the direction of the effect is the opposite of that for b. That is, a smaller open-loop pole *increases* the magnitude of the closed-loop pole.

Figure 8.18 displays the time-domain effects of having a fixed percentage change in both a and b. Because $a \approx b$ and $K_p > 1$, errors in estimating b dominate the effect on the closed-loop pole.

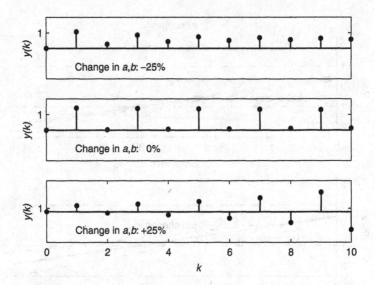

Fig. 8.18 *Time-domain effect of errors in estimating the open-loop pole and gain of a first-order target system with $a = 0.43$, $b = 0.47$, and $K_P = 3$.*

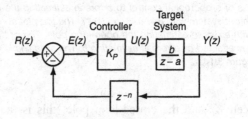

Fig. 8.19 *Proportional control of a first-order system with measurement delay.*

8.4.2 Measurement Delay

Measurement delays are common in computing systems. For example, the IBM Lotus Domino Server described in Chapter 1 has measurement delays due to RPCs not being recorded until their processing is completed. In this section we analyze the effect of measurement delays on closed-loop poles.

We study measurement delays in the context of Figure 8.19, which extends Figure 8.13 by including a delay block in the feedback loop. Measurement delays are one example of how the output signal may be transformed before it is seen by the controller. Such transformations are indicated in Figure 8.11 by the block labeled $H(z)$. In the case of measurement delays, $H(z) = z^{-n}$, where n is delay in units of sample times. Adjusting Equation (8.9), we have

$$F_R(z) = \frac{Y(z)}{R(z)} = \frac{K_P[b/(z-a)]}{1 + z^{-n}K_P[b/(z-a)]}$$

$$= \frac{z^n K_P b}{(z-a)z^n + K_P b}$$

Note that there are $n+1$ poles since the degree of z in the denominator is $n+1$. Also, note that measurement delays do not affect steady-state gain and hence accuracy. To see this, recall that steady-state gain of the measurement delay is $H(1) = 1^n = 1$.

Consider $n = 1$. Here, the poles are solutions to the characteristic equation $z^2 - za + K_p b = 0$. We denote these solutions by

$$p_1, p_2 = \frac{a}{2} \pm \frac{\sqrt{a^2 - 4K_p b}}{2}$$

Note that if $a^2 > 4K_p b$, the poles are real. Further, if $a > 0$ (which has been the most common case in our experience), the pole with the largest magnitude is

$$\frac{a}{2} + \frac{\sqrt{a^2 - 4K_p b}}{2}$$

We can use this pole in Equation (8.7) to approximate settling times. (The approximation works best if settling times are short and/or the two poles are far apart.) If $a^2 < 4K_p b$, there is a pair of complex conjugate poles. Since both poles have the same magnitude, k_s can be computed using either pole.

Figure 8.20 displays the effect of n on the position of the largest pole as K_p is varied for $a = 0.43$ and $b = 0.47$. With $n \geq 1$, we can get complex poles. Thus, we plot both the magnitude r and angle θ of the largest pole. Observe that increasing n increases r as well (at least within the region in which the system

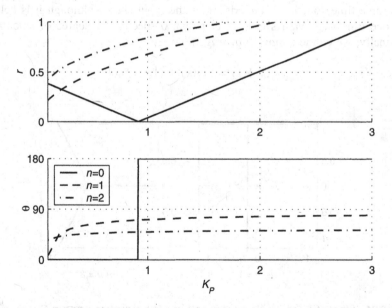

Fig. 8.20 Effect of K_P on the magnitude r and angle θ of the largest pole for different values of pure delay (n) and $G(z) = 0.47/(z - 0.43)$. Note that increasing n increases the magnitude of the largest pole and hence increases settling time.

is stable). Also observe that if K_p is sufficiently large, we have a nonzero pole angle. For $n = 0$, a large K_p results in an angle of 180 degrees, which means that the pole is negative. The solid line in Figure 8.20 is the same as Figure 8.14; there is only one pole and it is either positive or negative. For $n = 1, 2$, the angles indicate that the poles have a nonzero imaginary part. Another important observation is that increasing the measurement delay n *decreases* the region of K_p values where the closed-loop system is stable.

Another way to visualize the effect of K_p on the behavior of the closed-loop system is to plot the root locus, as in Figure 8.21. For $n = 1$, there are two poles (the roots of $z^2 - za + K_p b$), and for $n = 2$ there are three poles. This representation has the advantage of showing all the poles, not just the largest; on the other hand, it does not explicitly show the values of K_p.

8.4.3   Moving-Average Filter

As noted in the simulation in Figure 8.8, the presence of noise can severely impair the operation of the controller. In computing systems, noise typically takes the form of a random variations around a mean. An effective way to reduce such variations is to smooth the signal with a moving-average filter. In this section we extend the control system of Section 8.4.2 to include such a filter.

The input of the moving-average filter is the "raw" signal and its output is a smoothed signal. We begin by being more precise about the filter. Let $y(k)$ be the unfiltered signal and let $w(k)$ be its filtered version. The operation of the filter is described by a single constant, c, where $0 \leq c < 1$. If $c = 0$, the output has the same time-domain characteristics as the input signal, although it is delayed by one time step. Values of c greater than 0 specify the degree of smoothing. Formally, we define a *moving-average filter* as

$$w(k + 1) = cw(k) + (1 - c)y(k)$$

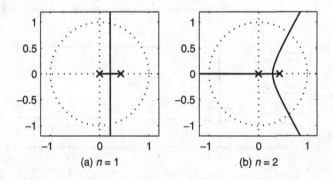

Fig. 8.21   *Effect of K_P on the closed-loop pole of a first-order target system $G(z) = \dfrac{0.47}{z - 0.43}$ with measurement delay. The $\times$ shows the location of the poles when $K_P = 0$. The unit circle is shown to indicate the stability boundary.*

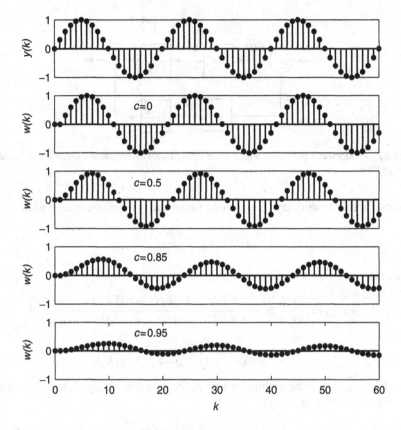

Fig. 8.22 *Effect of a moving-average filter on a sine wave for different values of the filter parameter c. Note that c = 0 corresponds to a delay of one sample time.*

This has the transfer function

$$H(z) = \frac{W(z)}{Y(z)} = \frac{1-c}{z-c}$$

Figure 8.22 illustrates the effect of a moving-average filter on a sine wave. Note that the frequency of the wave does not change, nor does its mean value. However, as c increases, the amplitude of the wave decreases. Also note that the phase of the wave shifts as c increases in that peaks and valleys move to the right. This indicates that the filter affects the transient response. Finally, observe that the steady-state gain of this filter is 1 (which is why the mean value of the output signal is the same as that of the input signal). This is by design so that the filter does not affect accuracy. Sometimes, variations on this filter are used, such as $w(k+1) = cw(k) + y(k)$. Such a filter has a transfer function of $1/(z-c)$, which can affect accuracy.

Figure 8.23 describes the system we analyze. It augments the one in Section 8.4.2 by including the filter just described. The measurement transducer

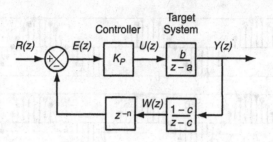

Fig. 8.23 *Proportional control of a first-order system with measurement delay and a moving-average filter.*

includes both a time delay of n sample times and a moving-average filter,

$$H(z) = z^{-n}\frac{1-c}{z-c}$$

Thus, the closed-loop transfer function is

$$F_R(z) = \frac{Y(z)}{R(z)} = \frac{K_P[b/(z-a)]}{1 + z^{-n}[(1-c)/(z-c)]K_P[b/(z-a)]}$$

$$= \frac{K_P b z^n (z-c)}{z^n (z-c)(z-a) + (1-c)K_P b}$$

As before, there may be multiple poles. Also, note that steady-state gain is unaffected by the value of c since

$$F_R(1) = \frac{K_P b(1-c)}{(1-c)(1-a) + (1-c)K_P b}$$

$$= \frac{K_P b}{(1-a) + K_P b}$$

Figure 8.24 shows how the filter parameter c affects the magnitude r and angle θ of the largest closed-loop pole. The top three plots show how the magnitude of the largest pole is affected by K_P, and the bottom three plots show the effect on the angle of the largest pole. We consider $c = 0, 0.5, 0.95$. Since $c = 0$ is a pure time delay, $(c = 0, n = 0)$ in Figure 8.24 is the same as $n = 1$ in Figure 8.20, and $(c = 0, n = 1)$ in Figure 8.24 is the same as $n = 2$ in Figure 8.20.

A few observations are of interest. First, note that within the region in which the system is stable (i.e., all poles have a magnitude less than 1), increasing the delay (n) increases the magnitude of the largest pole. This is consistent with the results of Section 8.4.2. Also note that increasing c causes r to decrease for $c \in \{0, 0.5\}$. However, the behavior for $c = 0.95$ is more complicated due to the relationship between the open-loop pole and the pole of the filter. (This is explored in more depth in an exercise at the end of the chapter.) Another effect of a larger c is to reduce θ. This is particularly noticeable for $c = 0.95$, where $\theta = 0$ until $K_P = 2$. Thus, increasing c increases the region over which

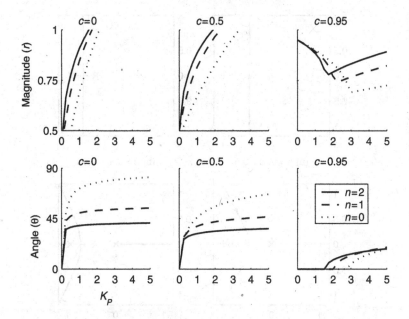

Fig. 8.24 Effect of controller gain K_P, number of time delays n, and filter parameter c on the magnitude r and angle θ of the largest closed-loop pole. The target system is first-order with $a = 0.43$ and $b = 0.47$.

the closed-loop system is stable. On the other hand, a moving-average filter with $c = 0.95$ introduces an open-loop pole at 0.95 and hence slows down the closed-loop response considerably, especially for small values of K_P.

Another way to visualize the effect of the filter on the closed-loop system is to plot all of the closed-loop poles simultaneously in the complex plane using the root locus. Since $c = 0$ is a pure time delay, we focus on $c = 0.5$ and $c = 0.95$. Figure 8.25 shows the pole locations as K_P varies. For $n = 0$, there are two poles in the closed-loop system, and for $n = 1$ there are three closed-loop poles. When $K_P = 0$, the closed-loop poles are at a, c, and 0 (if there is a time delay). As K_P increases, the poles move and eventually cross the unit circle (indicating an unstable closed-loop system).

8.5 DESIGN OF PROPORTIONAL CONTROLLERS

Thus far, our goal has been to determine closed-loop poles based on knowing one or more open-loop transfer functions. The next step is design—choosing K_P so that the resulting system has desirable properties, such as a small steady-state error and short settling times.

Considered first is pole placement design, which selects controller parameters that result in desired closed-loop poles. Pole placement starts by determining the desired poles based on the SASO properties of the closed-loop system. Then the closed-loop transfer function is constructed as a function of the proportional gain

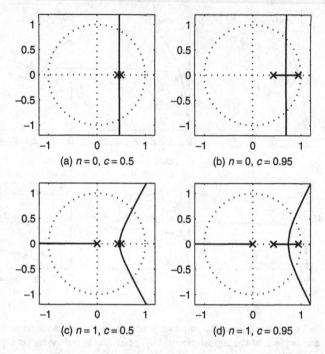

Fig. 8.25 Effect of K_P on the closed-loop pole of a first-order target system $G(z) = Y(z)/U(z) = 0.47/z - 0.43$ with measurement delay. The $\times$ shows the location of the poles when $K_P = 0$. The unit circle is shown to indicate the stability boundary.

K_P. Next, we solve for the closed-loop poles in terms of K_P. Last, the modeled poles are set equal to the desired poles, which allows us to derive K_P.

An alternative approach to determining K_P is to plot the properties of steady-state error, settling time, and maximum overshoot as a function of K_P. Note that since there is only one parameter K_P and there may be many desired properties, a solution may not exist. In this case, an alternative control strategy may be needed, or some of the design goals must be relaxed.

We illustrate the pole placement procedure with a simple example.

Example 8.3: Proportional control of the IBM Lotus Domino Server Consider the IBM Lotus Domino Server, with transfer function

$$G(z) = \frac{Y(z)}{U(z)} = \frac{0.47}{z - 0.43} \tag{8.13}$$

Recall that $y(k)$ is the offset of RPCs in the system (RIS) from the operating point, and $u(k)$ is the offset of MaxUsers from the operating point. We consider four design goals:

1. Stability
2. Steady-state error to unit step reference $e_{ss} < 0.1$

3. Settling time $k_s < 10$

4. Maximum overshoot to unit step reference $M_p < 0.1$

With proportional control (as in Figure 8.5), the closed-loop transfer function from the reference to the output is

$$F_R(z) = \frac{Y(z)}{R(z)} = \frac{0.47K_p}{z - 0.43 + 0.47K_p}$$

We consider the four design goals individually. First, for stability, we must have all closed-loop poles inside the unit circle. The closed-loop transfer function is first order, and hence there is only one closed-loop pole, $p_1 = 0.43 - 0.47\ K_p$. Considering the stability condition,

$$|p_1| = |0.43 - 0.47K_p| < 1$$

we solve for the conditions on K_p to be

$$-1.21 < K_p < 3.0$$

Now, consider steady-state error. From Equation (8.5) we have

$$e_{ss} = r_{ss}[1 - F_R(1)]$$

The condition is for a unit step reference, and hence $r_{ss} = 1$. Setting $e_{ss} < 0.1$, we have

$$e_{ss} = 1 - F_R(1) = 1 - \frac{0.47K_p}{1 - 0.43 + 0.47K_p} < 0.1$$

$$\frac{0.47K_p}{0.57 + 0.47K_p} > 0.9$$

$$K_p > 10.9$$

Recall that the steady-state error condition is derived from the final value theorem, and that theorem is valid only if the system is stable. From the first result we see that if $K_p > 3.0$, the system is unstable. Hence, the steady-state error condition cannot be satisfied with any value of K_p.

The settling time depends on the magnitude of the largest closed-loop pole. Since there is only one pole, we have from Equation (8.7) that

$$k_s \approx \frac{-4}{\log |0.43 - 0.47K_p|} < 10$$

$$-0.4 > \log |0.43 - 0.47K_p|$$

$$e^{-0.4} = 0.67 > |0.43 - 0.47K_p|$$

With the absolute value, we get two inequalities: $0.67 > 0.43 - 0.47K_p > -0.67$, which simplifies to $-0.51 < K_p < 2.3$.

Finally, we consider maximum overshoot. Since the system is first order, the pole is always real. If it is positive, there is no overshoot; there is overshoot only if it is negative. We use Equation (8.8) to estimate

$$M_P = |0.43 - 0.47K_P| < 0.1$$

which results in $K_P < 1.1$.

To summarize, the desired properties of the closed-loop system impose the following constraints on K_P:

1. Stability: $-1.21 < K_P < 3.0$
2. $e_{ss} < 0.1$: $K_P > 10.9$
3. $k_s < 10$: $-0.51 < K_P < 2.3$
4. $M_P < 0.1$: $K_P < 1.1$

While the desired bound on steady-state error cannot be achieved, the other properties are obtained if $-0.51 < K_P < 1.1$.

Root locus analysis provides considerable insight into how the closed-loop poles are affected by K_P. However, to use this information for design purposes, there is another step—showing the relationship between pole values and system properties of interest. Indeed, for some properties, knowing the values of the poles is not sufficient. In particular, e_{ss} depends on the steady-state gain.

These considerations motivate another approach in which we study the system properties of interest directly. Figure 8.26 plots the steady-state error (e_{ss}), settling time (k_s), and maximum overshoot (M_P) of the system in Equation (8.13) as K_P changes from 0 to 2. From Section 8.3, e_{ss} is a function of steady-state gain (which is computed from the transfer function). Settling time is computed by only considering the largest pole and using Equation (5.18). Maximum overshoot is obtained using the estimation in Equation (8.8).

A few observations are of interest. The ideal e_{ss} is 0, but we barely fall below 0.5 for the range of K_P values considered. The rationale for not considering larger K_P is clear from the plot of settling time. For $K_P > 1.5$, settling times increase dramatically. Also note that for this system, M_P increases almost linearly with K_P (at least for $K_P > 0.25$). Thus, we can reduce settling time and maximum overshoot by having a smaller K_P, although this is done at the expense of accuracy in that e_{ss} is larger.

The foregoing suggests a procedure for controller design:

1. Determine the K_P at which e_{ss} does not change much. In Figure 8.26, this is $K_P \in [0.75, 2.0]$.
2. Determine the K_P for which k_s is acceptable. In Figure 8.26, this is $K_P \in [0, 1]$.
3. Take the intersection of the two regions, which is $[0.75, 1.0]$ in our example.
4. Choose the K_P within this range such that M_P is minimized. In the figure, this is $K_P = 0.75$.

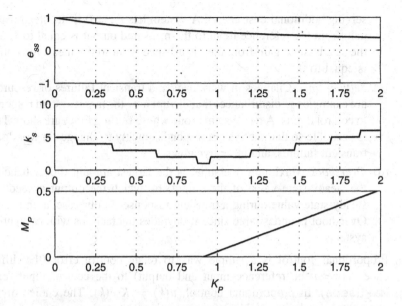

Fig. 8.26 *Plots used in analyzing trade-offs in the value of K_P for the IBM Lotus Domino Server, and a two-time-unit measurement delay ($n = 2$). Ideally, K_P is chosen so that $|e_{ss}|$, k_S, and M_P are small. In practice, trade-offs are required.*

Although such a procedure has appeal for a proportional controller, proportional control is rarely used in practice. In Chapter 9 we discuss design techniques for more commonly used controllers, especially the widely used proportional–integral (PI) controller.

8.6 SUMMARY

1. Regulatory feedback control provides a way to maintain a desired output value without precise knowledge of the characteristics of the target system. For example, Section 8.1 shows that feedback control can compensate for a disturbance of unknown magnitude.

2. The SASO properties of controllers are of most interest in computing systems.

   (a) *Stability.* Our formal definition of stability is that all bounded inputs produce bounded outputs. However, in practice, instabilities may be manifested as limit cycles in which the output alternates between extreme values.

   (b) *Accuracy.* An accurate system is one for which the output is equal to the reference input. Hence, $e_{ss} = 0$. Accuracy is desirable, for example, in service differentiation so that customers receive the service they paid for, but no more (e.g., if the service provider could obtain revenue by serving additional customers). A system has $e_{ss} = 0$ if its steady-state gain from the reference input to the measured output is equal to 1, and the steady-state gain from the disturbance input to the measured output is equal to 0.

(c) *Settling time*. Changes in workloads and transient failures of resources are examples of disturbances that disrupt how the target system responds to control inputs. A fast system is one whose settling times are short. This is desirable so that the system responds quickly to changes in workload, transient failures, and other dynamics.

(d) *Overshoot*. Maximum overshoot is the largest amount (normalized by the steady-state value of the output) by which the output exceeds its steady-state value during a transient response (in our case, a unit step). Overshoot is undesirable since it degrades interactions with computing systems.

3. Proportional control is a simple way to relate control error (the difference between the reference input and output) to the control input (e.g., MaxUsers). In proportional control, $u(k) = K_p e(k)$. The choice of K_p constitutes the design problem for proportional control.

4. Proportional control is inherently inaccurate in that $|e_{ss}| > 0$ for a step input. However, $|e_{ss}|$ decreases as K_p increases.

5. The properties of stability, settling times, and maximum overshoot are all related to the poles of the transfer function.

(a) The system is stable if the poles lie within the unit circle.

(b) Settling times are shorter for poles closer to 0.

(c) The approximation in Section 8.3.5 suggests that M_p increases with pole magnitude and increases with the angle of the pole.

6. Choosing K_p involves trade-offs. A larger K_p improves accuracy (i.e., decreases e_{ss}). However, a sufficiently large K_p increases the magnitude of the closed-loop pole. This causes settling time and possibly the maximum overshoot to increase and may cause instability.

7. Root locus analysis is a graphical approach to showing how poles change as K_p is varied.

8.7 EXTENDED EXAMPLES

In this section we present several examples of using proportional control and explore issues with its application.

8.7.1 IBM Lotus Domino Server with a Moving-Average Filter

The stochastic nature of resource consumption in computing systems typically results in substantial variability, especially for performance metrics such as response

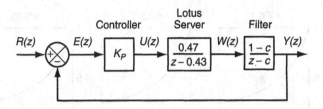

Fig. 8.27 Block diagram of feedback control of the IBM Lotus Domino Server. A moving-average filter is used to reduce the effect of stochastics.

times, queue lengths, and utilizations. Stochastics in a feedback loop make it difficult to separate the true dynamics (signal) from random variations (noise). Often, a moving-average filter is used to mitigate the effect of stochastics. In this example we study the effect of such a filter on the performance of a proportional controller for the IBM Lotus Domino Server.

Figure 8.27 displays a block diagram of a feedback loop that controls the IBM Lotus Domino Server. The control input, $u(k)$, is MaxUsers, and the server output RPCs in system (RIS) is $w(k)$. A proportional controller is employed, which has the transfer function K_P. Also present is a moving-average filter as described in Section 8.4.3. The filter constructs the smoothed signal $y(k)$ from the output by using $y(k+1) = cy(k) + (1-c)w(k)$, where $0 \le c \le 1$. The filter has the transfer function

$$H(z) = \frac{Y(z)}{W(z)} = \frac{1-c}{z-c}$$

The closed-loop transfer function from the reference input to the filtered output is

$$F_R(z) = \frac{Y(z)}{R(z)} = \frac{K_P 0.47(1-c)}{(z-0.43)(z-c) + 0.47(1-c)K_P} \tag{8.14}$$

Figure 8.28 displays the effect of the filter constant c on steady-state error e_{ss}, settling time k_s, and maximum overshoot M_P. Note that since the steady-state gain of $H(z)$ is 1, the steady-state error e_{ss} of the closed-loop system is unaffected by c. However, c does affect settling times and maximum overshoot M_P. For example, note that $K_P = 2$ is a reasonable value if $c = 0.5$ or 0.95. But this choice of K_P is a poor choice for $c = 0.1$, in that it results in huge settling times.

Studying Figure 8.28 more, we see that for small to moderate values of c, settling times increase with K_P. However, for large c, settling times *decrease* with K_P. It turns out the effect of K_P on settling times looks like an upward-facing parabola. For smaller c, we see only the increasing part of this effect (the rightmost part of the parabola) since $K_P > 0$. At $c = 0.95$, we see primarily a decrease in settling times for the range of K_P considered (the leftmost part of the parabola).

Finally, we see that $M_P \approx 0$ for $c = 0.95$. Intuitively, this make sense in that smoothing reduces variability, including overshoot. A more detailed understanding is obtained by examining the poles of Equation (8.14). It turns out that at

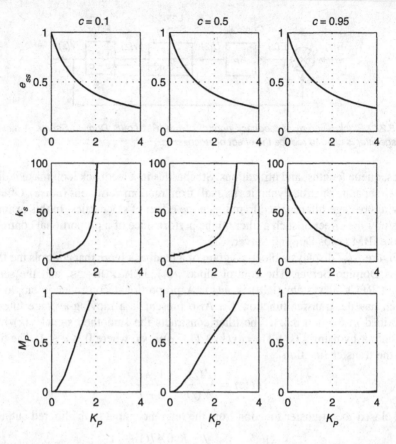

Fig. 8.28 *Effect of the filter constant c and the proportional gain K_P on the characteristics of the feedback system in Figure 8.27.*

large c, the poles have a very small imaginary part and thus are approximately positive real numbers. Hence, from Section 8.3.5 we know that $M_p \approx 0$.

8.7.2 Apache with Precompensation

In Chapter 1 we described how KeepAlive (the time that idle HTTP connections are held) can be manipulated so as to regulate CPU (CPU utilizations). In this example we investigate the use of precompensation to improve the accuracy of regulating CPU using proportional control.

Figure 8.29 displays block diagrams for controlling CPU using KeepAlive. The operating point is $(\overline{\text{CPU}}, \overline{\text{KA}}) = (0.58, 11)$, and the offset values are $u(k) = \text{KA}(k) - \overline{\text{KA}}$, and $y(k) = \text{CPU}(k) - \overline{\text{CPU}}$. The controller has the transfer function K_P, and the transfer function of the target system is

$$G(z) = \frac{Y(z)}{U(z)} = \frac{-0.014}{z - 0.59}$$

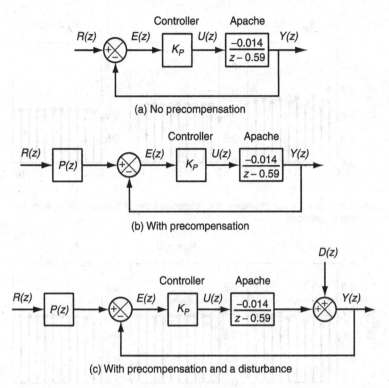

Fig. 8.29 Block diagrams of the Apache HTTP Server showing how precompensation is used and how a CPU disturbance can be modeled. $P(z)$ is the transfer function of the precompensator.

We begin with Figure 8.29(a). From Equation (4.1), the transfer function from the reference input to the output is

$$F_R(z) = \frac{Y(z)}{R(z)} = \frac{-0.014K_p}{z - 0.59 - 0.014K_p} \tag{8.15}$$

If there is a step change in the reference input with magnitude r_{ss}, the Z-transform of the output signal is

$$Y(z) = F_R(z)\frac{z}{z-1}r_{ss}$$

Then the time-domain signal is $CPU(k) = y(k) + \overline{CPU}$, where $y(k)$ is obtained from the Z-transform above. Figure 8.30(a) plots $CPU(k)$ for Figure 8.29(a) when the reference value is increased from 0.58 to 0.68 (so $r_{ss} = 0.1$). The dotted line is the reference value, and the dashed line is the steady-state output.

We begin by making two observations. First, we want $K_p < 0$ since we know that CPU increases as KeepAlive *decreases*. This relationship is apparent in Equation (8.15) in that the numerator is negative. Second, in Figure 8.30(a), the distance between the dashed and dotted lines is $|e_{ss}|$. We see that $|e_{ss}| > 0$ and that it increases as $|K_p|$ decreases.

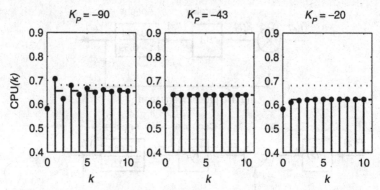

(a) Step response to a change in the reference input of Figure 8.29(a), a system with no precompensation

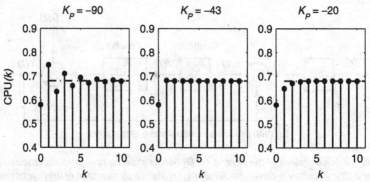

(b) Step response to a change in the reference input of Figure 8.29(b), a system with precompensation

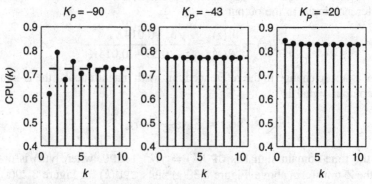

(c) Step response of a change in the reference input and a disturbance of Figure 8.29(c), a system with precompensation

Fig. 8.30 *Time-domain response to a change of reference value for the systems in Figure 8.29. The reference value changes from 0.58 to 0.68. For Figure 8.29(c), $d(k) = 0.3$.*

We can eliminate steady-state error (i.e., reduce the distance between the dashed and dotted lines) by using the system in Figure 8.29(b). This system includes a block labeled $P(z)$, the precompensator. $P(z)$ provides a way to adjust the reference signal $R(z)$ to correct for the steady-state gain of the closed-loop system. The transfer function from the reference input to the output is

$$F'_R(z) = \frac{Y(z)}{R(z)} = \frac{-0.014K_P P(z)}{z - 0.59 - 0.014K_P} \tag{8.16}$$

Note that $P(z)$ only appears in the numerator of F'_R and hence can be used to adjust the steady-state gain of the system without affecting its poles. In particular, we can make $F'_R(1) = 1$ by having a constant precompensator

$$P(z) = \frac{0.41 - 0.014K_P}{-0.014K_P}$$

which is the reciprocal of the steady-state gain of the system without the pre-compensator. That is,

$$\begin{aligned} F'_R(z) = \frac{Y(z)}{R(z)} &= \frac{-0.014K_P[(0.41 - 0.014K_P)/-0.014K_P]}{z - 0.59 - 0.014K_P} \\ &= \frac{0.41 - 0.014K_P}{z - 0.59 - 0.014K_P} \end{aligned}$$

Clearly, with $F'_R(1) = 1$, we have $e_{ss} = 0$. Figure 8.30(b) plots the step response of Figure 8.29(b) for the same change in reference value as in Figure 8.30(a). Note that we have eliminated the steady-state error for all three values of K_P. Also, observe that dynamics (e.g., k_S, M_P) are unaffected by precompensation.

Unfortunately, precompensation is not effective at eliminating steady-state errors introduced by disturbances. Consider Figure 8.29(c). Here, there is a disturbance that adds additional CPU utilization (e.g., due to the execution of non-Apache tasks). The transfer function from the disturbance to the output is

$$F'_D(z) = \frac{Y(z)}{D(z)} = \frac{z - 0.59}{z - 0.59 - 0.014K_P} \tag{8.17}$$

Note that $P(z)$ does not appear in this transfer function since, by definition, $R(z) = 0$ when we compute $F_D(z)$. The Z-transform of the output for a step increase in the reference and disturbance inputs is

$$Y(z) = F'_R(z)\frac{z}{z - 1}r_{ss} + F'_D(z)\frac{z}{z - 1}d_{ss}$$

where d_{ss} is the steady-state magnitude of the constant disturbance. Figure 8.30(c) plots the step response of Figure 8.29(c) for the same change in reference value as in Figure 8.29(a) and a disturbance of magnitude 0.3. We see that $|e_{ss}| > 0$. The reason for this is that

$$F'_D(1) = \frac{0.4}{0.4 - 0.014K_P} \neq 0$$

unless $K_P = 0$. But if $K_P = 0$, then $F_R(z) = 0$, so we cannot track the reference value.

One might ask, "Why not use precompensation for the disturbance as well as the reference inputs?" The difficulty here is that, by definition, the disturbance is something that is usually unknown a priori and cannot be controlled. For example, if the disturbance takes the form of non-Apache tasks executing on the same computer, we have no way to adjust their execution times. As a result, there is no way to implement a precompensator to correct for the effect of the disturbance.

8.7.3 Apache with Disturbance Rejection

This is a continuation of the last example to investigate response to a disturbance, especially steady-state error and settling time. Our starting point is Figure 8.29(c). The operating point is $(\overline{\text{CPU}}, \overline{\text{KA}}) = (0.58, 11)$, and the offsets are $u(k) = \text{KA}(k) - \overline{\text{KA}}$ and $y(k) = \text{CPU}(k) - \overline{\text{CPU}}$. Since the focus of this example is disturbance rejection, the reference value $r(k) = 0$. The controller has the transfer function K_P, and the transfer function of the target system is

$$G(z) = \frac{Y(z)}{U(z)} = \frac{-0.014}{z - 0.59}$$

The disturbance, $D(z)$, reflects additional CPU utilizations, such as the execution of non-Apache processes on the same server. From Equation (4.4), the transfer function from the disturbance input to the output is

$$F_D(z) = \frac{Y(z)}{D(z)} = \frac{z - 0.59}{z - 0.59 - 0.014K_P}$$

Figure 8.31 displays steady-state error and settling time for the system in Figure 8.29(c) with a unit step disturbance input. We see that $|e_{ss}|$ is smallest when $|K_P|$ is largest, which is consistent with Equation (8.17). Settling time has the shape of an upward-facing parabola. The minimum value of k_s occurs at $K_P = -43$ since $(-0.014)(-43) \approx 0.6$ and hence the pole is near 0.

Figure 8.32 displays the time-domain response to a step disturbance input of magnitude 0.3 for three values of K_P. We see that $k_s \approx 10, 1, 3$ for $K_P = -90, -43, -20$, which is consistent with Figure 8.31. Also in Figure 8.32, note that the steady-state error increases as the magnitude of K_P gets smaller, an effect that is clear from Figure 8.31.

8.7.4 Effect of Operating Region on $M/M/1/K$ Control

The relationship between control inputs and outputs in computing systems depends on operating parameters such as arrival rates and service times. However, such operating parameters may vary over time. For example, an e-commerce site may have a mixture of "browse" and "buy" requests, with the latter being more computer intensive than the former because of encrypting data for security purposes.

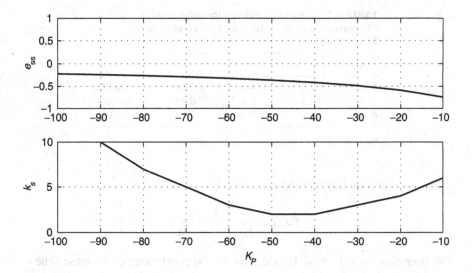

Fig. 8.31 *Assessment of steady-state error and settling time for the Apache HTTP Server in Figure 8.29(c).*

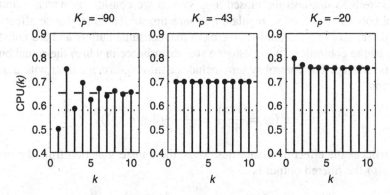

Fig. 8.32 *Time-domain response of a step disturbance input in Figure 8.29(c). $r(k) = 0$ and $d(k) = 0.3$, $k \geq 0$. The dashed line is the steady-state output.*

So changes in the relative proportion of the two request types (e.g., due to last-minute shopping for Christmas) affects operating parameters. Hence, there is a need to ensure that controller characteristics are robust to changes in operating parameters. This example investigates such considerations in the context of the $M/M/1/K$ queueing system.

Recall that the static and dynamic characteristics of $M/M/1/K$ are determined by the arrival rate λ, the service rate μ, and the buffer size K. In this example, λ is fixed at 1 second. K is the control input, and response time is the output. We consider changes in μ (e.g., the CPU required to process a Web request). Because it is more natural to think in terms of service times than service rates, we use $1/\mu$ in the sequel.

TABLE 8.1   Results of System Identification for Response Times in $M/M/1/K$ at Different Service Times $(1/\mu)^a$

$1/\mu$	$\overline{K}$	$\overline{R}$	a	b
0.85	15	4.4	0.83	0.0015
0.95	15	6.4	0.93	0.0023
0.99	15	7.3	0.97	0.0016

$^a\lambda = 1$ and $T_s = 10$. All time units are in seconds.

We assume a first-order model for $M/M/1/K$, so

$$G(z) = \frac{Y(z)}{U(z)} = \frac{b}{z - a}$$

The operating point is $\overline{K} = 15$ and $\overline{R}$ is the expected value of response time at the value of λ, μ, and K used. Let $u(k) = K(k) - \overline{K}$ and $y(k) = R(k) - \overline{R}$. Table 8.1 contains the results of system identification at several values of $1/\mu$ in which $K(k)$ is increased in steps from 10 to 23.

Figure 8.33 displays the closed-loop system we consider in which a proportional controller is used to regulate response times.[1] The disturbance affects the true buffer size (e.g., administrative tasks that consume buffers and are not regulated by the controller). We consider a step disturbance in which the actual buffer size is reduced. The control system includes a moving-average filter with transfer function

$$H(z) = \frac{Y(z)}{W(z)} = \frac{1 - c}{z - c}(0 \leq c < 1)$$

that reduces the effect of stochastics. Thus, the transfer function from the disturbance to the filtered output is

$$F_D(z) = \frac{Y(z)}{D(z)} = \frac{b(1 - c)}{(z - a)(z - c) + bK_P(1 - c)} \tag{8.18}$$

Figure 8.34 studies controller performance at different average service times $1/\mu$ as K_P is varied. We see that settling times change considerably with $1/\mu$, as does steady state error.

Figure 8.35 studies the time-domain effects of changes in $1/\mu$ and K_P. The solid lines are the results of $M/M/1/K$ simulations (averaged over multiple replications), and the dashed lines are predictions from Equation (8.18). The disturbance occurs at $k = 100$ with $d(k) = -4$ for $k \geq 100$. Due to the stochastic nature of $M/M/1/K$, the correspondence between the predicted and actual values is a bit rough. In particular, many of the plots evidence a rapid drop in $\overline{R}(k)$

---

[1] Using buffer size to regulate response times means that some requests are not served. In practice, this may mean that requests are sent elsewhere using a load-balancing scheme.

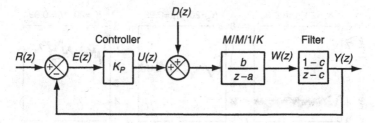

Fig. 8.33 *Block diagram of the $M/M/1/K$ example. The control input is buffer size, and the output is response time. The disturbance affects the control input. A moving-average filter is used to reduce variability seen by the controller. The parameters a and b are determined by system identification at different workload intensities as specified in Table 8.1.*

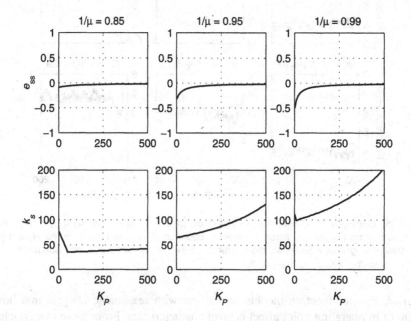

Fig. 8.34 *Effect of K_P in Figure 8.33 on steady-state error and settling time. $1/\mu$ is in seconds.*

after the disturbance, but the values predicted show a much more gradual decline. Even so, the simulations generally track the predictions.

Returning to Figure 8.34, we see that $|e_{ss}|$ increases with service time, which is reflected in Figure 8.35 as well. Note that $e_{ss} < 0$, which means that a unit step disturbance causes $y(k)$ to be larger than the reference. Thus, a negative disturbance (decreasing the buffer size) should result in lower response times, which is the case in Figure 8.35.

From the foregoing we draw three conclusions. First, the operating region has a strong effect on how K_P affects the control of $M/M/1/K$ (which very likely suggests a strong effect in real computing systems as well). Second, properly

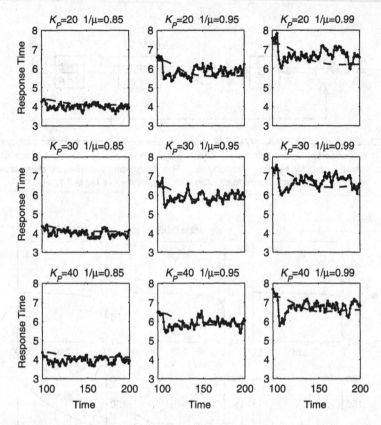

Fig. 8.35 Comparison of time-domain response to a disturbance in $M/M/1/K$ with the predictions from the transfer function model in Equation (8.18). Solid lines are the $M/M/1/K$ response averaged over 500 replications with $c = 0.95$. The dashed line is the value predicted. $d(k) = -4$ for $k \geq 100$. $T_s = 10$ seconds.

applied, transfer function models provide us with reasonable insights into how changes in operating point affect control characteristics. From these two conclusions we draw a third conclusion—that transfer function models should be used to explore control characteristics for a range of operating points.

*8.8 DESIGNING P-CONTROLLERS IN MATLAB

In this section we illustrate how MATLAB can be used to analyze control systems. We use Equation (8.14) as a running example. We begin by observing that Equation (8.14) is constructed from three transfer functions:

- The controller has the transfer function K_P. In the following, we use $K_P = 2$.
- The target system (the IBM Lotus Domino Server) has the transfer function $0.47/(z - 0.43)$.

- The filter has the transfer function $(1-c)/(z-c)$. In the following, we use $c = 0.95$.

The closed-loop transfer function is

$$\frac{K_p 0.47(1-c)}{(z-0.43)(z-c)+(1-c)K_p 0.47}$$

We can construct this directly as follows:

```
>>Kp=2; c=0.95;

>>tf(Kp*0.47*[1-c],[1-(0.43+c)0.43*c+(1-c)*Kp*0.47],-1)

Transfer function:

   0.047
----------------------
z^2 - 1.38 z + 0.4555
```

Lines beginning with >> are user inputs, and those beginning with a space are the MATLAB response to these inputs. The MATLAB function tf takes as arguments the numerator of the transfer function, its denominator, and a time specification. The numerator and denominator are expressed as polynomials in z. For example, [1 -c] represents $z - c$. A -1 for the time specification means that time is unspecified.

MATLAB provides a convenient way to construct feedback loops from transfer functions for the feedforward loop and the filter. We start by constructing the transfer function of the IBM Lotus Domino Server:

```
>> lotus=tf(0.47,[1 -0.43],-1)

Transfer function:

 0.47
--------
z - 0.43
```

and the transfer function for the filter:

```
>> filter = tf(1-c, [1 -c],-1)

Transfer function:

 0.05
--------
z - 0.95
```

The feedback loop has the product of the proportional gain K_P and the IBM Lotus Domino Server in feedforward (from the reference to the output) and the filter in feedback. Hence, the closed-loop transfer function from the reference to the output is

```
>> sys_cl = feedback(Kp*lotus,filter)
```

Transfer function:

```
  0.047
---------------------
z^2 - 1.38 z + 0.4555
```

which is the same as before.

MATLAB also provides functions to extract poles, zeros, and steady-state gain from transfer functions. For example:

```
>> pole(sys_cl)

ans =

  0.8335

  0.5465

>> zero(sys_cl)

ans =

Empty matrix: 0-by-1
```

The latter is because sys_cl has no finite zeros.

```
>> dcgain(sys_cl)

ans =


  0.6225
```

We can also use MATLAB to plot the root locus of the system; note that here we use the product of the *loop* transfer functions, since the root locus plots the poles for all possible values of K_P.

```
>> rlocus(lotus*filter)
```

Finally, MATLAB provides a way to simulate the response to a step input. For example,

```
>> step(sys_cl)
```

results in a plot in which the horizontal axis is time and the vertical axis is the output $y(k)$.

8.9 EXERCISES

1. Consider a system with transfer function

$$G(z) = \frac{Y(z)}{U(z)} = \frac{0.5}{z - 0.75}$$

and proportional control, as in Figure 8.5. Find the range of values of K_P such that the closed-loop system

 (a) Is stable

 (b) Has steady-state error e_{ss} to a unit step reference less than 0.1

 (c) Has setting time $k_s < 10$

 (d) Has maximum overshoot $M_P < 0.1$

 (*Note:* It may not be possible to satisfy all criteria.) Repeat with one time delay in the feedback loop. Explain the change, if any, in K_P.

2. Repeat Exercise 1 with an uncertain transfer function. That is,

$$G(z) = \frac{0.5}{z - a} \qquad \text{where } a = 0.75 \pm 0.1$$

3. Plot the root locus of $G(z) = 0.5/(z - 0.75)$ and indicate on the plot the value(s) of K_P at which instability results. Repeat with one time delay in the feedback loop.

4. Consider a system with transfer function $G(z) = 0.5/(z - 0.75)$ and proportional control. Plot e_{ss}, k_s, and M_P as functions of K_P for the range of K_P in which the closed-loop system is stable. Repeat with one and two time delays in the loop.

5. Consider a system $G(z) = 0.4/(z - 0.25)$. Design a proportional controller to result in $k_s < 2$. Add a precompensator to achieve zero steady-state error to a step reference. Verify your control design by simulation. What is the steady-state output of the system if there is a unit step disturbance entering as in Figure 8.5?

6. Consider a system $G(z) = -0.4/(z + 0.25)$. Design a moving-average filter and a proportional controller to result in $M_P < 0.1$. Add a precompensator to achieve zero steady-state error to a step reference. Verify your control design by simulation.

7. Consider a closed-loop system consisting of a target system with transfer function $G(z)$ and a proportional controller. Prove that if $G(z)$ has at least one zero at infinity, there exists a sufficiently large K_P such that the closed-loop system is unstable.

8. Figure 8.8 can be divided into three sections: (1) $k \in [0, 5)$, during which $d(k) = 0 = n(k)$; (2) $k \in [5, 10)$, during which $d(k) \neq 0 = n(k)$; and (3) $k \in [10, 15]$, during which $d(k) \neq 0 \neq n(k)$. For each section, find the steady-state values of $u(k)$, $e(k)$, and $t(k)$ for the inputs in each section.

9. Consider control systems with various placements of a moving-average filter as depicted in Figure 8.36. How does the filter placement affect the poles of the transfer functions for the reference and disturbance inputs? What is the effect on settling times and maximum overshoot?

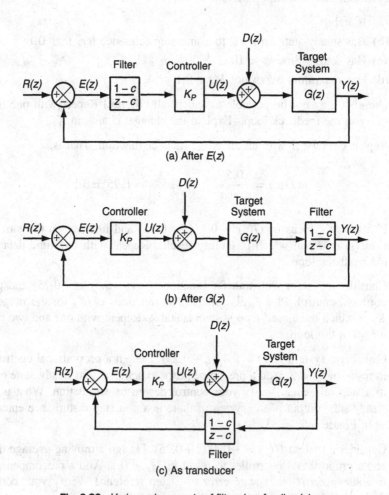

(a) After $E(z)$

(b) After $G(z)$

(c) As transducer

Fig. 8.36 *Various placements of filters in a feedback loop.*

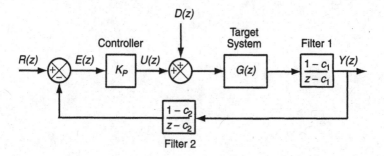

Fig. 8.37 Block diagram of proportional control system with multiple filters.

10. The system in Figure 8.37 has two filters. How do the transfer functions of this system differ from those in Figure 8.36(b) and 8.36(c)? What are the advantages and disadvantages of the design in Figure 8.37?

11. Explain the effect of K_p on the magnitude of the largest pole in Figure 8.24 for $c = 0.95$.

9

PID Controllers

The proportional controller discussed in Chapter 8 reduces steady-state errors. However, it cannot drive the steady-state error to zero. In this chapter we introduce the integral and derivative control actions. Integral control can drive the steady-state error to zero, although it may also slow controller response. Derivative control provides a way to respond quickly. Also addressed are various combinations of proportional, integral, and derivative control actions, especially the PID controller (which includes all three). PID control is widely used in the process control industry [8]. Various approaches to controller design are discussed, with an emphasis on pole placement design.

9.1 INTEGRAL CONTROL

As shown in Section 8.3.3, steady-state error is unavoidable with proportional control. This is because the output of a proportional controller is proportional to the control error, a zero error implies a zero controller output. A constant reference requires a nonzero control input and hence cannot be tracked exactly. As shown in Section 8.7.2, a precompensator can be used to eliminate steady-state error to a reference input, but this relies on a precise knowledge of the system model and cannot eliminate steady-state error to a disturbance. In contrast, for integral controllers, the *change* of the controller output is proportional to the error, or equivalently, the controller output is proportional to the *integral* of the

Feedback Control of Computing Systems, by Joseph L. Hellerstein, Yixin Diao, Sujay Parekh, and Dawn M. Tilbury
ISBN 0-471-26637-X   Copyright © 2004 John Wiley & Sons, Inc.

control error. Once a nonzero error exists, the controller output keeps changing to reduce the error. The larger the error, the more the change. It is this integral effect that can drive the steady-state error to zero.

The integral control law has the form

$$u(k) = u(k-1) + K_I e(k) \tag{9.1}$$

where $u(k)$ is the output of the integral controller and $e(k)$ is the control error. The controller parameter K_I defines the ratio of control change (the difference between the current and past inputs) to the control error. Note that unlike proportional control, the control input $u(k)$ can be nonzero even when the current error $e(k)$ is zero. This allows the system to have zero steady-state error in the presence of a step change in reference and/or disturbance inputs.

The term *integral control* refers to the fact that the controller output is proportional to the integral of all past errors. This can be seen by computing the kth input $u(k)$, as follows:

$$u(1) = u(0) + K_I e(1)$$

$$u(2) = u(1) + K_I e(2) = u(0) + K_I e(1) + K_I e(2)$$

$$\vdots$$

$$u(k) = u(k-1) + K_I e(k) = u(0) + K_I e(1) + \cdots + K_I e(k)$$

$$= u(0) + K_I \sum_{j=1}^{k} e(j)$$

The transfer function of the integral controller can be found by taking the Z-transform of Equation (9.1) with zero initial conditions:

$$U(z) = z^{-1}U(z) + K_I E(z) \tag{9.2}$$

$$(1 - z^{-1})U(z) = K_I E(z) \tag{9.3}$$

$$\frac{U(z)}{E(z)} = \frac{K_I}{1 - z^{-1}} \tag{9.4}$$

$$= \frac{K_I z}{z - 1} \tag{9.5}$$

Note that the integrator has a pole at $z = 1$. In open loop, the integrator is not BIBO stable. The integrator also has a zero at $z = 0$.

9.1.1 Steady-State Error with Integral Control

To show how the steady-state error of a system with integral control can be zero, even with constant reference or disturbance inputs, we start with an example.

Example 9.1: Steady-state error of the IBM Lotus Domino Server with I control Consider the IBM Lotus Domino Server with an integral controller. Its control input is MaxUsers, and the output is RIS, the number of RPCs in the Notes Server. The operating point of the IBM Lotus Domino Server is $(\overline{\text{MaxUsers}}, \overline{\text{RIS}})$. In our case, $(\overline{\text{MaxUsers}}, \overline{\text{RIS}}) = (375, 325)$. The kth offset value of the input is $u(k) = \text{MaxUsers}(k) - \overline{\text{MaxUsers}}$, and for the output it is $y(k) = \text{RIS}(k) - \overline{\text{RIS}}$. The block diagram is shown in Figure 9.1. As derived in Example 3.7, the transfer function of the IBM Lotus Domino Server is

$$G(z) = \frac{Y(z)}{U(z)} = \frac{0.47}{z - 0.43}$$

Referring to Figure 9.1, the closed-loop transfer function from the reference input to the measured output is

$$F_R(z) = \frac{Y(z)}{R(z)} = \frac{[K_I z/(z-1)][0.47/(z-0.43)]}{1 + [K_I z/(z-1)][0.47/(z-0.43)]}$$

$$= \frac{0.47 K_I z}{z^2 + (0.47K_I - 1.43)z + 0.43}$$

Note that for *any* value of K_I, the steady-state gain of this transfer function is 1:

$$F_R(1) = \frac{0.47 K_I}{1 + (0.47K_I - 1.43) + 0.43} = 1$$

From Equation (8.5), the steady-state error to a constant reference of magnitude r_{ss} is

$$e_{ss} = r_{ss}[1 - F_R(1)] = 0$$

and thus, for any value of K_I such that the closed-loop system is stable, the steady-state error to a constant reference input is zero.

It turns out that the steady-state gain of a system with integral control does not depend on the target system as long as the closed-loop system is stable. Indeed, for a stable closed-loop system with integral control, the steady-state gain is 1. This is a key result since having a steady-state gain of 1 means that there is no

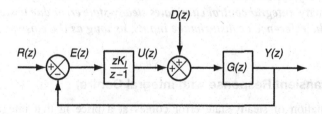

Fig. 9.1 *Feedback loop with integral control.*

steady-state error in response to step changes in the reference and disturbance inputs.

The foregoing can be proved in a straightforward way. Referring to Figure 9.1, we see that

$$F_R(z) = \frac{Y(z)}{R(z)} = \frac{[K_I z/(z-1)]G(z)}{1+[K_I z/(z-1)]G(z)}$$

$$= \frac{K_I z G(z)}{(z-1)+K_I z G(z)}$$

Now observe that

$$F_R(1) = \frac{K_I G(1)}{0+K_I G(1)} = 1$$

Note that this result does not depend on K_I as long as the closed-loop system is stable.

Integral control also eliminates errors due to disturbance inputs. Consider again the integral control system of Figure 9.1. The closed-loop transfer function for a disturbance input is the forward gain from $D(z)$ to $Y(z)$ divided by 1 plus the loop gain,

$$F_D(z) = \frac{Y(z)}{D(z)} = \frac{G(z)}{1+[K_I z/(z-1)]G(z)}$$

$$= \frac{(z-1)G(z)}{(z-1)+K_I z G(z)}$$

and the steady-state gain of this disturbance transfer function is

$$F_D(1) = \frac{0}{0+K_I G(1)} = 0$$

From Equation (8.6), the steady-state error to a constant disturbance of magnitude d_{ss} is

$$e_{ss} = d_{ss}F_D(1) = 0$$

Again, the steady-state error to a constant disturbance is zero for any value of K_I and for any system model $G(z)$, such that the closed-loop system is stable.

In summary, *integral control eliminates steady-state error due to step changes in either the reference or disturbance inputs, as long as the closed-loop system is stable.*

9.1.2   Transient Response with Integral Control

The elimination of steady-state error comes at a price in that integral control slows system response. The reason for this is that the integrator adds an open-loop pole at $z = 1$. Thus, the closed-loop system has one more pole than the open-loop transfer function $G(z)$. This additional pole is typically closer to the unit circle than any of the open-loop poles, and hence results in a slower closed-loop response.

Example 9.2: Closed-loop poles of the IBM Lotus Domino Server with integral control   Consider the closed-loop system in Figure 9.1 in which $G(z) = 0.47/(z-0.43)$. The closed-loop system has two poles, one from the IBM Lotus Domino Server and one from the integrator. Instead of computing their locations directly, we can plot the root locus—all possible locations of the closed loop poles as K_I varies from 0 to ∞. In Figure 9.2, the root locus of the IBM Lotus Domino Server alone is shown on the left, and the root locus of the IBM Lotus Domino Server plus an integrator is shown on the right. Since the integrator adds an open-loop pole at $z = 1$, there are two branches to the root locus. One branch ends at the finite zero ($z = 0$), and the other at the zero at infinity. The largest closed-loop pole is always closer to the unit circle than the open-loop pole 0.43.

Another way to view the effect of integral control is to plot the magnitude of the largest closed-loop pole versus the control gain. Figure 9.3 shows this plot for both the IBM Lotus Domino Server with P control (top) and the IBM Lotus Domino Server with I control (bottom). Recall that the settling time of the system depends on the magnitude of the dominant closed-loop pole, as $k_s = -4/\log|p|$, where p is the dominant pole. Since the magnitude of the largest closed-loop pole with I control is always greater than the magnitude of the open-loop pole (0.43), and the settling time increases with the pole magnitude, the closed-loop response will always be slower than the open-loop response, no matter what value of K_I is chosen. This trade-off between accuracy and speed is one of the many choices that must be made in control design.

Consider three different choices for K_I: $K_I = 1, 3, 5$. According to Figure 9.3, each of these choices results in a stable closed-loop system. The closed-loop poles are shown in Table 9.1, along with the predicted settling time and maximum overshoot. The predicted settling time is the same for all cases but is twice

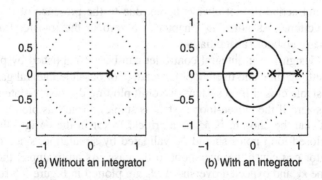

(a) Without an integrator   (b) With an integrator

Fig. 9.2   *Root locus of the IBM Lotus Domino Server without and with an integrator in the loop.*

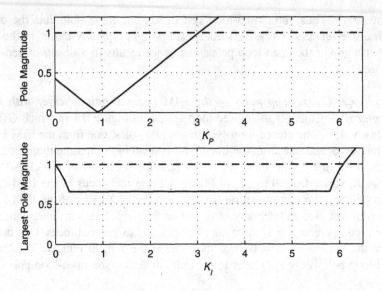

Fig. 9.3 *Magnitude of largest closed-loop pole, the IBM Lotus Domino Server with P control (top) and I control (bottom).*

TABLE 9.1 Closed-Loop Poles with Predicted and Actual Transient Behavior for the IBM Lotus Domino Server with Integral Control[a]

Gain K_I	Closed-Loop Poles	Error e_{ss}	k_s (predicted)	M_P (predicted)	M_P (actual)
1	$0.48 \pm 0.45j = 0.66e^{\pm j(\pi/4)}$	0	10	0.19	0.18
3	$0.01 \pm 0.66j = 0.66e^{\pm j(\pi/2)}$	0	10	0.44	0.44
5	$-0.46 \pm 0.47j = 0.66e^{\pm j(3\pi/4)}$	0	10	0.57	1.35

[a] See Figure 9.1.
Simulation results are shown in Figure 9.4.

as long as the settling time of the open-loop system $[-4/\log(0.43) = 4.7]$. The actual maximum overshoot is computed from the simulations as shown in Figure 9.4, for a reference change of 20 (increasing RIS from 325 to 345). The estimated and actual do not always agree, due to the presence of a zero in the transfer function. As noted in Chapter 6, a zero in the transfer function can increase the overshoot substantially.

Control design for an integral controller can be accomplished by plotting the expected settling time and overshoot for a range of possible integral gains K_I that result in a stable closed-loop system (we omit plotting the steady-state error since it is always zero if the closed-loop system is stable). From this plot, a reasonable value of K_I can be chosen. If M_P is a critical factor in the design, the estimate from the closed-loop poles should be validated by simulation, since the zero in the integrator can cause the overshoot to increase. As an example, the expected settling time k_s and expected overshoot M_P are plotted in Figure 9.5 for the IBM Lotus Domino Server with integral control.

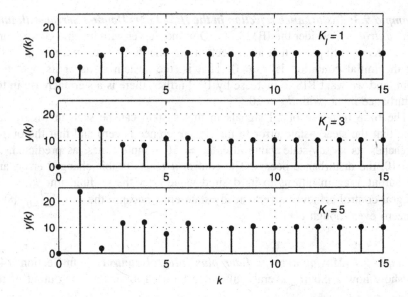

Fig. 9.4 *Transient response of the IBM Lotus Domino Server and integral control to a step reference change of $r_{ss} = 10$ for three different values of K_1. The closed-loop poles and transient performance metrics are shown in Table 9.1.*

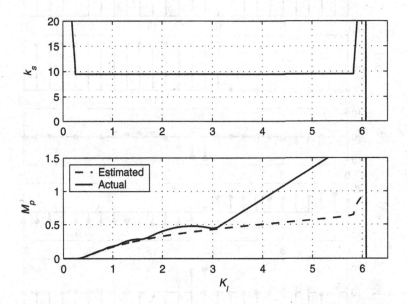

Fig. 9.5 *Settling time k_s and maximum overshoot M_P estimated from the dominant pole for the system of the IBM Lotus Domino Server with integral control. The stability boundary is indicated by the solid vertical line.*

Example 9.3: Disturbance rejection in the IBM Lotus Domino Server with integral control   Consider the IBM Lotus Domino Server with integral control, and choose $K_I = 1$. Suppose that as in Section 8.1, the desired reference is $r_{ss} = 10$, but the initial condition is $y = 0$. That is, the system starts at its operating point, and we want RIS to increase by 10. Further, there is a step increase in the disturbance input, with $d_{ss} = 20$.

The time response of all signals in this system can be seen in Figure 9.6. Note that the steady-state error to the step reference is zero and that the output y reaches its steady-state value after $k_s = 10$ sample times, as predicted. At $k = 10$, the disturbance occurs. The control u reacts to this changed error, and the output y again returns to its desired value after the settling time $k_s = 10$. Integral control achieves a zero steady-state error because the sum $\sum_{i=0}^{k} e(i)$ is nonzero even though $e(k) = 0$.

Example 9.4: Moving-average filter plus integral control   In Section 8.4.3 we show how a moving-average filter can be used to smooth the output of the

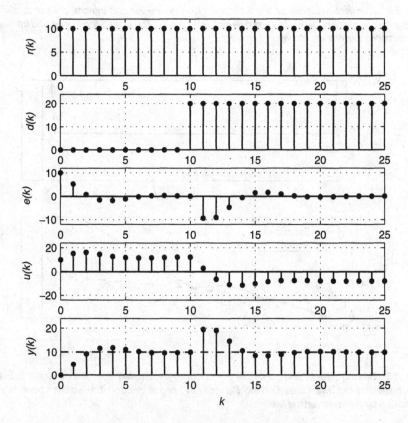

Fig. 9.6   *Reference tracking ($r_{ss} = 10$) and disturbance rejection ($d_{ss} = 20$) in the IBM Lotus Domino Server with integral control, $K_I = 1$.*

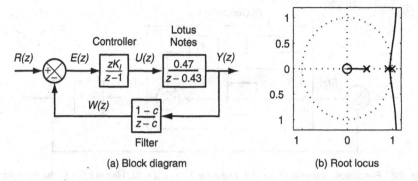

Fig. 9.7 *Block diagram and root locus of the IBM Lotus Domino Server with integral control and a moving-average filter (c = 0.9).*

system before it is fed back to the controller. Such an approach is depicted in Figure 9.7(a) for the IBM Lotus Domino Server. One consequence of a moving-average filter is to slow the system response so that it reacts only to sustained changes in the reference and disturbance inputs.

Since an integral controller also slows down the system response, the combination of a moving-average filter with integral control can lead to undesirable or overly slow behavior. To see this, consider the root locus of the IBM Lotus Domino Server plus a moving-average filter and an integral controller, as shown in Figure 9.7(b). There are in total three closed-loop poles: the integral controller contributes a pole at $z = 1$, the moving-average filter contributes a pole at $z = c$ (here $c = 0.9$), and the IBM Lotus Domino Server contributes a pole at $z = 0.43$. As can be seen in the root locus plot, the region of controller gains K_I that result in a stable closed-loop system is very small. In addition, since in the stable region the dominant closed-loop pole is very close to the unit circle (magnitude greater than 0.95, or halfway in between c and 1), the settling time will necessarily be very long (here, $k_s > 78$).

In essence, an integral controller acts like a moving-average filter. A short transient disturbance contributes only slightly to the integral of the error, while a sustained change in the output has a more substantial effect on the integral of the error. The difference is that an integral controller can drive the steady-state error to zero, whereas a moving-average filter, with a steady-state gain of 1, cannot change the steady-state behavior of the system.

9.2 PROPORTIONAL–INTEGRAL CONTROL

Proportional–integral (PI) control combines the advantages of integral control (zero steady-state error) with those of proportional control (increasing the speed of the transient response). As shown in Figure 9.8, the control input is the sum of the proportional and integral terms. For proportional control, the control input is proportional to the control error, and for integral control, the change in control

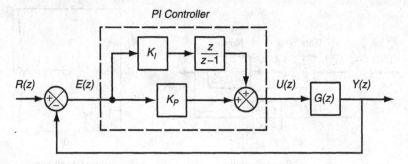

Fig. 9.8 *Feedback loop with PI control. The error $E(z) = R - Y(z)$ is the input to the controller. The control input $U(z)$ is a sum of the proportional term $K_P E(z)$ and the integral term $K_1[z/(z-1)]$.*

input is proportional to the control error:

$$u_P(k) = K_P e(k)$$

$$u_I(k) = u_I(k-1) + K_I e(k)$$

The PI controller adds these two terms together,

$$u(k) = u_P(k) + u_I(k)$$
$$= K_P e(k) + u_I(k-1) + K_I e(k)$$

To eliminate the u_I term algebraically, it is simplest to write out the equation for the change of $u(k)$:

$$u(k) - u(k-1) = u_P(k) - u_P(k-1) + u_I(k) - u_I(k-1)$$
$$= K_P e(k) - K_P e(k-1) + K_I e(k)$$

Thus, the PI control law has the form

$$u(k) = u(k-1) + (K_P + K_I)e(k) - K_P e(k-1) \qquad (9.6)$$

Note that to compute the current control input $u(k)$, the controller needs to know the current value of the control error $e(k)$ along with the past value of the error $e(k-1)$ and the past value of the control input $u(k-1)$. It is this memory inherent in the PI controller that makes it dynamic (in contrast to the static P controller).

The transfer function of the PI controller can be found by taking the Z-transform of Equation (9.6) with zero initial conditions:

$$U(z) = z^{-1}U(z) + (K_P + K_I)E(z) - K_P z^{-1} E(z)$$

$$(1 - z^{-1})U(z) = \left(K_P + K_I - K_P z^{-1} \right) E(z)$$

$$\frac{U(z)}{E(z)} = \frac{(K_P + K_I)z - K_P}{z - 1} = K_P + \frac{K_I z}{z - 1} \qquad (9.7)$$

The transfer function given in Equation (9.7) is written in two different ways. One form emphasizes the separate contributions of the proportional and integral terms, as shown in Figure 9.8, and the other emphasizes the pole and zero of the controller. Similarly to the integral controller, the PI controller also has a pole at $z = 1$; this corresponds to the integral action. The control transfer function also has a finite zero, but instead of being at $z = 0$, as in the integral case, it is at $z = K_P/(K_P + K_I)$. If K_P and K_I have the same sign (as is usually the case), the zero is always on the real line between 0 and 1. When the zero is exactly at 0, PI control reduces to the pure integral control case. When the zero is exactly at 1, it cancels the pole at $z = 1$, negating the effect of the integral control, and reduces to the pure proportional control case. A PI control loop is shown in Figure 9.9.

9.2.1 Steady-State Error with PI Control

Consider the steady-state error for a system with PI controller. Since PI includes an integral control term, we expect the steady-state error to be zero. This can be confirmed by finding the closed-loop transfer function of the system in Figure 9.9 for a generic transfer function $G(z)$. The closed-loop transfer function is computed as the forward gain from R to Y divided by 1 plus the loop gain:

$$F_R(z) = \frac{Y(z)}{R(z)} = \frac{\{[(K_P + K_I)z - K_P]/(z - 1)\}G(z)}{1 + \{[(K_P + K_I)z - K_P]/(z - 1)\}G(z)}$$

$$= \frac{[(K_P + K_I)z - K_P]G(z)}{(z - 1) + [(K_P + K_I)z - K_P]G(z)} \qquad (9.8)$$

$$F_R(1) = \frac{(K_P + K_I - K_P)G(z)}{0 + (K_P + K_I - K_P)G(z)} = 1$$

That is, PI control has a zero steady-state error in response to a step change in the reference input, if the closed-loop system is stable. This statement does not depend on the choice of K_P or K_I. It turns out that the same holds for a step change in the disturbance input. The proof of this is left as an exercise.

9.2.2 PI Control Design by Pole Placement

Consider the closed-loop system with PI control in Figure 9.9. We have four design goals for the PI controller: (1) the closed-loop system is stable; (2) steady-state error is minimized; (3) settling time does not exceed k_s^*; and (4) maximum

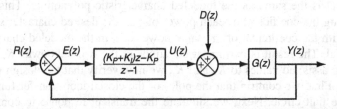

Fig. 9.9 *Block diagram of a computing system $G(z)$ with proportional–integral control.*

overshoot does not exceed M_p^*. The first design goal is achieved by ensuring that all poles lie within the unit circle. The second goal is achieved by using a PI controller, at least for a step change in the reference and/or disturbance inputs. Thus, the design problem is reduced to goals 3 and 4. These control goals can be achieved by properly selecting the parameters K_P and K_I of the PI controller.

Our approach assumes that $G(z)$ is a first-order system. If $G(z)$ is a higher-order system, we can use Equation (3.30) to construct a first-order approximation of $G(z)$. The case of $G(z)$ having order 0 is considered in the problems at the end of the chapter. Note that if $G(z)$ is first order, the closed-loop system is second order since the PI controller is a first-order system. Hence, the closed-loop system has two poles.

Table 9.2 details the steps in our procedure for pole placement design. The first step is to compute the desired poles of the closed-loop system based on k_s^* and M_p^*. We assume that the poles are complex conjugates $re^{\pm j\theta}$. From Equation (8.7) we know that $k_s < -4/\log r$. Thus, an upper bound for r is

$$r = e^{-4/k_s^*} \tag{9.9}$$

Equation (8.8) relates M_p to θ as $M_p \approx r^{\pi/\theta}$ (for $\theta \geq 0$) so

$$\theta = \pi \frac{\log r}{\log M_p^*} \tag{9.10}$$

Note that both r and θ are constructed so that smaller (absolute) values will also satisfy the design goals.

The next step is to construct the *desired characteristic polynomial*, which is the characteristic polynomial that we want for the closed-loop system. The desired characteristic polynomial is

$$(z - re^{j\theta})(z - re^{-j\theta}) = z^2 - 2r\cos\theta z + r^2 \tag{9.11}$$

The third step is to construct the *modeled characteristic polynomial*, which is the denominator of the transfer function of the closed-loop system. In Figure 9.9 this is the denominator of

$$\frac{((K_P + K_I)z - K_P)G(z)}{z - 1 + ((K_P + K_I)z - K_P)G(z)}$$

In the fourth step we solve for K_P and K_I so that the desired characteristic polynomial is the same as the modeled characteristic polynomial. This is done by equating the coefficient of each power of z in the desired characteristic polynomial with the coefficient of the same power of z in the modeled characteristic polynomial. The result is two linear equations in the two unknowns K_P and K_I.

Having assigned values to K_P and K_I, we now verify that the design goals are achieved. First, we confirm that the poles of the closed-loop transfer function lie within the unit circle. Next, we simulate the transient response to confirm that settling times do not exceed k_s^* and the maximum overshoot does not exceed M_p^*.

TABLE 9.2   Procedure for Pole Placement Design for a PI Controller

The design goals are that settling time does not exceed k_s^* and that the maximum overshoot does not exceed M_P^*.

1. Compute the desired closed-loop poles $re^{\pm j\theta}$:

   - Compute r based on k_s^* using Equation (9.9).
   - Compute θ based on M_P using Equation (9.10).

2. Construct and expand the desired characteristic polynomial.

   - From Equation (9.11), the desired characteristic polynomial is $z^2 - 2r\cos\theta z + r^2$, as specified in Equation (9.11).

3. Construct and expand the modeled characteristic polynomial.

   - The modeled characteristic polynomial is the denominator of

$$\frac{K(z)G(z)}{1 + K(z)G(z)}$$

   where

$$K(z) = \frac{(K_P + K_I)z - K_P}{z - 1}$$

   - Eliminate all fractions in the denominator (by multiplication) and expand the polynomial.

4. Find K_P and K_I.

   - Equate the coefficients of the desired characteristic polynomial with the coefficient of the modeled characteristic polynomial of the same degree.
   - Solve for K_P and K_I.

5. Verify the result.

   - Check that the closed-loop poles lie within the unit circle.
   - Simulate transient response to assess if the design goals are met.

Below we give an example of applying the procedure in Table 9.2.

Example 9.5: PI control design by pole placement   Consider the IBM Lotus Domino Server, with transfer function

$$G(z) = \frac{Y(z)}{U(z)} = \frac{0.47}{z - 0.43} \qquad (9.12)$$

Recall that $y(k)$ is the offset of RPC's in the system (RIS) from the operating point, and $u(k)$ is the offset of MaxUsers from the operating point. We use the procedure in Table 9.2 to design a PI controller so that $k_s^* = 10$ and $M_P^* = 10\%$.

1. Compute the dominant poles. Using Equation (9.9), we have $r = e^{-4/10} = 0.67$. Using Equation (9.10), we determine that $\theta = \pi(\ln r/\ln 0.1) = 0.70$. To be conservative, we round this to $r = 0.6$ and $\theta = 0.6$.

2. Construct and expand the desired characteristic polynomial. The desired characteristic polynomial is $z^2 - 2r\cos\theta z + r^2 = z^2 - z + 0.36$.

3. Construct and expand the modeled characteristic polynomial. With PI control (as in Figure 9.9), the closed-loop transfer function from the reference input to the measured output is

$$F_R(z) = \frac{Y(z)}{R(z)} = \frac{\{[(K_P + K_I)z - K_P]/(z-1)\}G(z)}{1 + \{[(K_P + K_I)z - K_P]/(z-1)\}G(z)}$$

$$= \frac{0.47(K_P + K_I)z - 0.47K_P}{z^2 + [0.47(K_P + K_I) - 1.43]z + 0.43 - 0.47K_P} \quad (9.13)$$

The modeled characteristic polynomial is the denominator of Equation (9.13), which is $z^2 + [0.47(K_P + K_I) - 1.43]z + 0.43 - 0.47K_P$.

4. Solve for K_P and K_I. We want the desired characteristic polynomial to equal the modeled characteristic polynomial. That is,

$$z^2 - z + 0.36 = z^2 + [0.47(K_P + K_I) - 1.43]z + 0.43 - 0.47K_P$$

This is true if

$$0.47(K_P + K_I) - 1.43 = -1$$

$$0.43 - 0.47K_P = 0.36$$

Solving this system of equations, we have

$$K_P = 0.15$$

$$K_I = 0.76$$

5. Verify the result. Substituting into Equation (9.13), we have

$$F_R(z) = \frac{0.47(0.15 + 0.76)z - (0.47)(0.15)}{z^2 + [0.47(0.15 + 0.76) - 1.43]z + 0.43 - (0.47)(0.15)}$$

$$= \frac{0.43z - 0.07}{z^2 - z + 0.36}$$

As expected, the poles of $F_R(z)$ are 0.5 ± 0.33, so the system is stable. $F_R(1) = 1$ and hence there is no steady-state error to a step change in the reference or disturbance inputs. Figure 9.10 displays simulation results to a step increase of 10 in the reference input and an increase of 20 in the disturbance input. We see that the design criteria are satisfied in that settling times are well under the objective of 10, and the maximum overshoot is well under 10%. Also shown in the figure are the magnitudes of the proportional and integral components of the control signal $u(k)$. Note that the integral controller has the most effect on $u(k)$.

Recall that the foregoing procedure handles higher-order $G(z)$ by using a first-order approximation. Another approach is to increase the number of controller

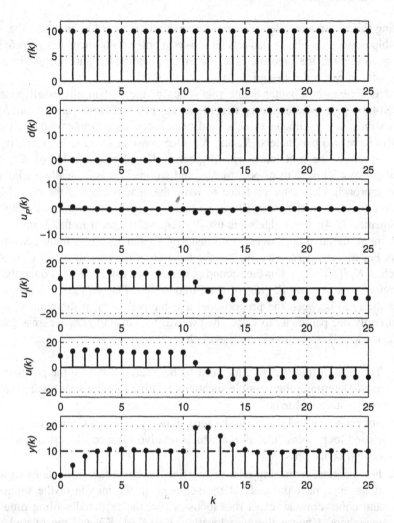

Fig. 9.10 *PI control of the IBM Lotus Domino Server with $K_P = 0.15$, $K_I = 0.76$. The reference is 10 and there is a disturbance of 20. The design objectives are satisfied in that settling time less than $k = 10$ and overshoot less than 0.1 (10%). The proportional and integral contributions to the controller are shown separately, along with their sum: $u(k) = u_P(k) + u_I(k)$.*

parameters so that they are equal to the order of the system. This approach is used in Chapter 10 in the discussion of pole placement design for state-space feedback control.

9.2.3 PI Control Design Using Root Locus

In pole placement design, the desired closed-loop poles are determined based on an a priori specification of desired properties of the closed-loop system (e.g., settling time and maximum overshoot). However, it could be that even shorter settling times and a smaller maximum overshoot are possible based on the relationship between control gains and closed-loop poles. Root locus design provides a way to explore the possible pole placements and hence gain insight into the trade-offs in controller design.

As described in Chapter 8, the root locus of the system allows all possible closed-loop pole locations to be considered at one time. However, the root locus allows only one parameter to be varied, which creates a problem since PI controllers have two parameters: K_P and K_I. One possible solution is to first fix K_P and then draw the root locus with respect to K_I, choose a value of K_I, then draw the root locus with respect to K_P, and so on. This is basically a trial-and-error approach. Care must be taken to write the denominator of the closed-loop transfer function in the correct form so that it matches the root locus definition of Equation (8.4); some algebra is usually required to get it in this form.

A more effective approach is to transform K_P and K_I into a more convenient form. For the first parameter, we use the location of the zero of the PI controller, which is $K_P/(K_P + K_I)$. For the second parameter we use $K_P + K_I$, a quantity that we refer to as the *overall gain* of the PI controller. Placing the zero effectively fixes the ratio between the proportional and integral parts of the controller and leaves only one parameter to vary. Then we vary the overall gain to assess control performance. This method is outlined below.

1. The zero of the PI controller must be between 0 and 1 on the positive real axis. Determine the possible locations relative to other poles and zeros on the positive real axis.
2. For each relative location of the zero, draw the root locus. Study the possible closed-loop poles. Determine which relative location is best to meet the design constraints.
3. For the most promising relative location, choose a few possible exact locations (e.g., near the ends of the segment, in the middle of the segment), and either draw an exact root locus or plot the expected settling time and overshoot. Choose the zero location $K_P/(K_P + K_I)$ and the overall gain $(K_P + K_I)$.
4. Simulate to verify the design, since the zero introduced by the PI controller and any zeros present in $G(z)$ can affect the system overshoot.

This design method is illustrated in the following example.

Example 9.6: PI control using root locus   Consider again the IBM Lotus Domino Server. The open-loop pole is at $z = 0.43$. The zero can be placed either to the right or to the left of the open-loop pole; the two different root locus plots are shown in Figure 9.11. If the zero is to the right of the pole, there is always a closed-loop pole between the zero location and $z = 1$. This closed-loop pole near the unit circle results in a slow closed-loop response. If the zero is placed to the left of the open-loop pole, the closed-loop response can be faster

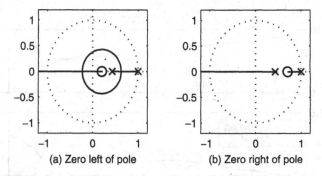

Fig. 9.11 *Root locus of the IBM Lotus Domino Server and PI control. The zero can be placed either to the left or to the right of the pole at 0.43. The root locus has a similar form no matter where exactly the zero is placed.*

than the open-loop response (the closed-loop poles can be closer to the origin). However, since the closed-loop poles can be complex, there could be a significant amount of overshoot in the closed-loop response, which may be undesirable.

We consider three different locations of the zero on the segment between the origin and the open-loop pole: 0.1, 0.2, 0.4. The first is very near the origin, the second is in the middle of the segment, and the third is near the open-loop pole. For each of these zero locations, and a range of overall gains, we compute the expected settling time and overshoot as predicted by the closed-loop poles. We also compute the actual overshoot by simulation. The results are shown in Figure 9.12.

The minimum settling time occurs with the zero at 0.2 and the overall gain of 4. However, the overshoot at this point is large (almost 90%). We choose to place the zero at 0.4, since it gives a larger region of gains with no overshoot. A choice of overall gain at 1.5 results in overshoot $M_p = 0$ and settling time $k_s = 4.2$. From the zero location and overall gain, we can find the gains K_P and K_I as

$$\left.\begin{array}{rcl} \dfrac{K_P}{K_P + K_I} &=& 0.4 \\[2mm] K_P + K_I &=& 1.5 \end{array}\right\} \implies \left\{\begin{array}{rcl} K_P &=& 0.6 \\ K_I &=& 0.9 \end{array}\right.$$

The simulation results of Figure 9.13 show the response to a step reference of 10. As predicted, the settling time is less than 5 and the maximum overshoot is zero. Comparing these results with those in Figure 9.10, we see that the larger proportional gain results in a faster response. The contribution of the proportional controller $u_P(k)$ is also much larger, as can be seen in the figures.

9.2.4   PI Control Design Using Empirical Methods

In many cases, the system model $G(z)$ is unknown. One approach is to use the system identification techniques described in Chapter 2 and then apply pole placement design or root locus analysis to the estimated transfer function. Here,

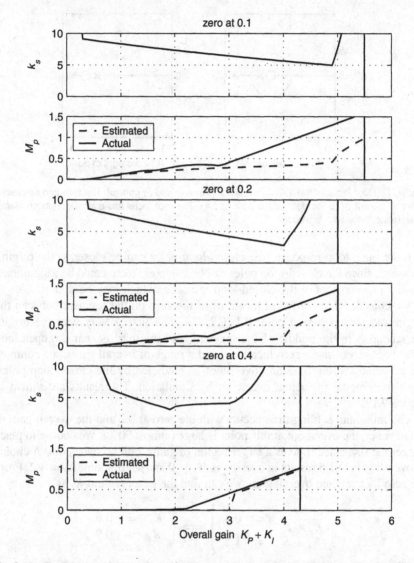

Fig. 9.12 Predicted settling times and maximum overshoot for the IBM Lotus Domino Server with PI control, for three different zero locations and a range of overall gains $K_P + K_I$. The stability boundary is indicated by the solid vertical line. Note that M_P is expressed as a fraction.

we describe an alternative approach in which the controller gains are computed in a more direct manner.

The starting point is to obtain the step response of the target system by applying a *bump test*, a step change in the control input. For computing systems, multiple replications of the bump test are needed because of stochastics. Also, the step input should be scaled by a factor u_{ss} so that the output response covers the desired operating region of the system.

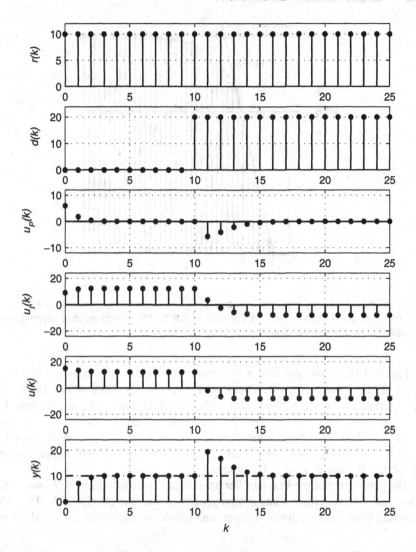

Fig. 9.13 *PI control of the IBM Lotus Domino Server with $K_P = 0.6$, $K_I = 0.9$. The reference is 10 and there is a disturbance of 20. The proportional and integral contributions to the controller are shown separately, along with their sum: $u(k) = u_P(k) + u_I(k)$. Compare these results to those in Figure 9.10. Here the proportional gain is larger, and this larger proportional gain drives the error to zero faster.*

Our focus is the *CHR controller design method* developed by Hrones and others [14]. (A good description of this method can also be found in [8].) This method assumes that system dynamics can be approximated by a first-order model with a delay of n sample times. That is, $y(k + n) = ay(k) + bu(k)$. These parameters are determined from a plot of the results of the bump test. However, instead of using a, b, and n, it is more common to use an alternative set of three parameters: L, R, and T. The definitions of these three parameters are shown

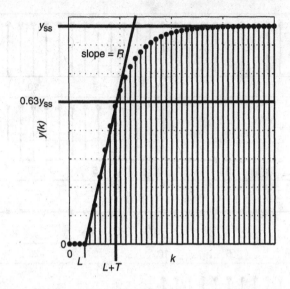

Fig. 9.14 *Step response curve for the CHR design method. The tangent line to the output has maximum slope R and intersects the time axis at L. The system reaches approximately two-thirds of its final value at time T + L.*

in Figure 9.14. A tangent line with maximum slope is drawn at the inflection point of the system response curve. The slope of the tangent line is R, and the intersection of the tangent line with the time axis is L, or the time lag of the system. The time constant T is the time needed by the system to reach $1 - e^{-1} \approx 0.63$ of its final value after it starts to react. The system reaches this point at time $T + L$. Note that T and L are expressed in terms of samples and that R has the same units as the output.

The parameters of the PI controller are computed directly from R, L, and T for a specific control objective and design goal using the formulas in Table 9.3. The approach taken is to minimize settling time subject to constraints on overshoot for

TABLE 9.3 CHR Rules for Designing a PI Controller

Design Goal	Overshoot Specification	Controller Gains K_P	K_I
Disturbance rejection	0%	$\dfrac{0.6}{RL}$	$\dfrac{0.15}{RL^2}$
Disturbance rejection	20%	$\dfrac{0.7}{RL}$	$\dfrac{0.3}{RL^2}$
Reference tracking	0%	$\dfrac{0.35}{RL}$	$\dfrac{0.3}{RLT}$
Reference tracking	20%	$\dfrac{0.6}{RL}$	$\dfrac{0.6}{RLT}$

Source: [27].

a change in either the reference or disturbance inputs.[1] The table considers two control objectives: disturbance rejection and reference tracking. The design goal is expressed in terms of maximum overshoot, which is either 0% or 20%. K_P and K_I are chosen so that the closed-loop system has the shortest settling time within the overshoot constraints. Note that the controller gains are larger if a 20% overshoot is permitted, which will result shorter settling times. Since all of the integral control gains are nonzero, there is a zero steady-state error in response to a step change in either the disturbance or reference inputs. The closed-loop system will be stable if the first-order system with delay is a reasonable approximation to the actual system. If the open-loop response is qualitatively different than that shown in Table 9.3, a stability analysis should be performed before an empirically designed controller is implemented.

Example 9.7: Controller design using the CHR rules   Figure 9.15 displays the results of an experiment conducted on a fourth-order system in open loop by applying a unit step to the control input $u(k)$. From the data plotted, it appears that the steady-state output is approximately 15, and the line of steepest slope (which is drawn on the plot) is approximately $R = 15/9 = 1.7$. This line intersects the time axis at $L = 4$. Since the final value is 15 and the initial value is 0, the time constant is found at the time when the response reaches $0.63(15) = 10$.

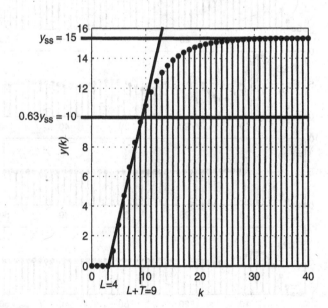

Fig. 9.15 *Open-loop response of a fourth-order system to a unit step input $u(k)$. The estimates of the parameters L, T are shown on the plot. R is estimated as the slope of the line, approximately $15/9$.*

---

[1][14] extends the definition of overshoot to apply to changes in either the reference or the disturbance inputs.

This happens at approximately $k = 9$. Thus, $L + T = 9$ and the time constant is estimated to be $T = 5$.

Using these estimates of R, L, and T, we can compute the control gains for a PI controller from Table 9.3. The results are shown in Table 9.4. Figure 9.16 displays the closed-loop response to a five-unit-step change in the reference input. Observe that the reference tracking controllers RT:00 and RT:20 have shorter

TABLE 9.4   PI Controller Gains Obtained by Applying the Example of Table 9.3 to Figure 9.15

Symbol	Design Goal	Overshoot Specification (%)	Controller Gains K_P	K_I
DR:00	Disturbance rejection	0	0.09	0.0056
DR:20	Disturbance rejection	20	0.11	0.011
RT:00	Reference tracking	0	0.053	0.009
RT:20	Reference tracking	20	0.09	0.018

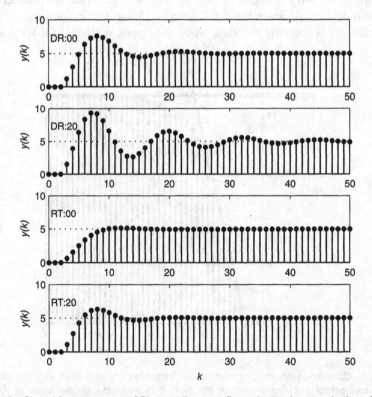

Fig. 9.16 *Closed-loop response of PI controllers to a five-unit-step increase in the reference input. The controller designs are given in Table 9.4. The design goals are disturbance rejection with 0% overshoot (DR:00), disturbance rejection with 20% overshoot (DR:20), reference tracking with 0% overshoot (RT:00), and reference tracking with 20% overshoot (RT:20).*

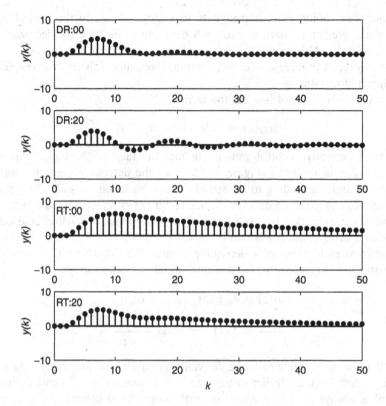

Fig. 9.17 *Closed-loop response of PI controllers to a 50-unit-step increase in the disturbance input. The controller designs are specified in Table 9.4. The design goals are disturbance rejection with 0% overshoot (DR:00), disturbance rejection with 20% overshoot (DR:20), reference tracking with 0% overshoot (RT:00), and reference tracking with 20% overshoot (RT:20).*

settling times and smaller overshoot than the disturbance rejection controllers DR:00 and DR:20. Also observe that the effect of permitting a larger overshoot is to reach the steady-state value faster. This is the case in part because the true system is a fourth-order system as opposed to the first-order system that is assumed by the CHR method. Figure 9.17 plots the closed-loop response to a 50-unit-step change in the disturbance input. Here, controllers DR:00 and DR:20, which designed for disturbance rejection, have shorter settling times and smaller overshoot than RT:00 and RT:20. As before, the effect of permitting a larger maximum overshoot is that the system reaches its steady-state value faster, although this does not necessarily mean that settling times are shorter.

9.3 PROPORTIONAL–DERIVATIVE CONTROL

The control actions of the proportional or integral controllers are based on the current error or past errors. In derivative control the controller output is proportional to the *rate of change* of the error. The idea behind derivative control is that the controller should react immediately to a large change in the control error; in essence, predicting that the error will continue to increase (or decrease) and act accordingly. Although this quick reaction can result in fast response times, it can also result in undesirable overreaction, especially if the system output has significant stochastics.

The derivative control law has the form

$$u_D(k) = K_D[e(k) - e(k-1)] \tag{9.14}$$

where the derivative control gain K_D defines the ratio of the input magnitude to the change in the error (Figure 9.18). Since the derivative controller adjusts the control input according to the speed of error variation, it is able to make an adjustment prior to the appearance of even larger errors. Practically, the derivative controller is never used by itself since if the error remains constant, the output of the derivative controller would be zero.

The transfer function of a derivative controller can be found by taking the Z-transform of Equation (9.14) with zero initial conditions to get

$$U_D(z) = K_D E(z) - K_D z^{-1} E(z)$$
$$\frac{U_D(z)}{E(z)} = K_D(1 - z^{-1}) = \frac{K_D(z-1)}{z}$$

Note that the steady-state gain of a derivative controller is equal to zero. As noted above, a derivative controller cannot react to a constant error. Thus, derivative control is always used in conjunction with proportional control and sometimes also with integral control.

The proportional–derivative (PD) control law has two terms: one proportional to the current error, and the other proportional to the change in error:

$$u(k) = K_P e(k) + K_D(e(k) - e(k-1)) \tag{9.15}$$

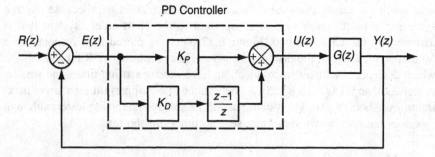

Fig. 9.18 Feedback loop with PD control. The error $E(z) = R - Y(z)$ is the input to the controller. The control input $U(z)$ is a sum of the proportional term $K_P E(z)$ and the derivative term $K_D[(z-1)/z]$.

Its transfer function can be found by taking the Z-transform with zero initial conditions and rearranging terms to get

$$\frac{U(z)}{E(z)} = K_P + \frac{K_D(z-1)}{z} = \frac{(K_P + K_D)z - K_D}{z} \qquad (9.16)$$

The controller has a pole at $z = 0$; this pole is fast and hence does not slow down the transient response like the pole at $z = 1$ does in integral control. The control transfer function also has a finite zero at $z = K_D/(K_P + K_D)$. If K_P and $K_D > 0$ have the same sign, the zero is always on the real line between 0 and 1. When the zero is exactly at 0, it cancels the pole at 0 and PD control reduces to the pure proportional control case. When the zero is exactly at 1, it reduces to the pure derivative control case.

PD controllers can be designed using the root locus method as in Section 9.2.3. However, PD controllers are not appropriate for first-order systems because pole placement is quite limited. For example, Figure 9.19 shows the root locus plots of a first-order system with PD control with two different zero locations. Observe that the poles are restricted to a limited section of the real axis. Compare these plots with the root locus of a first-order system and P control, as shown in Figure 8.12. Note that P control allows the closed-loop pole to be placed anywhere on the real axis to the left of the open-loop pole.

With their predictive ability, PD controllers can be used effectively to reduce the overshoot for a system that exhibits a significant amount of oscillation with P control. For example, consider a second-order system with transfer function

$$G(z) = \frac{1}{z^2 - 1.3z + 0.49}$$

The root locus of this system is shown in Figure 9.20. As the proportional gain increases, the closed-loop poles move farther away from the origin. Both the settling time and overshoot increase as K_P increases.

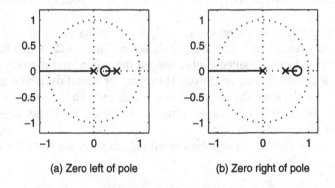

(a) Zero left of pole   (b) Zero right of pole

Fig. 9.19 *Root locus of PD control for a first-order system.*

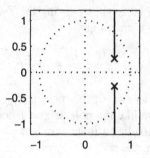

Fig. 9.20 Root locus of $G(z) = \dfrac{1}{z^2 - 1.3z + 0.49}$ considering only proportional control.

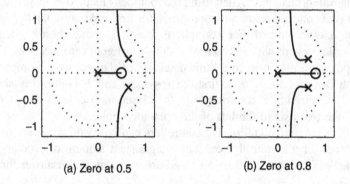

(a) Zero at 0.5

(b) Zero at 0.8

Fig. 9.21 Root locus of $G(z) = \dfrac{1}{z^2 - 1.3z + 0.49}$ and PD control for two different zero locations.

If we add a PD controller to this system, we add a zero and a pole to the open-loop system. The pole is at $z = 0$, and the zero can be placed anywhere along the positive real axis. Figure 9.21 shows the root locus for two different zero locations. When the zero is farther to the right, the root locus moves farther to the left.

For each of these two choices of zero location, settling time and overshoot are a function of overall gain ($K_P + K_D$), as shown in Figure 9.22. When the zero is at 0.8, the root locus is pulled farther toward the origin, and thus the expected overshoot and settling time are lower. However, the actual overshoot is greater. This difference between the estimated and actual overshoot is due to the effect of the zero. The zero has the largest effect on the actual overshoot when it is to the right of the closed-loop poles.

Choosing the zero at 0.5 and the overall gain at 0.18, we solve for the gains K_P and K_D as follows:

$$\left. \begin{array}{rcl} \dfrac{K_D}{K_P + K_D} & = & 0.5 \\[2mm] K_P + K_D & = & 0.18 \end{array} \right\} \implies \left\{ \begin{array}{rcl} K_P & = & 0.09 \\[2mm] K_D & = & 0.09 \end{array} \right.$$

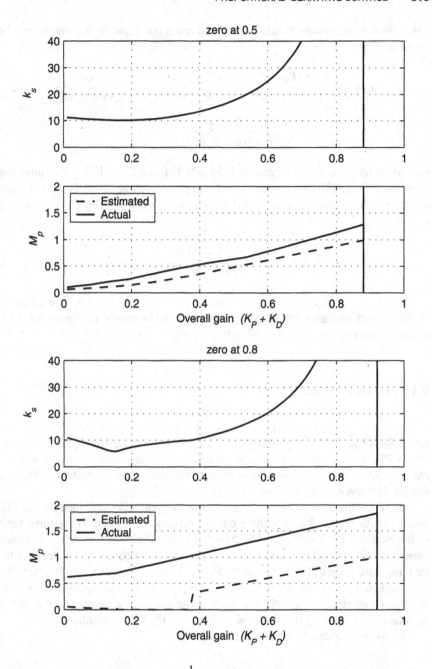

Fig. 9.22 *PD control of* $G(z) = \dfrac{1}{z^2 - 1.3z + 0.49}$ *for two different zero locations. Predicted settling times and overshoots are computed from the dominant closed loop poles. Actual overshoots are computed by simulation. The stability limit is shown by the solid vertical line. Overshoot is shown as a fraction.*

The closed-loop transfer function from the reference input to the output can be found as

$$F_R(z) = \frac{\{[(K_P + K_D)z - K_D]/z\}[1/(z^2 - 1.3z + 0.49)]}{1 + \{[(K_P + K_D)z - K_D]/z\}[1/(z^2 - 1.3z + 0.49)]}$$

$$= \frac{0.18z - 0.09}{z^3 - 1.3z^2 + 0.67z - 0.09}$$

the closed-loop poles are located at $0.55 \pm 0.39j$ and 0.20. Using the dominant poles of $0.55 \pm 0.39j = 0.67e^{\pm j\pi/5}$, the expected settling time is $k_s = 10$ and the estimated overshoot is $M_P = 0.13$. The steady-state gain of the closed-loop system is

$$F_R(1) = \frac{0.18 - 0.09}{1 - 1.29 + 0.67 - 0.09} = 0.31$$

which gives a steady-state error of almost 70% $(1 - 0.31/100)$. The response of the system to a step reference of magnitude 10 is shown in Figure 9.23. PD control cannot eliminate the steady-state error.

9.4 PID CONTROL

Proportional–integral–differential control (*PID control*) combines the three control actions that we have studied thus far. Figure 9.24 contains a block diagram of the PID controller. There is one parameter for each control action: K_P, K_I, and K_D. Since PID controllers have more parameters, there is more flexibility in design. However, there is more complexity as well.

Before continuing, we want to underscore the generality provided by the PID controller. In Figure 9.24 the three control actions correspond to the three rows of boxes in the PID controller. Observe that a proportional controller is a special case of a PID controller in which $K_I = K_D = 0$. This is equivalent to deleting the first and third rows of boxes inside the PID controller. Similarly, the PI controller is constructed by having $K_D = 0$, which corresponds to deleting the third row in the PID controller, and the PD controller is constructed by having $K_I = 0$, which is obtained by deleting the first row of boxes in the PID controller.

The difference equation for a PID controller is

$$u(k) = u_P(k) + u_I(k) + u_D(k)$$

$$= K_P e(k) + K_I \sum_{i=0}^{k-1} e(i) + K_I e(k) + K_D [e(k) - e(k-1)] \qquad (9.17)$$

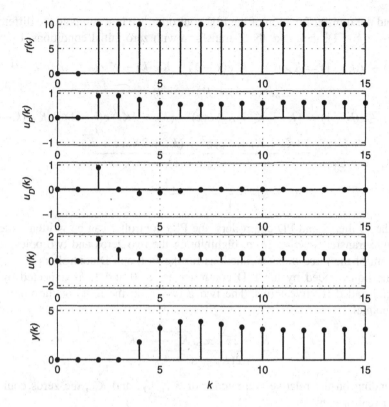

Fig. 9.23 Transient response of $G(z) = \dfrac{1}{z^2 - 1.3z + 0.49}$ with PD control to a step reference of magnitude 10. The contributions of the proportional and derivative parts of the control are shown separately, along with their sum. The derivative control $u_D(k)$ is only active initially, when the change in the error is large. Because the system $G(z)$ is second order, it takes two time steps before the control input $u(k)$ affects the output $y(k)$.

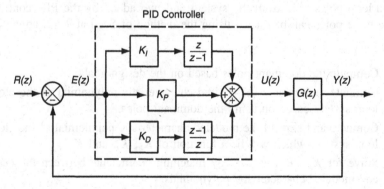

Fig. 9.24 Feedback loop with PID control. The error $E(z) = R - Y(z)$ is the input to the controller. The control input $U(z)$ is a sum of the proportional term $K_P E(z)$, the integral term $K_I[z/(z-1)]$ and the derivative term $K_D[(z-1)/z]$.

To find the transfer function of the PID controller, we first compute the difference $u(k) - u(k - 1)$, then take the Z-transform with zero initial conditions, to get

$$u(k) - u(k-1) = K_P e(k) - K_P e(k-1) + K_I e(k) + K_D e(k) - K_D e(k-1)$$
$$- K_D e(k-1) + K_D e(k-2)$$

$$u(k) - u(k-1) = (K_P + K_I + K_D)\, e(k) - (K_P + 2K_D)\, e(k-1) + K_D e(k-2)$$

$$\frac{U(z)}{E(z)} = \frac{(K_P + K_I + K_D)\, z^2 - (K_P + 2K_D)\, z + K_D}{z(z-1)}$$

$$= K_P + K_I \frac{z}{z-1} + K_D \frac{z-1}{z} \tag{9.18}$$

Similar to the PI and PD controllers, the PID controller can be written either in a single transfer function form, highlighting the two zeros and two poles, or as the sum of the three transfer functions for the P, I, and D controllers.

The poles added by the PID controller are at 0 and 1, as expected by the integral and derivative terms. The two zeros are at the roots of the numerator polynomial,

$$\frac{K_P + 2K_D \pm \sqrt{K_P^2 - 4K_I K_D}}{2(K_P + K_I + K_D)}$$

Depending on the relative magnitudes of K_P, K_I, and K_D, the zeros could be either real or complex.

As expected by the presence of the integral term, a PID controller results in zero steady-state error to both a constant reference and a constant disturbance input, as long as the system is stable in closed loop. The calculations of these errors are left as exercises for the reader.

Because there are three parameters in the PID controller, controller design is more complicated. For a first-order system with PID control, there are three closed-loop poles: one from the system and two added by the PID controller. These three poles can be placed using the method of Section 9.2.2, abbreviated here:

1. Compute the dominant poles based on the design goals.
2. Compute and expand the desired characteristic polynomial of the closed-loop system based on using the dominant poles.
3. Compute and expand the modeled characteristic polynomial of the closed-loop system, which will be a function of K_P, K_I, and K_D.
4. Solve for K_P, K_I, and K_D by matching coefficients between the desired and modeled characteristic polynomials.
5. Verify the result (e.g., by simulation).

Typically, the two dominant poles can be chosen based on the design goals; the third pole must be chosen smaller than the dominant one(s). For a second-order system with PID control, there are four closed-loop poles. Only three of these can be arbitrarily placed using the three parameters in a PID controller. Similarly, for higher-order systems, the method does not always yield a feasible solution. There are also empirical design methods for PID controllers similar to those discussed in Section 9.2.4; a good reference for these methods is [8].

It is worth mentioning that even if the derivative control law can help to add certain predictability to the controller, it may also be sensitive to the stochastic variations in the system output. This may become a serious problem for computing systems because they typically have a significant stochastic component. One way to solve this problem is to apply a low-pass filter to smooth the system output so that the derivative control term will respond only to large system changes, not to small stochastic variations. However, this additional filter may slow down the system response, which is contrary to the purpose of introducing the derivative control term. Hence, in practice, PI controllers are preferred over PID controllers.

Example 9.8: PID control design by pole placement   Consider the IBM Lotus Domino Server, as in Example 9.5, with the same design goals. For a PID control design, we must choose three closed-loop poles. We choose the dominant poles p_1 and $p_2 = 0.6e^{\pm j0.6} = 0.5 \pm 0.34j$. The third pole is chosen to have a smaller magnitude than the dominant ones, $p_3 = -0.3$. As shown by the algebra, this last pole must be chosen to be negative if all of the control gains are to be positive. The desired characteristic polynomial is $(z - p_1)(z - p_2)(z - p_3) = (z^2 - z + 0.36)(z + 0.3) = z^3 - 0.70z^2 + 0.063z + 0.11$.

With PID control (as in Figure 9.24), the closed-loop transfer function from the reference to the output is

$$
\begin{aligned}
F_R(z) &= \frac{Y(z)}{R(z)} \\[4pt]
&= \frac{\dfrac{(K_P + K_I + K_D)\,z^2 - (K_P + 2K_D)\,z + K_D}{z(z-1)}\left(\dfrac{0.47}{z-0.43}\right)}{1 + \dfrac{(K_P + K_I + K_D)\,z^2 - (K_P + 2K_D)\,z + K_D}{z(z-1)}\left(\dfrac{0.47}{z-0.43}\right)} \\[4pt]
&= \frac{(0.47)\left((K_P + K_I + K_D)z^2 - (K_P + 2K_D)z + K_D\right)}{D(z)}
\end{aligned}
\tag{9.19}
$$

where

$$
D(z) = z^3 + (0.47(K_P + K_I + K_D) - 1.43)\, z^2 \\
+ (0.43 - 0.47(K_P + 2K_D))\, z + 0.47K_D
$$

Note that this closed-loop transfer function depends on K_P, K_I, and K_D.

To find the values of K_P, K_I, and K_D that result in this characteristic polynomial, we match terms with the closed-loop transfer function of Equation (9.19), to get three equations in three unknowns:

$$z^3 - 0.70z^2 + 0.063z + 0.11$$
$$= z^3 + (0.47(K_P + K_I + K_D) - 1.43)\, z^2$$
$$+ (0.43 - 0.47(K_P + 2K_D)) + 0.47K_D$$

$$\left. \begin{array}{rcl} 0.47K_D &=& 0.11 \\ 0.43 - 0.47(K_P + 2K_D) &=& 0.063 \\ 0.47(K_P + K_I + K_D) - 1.43 &=& -0.7 \end{array} \right\} \implies \left\{ \begin{array}{rcl} K_P &=& 0.31 \\ K_I &=& 1.01 \\ K_D &=& 0.23 \end{array} \right.$$

If the third pole p_3 had been chosen to be positive and real, the derivative gain K_D would necessarily be negative. Negative gains are undesirable (except in the case when the system transfer function has a negative gain—and then *all* control gains should be negative).

Since the system model is only first order, there are no extra pole locations to solve for. Simulation results in Figure 9.25 for a step reference of 10 show that with this choice of gains, the design criteria are satisfied. The response to a disturbance of magnitude 20 is also shown. The proportional, integral, and derivative components of the control signal $u(k)$ are shown individually, along with their sum $u(k) = u_P(k) + u_I(k) + u_D(k)$. Since the proportional gain is small, the proportional control does not contribute very much to the response. Also note that the derivative term is active only when the error changes abruptly, but it does serve to speed up the response (comparing to Figure 9.10).

9.5 SUMMARY

1. Integral controllers adjust the control input based on K_I times the sum of the control errors. Integral control can eliminate steady-state error but can also increase settling times.

2. Derivative controllers adjust the control input based on K_D times the change in control error. Derivative control can decrease settling times, but this technique is quite sensitive to noise.

3. Proportional, integral, and derivative control can be used in combination. Examples are proportional–integral (PI) controllers, proportional–derivative controllers (PD), and proportional–integral–derivative (PID) controllers.

4. Pole placement design provides a way to find the values of control parameters based on a specification of desired closed-loop properties (e.g., settling time, maximum overshoot).

5. Root locus design proceeds by observing how closed-loop poles change as controller parameters are adjusted.

6. The values of the controller parameters (e.g., K_P, K_I) can be determined by empirical methods based on the step response of the open-loop system.

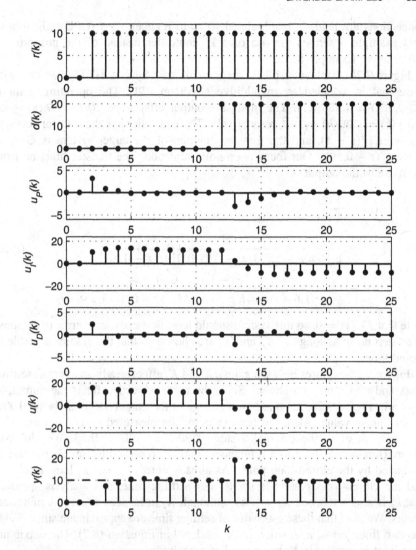

Fig. 9.25 *PID control of the IBM Lotus Domino Server with $K_P = 0.31$, $K_I = 1.01$, and $K_D = 0.23$. The reference is 10 and there is a disturbance of 20. The design goals of a settling time less than $k = 10$ and an overshoot less than 0.1 (10%) are satisfied. The proportional, integral, and derivative contributions to the controller are shown separately, along with their sum: $u(k) = u_P(k) + u_I(k) + u_D(k)$.*

9.6 EXTENDED EXAMPLES

9.6.1 PI Control of the Apache HTTP Server Using Empirical Methods

This example extends Section 8.7.2 in which proportional control is used to manage the Apache HTTP Server. As before, KeepAlive (the time that idle HTTP connections are held) is manipulated so as to regulate CPU (CPU utilizations). This example describes the use of a PI controller instead of the proportional controller of Example 8.7.2.

Figure 9.26 displays a block diagram of the Apache HTTP Server with noise that is modeled as an additive effect on CPU. The operating point is $(\overline{\text{CPU}}, \overline{\text{KA}}) = (0.58, 11)$. The input and output offsets are $u(k) = \text{KA}(k) - \overline{\text{KA}}$ and $y(k) = \text{CPU}(k) - \overline{\text{CPU}}$, respectively. The controller has the transfer function $K_P + zK_I/(z - 1)$, and the transfer function of the target system is $G(z) = -0.014/(z - 0.59)$. Our focus is on noise rejection. The transfer function from the noise to the output is

$$F_N(z) = \frac{T(z)}{N(z)}$$

$$= \frac{1}{1 + [K_P + zK_I/(z - 1)][-0.014/(z - 0.6)]} \tag{9.20}$$

$$= \frac{(z - 1)(z - 0.6)}{z^2 - (1.6 + 0.014K_I + 0.014K_P)z + 0.014K_P + 0.6} \tag{9.21}$$

Note that $F_N(1) = 0$, so this system should have no steady-state error in response to a step noise as long as K_p and K_I are chosen so that the system is stable in closed loop.

Figure 9.27 explores how the gains K_p and K_I affect steady-state error, settling time, and maximum overshoot. Since the noise directly affects the output, as shown in Figure 9.26, the maximum change in the output value is always 100% of the noise value. Also, the final value of the measured output is zero. That is, $y_{ss} = 0$; or in the original system, $\text{CPU}_{ss} = \overline{\text{CPU}} = 0.58$. We also plot the maximum overshoot to a reference input, as computed by simulation and as estimated by the closed-loop poles. As already noted, $e_{ss} = 0$ as long as $K_I \neq 0$ and the closed-loop system is stable. For settling time, this analysis predicts that k_s is smallest when $K_P = -43$, although K_I influences when this minimum occurs. We note that these estimates of settling time are approximate since $F_N(z)$ has two finite zeros, a situation not considered in Equation (8.7). The maximum overshoot is smaller if K_I has a smaller magnitude.

Figure 9.28 displays the transient response of $F_N(z)$ to a noise input of magnitude 0.2. When the noise occurs, the output immediately increases by the

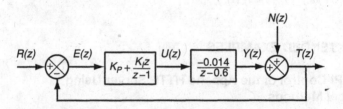

Fig. 9.26 Block diagram of the Apache HTTP Server using PI control. The control input is KeepAlive, and the output is CPU. The noise has an additive effect on CPU.

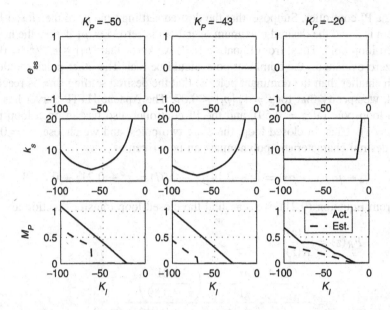

Fig. 9.27   *Effect of K_P and K_I in Figure 9.26 on steady-state error, settling time, and maximum overshoot. The actual overshoot is computed for a step reference change, and the estimated overshoot is based on the closed-loop pole locations.*

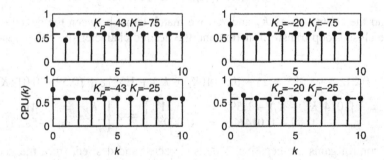

Fig. 9.28   *Effect of K_P and K_I in Figure 9.26 on transient response to a noise input. $n(k) = 0.2$. The dashed line is the reference value.*

magnitude of the noise. The PI controller then adjusts the control input (here, KA) based on the difference between the output and the reference. The dashed line is the reference value. As predicted by analysis, there is no steady-state error.

9.6.2   Designing a PI Controller for the Apache HTTP Server Using Pole Placement Design

This example applies the analytic techniques developed in Section 9.2.4 to the Apache HTTP Server of Section 9.6.1. We proceed from the perspective of design using a PI controller. Suppose that the desired settling time k_s of the closed-loop system is 2 and the desired maximum overshoot is zero. Let p_1 denote the largest closed-loop pole. Thus, from Equation (8.7) we know that $|p_1| \leq e^{-4/k_s} = 0.14$. For zero overshoot, the dominant pole should be real. The other poles should be much smaller than the dominant pole, so that the desired settling time is reached. Thus, we specify that for $i \neq 1$, $|p_i| \leq 0.07$. The Apache HTTP Server has one open-loop pole (at $z = 0.59$), and the PI controller also has an open-loop pole (at $z = 1$). Thus, in closed loop, there are two poles, and we choose $p_2 = 0.07$. The desired characteristic polynomial can be written as

$$(z - p_1)(z - p_2) = (z - 0.14)(z - 0.07) = z^2 - 0.21z + 0.0098$$

From Equation (9.21), we can find the closed-loop transfer function as

$$F_R(z) = \frac{Y(z)}{R(z)}$$

$$= \frac{\dfrac{(K_P + K_I)z - K_P}{z - 1}\left(\dfrac{-0.014}{z - 0.59}\right)}{1 + \dfrac{(K_P + K_I)z - K_P}{z - 1}\left(\dfrac{-0.014}{z - 0.59}\right)}$$

$$= \frac{-0.014(K_P + K_I)z + 0.014K_P}{z^2 - (0.014(K_P + K_I) + 1.59)z + (0.59 - 0.014K_P)}$$

To find the control gains K_P and K_I, we match terms between the denominator of the closed-loop transfer function and the desired characteristic polynomial, to get

$$z^2 - 0.21z + 0.0098 = z^2 - [0.014(K_P + K_I) + 1.59]z + (0.59 - 0.014K_P)$$

$$\left.\begin{array}{rcl} -0.014(K_P + K_I) - 1.59 & = & -0.21 \\ 0.59 - 0.014K_P & = & 0.0098 \end{array}\right\} \implies \left\{\begin{array}{rcl} K_P & = & -41 \\ K_I & = & -58 \end{array}\right.$$

Both control gains are negative. This is expected and desired, since the gain of the system is also negative. If the gain of the system is positive, the control gains should also be positive.

These results are consistent with Figure 9.27 in that when $K_P = -43$ and $K_I = -57$, $k_s \approx 2$. Indeed, we could use plots such as those in Section 9.6.1 for design. However, pole placement design provides a way to obtain controller parameters that achieve a variety of design goals.

9.6.3 IBM Lotus Domino Server with a Sensor Delay

This example studies integral control of the IBM Lotus Domino Server. The objective is to regulate RIS, the number of RPCs waiting for or receiving service (which is approximately the same as the number of active users). This is done by adjusting the tuning parameter MaxUsers. Presented below is a summary and refinement of results reported in [53] in which integral control is used for a product-level server.

Reference [53] models the IBM Lotus Domino Server in terms of the server itself and a measurement sensor. In particular, this analysis concludes that it is important to consider the manner in which measurements are collected (the sensor) since this affects their accuracy and can introduce delays. The transfer functions of the controller, the IBM Lotus Domino Server, and the sensor are shown in the block diagram in Figure 9.29. The operating point is $\overline{\text{MaxUsers}} = 375$, $\overline{\text{RIS}} = 325$, and $u(k) = \text{MaxUsers}(k) - \overline{\text{MaxUsers}}$, $y(k) = \text{RIS}(k) - \overline{\text{RIS}}$. Note that the closed-loop transfer function from the reference to the output is

$$F_R(z) = \frac{Y(z)}{R(z)}$$

$$= \frac{zK_I(0.47)(0.17z - 0.11)}{(z - 1)(z - 0.43)(z - 0.64) + zK_I(0.47)(0.17z - 0.11)} \tag{9.22}$$

Figure 9.30 studies the effect of the integral control parameter K_I. Each subfigure contains two plots, one for RIS(k) (which also displays the reference value) and a second plot that shows the associated value of MaxUsers(k). Consider $K_I = 0.1$. We see that there is a slow convergence to the reference value. If $K_I = 1$, the convergence is faster. If $K_I = 5$, there are substantial oscillations.

First consider steady-state error. Observe that for all three values of K_I considered in Figure 9.30, the controller is accurate in that RIS(k) is centered around the reference value. This suggests that $e_{ss} = 0$. Such a conclusion is consistent with Equation (9.22) in that $F_R(1) = 1$.

Figure 9.31 provides insights into the transient behavior displayed in Figure 9.30. The figure plots the magnitude and angle of the poles of Equation (9.22) as K_I is varied. Note that there are three poles because the power of z in the denominator of $F_R(z)$ is 3. We see that when $K_I \approx 0$, the dominant closed-loop pole is close to 1, which explains the long settling time for $K_I = 0.1$ in Figure 9.30(a). As K_I increases, the magnitude of the dominant pole is reduced. For example, at $K_I = 1$, this magnitude is approximately 0.75. This is why Figure 9.30(b) has a much shorter settling time than Figure 9.30(a). However, for $K_I > 1.5$, we have a pair of complex poles. These poles result in controller-induced oscillations, as is evident in Figure 9.30(c).

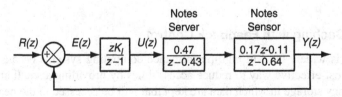

Fig. 9.29 Block diagram for integral control of the IBM Lotus Domino Server. The measurement sensor is modeled explicitly.

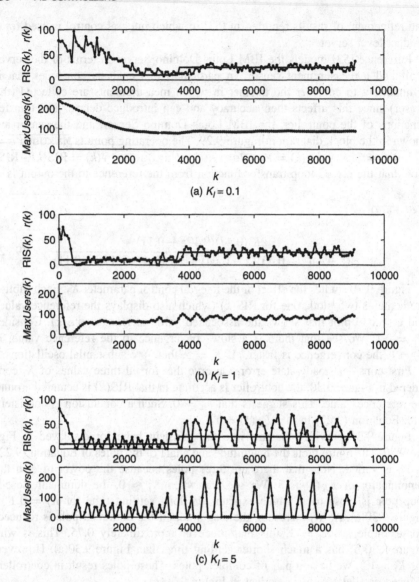

Fig. 9.30 Transient response of a control system incorporating a product-level Lotus Notes Server with an external integral controller to a synthetic workload for different values of K_I. There is a step increase in the reference value $r(k)$, as shown in the first of each paired subfigure.

9.6.4 Caching with Feedback Control

Caching is widely used in high-performance computing systems because it provides a cost-effective way to reduce access times by providing a small amount of low-latency storage in which data are kept that will be accessed in the near future. Low-latency storage is relatively expensive and is therefore a scarce resource. As such, controlling the allocation of this storage is of concern.

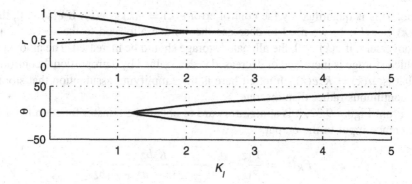

Fig. 9.31 *Magnitude and angle of the poles for the closed-loop system for the IBM Lotus Domino Server in Figure 9.29. The integral control parameter is K_I, and the angle is plotted in degrees.*

One way to allocate cache storage is based on business-oriented policies (e.g., as in [44]). For example, gold class service might ensure a 1-second response time, whereas silver class might only guarantee a 3-second response time for the same type of request. One element of enforcing such service differentiation is for preferred classes (e.g., gold) to have a higher hit rate. (*Hit rate* is the probability that the data requested are in low-latency storage.) The hit rate for a service class can be increased (decreased) by allocating more (less) low-latency storage for that service class.

Figure 9.32 displays the block diagram of a system that regulates hit rate for a service class using proportional control. $R(z)$ specifies the reference (desired) hit rate, which may vary over time. The actual (measured) hit rate is $Y(z)$, which is the output of the system. The operation of the cache (as perceived by the service class under consideration) is modeled as an integrator that front-ends a first-order system. The integrator models the fact that the control input is the *change* in cache allocation, not the absolute amount of cache space allocated. Thus, the cache transfer function is

$$\frac{z}{z-1}\frac{b}{z-a}$$

The control input $U(z)$ is the change in low-latency storage allocated for the service class. We want the measured hit rate to be very close to the reference hit

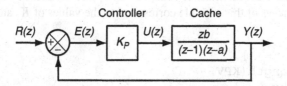

Fig. 9.32 *Block diagram for control of a cache using proportional control.*

rate. This is quantified by the control error $e(k) = r(k) - y(k)$. If $e(k) < 0$, then $y(k) > r(k)$, so we need to decrease the storage allocated to the service class. Conversely, if $e(k) > 0$, the allocated storage should be increased. The amount by which storage is increased or decreased is determined by a proportional controller. That is, $u(k) = K_p e(k)$. Implicit here is the simplifying assumption that storage is continuous rather than discrete.

From Figure 9.32, it is straightforward to obtain the transfer function from the reference input to the output:

$$F_R(z) = \frac{Y(z)}{R(z)} = \frac{K_p bz}{(z-1)(z-a) + K_p bz}$$

Observe that the steady gain of this system is $F_R(1) = 1$, so there is no steady-state error. At first glance, this may seem surprising since we use proportional control, and we know that proportional control has $|e_{ss}| > 0$ unless K_p is very large. Further, there is no precompensation. Rather, the reason why $e_{ss} = 0$ is that the cache system itself includes an integrator.

*9.7 DESIGNING PI CONTROLLERS IN MATLAB

In this section we describe ways to use MATLAB in controller design. In Section 8.8 we introduce the MATLAB functions feedback, pole, zero, dcgain, and rlocus. Here we show how to construct transfer functions for sets of controller parameters and how to estimate the settling time and overshoot from the closed-loop transfer function.

Our starting point is Figure 9.27 in which we plot e_{ss}, k_s^*, and M_p for many combinations of K_P and K_I. In MATLAB, each K_P, K_I pair results in a different transfer function. Thus, we must construct a matrix of transfer functions to produce Figure 9.27.

Our approach is as follows. We first define vectors for the set of K_I and K_P values to consider.

```
KIV = (-150:-10)';
KPV = [-50; -43; -30];
```

Next, we define the transfer function for the Apache HTTP Server.

```
apache = tf(-.014, [1 -.59],-1);
```

Now we construct the transfer functions and place the results into the variable sys_m. The rows of this variable correspond to the values of K_P and the columns to K_I.

```
sys_matrix = [];
for i=1:length(KPV)
 sys_vector = [];
 for k = 1:length(KIV)
```

```
control = tf([KIV(k) 0], [1 -1], -1) + KPV(i);
sys_vector = [sys_vector feedback(apache*control,1)];
end
sys_matrix = [sys_matrix; sys_vector];
end
```

The outer loop varies K_P, and the inner loop changes K_I. sys_matrix is initialized to the empty vector. Each iteration of the outer loop constructs a row vector of transfer functions for the values of K_I. These are then appended to sys_matrix.

To estimate the settling time and overshoot, we need the dominant poles of the closed-loop transfer function. These are the ones with the largest magnitude.

```
cl = feedback(apache*control,1);
clpoles = poles(cl);
[r,index] = max(abs(clpoles));
```

The system is stable in closed loop if the magnitude of the dominant pole is less than 1. In this case, we can estimate the settling time and maximum overshoot, and compute the actual overshoot using the step command.

```
if r < 1
    ks(i) = -4/log(r);
    theta = angle(clpoles(index));

    % check pole too close to zero
    if abs(theta)< 0.00 mp(i) =0;

    % check for negative pole
    elseif abs(theta - pi)< 0.001 mp(i) = r;

    % largest pole is complex
    else mp(i) = r^(pi/theta);
    end

    [y,t] = step(cl);
    mp_actual(i) = (max(y) - dcgain(cl))/dcgain(cl);
end % if
```

Inside a loop, this set of commands creates a vector of values for k_s and M_P (actual and estimated), which can then be plotted.

9.8 EXERCISES

1. Compute the steady-state error to a step reference and a constant (step) disturbance for a system $G(z)$ with the following controllers. Refer to Figure 9.24,

and let the disturbance enter at the same place as the reference input. For what values of K_P, K_I, and K_D do your results hold?

(a) PI control, Equation (9.6).

(b) PD control, Equation (9.14).

(c) PID control, Equation (9.17).

2. Consider the IBM Lotus Domino Server

$$G(z) = \frac{Y(z)}{U(z)} = \frac{0.47}{z - 0.43}$$

with a PI controller, as shown in Figure 9.9. Let $K_P = 2$, $K_I = 1$.

(a) Find the closed-loop transfer function $F_R(z) = Y(z)/R(z)$.

(b) From the dominant closed-loop poles, estimate the settling time k_s and maximum overshoot M_P.

(c) Simulate the system to find the maximum overshoot to a step reference of magnitude 10. Does this agree with your previous estimate?

(d) Simulate the response of the system to a disturbance of magnitude 20.

3. Repeat Exercise 2 with $K_P = 0.5$, $K_I = 1$.

4. Consider the Apache HTTP Server with transfer function

$$G(z) = \frac{Y(z)}{U(z)} = \frac{-0.014}{z - 0.59}$$

with a PI controller, as shown in Figure 9.26. Design a PI controller so that the closed-loop poles are at $0.5e^{\pm j(\pi/4)}$. Simulate the closed-loop system to a step reference of magnitude 0.2, and a step disturbance of 0.3.

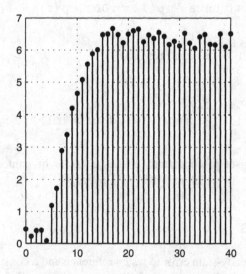

Fig. 9.33 Output response to a unit step input.

5. When using empirical methods for tuning, the output does not always exactly match the form of Table 9.3. Consider the system response (to a unit step input) shown in Figure 9.33. Estimate (as best as possible) the parameters L, R, and T for this system, and use these to design a PI controller. Simulate the resulting PI controller on the following system:

$$G(z) = \frac{Y(z)}{U(z)} = \frac{1}{z^5 - 0.47z^4 - 0.85z^3 + 0.33z^2 + 0.15z}$$

6. Consider the feedback loop with integral control in Figure 9.1 in which the target system has the transfer function $G(z) = G$. How should Figure 9.2.2 be modified to do pole placement design? What difficulties will arise if instead we wanted to do PI control (i.e., Figure 9.9) and the target system has the transfer function $G(z) = G$?

10

State-Space Feedback Control

State-space models such as those described in Chapter 7 arise in many settings, especially multiple-input, multiple-output (MIMO) systems. In this chapter we describe several approaches to the design of feedback controllers for systems modeled in state space. Three architectures are considered. The first, static state feedback, is a multidimensional extension of proportional control in which the reference input is fixed at the system's operating point. A second architecture, precompensated static control, extends the first architecture by including a precompensator to accomplish reference tracking. The third architecture, dynamic state feedback, can be viewed as the state-space analog to PI (proportional integral) control and hence has good disturbance rejection properties (although settling times may be longer). For all three architectures, the design problem is to select feedback gains that yield the desired controller properties, especially settling times and maximum overshoot. Two design techniques are discussed. The first, pole placement design, determines the poles needed to achieve the desired closed-loop properties and then computes the feedback gains required. The second approach, linear quadratic regulation (LQR), employs an optimization technique that parameterizes the trade-off between control errors and control effort (i.e., how big an adjustment must be made).

10.1 STATE-SPACE ANALYSIS

In this section we review the basics of state-space models using the tandem queue example. (See Chapter 7 for more details on both topics.)

Feedback Control of Computing Systems, by Joseph L. Hellerstein, Yixin Diao, Sujay Parekh, and Dawn M. Tilbury
ISBN 0-471-26637-X Copyright © 2004 John Wiley & Sons, Inc.

State-space models employ state variables to describe system dynamics. These variables are typically denoted by the vector $\mathbf{x}(k) = [x_1, \ldots, x_n]^\top = \begin{bmatrix} x_1 \\ \vdots \\ x_n \end{bmatrix}$. This is illustrated in the following example.

Example 10.1: Tandem queue   Figure 10.1 displays the tandem queue system that consists of two queueing systems connected in series. Requests that complete processing in the first queue flow into the second queue. Recall that the buffer size of the first queueing system is used as the actuator, and the sum of the response times of the two queues is the measured output. Although this is a SISO system, it is useful to employ the response times of the individual queues as state variables. Thus, the state $\mathbf{x}(k)$ is $\begin{bmatrix} x_1(k) \\ x_2(k) \end{bmatrix} = \begin{bmatrix} R_1(k) - \overline{R}_1 \\ R_2(k) - \overline{R}_2 \end{bmatrix}$, where $R_i(k)$ is the response time of queueing system i at time k, and $\overline{R}_i$ is the operating point of queue i. In this example, $\overline{R}_1 = 2.5$ and $\overline{R}_2 = 6.5$.

Typically, state-space descriptions are multidimensional, such as the use of the response times of the individual queueing systems in Example 10.1. This leads to a vector and matrix representation of models. In particular,

$$\mathbf{x}(k+1) = \mathbf{A}\mathbf{x}(k) + \mathbf{B}u(k)$$

$$y(k) = \mathbf{C}\mathbf{x}(k) \tag{10.1}$$

where $\mathbf{x}(k)$ is an $n \times 1$ vector to represent n system states, $u(k)$ is a scalar input, and $y(k)$ is a scalar output. $\mathbf{A}$ is an $n \times n$ matrix, $\mathbf{B}$ is an $n \times 1$ vector, and $\mathbf{C}$ is a $1 \times n$ vector. The first equation describes the dynamics of the state vector. The second equation shows how measured outputs are computed from the state vector. In MIMO systems, $u(k)$ and $y(k)$ are vectors [which are denoted by $\mathbf{u}(k)$ and $\mathbf{y}(k)$], and $\mathbf{B}$ and $\mathbf{C}$ are matrices.

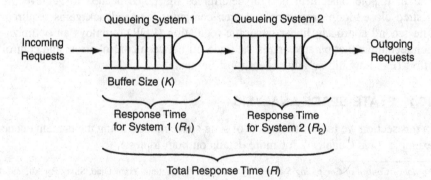

Fig. 10.1 *Architecture diagram of a tandem queue as shown in Figure 7.1.*

Example 10.2: State-space model of a tandem queue   Define the state vector

$$\mathbf{x}(k) = \left[\begin{array}{c} x_1(k) \\ x_2(k) \end{array} \right] = \left[\begin{array}{c} R_1(k) - \overline{R}_1(k) \\ R_2(k) - \overline{R}_2(k) \end{array} \right]$$

From Chapter 7 we have

$$\mathbf{A} = \left[\begin{array}{cc} a_{11} & 0 \\ a_{21} & a_{22} \end{array} \right] = \left[\begin{array}{cc} 0.13 & 0 \\ 0.46 & 0.63 \end{array} \right]$$

$$\mathbf{B} = \left[\begin{array}{c} b \\ 0 \end{array} \right] = \left[\begin{array}{c} 0.069 \\ 0 \end{array} \right]$$

$$\mathbf{C} = \left[\begin{array}{cc} c_1 & c_2 \end{array} \right] = \left[\begin{array}{cc} 1 & 1 \end{array} \right]$$

Then we see from Equation (10.1) that $\mathbf{x}(k+1) = \mathbf{A}\mathbf{x}(k) + \mathbf{B}u(k)$ and $y(k) = \mathbf{C}\mathbf{x}(k)$.

Last, recall from Chapter 7 that the settling time of a system is determined by its poles, and the poles of a state-space model are the eigenvalues of $\mathbf{A}$ in Equation (10.1). As in Chapter 6, we focus on the dominant pole.

Example 10.3: Open-loop settling time of a tandem queue   The poles of Equation (10.1) are the solutions to its characteristic equation, which is obtained by setting the characteristic polynomial to 0. That is,

$$
\begin{aligned}
0 &= \det(z\mathbf{I} - \mathbf{A}) \\
&= \det \left[\begin{array}{cc} z - 0.13 & 0 \\ -0.46 & z - 0.63 \end{array} \right] \\
&= (z - 0.13)(z - 0.63)
\end{aligned}
$$

Clearly, the poles are 0.13 and 0.63, and the latter is the dominant pole. So the settling time of the system is

$$k_s \approx \frac{-4}{\log 0.63} = 9$$

Figure 10.2 plots the open-loop step response of the tandem queue example. We see that the estimated value of k_s closely approximates the observed settling time.

10.2   STATE FEEDBACK CONTROL SYSTEMS

In this section we present three architectures for feedback control: static state feedback, which is similar to proportional control; precompensated static feedback, which provides a way to change the reference value; and dynamic state feedback, which is similar to PI control.

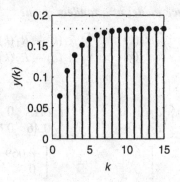

Fig. 10.2 *Step response of the tandem queue.*

10.2.1 Static State Feedback

A simple approach to controller design is to employ *static state feedback*. The intuition is that the control input $u(k)$ should be proportional to the state but with an opposite sign. Thus, as the closed-loop system moves away from its operating point $\mathbf{x}(k) = 0$, the control action pushes it back.

Static state feedback uses the control law

$$u(k) = -\mathbf{K}\mathbf{x}(k). \tag{10.2}$$

The $\mathbf{K}$ are the *controller gains* for static state feedback. In general, the $\mathbf{K}$ are chosen so that $-\mathbf{K}\mathbf{x}(k)$ drives $\mathbf{x}(k)$ to $\mathbf{0}$.

Figure 10.3 displays a block diagram of static state feedback. The target system has scalar control input $u(k)$. Based on this and the values of the state variables $\mathbf{x}(k)$, the (scalar) measured output $y(k)$ is determined. The double lines labeled $\mathbf{x}(k)$ indicate that a vector is output from the target system and input to the controller block labeled $\mathbf{K}$. Also, there is a disturbance input $d(k)$ that affects the control input.

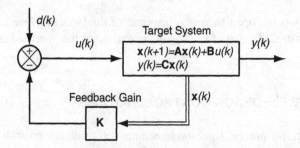

Fig. 10.3 *Block diagram of a static state feedback controller. The control input $u(k)$, disturbance input $d(k)$, and the measured output $y(k)$ are scalars. The state vector $\mathbf{x}(k)$ is a vector.*

We describe the behavior of static state feedback by substituting Equation (10.2) into Equation (10.1):

$$x(k + 1) = \mathbf{A}x(k) - \mathbf{BK}x(k)$$
$$= (\mathbf{A} - \mathbf{BK})x(k)$$

So the characteristic polynomial of the closed-loop system is

$$\det(z\mathbf{I} - (\mathbf{A} - \mathbf{BK})) \tag{10.3}$$

and the closed-loop poles are the solution to $\det\{z\mathbf{I} - (\mathbf{A} - \mathbf{BK})\} = 0$. Hence, we can place the poles of the closed-loop system by properly selecting the feedback gains in $\mathbf{K}$ (as discussed in Sections 10.3.1 and 10.3.2).

Example 10.4: Static state feedback for a tandem queue This example illustrates how properly selected feedback gains can result in a static feedback controller with good transient response. Our control objective is to regulate response times of both queueing systems at the operating point $\overline{R}_1 = 2.5$, $\overline{R}_2 = 6.5$ (and hence $\overline{R} = 9$). We use the feedback gains

$$\mathbf{K} = [K_1 \quad K_2] = [2.3 \quad 6.9]$$

Figure 10.4 displays a block diagram of this system.

Now consider a situation in which the initial conditions are $x(0) = [1, 1]^\top$; that is, $R_1(0) = 3.5$ and $R_2(0) = 7.5$. Figure 10.5 displays the simulation results. Note that both state variables converge quickly to their operating point. Also, the buffer size $K(k)$ initially decreases in order to lower the response time, and then there is some overshoot of $R_1(k)$ in order to facilitate fast convergence.

Although static state feedback is a simple scheme, it suffers from a major drawback—it cannot be used for tracking a reference input. Indeed, the architecture does not include a reference input. Further, it turns out that static state feedback also has poor disturbance rejection characteristics.

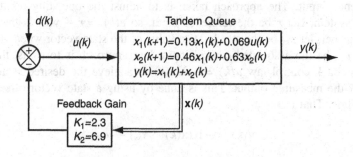

Fig. 10.4 *Block diagram of a static state feedback controller for a tandem queue.* $x_1(k) = R_1(k) - 2.5$, $x_2(k) = R_2(k) - 6.5$, $u(k) = K(k) - 25$, $y(k) = R(k) - 9$.

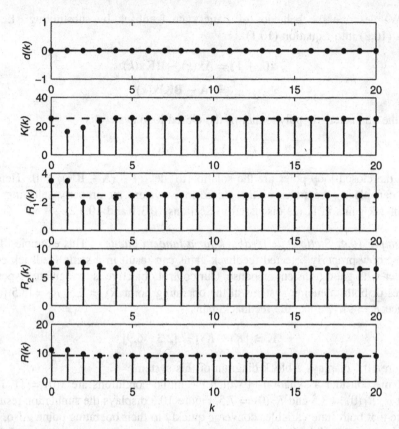

Fig. 10.5 *Response of a system with static state feedback control to initial conditions. The objective is to regulate the system at its operating point for response time, where $\overline{R}_1(0) = 2.5$ seconds and $\overline{R}_2(0) = 6.5$ seconds. The operating point of all variables is indicated by the dashed lines. The disturbance input is zero.*

10.2.2 Precompensated Static State Feedback

In this section we describe a variation of static state feedback that can track a reference input. The approach taken is to adjust the operating point of the control system. Let r be the reference input, so $e(k) = r - y(k)$ is the control error. Further, let $\mathbf{x}_{ss}$ be the steady-state value of the state vector when $e(k) = 0$, and let u_{ss} be the associated control input. Our approach is to adjust the static state feedback control law $u(k) = -\mathbf{K}\mathbf{x}(k)$ to achieve the desired steady-state value of the measured output. This is done by using a state vector offset in the control law. That is,

$$u(k) = -\mathbf{K}(\mathbf{x}(k) - \mathbf{x}_{ss}) + u_{ss} \tag{10.4}$$

In essence, we reset the operating point so that it yields a measured output that is equal to the reference input.

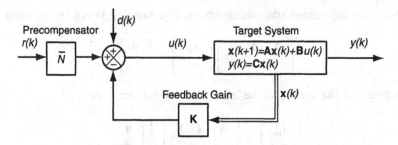

Fig. 10.6 *Block diagram of a precompensated static state feedback control system. $\overline{N}$ is computed from Equation (10.6).*

Figure 10.6 displays the architecture for precompensated state feedback. Observe that this diagram includes a new block labeled $\overline{N}$ whose input is r and whose output is used to compute the control input.

We proceed as follows. From Equations (10.1) and 10.4 we know that

$$\mathbf{x}(k+1) = \mathbf{A}\mathbf{x}(k) + \mathbf{B}u(k)$$

$$= \mathbf{A}\mathbf{x}(k) - \mathbf{B}\mathbf{K}(\mathbf{x}(k) - \mathbf{x}_{ss}) + \mathbf{B}u_{ss}$$

Further, in steady state, $\mathbf{x}_{ss} = \mathbf{A}\mathbf{x}_{ss} + \mathbf{B}u_{ss}$, or $\mathbf{B}u_{ss} = \mathbf{x}_{ss} - \mathbf{A}\mathbf{x}_{ss}$. So

$$\mathbf{x}(k+1) = \mathbf{A}\mathbf{x}(k) - \mathbf{B}\mathbf{K}(\mathbf{x}(k) - \mathbf{x}_{ss}) + \mathbf{x}_{ss} - \mathbf{A}\mathbf{x}_{ss}$$

That is,

$$\mathbf{x}(k+1) - \mathbf{x}_{ss} = (\mathbf{A} - \mathbf{B}\mathbf{K})(\mathbf{x}(k) - \mathbf{x}_{ss})$$

This equation can be interpreted as applying static state feedback to the state vector $\mathbf{x}(k) - \mathbf{x}_{ss}$. Hence, if $\mathbf{x}(k) = \mathbf{x}_{ss}$, then $r = y(k)$. Thus, properly selecting the precompensator $\overline{N}$ causes the control system to converge to **0**. We note in passing that including a precompensator does not affect the poles of the system in that the characteristic polynomial is still Equation (10.3).

We compute $\overline{N}$ by observing that the following should hold in steady state:

$$\mathbf{x}_{ss} = \mathbf{A}\mathbf{x}_{ss} + \mathbf{B}u_{ss}$$

$$y_{ss} = \mathbf{C}\mathbf{x}_{ss}$$

$$y_{ss} = r$$

Substituting the second equation into the third equation and rearranging terms, we have

$$(\mathbf{A} - \mathbf{I})\mathbf{x}_{ss} + \mathbf{B}u_{ss} = 0$$

$$\mathbf{C}\mathbf{x}_{ss} = r \tag{10.5}$$

Using the augmented state vector above, Equation (10.5) can be rewritten as

$$\begin{bmatrix} A - I & B \\ C & 0 \end{bmatrix} \begin{bmatrix} x_{ss} \\ u_{ss} \end{bmatrix} = \begin{bmatrix} 0 \\ r \end{bmatrix}$$

Assuming that the matrix on the left is nonsingular, we have

$$\begin{bmatrix} x_{ss} \\ u_{ss} \end{bmatrix} = \begin{bmatrix} A - I & B \\ C & 0 \end{bmatrix}^{-1} \begin{bmatrix} 0 \\ r \end{bmatrix}$$

(The superscript -1 denotes a matrix inverse, which is meaningful only if the matrix is nonsingular.) Substituting the foregoing equation into Equation (10.4), we obtain the following for the feedback control law:

$$u(k) = -\mathbf{K}x(k) + \mathbf{K}x_{ss} + u_{ss}$$

$$= -\mathbf{K}x(k) + \begin{bmatrix} \mathbf{K} & 1 \end{bmatrix} \begin{bmatrix} x_{ss} \\ u_{ss} \end{bmatrix}$$

$$= -\mathbf{K}x(k) + \begin{bmatrix} \mathbf{K} & 1 \end{bmatrix} \begin{bmatrix} A - I & B \\ C & 0 \end{bmatrix}^{-1} \begin{bmatrix} 0 \\ r \end{bmatrix}$$

This complicated expression can be simplified by making the substitution

$$\overline{N} = \begin{bmatrix} \mathbf{K} & 1 \end{bmatrix} \begin{bmatrix} A - I & B \\ C & 0 \end{bmatrix}^{-1} \begin{bmatrix} 0 \\ 1 \end{bmatrix} \tag{10.6}$$

This leads to the following control law for precompensated static feedback:

$$u(k) = -\mathbf{K}x(k) + \overline{N}r \tag{10.7}$$

Thus, $\overline{N}$ in Figure 10.6 is obtained from Equation (10.6).

Example 10.5: Static state feedback with precompensation for a tandem queue
This example extends Example 10.4 by including the precompensation component $\overline{N}$ in Figure 10.6.

Figure 10.7 displays a block diagram of the feedback control system we consider. We see that

$$A = \begin{bmatrix} 0.13 & 0 \\ 0.46 & 0.63 \end{bmatrix}$$

$$B = \begin{bmatrix} 0.069 \\ 0 \end{bmatrix}$$

$$C = \begin{bmatrix} 1 & 1 \end{bmatrix}$$

$$K = \begin{bmatrix} 2.31 & 6.95 \end{bmatrix}$$

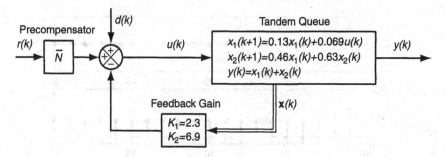

Fig. 10.7 Block diagram of a static state feedback controller with precompensation for a tandem queue.

So

$$A - I = \begin{bmatrix} -0.87 & 0 \\ 0.46 & -0.37 \end{bmatrix}$$

Thus,

$$\begin{bmatrix} A - I & B \\ C & 0 \end{bmatrix}^{-1} = \begin{bmatrix} -0.87 & 0 & 0.069 \\ 0.46 & -0.37 & 0 \\ 1 & 1 & 0 \end{bmatrix}^{-1}$$

Hence, from Equation (10.6),

$$\overline{N} = \begin{bmatrix} K & 1 \end{bmatrix} \begin{bmatrix} A - I & B \\ C & 0 \end{bmatrix}^{-1} \begin{bmatrix} 0 \\ 1 \end{bmatrix}$$

$$= \begin{bmatrix} 2.31 & 6.95 & 1 \end{bmatrix} \begin{bmatrix} -0.87 & 0 & 0.069 \\ 0.46 & -0.37 & 0 \\ 1 & 1 & 0 \end{bmatrix}^{-1} \begin{bmatrix} 0 \\ 0 \\ 1 \end{bmatrix}$$

$$= 0.16$$

Figure 10.8 displays the results of a simulation of the system in Figure 10.7 with the values of $\overline{N}$, A, B, C, and K described above in which the reference value is changed from 9 seconds to 19 seconds and there is no disturbance. We see that the system performs well in that the measured output quickly converges to the reference input.

Now consider what happens when a disturbance is present. Figure 10.9 simulates the same system in the presence of a disturbance $d(k) = 1$, $k \geq 1$ with the reference value at the operating point. Once again, the system settles quickly. However, the steady-state value is not equal to the reference input.

From this example we see that static state feedback with precompensation does well with tracking a reference input if *there is no disturbance*. However, if a disturbance is present, tracking performance is poor.

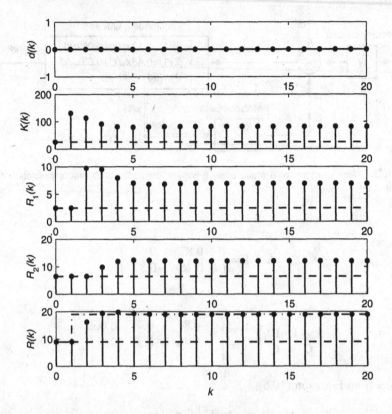

Fig. 10.8 *Response of a system with static state feedback control and a precompensator to a step increase in the reference input. The dashed lines in the plots of $K(k)$, $R_1(k)$, $R_2(k)$, and $R(k)$ indicate the operating points. The system quickly converges to the reference input $R(k)$ (denoted by the dashed-dotted line). The disturbance input is zero.*

10.2.3 Dynamic State Feedback

In this section we describe a state-space architecture that both tracks the reference input and rejects disturbances. The approach can be viewed as a generalization of proportional integral (PI) control as described for SISO systems in Chapter 9.

Our starting point is to augment the state vector to include the control error $e(k) = r - y(k)$. Specifically, we use the *integrated control error*, which describes the accumulated control error. Denoted by $x_I(k)$, the integrated control error is computed as

$$x_I(k+1) = x_I(k) + e(k) \tag{10.8}$$

The augmented state vector is $\begin{bmatrix} \mathbf{x}(k) \\ x_I(k) \end{bmatrix}$. The control law becomes

$$u(k) = -\begin{bmatrix} \mathbf{K}_p & K_I \end{bmatrix} \begin{bmatrix} \mathbf{x}(k) \\ x_I(k) \end{bmatrix} \tag{10.9}$$

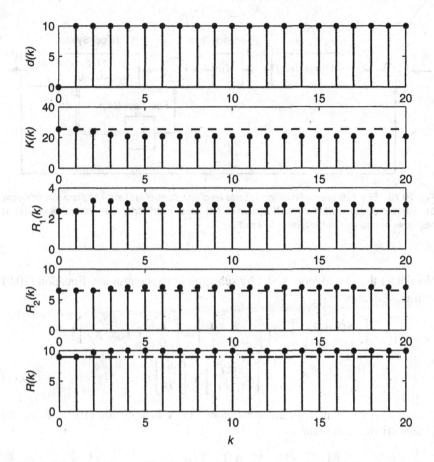

Fig. 10.9 *Response of a system with static state feedback control and precompensator to a step increase in the disturbance input. The dashed lines in the plots of $K(k)$, $R_1(k)$, $R_2(k)$, and $R(k)$ indicate the operating points. The system cannot reject the disturbance, as indicated by $R(k)$ deviating from the reference input (dashed-dotted line).*

where $\mathbf{K}_P$ denotes the feedback gain for $\mathbf{x}(k)$ and K_I is the gain associated with $x_I(k)$.

Figure 10.10 displays a block diagram of a system that uses the dynamic feedback control law in Equation (10.9). This system differs from the precompensated state feedback in that (1) the $\overline{N}$ component is removed, and (2) blocks are added for the $x_I(k)$ dynamics and the integral feedback gain K_I.

To understand the characteristics of dynamic state feedback control, we proceed as follows. The augmented state-space model is

$$\begin{bmatrix} \mathbf{x}(k+1) \\ x_I(k+1) \end{bmatrix} = \begin{bmatrix} \mathbf{A} & \mathbf{0} \\ -\mathbf{C} & 1 \end{bmatrix} \begin{bmatrix} \mathbf{x}(k) \\ x_I(k) \end{bmatrix} + \begin{bmatrix} \mathbf{B} \\ 0 \end{bmatrix} u(k) + \begin{bmatrix} \mathbf{0} \\ 1 \end{bmatrix} r \qquad (10.10)$$

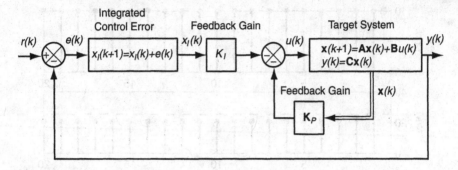

Fig. 10.10 *Block diagram of a dynamic state feedback control system. The state x_I computes the integral of the control error. It dynamics are used in adjusting the control input $u(k)$ in response to changes in the reference input r.*

We obtain the closed-loop model by substituting the control law Equation (10.9) into this equation:

$$
\begin{bmatrix} \mathbf{x}(k+1) \\ x_I(k+1) \end{bmatrix} = \left(\begin{bmatrix} \mathbf{A} & 0 \\ -\mathbf{C} & 1 \end{bmatrix} - \begin{bmatrix} \mathbf{B} \\ 0 \end{bmatrix} \begin{bmatrix} \mathbf{K}_p & K_I \end{bmatrix} \right)
$$

$$
\times \begin{bmatrix} \mathbf{x}(k) \\ x_I(k) \end{bmatrix} + \begin{bmatrix} 0 \\ 1 \end{bmatrix} r \tag{10.11}
$$

The expression in parentheses corresponds to $\mathbf{A}$ in Equation (10.1). Thus, the characteristic polynomial is

$$
\det \left\{ z\mathbf{I} - \left(\begin{bmatrix} \mathbf{A} & 0 \\ -\mathbf{C} & 1 \end{bmatrix} - \begin{bmatrix} \mathbf{B} \\ 0 \end{bmatrix} \begin{bmatrix} \mathbf{K}_p & K_I \end{bmatrix} \right) \right\} \tag{10.12}
$$

Hence, by properly choosing $\mathbf{K}_p$ and K_I, we can determine the dynamics of the closed-loop system.

It turns out that with dynamic state feedback the measured output converges to the reference input. This can be shown as follows. From Equation (10.8) we know that at steady state $x_{I,ss} = x_{I,ss} + e_{ss}$. That is, $0 = e_{ss}$. This property holds regardless of the feedback gains $\mathbf{K}_p$ and K_I, (as long as the closed-loop system is stable).

Example 10.6: Dynamic state feedback for a tandem queue   This example uses dynamic state feedback control to regulate end-to-end response time in the tandem queue example in Example 10.1.

The states used in the tandem queue example are $x_1(k) = R_1(k) - \overline{R}_1$ and $x_2(k) = R_2(k) - \overline{R}_2$. The augmented state vector includes the integrated (summed) control error as specified in Equation (10.8). That is, $\begin{bmatrix} x_1(k) \\ x_2(k) \\ x_I(k) \end{bmatrix}$.

Recall that

$$A = \begin{bmatrix} 0.13 & 0 \\ 0.46 & 0.63 \end{bmatrix}$$

$$B = \begin{bmatrix} 0.069 \\ 0 \end{bmatrix}$$

$$C = \begin{bmatrix} 1 & 1 \end{bmatrix}$$

Substituting into Equation (10.10), the augmented state-space model is

$$\begin{bmatrix} \mathbf{x}(k+1) \\ x_I(k+1) \end{bmatrix} = \begin{bmatrix} \mathbf{A} & \mathbf{0} \\ -\mathbf{C} & 1 \end{bmatrix} \begin{bmatrix} \mathbf{x}(k) \\ x_I(k) \end{bmatrix} + \begin{bmatrix} \mathbf{B} \\ 0 \end{bmatrix} u(k)$$

$$+ \begin{bmatrix} \mathbf{0} \\ -1 \end{bmatrix} r$$

$$\begin{bmatrix} x_1(k+1) \\ x_2(k+1) \\ x_I(k+1) \end{bmatrix} = \begin{bmatrix} 0.13 & 0 & 0 \\ 0.46 & 0.63 & 0 \\ -1 & -1 & 1 \end{bmatrix} \begin{bmatrix} x_1(k) \\ x_2(k) \\ x_I(k) \end{bmatrix} + \begin{bmatrix} 0.069 \\ 0 \\ 0 \end{bmatrix} u(k)$$

$$+ \begin{bmatrix} 0 \\ 0 \\ -1 \end{bmatrix} r$$

The closed loop model is obtained by substituting into Equation (10.11).

$$\begin{bmatrix} \mathbf{x}(k+1) \\ x_I(k+1) \end{bmatrix} = \left(\begin{bmatrix} \mathbf{A} & \mathbf{0} \\ -\mathbf{C} & 1 \end{bmatrix} - \begin{bmatrix} \mathbf{B} \\ 0 \end{bmatrix} \begin{bmatrix} \mathbf{K}_p & K_I \end{bmatrix} \right) \begin{bmatrix} \mathbf{x}(k) \\ x_I(k) \end{bmatrix}$$

$$+ \begin{bmatrix} \mathbf{0} \\ -1 \end{bmatrix} r$$

$$\begin{bmatrix} x_1(k+1) \\ x_2(k+1) \\ x_I(k+1) \end{bmatrix} = \left(\begin{bmatrix} 0.13 & 0 & 0 \\ 0.46 & 0.63 & 0 \\ -1 & -1 & 1 \end{bmatrix} - \begin{bmatrix} 0.069 \\ 0 \\ 0 \end{bmatrix} \begin{bmatrix} K_p^1 & K_p^2 & K_I \end{bmatrix} \right)$$

$$\begin{bmatrix} x_1(k) \\ x_2(k) \\ x_I(k) \end{bmatrix} + \begin{bmatrix} 0 \\ 0 \\ -1 \end{bmatrix} r$$

where $\mathbf{K}_p = [K_p^1, K_p^2]$. Simplifying, we have

$$\begin{bmatrix} x_1(k+1) \\ x_2(k+1) \\ x_I(k+1) \end{bmatrix} = \begin{bmatrix} 0.13 - 0.069K_p^1 & -0.069K_p^2 & -0.069K_I \\ 0.46 & 0.63 & 0 \\ -1 & -1 & 1 \end{bmatrix} \begin{bmatrix} x_1(k) \\ x_2(k) \\ x_I(k) \end{bmatrix}$$

$$+ \begin{bmatrix} 0 \\ 0 \\ -1 \end{bmatrix} r$$

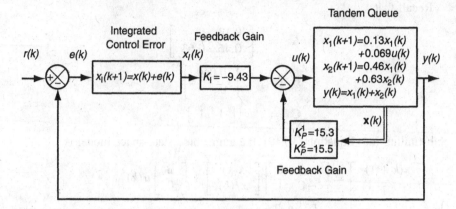

Fig. 10.11 Block diagram of a dynamic state feedback control system for the tandem queue example.

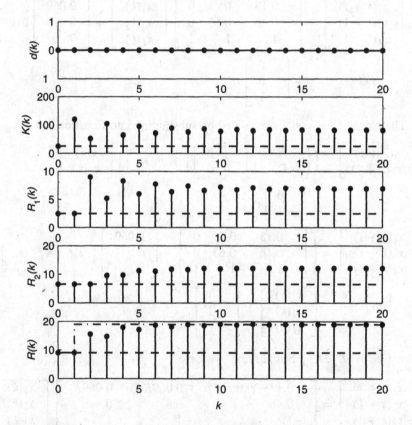

Fig. 10.12 Response of a system with dynamic state feedback controller to a step increase in the reference input. The system is designed using pole placement with $k_s^* = 5$ and $M_P^* = 0.05$. The dashed lines indicate the operating points. The system operates within its k_s^*, M_P^* specifications. The disturbance input is zero.

Now consider the dynamic feedback controller with $\mathbf{K} = [K_p^1 \quad K_p^2 \quad K_I] =$ [15.3 15.5 −9.43]. Figure 10.11 contains a block diagram of dynamic state feedback for the tandem queue. Figure 10.12 shows the step response with no disturbance, and Figure 10.13 simulates the controller's response to a disturbance. We observe that dynamic state feedback not only tracks the reference input, it also does a good job of tracking in the presence of a disturbance.

10.2.4 Comparison of Control Architectures

Figure 10.14 summarizes the results of simulations done on the three architectures. Note that static feedback cannot track the reference input, but precompensated state and dynamic state feedback can. Both static architectures have poor disturbance rejection. Dynamic state feedback has good disturbance rejection, but it has longer settling times.

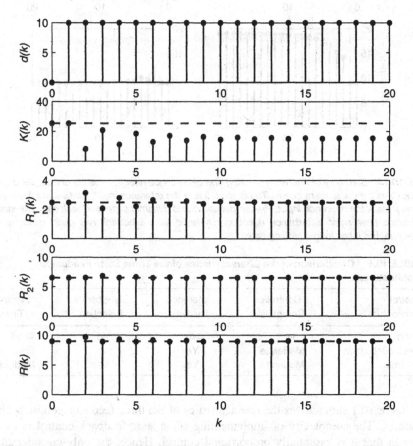

Fig. 10.13 *Response of a system with dynamic state feedback controller to a step increase in the disturbance. The system is designed using pole placement with $k_s^* = 5$ and $M_P^* = 0.05$. The dashed lines indicate the operating points. The system has good disturbance rejection.*

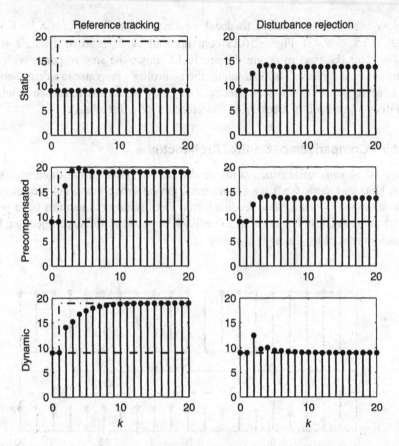

Fig. 10.14 *Summary of reference tracking and disturbance rejection results of state feedback controllers for the tandem queue. The dashed line is the reference input. Static state feedback cannot track the reference input. Precompensated and dynamic state feedback can. The static schemes have poor disturbance rejection. Dynamic state feedback has good disturbance rejection, but it has longer settling times.*

TABLE 10.1   Comparison of the Characteristics of the Three State Feedback Architectures

Control Architecture	Controller Complexity	Reference Tracking	Disturbance Rejection	Settling Time
Static	Low	No	No	Short
Precompensation	Moderate	Yes	No	Short
Dynamic	Moderate	Yes	Yes	Moderate

Table 10.1 summarizes the characteristics of the three feedback control architectures. The complexity of implementing static state feedback control is quite low in that it is essentially proportional control. Hence, the only consideration is selecting the feedback gains. Static state feedback with precompensation is more complicated to implement because of the precompensator. Dynamic state

feedback requires that the state vector be augmented with the integrated control error x_I.

10.3 DESIGN TECHNIQUES

Having presented three architectures for state-space feedback control, we now describe approaches to their design. By *design*, we mean choosing the feedback gains. For static state feedback (with and without precompensation), the gains are given in the vector **K**. For dynamic state feedback, we must select K_I as well. In Section 10.3.1 we describe pole placement design, and in Section 10.3.2 we describe an optimization based approach called *linear quadratic regulation*.

10.3.1 Pole Placement Design

In this section we detail an approach to the design of state-space feedback control based on properly placing all poles of the closed-loop system. The approach taken is an extension of pole placement design for transfer functions as detailed in Table 9.2.

Our approach to pole placement design starts with a specification of the desired settling time k_s^* and the desired maximum overshoot M_p^* of the closed-loop system. The first step computes the desired poles of the closed-loop system based on k_s^* and M_p^*. To do this, we assume that the dominant poles are complex conjugates $re^{\pm j\theta}$. We proceed as in Chapter 9 using Equation (9.9) to set r to its upper bound $r = e^{-4/k_s^*}$. Similarly, θ is obtained using Equation (9.10) to set θ to its upper bound $\theta = \pi[\log(r)/\log(M_p^*)]$. The remaining $n-2$ poles should have sufficiently small magnitudes so that the closed-loop system has the desired settling time and maximum overshoot. We use $0.25r$.

The second step constructs and expands the desired characteristic polynomial. From step 1 we know that this polynomial is $(z^2 - 2r\cos\theta z + r^2)(z - 0.25r)^{n-2}$. The expanded polynomial has $n+1$ terms. Note that the number of poles is equal to the number of states in the state vector, and the latter is the same as the number of terms in the (expanded) desired characteristic polynomial (excluding z^n).

In the third step we obtain the modeled characteristic polynomial, which is the characteristic polynomial expressed in terms of the feedback gain variables **K** (and K_I in the case of dynamic state feedback). To relate the feedback gains to the desired closed-loop poles, we expand the modeled characteristic polynomial. For the static state architectures, the modeled characteristic polynomial is

$$\det[z\mathbf{I} - (\mathbf{A} - \mathbf{BK})] \tag{10.13}$$

This polynomial can be expanded to obtain the coefficients of each power of z, and these coefficients will contain the unknown feedback gains.

The fourth step is to solve for the control gains. The fifth step is to verify the resulting design. Since $n-2$ poles are chosen arbitrarily, we need to make sure that the closed-loop system achieves the design goals specified by k_s^* and M_p^*.

Example 10.7: Expanding the modeled characteristic polynomial Using **A** and **B** in Example 10.4, we have

$$z\mathbf{I}-(\mathbf{A}-\mathbf{BK}) = z\begin{bmatrix} 1 & 0 \\ 0 & 1 \end{bmatrix}$$

$$-\left(\begin{bmatrix} 0.13 & 0 \\ 0.46 & 0.63 \end{bmatrix} - \begin{bmatrix} 0.069 \\ 0 \end{bmatrix}\begin{bmatrix} K_P^1 & K_P^2 \end{bmatrix}\right)$$

$$= \begin{bmatrix} z & 0 \\ 0 & z \end{bmatrix} - \begin{bmatrix} 0.13 - 0.069K_P^1 & -0.069K_P^2 \\ 0.46 & 0.63 \end{bmatrix}$$

$$= \begin{bmatrix} z - 0.13 + 0.069K_P^1 & 0.069K_P^2 \\ -0.46 & z - 0.63 \end{bmatrix}$$

So

$$\det[z\mathbf{I}-(\mathbf{A}-\mathbf{BK})] = z^2 + (0.069K_P^1 - 0.76)z - 0.043K_P^1$$
$$+ 0.032K_P^2 + 0.082 \tag{10.14}$$

The coefficient of z^2 is 1, the coefficient of z^1 is $0.069K_P^1 - 0.76$, and the coefficient of z^0 is $-0.043K_P^1 + 0.032K_P^2 + 0.082$.

For dynamic state feedback in Equation (10.11), the modeled characteristic polynomial is

$$\det\left\{z\mathbf{I} - \left(\begin{bmatrix} \mathbf{A} & \mathbf{0} \\ -\mathbf{C} & 1 \end{bmatrix} - \begin{bmatrix} \mathbf{B} \\ 0 \end{bmatrix}\begin{bmatrix} \mathbf{K}_P & K_I \end{bmatrix}\right)\right\}$$

Here too, the characteristic polynomial can be expanded (although doing so can be tedious). Note that the degree of this polynomial is $n + 1$ since we add the state variable x_I and must solve for K_I.

Solving for the feedback gains requires equating the coefficients of the desired characteristic polynomial to the coefficients of the modeled characteristic polynomial. The former are constants, and the latter include the feedback gains.

A complete example of pole placement design is described below.

Example 10.8: Pole placement design for static state feedback of a tandem queue This example designs a static state feedback controller for Example 10.4 (tandem queue) using pole placement design. The control objective is to maintain response times at their operating points, where $\overline{R}_1 = 2.5$, $\overline{R}_2 = 6.5$, and $\overline{R} = \overline{R}_1 + \overline{R}_2 = 9$. The specifications for this system are that settling time is no greater than 5 minutes and the maximum overshoot does not exceed 5%. So $k_s^* = 5$ and $M_P^* = 0.05$.

We begin by determining the desired location of the poles based on k_s^* and M_P^*. Since this system has two states (i.e., response time offset of the two queues), there are two poles. We assume that these poles are complex conjugates of the form $re^{\pm j\theta}$. From Equation (9.9) we have that $r = e^{-4/k_s^*} = e^{-4/5} = 0.45$, and from Equation (9.10), we use

$$\theta = \pi \frac{\log(r)}{\log(M_p)} = \pi \frac{\log(0.45)}{\log(0.05)} = 0.84$$

Hence, the desired characteristic polynomial is

$$z^2 - 2r\cos\theta z + r^2 = z^2 - 0.6z + 0.2 \tag{10.15}$$

Next, we construct the modeled characteristic polynomial. Since this is static state feedback, we use Equation (10.13) as follows:

$$\det[z\mathbf{I} - (\mathbf{A} - \mathbf{BK})]$$

$$= \det\left\{\begin{bmatrix} z & 0 \\ 0 & z \end{bmatrix} - \begin{bmatrix} 0.13 & 0 \\ 0.46 & 0.63 \end{bmatrix} + \begin{bmatrix} 0.069 \\ 0 \end{bmatrix}\begin{bmatrix} K_p^1 & K_p^2 \end{bmatrix}\right\}$$

$$= \det\begin{bmatrix} z - 0.13 + 0.069K_p^1 & 0.069K_p^2 \\ -0.46 & z - 0.63 \end{bmatrix}$$

$$= z^2 + (0.069K_p^1 - 0.76)z + 0.082 - 0.0435K_p^1 + 0.0317K_p^2 \tag{10.16}$$

To determine the values of K_p^1 and K_p^2, we equate the coefficients of the powers of z in Equation (10.15) with those in Equation (10.16). This results in the following two equations:

$$0.069K_p^1 - 0.76 = -0.6$$

$$0.082 - 0.0435K_p^1 + 0.0317K_p^2 = 0.2$$

Solving these, we determine that the feedback gains are

$$\mathbf{K} = [K_p^1 \quad K_p^2] = [2.31 \quad 6.95]$$

These are the same gains that are used in Example 10.4.

Table 10.2 summarizes our approach to pole placement design for state-space feedback. Comparing this with the design of PI controllers for SISO systems (as described in Figure 9.2), we see that the state-space approach allows us to address high-order target systems directly. That is, for SISO PI control, we had to use a first-order approximation of higher-order target systems so that the closed-loop system is second order. By so doing, we end up with two equations in two unknowns in step 4 of Table 9.2. In contrast, the state-space approach allows us to deal with higher-order target systems without a first-order approximation. This is accomplished by having $\mathbf{K}$ be of dimension $1 \times n$ so that there are sufficient controller parameters to solve the set of linear equations in step 4 of Table 10.2.

Intuitively, the magnitude of the feedback gains reflects the control effort required. This effort typically relates to how far the closed-loop poles are from

TABLE 10.2   Procedure for Pole Placement Design for State-Space Feedback

The design goals are that settling time does not exceed k_s^* and that the maximum overshoot does not exceed M_p^*.

1. Compute the closed-loop poles $re^{\pm j\theta}$.

   - Compute r based on k_s^* using Equation (9.9).
   - Compute θ based on M_p^* using Equation (9.10).

2. Construct the desired characteristic polynomial.

   - The desired characteristic polynomial is $\left(z^2 - 2r\cos\theta z + r^2\right)(z - 0.25r)^{n-2}$, where n is the dimension of the state space.

3. Construct and expand the modeled characteristic polynomial for $\mathbf{x}(k + 1) = \mathbf{Ax}(k) - \mathbf{BKx}(k)$.

   - $\mathbf{K} = [K_1, \ldots, K_n]$.
   - The modeled characteristic polynomial is $\det[z\mathbf{I} - (\mathbf{A} - \mathbf{BK})]$.

4. Solve for the K_i in $\mathbf{K}$.

   - Equate the coefficients of the desired characteristic polynomial with the coefficient of the modeled characteristic polynomial of the same degree.
   - Solve the system of equations.

5. Verify the result.

   - Check that the closed-loop poles lie within the unit circle.
   - Simulate transient response to assess if the design goals are met.

---

the open-loop poles. Large control gains are a concern in computing systems in that large gains will cause the system to overreact, resulting in controller-induced variability and possibly limit cycles.

The following is a second example of pole placement design.

Example 10.9: Pole placement design for static state feedback with short settling times   This example modifies the specification used in Example 10.8 to show the implications of having a small settling time. Specifically, $k_s^* = 1$. We keep $M_p^* = 0.05$. We note in passing that the open-loop poles of the tandem queue suggest a settling time of 9. Hence, the closed-loop poles will need to be far from the open-loop poles.

The magnitude of the desired closed-loop poles is obtained from Equation (9.9) as $r = e^{-4/k_s^*} = e^{-4/1} = 0.018$, and the angle of the desired closed-loop poles is obtained from Equation (9.10) as

$$\theta = \pi \frac{\log(r)}{\log(M_p^*)} = \pi \frac{\log(0.018)}{\log(0.05)} = 4.19$$

Hence, the desired pole location is $-0.0091 \pm 0.016i$ and the desired characteristic polynomial is

$$(z + 0.0091 - 0.016i)(z + 0.0091 + 0.016i) = z^2 + 0.018z + 0.0003$$

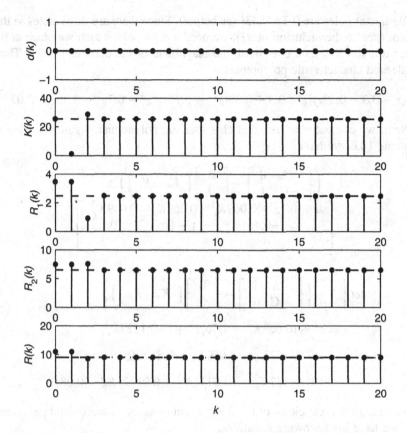

Fig. 10.15 *Transient response of static state feedback control with short settling times and no disturbance. The initial conditions are 1 second above the operating point (which are indicated by dashed lines).*

By equating the coefficients in this desired characteristic polynomial with those in Equation (10.16), we have

$$\mathbf{K} = [K_p^1 \quad K_p^2] = [11.28 \quad 12.88]$$

Figure 10.15 displays the response to initial conditions of this controller. Clearly, this system settles much faster than the system in Example 10.8, whose response to initial conditions is shown in Figure 10.5. Note, however, having large feedback gains causes large changes in the buffer size $K(k)$. A concern here is that if the system has noise or other stochastics, the controller may overreact and enter a limit cycle.

Example 10.10: Pole placement design for dynamic state feedback control of a tandem queue This example designs a dynamic state feedback controller for the tandem queue. Example 10.6 describes the structure of the control system. The specifications of the control system are that $k_s^* = 5$ and $M_p^* = 0.05$. Thus, the dominant poles are $0.3 \pm 0.33i$ (as before). Since there are three states in this system (due to the inclusion of x_I), we need a third pole, which we place at 0.1 (since this has less than one-fourth the magnitude of the dominant pole). Thus, the desired characteristic polynomial is

$$(z - 0.3 - 0.33i)(z - 0.3 + 0.33i)(z - 0.1) = z^3 - 0.7z^2 + 0.26z - 0.02$$

Next, we compute the modeled characteristic polynomial. Again referring to Example 10.6, we have

$$z\mathbf{I} - \left(\begin{bmatrix} \mathbf{A} & 0 \\ -\mathbf{C} & 1 \end{bmatrix} - \begin{bmatrix} \mathbf{B} \\ 0 \end{bmatrix} \begin{bmatrix} \mathbf{K}_P & K_I \end{bmatrix} \right)$$
$$= \begin{bmatrix} z - 0.13 + 0.069K_P^1 & 0.069K_P^2 & 0.069K_P^3 \\ -0.46 & z - 0.63 & 0 \\ 1 & 1 & z - 1 \end{bmatrix}$$

$$\det \left\{ z\mathbf{I} - \left(\begin{bmatrix} \mathbf{A} & 0 \\ -\mathbf{C} & 1 \end{bmatrix} - \begin{bmatrix} \mathbf{B} \\ 0 \end{bmatrix} \begin{bmatrix} \mathbf{K}_P & K_I \end{bmatrix} \right) \right\}$$
$$= z^3 + (0.069K_P^1 - 1.76)z^2 + (-0.1125K_P^1$$
$$+ 0.03177K_P^2 - 0.069K_P^3 + 0.8419)z$$
$$+ 0.04347K_P^1 - 0.03174K_P^2 + 0.01173K_P^3 - 0.0819$$

Matching the coefficients of the desired and modeled characteristic polynomials, we have the following equations:

$$0.069K_P^1 - 1.76 = -0.7$$
$$-0.1125K_P^1 + 0.03177K_P^2 - 0.069K_P^3 + 0.8419 = 0.26$$
$$0.04347K_P^1 - 0.03174K_P^2 + 0.01173K_P^3 - 0.0819 = -0.02$$

Solving these equations yields the feedback gains

$$\mathbf{K} = [15.3 \quad 15.5 \quad -9.43]$$

10.3.2 LQR Optimal Control Design

Pole placement design constructs a controller with desired poles. However, we must still consider the resulting control gains since higher gains can increase variability, possibly resulting in limit cycles. An alternative approach to controller design is to focus on the trade-off between control effort and control errors. Control errors are quantified by the squared values of state variables, which are typically offsets from the operating point. Control effort is quantified by the square of $u(k)$, the offset of the control input from its operating point. By minimizing control errors, we improve accuracy and reduce both settling times and overshoot. By minimizing control effort, we reduce the system's sensitivity to noise since we do not take large control actions (e.g., MaxClients does not change much). In general, there is a trade-off between control effort and control error. Specifically, reducing control errors requires more control effort, and reducing control effort means that control errors will be larger.

The LQR design problem is specified in terms of the relative "cost" of control errors and control effort. This is quantified by two input parameters, a matrix **Q** and a second matrix **R**. **Q** quantifies the cost of individual (and combinations of) state variables diverging from their operating point, and **R** specifies the cost of control effort.

Our formulation of LQR is more general than for pole placement in that we consider MIMO systems. This has two implications. First, the control input is a vector, which we denote by $\mathbf{u}(k)$. Hence, the state dynamics are $\mathbf{x}(k + 1) = \mathbf{A}\mathbf{x}(k) + \mathbf{B}\mathbf{u}(k)$. Second, the feedback gains **K** are a matrix instead of a vector. For the static feedback controller (with and without precompensation) the control law is $\mathbf{u}(k) = -\mathbf{K}\mathbf{x}(k)$. For dynamic state feedback, the terms in Equation (10.11) should be substituted for **A** and **B** in the analysis below.

The technical details of LQR are as follows. The objective function to minimize is J, where

$$J = \frac{1}{2} \sum_{k=0}^{\infty} \left[\mathbf{x}^\top(k)\mathbf{Q}\mathbf{x}(k) + \mathbf{u}^\top(k)\mathbf{R}\mathbf{u}(k) \right] \qquad (10.17)$$

It is required that **Q** be positive semidefinite and that **R** be positive definite. These conditions ensure that $J \geq 0$. The positive semidefinite condition holds for a matrix **F** if the eigenvalues of **F** are nonnegative. **F** is positive definite if all of its eigenvalues are positive.

The details of computing **K** using LQR are somewhat involved. Typically, analysts employ tools such as the MATLAB command dlqr. However, for completeness, we describe how to do the LQR computations.

Assume that the system [**A**, **B**] is stabilizable (i.e., [**A**, **B**] is either controllable or its uncontrollable subsystem is stable) and [**A**, **D**] is observable where $\mathbf{D}^\top\mathbf{D} = \mathbf{Q}$. The optimal feedback gains can be obtained following the steps shown in Table 10.3. (The derivation of this optimal law can be found in books such as [21].)

The steps in LQR design are summarized as follows:

1. Select the weighting matrices **Q** and **R**.
2. Compute the feedback gain **K** using the algorithm shown in Table 10.3 or using MATLAB command dlqr.
3. Predict control system performance based on the closed-loop system model, or run a computer simulation to verify the closed-loop performance.
4. Choose new **Q** and **R** and repeat the steps above if the performance is not suitable.

TABLE 10.3   Algorithm for LQR Design

1. Initialization:

   - Define the state-space model of the open-loop system by matrices **A** and **B**. For a system with n system states and m control inputs, **A** is an $n \times n$ matrix and **B** is an $n \times m$ matrix.

   - Define the weighting matrices **Q** and **R**, where **Q** is an $n \times n$ matrix and **R** is an $m \times m$ matrix. The eigenvalues of matrix **Q** must be nonnegative and the eigenvalues of matrix **R** must be positive.

   - The optimal feedback gain **K** is an $m \times n$ matrix. It is computed iteratively. Define the optimal feedback gain at step k as $\mathbf{K}(k)$.

   - Define an $n \times n$ auxiliary matrix S. The value of S is computed iteratively, so that its value is further defined at step k as $\mathbf{S}(k)$.

2. Iteration:

   (a) Initially, $i = 0$. Set $\mathbf{S}(0)$ and $\mathbf{K}(0)$ as zero matrices.

   (b) Compute an $m \times m$ temporary matrix $\mathbf{M_1} = \left[\mathbf{B}^\top \mathbf{S}(i)\mathbf{B} + \mathbf{R}\right]^{-1}$.

   (c) Compute another $n \times n$ temporary matrix $\mathbf{M_2} = \mathbf{S}(i) - \mathbf{S}(i)\mathbf{B}\mathbf{M_1}\mathbf{B}^\top\mathbf{S}(i)$.

   (d) Compute the auxiliary matrix for the next step, $\mathbf{S}(i+1) = \mathbf{A}^\top \mathbf{M_2}\mathbf{A} + \mathbf{Q}$.

   (e) Compute the feedback gain for the next step, $\mathbf{K}(i+1) = \mathbf{M_1}\mathbf{B}^\top\mathbf{S}(i+1)\mathbf{A}$.

   (f) If $|\mathbf{K}(i+1) - \mathbf{K}(i)|$ is small enough, stop the iteration; otherwise, $i = i+1$ and go to step 2b.

Example 10.11: LQR design for dynamic state feedback control of a tandem queue   We follow the steps in Table 10.3 to do LQR design for dynamic state feedback control of the tandem queue example. (An alternative approach using the MATLAB command `dlqr` is described in a later MATLAB section.)

Recall that for dynamic state feedback, the state vector is augmented to include the integrated error x_I. That is, $\mathbf{x}(k) = \begin{bmatrix} x_1(k) \\ x_2(k) \\ x_I(k) \end{bmatrix}$. Further, for dynamic state feedback,

$$\mathbf{A} = \begin{bmatrix} 0.13 & 0 & 0 \\ 0.46 & 0.63 & 0 \\ 1 & 1 & 1 \end{bmatrix}$$

$$\mathbf{B} = \begin{bmatrix} 0.069 \\ 0 \\ 0 \end{bmatrix}$$

We begin by specifying the LQR inputs **Q** and **R**. We choose

$$\mathbf{Q} = \begin{bmatrix} 1 & 0 & 0 \\ 0 & 1 & 0 \\ 0 & 0 & 100 \end{bmatrix}$$

and

$$\mathbf{R} = 1$$

The eigenvalues of matrix $\mathbf{Q}$ are $1, 100 > 0$, and eigenvalue of $\mathbf{R}$ is $1 > 0$. So these matrices satisfy the LQR assumptions. $\mathbf{Q}$ is structured so that interactions between elements of the state vector are ignored (in that the corresponding elements of $\mathbf{Q}$ are 0). $q_{1,1}$ and $q_{2,2}$ are the weights for x_1 and x_2 (the offsets of the response times for the queueing systems). Since $q_{1,1} = 1 = q_{2,2}$, these states are weighted equally. $q_{3,3}$ corresponds to x_I, the integrated control error. This has a large weight (100), so will strongly influence the choice of $\mathbf{K}$. That $R = 1$ implies that control effort is as important as control error.

From Figure 10.3, we initialize $\mathbf{S}$ and $\mathbf{K}$ as follows:

$$\mathbf{S}(0) = \begin{bmatrix} 0 & 0 & 0 \\ 0 & 0 & 0 \\ 0 & 0 & 0 \end{bmatrix}$$

$$\mathbf{K}(0) = \begin{bmatrix} 0 & 0 & 0 \end{bmatrix}$$

We first compute two temporary matrices:

$$\mathbf{M_1} = \left(\mathbf{B}^\top \mathbf{S}(0)\mathbf{B} + \mathbf{R} \right)^{-1}$$

$$= \left(\begin{bmatrix} 0.069 & 0 & 0 \end{bmatrix} \begin{bmatrix} 0 & 0 & 0 \\ 0 & 0 & 0 \\ 0 & 0 & 0 \end{bmatrix} \begin{bmatrix} 0.069 \\ 0 \\ 0 \end{bmatrix} + 1 \right)^{-1}$$

$$= 1$$

and

$$\mathbf{M_2} = \mathbf{S}(0) - \mathbf{S}(0)\mathbf{B}\mathbf{M_1}\mathbf{B}^\top \mathbf{S}(0)$$

$$= \begin{bmatrix} 0 & 0 & 0 \\ 0 & 0 & 0 \\ 0 & 0 & 0 \end{bmatrix} - \begin{bmatrix} 0 & 0 & 0 \\ 0 & 0 & 0 \\ 0 & 0 & 0 \end{bmatrix} \begin{bmatrix} 0.069 \\ 0 \\ 0 \end{bmatrix} \cdot 1$$

$$\cdot \begin{bmatrix} 0.069 & 0 & 0 \end{bmatrix} \begin{bmatrix} 0 & 0 & 0 \\ 0 & 0 & 0 \\ 0 & 0 & 0 \end{bmatrix}$$

$$= \begin{bmatrix} 0 & 0 & 0 \\ 0 & 0 & 0 \\ 0 & 0 & 0 \end{bmatrix}$$

Thus, the auxiliary matrix $S(1)$ is computed as

$$S(1) = A^\top M_2 A + Q$$

$$= \begin{bmatrix} 0.13 & 0.46 & 1 \\ 0 & 0.63 & 1 \\ 0 & 0 & 1 \end{bmatrix} \begin{bmatrix} 0 & 0 & 0 \\ 0 & 0 & 0 \\ 0 & 0 & 0 \end{bmatrix} \begin{bmatrix} 0.13 & 0 & 0 \\ 0.46 & 0.63 & 0 \\ -1 & -1 & 1 \end{bmatrix}$$

$$+ \begin{bmatrix} 1 & 0 & 0 \\ 0 & 1 & 0 \\ 0 & 0 & 100 \end{bmatrix}$$

$$= \begin{bmatrix} 1 & 0 & 0 \\ 0 & 1 & 0 \\ 0 & 0 & 100 \end{bmatrix}$$

and the feedback gain for the next step is

$$K(1) = M_1 B^\top S(1) A$$

$$= 1 \cdot \begin{bmatrix} 0.069 & 0 & 0 \end{bmatrix} \begin{bmatrix} 1 & 0 & 0 \\ 0 & 1 & 0 \\ 0 & 0 & 100 \end{bmatrix} \begin{bmatrix} 0.13 & 0 & 0 \\ 0.46 & 0.63 & 0 \\ 1 & 1 & 1 \end{bmatrix}$$

$$= \begin{bmatrix} 0.009 & 0 & 0 \end{bmatrix}$$

The steps above are repeated until the feedback gains converge as shown in Figure 10.16. This gives the optimal feedback gains

$$K = [K_1 \quad K_2 \quad K_3] = [11.54 \quad 11.92 \quad -6.21] \tag{10.18}$$

Substituting K in Equation (10.18) into Equation (10.12), we determine that the poles of the closed-loop system are $0.42 \pm 0.26i$ and 0.13, which makes the former dominant poles. Thus, the estimated settling time of this system is $k_s = 6$, and its estimated maximum overshoot is $M_p = 2\%$. Figure 10.17 assesses the controller's tracking performance for a step change in the reference input, and Figure 10.18 assesses the controller's performance for disturbance rejection. Note that the controller provides both good tracking and disturbance rejection.

10.4 SUMMARY

1. The state feedback control law is $u(k) = -Kx(k)$, where $u(k)$ is the (scalar) control input, $x(k)$ is the state vector, and K is the vector of feedback gains. The design problem is to choose the vector K of feedback gains. For MIMO systems, $u(k)$ is a vector and K is a matrix.

2. Three architectures are described for state feedback: static state feedback, static state feedback with precompensation, and dynamic state feedback.

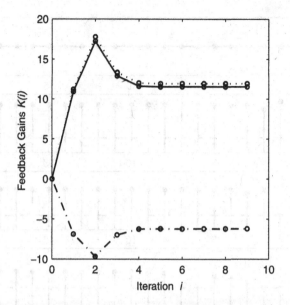

Fig. 10.16 *Convergence of feedback gains that are iteratively computed using LQR design for a dynamic state feedback controller. $K_1(i)$, $K_2(i)$, and $K_3(i)$ are indicated by the solid, dotted, and dashed-dotted lines. Note that the difference between successive estimates of the gains becomes quite small after iteration 5.*

3. Static state feedback is similar to proportional control. It is used to regulate measured outputs at their operating point. This architecture does not include a reference input.

4. Precompensated static state feedback can be used to track reference inputs. However, this architecture has poor disturbance rejection.

5. Dynamic state feedback augments the state vector with the variable x_I, the integrated control error. The approach taken is similar to that used in PI controllers of SISO systems. Dynamic state feedback can track reference inputs and reject disturbances. However, settling times may be longer than the static architectures because of the slower dynamics introduced by x_I.

6. Two approaches to designing state feedback controllers are presented: pole placement and linear quadratic regulation (LQR).

7. Our approach to pole placement design starts with a specification of the maximum settling time and overshoot of the closed-loop system. This specification is used to obtain the desired dominant poles of the closed-loop system. (The remaining poles are chosen to be sufficiently small.) Feedback gains are obtained by equating the coefficients of the desired and modeled characteristic polynomials.

8. Linear quadratic regulator (LQR) design chooses feedback gains that minimize a weighted sum of the control error and control effort. This approach minimizes the combined "cost" of control errors and control effort.

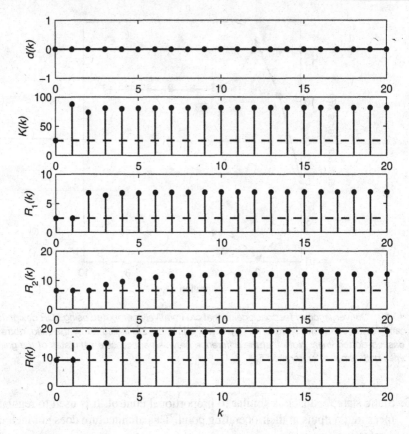

Fig. 10.17 *Response of a system with dynamic state feedback control designed using LQR to a step increase in the reference input (and no disturbance input). The operating point is indicated by the dashed lines in the plots of $K(k)$, $R_1(k)$, $R_2(k)$, and $R(k)$. The reference value is indicated by the dashed-dotted line in the $R(k)$ plot.*

10.5 EXTENDED EXAMPLES

In this section we present more detailed examples of designing state feedback controllers. The first designs a dynamic state feedback system for the Apache HTTP Server. The second example studies the effect of the LQR specification parameters $\mathbf{Q}$ and R on the transient performance of a feedback system for the tandem queue example.

10.5.1 MIMO Control of the Apache HTTP Server

This example designs a dynamic state feedback controller for the Apache HTTP Server. We consider a MIMO system in which the goal is to regulate CPU utilization (CPU) and memory utilization (MEM) using the control inputs MaxClients (MC) and KeepAlive(KA).

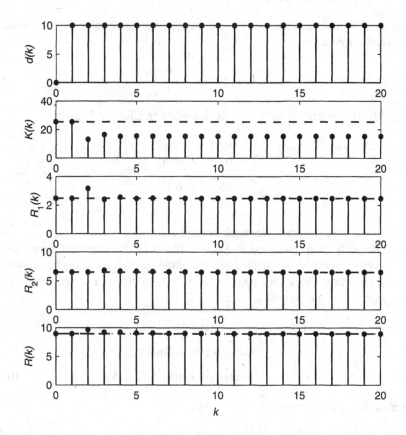

Fig. 10.18 *Response of a system with dynamic state feedback control designed using LQR to a step increase in the disturbance input. The dashed lines in the plots of $K(k)$, $R_1(k)$, $R_2(k)$, and $R(k)$ indicate the operating point values. The dashed-dotted line in the $R(k)$ plot shows the reference value for total response time.*

We consider the Apache HTTP Server at the operating point $\overline{\text{CPU}} = 0.52$, $\overline{\text{MEM}} = 0.53$, $\overline{\text{KA}} = 11$, and $\overline{\text{MC}} = 600$. We want to construct a control system with reference input $\mathbf{r} = [r_1, r_2]^\top$, where $r_1 = \text{CPU}^* - \overline{\text{CPU}}$, $r_2 = \text{MEM}^* - \overline{\text{MEM}}$, and CPU^*, MEM^* are the desired outputs. The state vector is

$$\mathbf{x}(k) = \begin{bmatrix} x_1(k) \\ x_2(k) \end{bmatrix} = \begin{bmatrix} \text{CPU} - \overline{\text{CPU}} \\ \text{MEM} - \overline{\text{MEM}} \end{bmatrix}$$

and the control input is

$$\mathbf{u}(k) = \begin{bmatrix} u_1(k) \\ u_2(k) \end{bmatrix} = \begin{bmatrix} \text{KA} - \overline{\text{KA}} \\ \text{MC} - \overline{\text{MC}} \end{bmatrix}$$

The state-space model is

$$\mathbf{x}(k+1) = \mathbf{A}\mathbf{x}(k) + \mathbf{B}\mathbf{u}(k)$$

$$\mathbf{y}(k) = \mathbf{C}\mathbf{x}(k).$$

(Note that the measured output is a vector.) Since state variables are the same as the outputs, we have

$$C = I = \begin{bmatrix} 1 & 0 \\ 0 & 1 \end{bmatrix}$$

Using MIMO system identification as described in Chapter 7 yields

$$A = \begin{bmatrix} 0.54 & -0.11 \\ -0.026 & 0.63 \end{bmatrix}$$

$$B = \begin{bmatrix} -85 & 4.4 \\ -2.5 & 2.8 \end{bmatrix} \times 10^{-4}$$

We use a dynamic state feedback control architecture. However, this is done a bit differently than described in Section 10.2.3 in that the state vector of the control system is not an augmented version of the state vector of the target system. Rather, the control error vector $e(k)$ is used, where $e(k) = r - y(k) = r - x(k)$. The dynamics of the control error are

$$e(k + 1) = r - x(k + 1)$$
$$= r - Ax(k) - Bu(k)$$
$$= Ae(k) - Bu(k) + (I - A)r \tag{10.19}$$

We also define the integrated control error:

$$x_I(k + 1) = x_I(k) + e(k) \tag{10.20}$$

The augmented state-space model can be written as

$$\begin{bmatrix} e(k) \\ x_I(k) \end{bmatrix} = \begin{bmatrix} e_1(k) \\ e_2(k) \\ x_{I,1}(k) \\ x_{I,2}(k) \end{bmatrix}$$

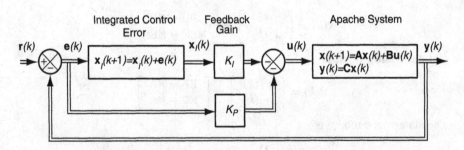

Fig. 10.19 Block diagram of a dynamic state feedback control system that regulates CPU and MEM in the Apache HTTP Server.

From Equations (10.19) and (10.20), we can construct the augmented state model for the control system.

$$\begin{bmatrix} e(k+1) \\ e_I(k+1) \end{bmatrix} = \begin{bmatrix} A & 0 \\ I & I \end{bmatrix} \begin{bmatrix} e(k) \\ e_I(k) \end{bmatrix} + \begin{bmatrix} -B \\ 0 \end{bmatrix} u(k) + \begin{bmatrix} I-A \\ 0 \end{bmatrix} r$$

That is,

$$\begin{bmatrix} e_1(k+1) \\ e_2(k+1) \\ x_{I,1}(k+1) \\ x_{I,2}(k+1) \end{bmatrix} = \begin{bmatrix} 0.54 & -0.11 & 0 & 0 \\ -0.026 & 0.63 & 0 & 0 \\ 1 & 0 & 1 & 0 \\ 0 & 1 & 0 & 1 \end{bmatrix} \begin{bmatrix} e_1(k) \\ e_2(k) \\ x_{I,1}(k) \\ x_{I,2}(k) \end{bmatrix}$$

$$+ \begin{bmatrix} 0.0085 & -0.00044 \\ 0.00025 & -0.00028 \\ 0 & 0 \\ 0 & 0 \end{bmatrix} \begin{bmatrix} u_1(k) \\ u_2(k) \end{bmatrix}$$

$$+ \begin{bmatrix} 0.46 & 0.11 \\ 0.026 & 0.37 \\ 0 & 0 \\ 0 & 0 \end{bmatrix} \begin{bmatrix} r_1 \\ r_2 \end{bmatrix}$$

Figure 10.19 displays a block diagram of the dynamic state feedback control system for the Apache HTTP Server. This system uses the control law

$$u(k) = -K \begin{bmatrix} e(k) \\ e_I(k) \end{bmatrix} = -\begin{bmatrix} K_P & K_I \end{bmatrix} \begin{bmatrix} e(k) \\ x_I(k) \end{bmatrix}$$

where K_P and K_I are 2×2 matrices and hence K is a 2×4 matrix. With this, the closed-loop model is

$$\begin{bmatrix} e(k+1) \\ x_I(k+1) \end{bmatrix} = \left(\begin{bmatrix} A & 0 \\ I & I \end{bmatrix} - \begin{bmatrix} -B \\ 0 \end{bmatrix} \begin{bmatrix} K_P & K_I \end{bmatrix} \right) \begin{bmatrix} e(k) \\ x_I(k) \end{bmatrix}$$

$$+ \begin{bmatrix} I-A \\ 0 \end{bmatrix} r$$

Now, we consider the design problem—how to choose the eight feedback gains in K_P and K_I. We begin with a pole placement design. Our specifications for transient performance are that (a) settling time be no more than 60 seconds and (b) maximum overshoot be no more than 5%. That is, $M_P^* = 0.05$ and $k_s^* = 12$ (since the sampling time is 5 seconds). The magnitude v of the dominant poles is

$$v = e^{-4/k_s^*} = e^{-4/12} = 0.72$$

and the angle is

$$\theta = \pi \frac{\log(v)}{\log(M_P^*)} = \pi \frac{\log(0.72)}{\log(0.05)} = 0.35$$

Thus, the two dominant poles are $0.67 \pm 0.25j$. There are a total of four poles in the closed-loop system since there are four state variables (and hence the characteristic polynomial has degree four). We choose the two nondominant poles to be $0.53 \pm 0.3j$. Thus, the desired characteristic polynomial is $(z - 0.67 - 0.25j)(z - 0.67 + 0.25j)(z - 0.53 - 0.3j)(z - 0.53 + 0.3j)$. The modeled characteristic polynomial is found by expanding

$$\det\left(z\mathbf{I} - \begin{bmatrix} \mathbf{A} & \mathbf{0} \\ \mathbf{I} & \mathbf{I} \end{bmatrix} + \begin{bmatrix} -\mathbf{B} \\ \mathbf{0} \end{bmatrix} \begin{bmatrix} \mathbf{K}_p & \mathbf{K}_I \end{bmatrix} \right)$$

Equating the coefficients of the desired and modeled characteristics polynomials results in four equations (the degree of these polynomials) in eight unknowns. Solving such an underconstrained system requires that additional assumptions be made. Rather than going through these technical details, we use the MATLAB place command, which yields the following gains:

$$\mathbf{K}_p = \begin{bmatrix} 31 & -114 \\ 106 & -2121 \end{bmatrix}$$

$$\mathbf{K}_I = \begin{bmatrix} 22 & -44 \\ 14 & -921 \end{bmatrix}$$

Figure 10.20 shows the tracking performance of the controller designed using pole placement. The dashed lines are the desired values of the output metrics, dashed-dotted lines are what the model predicts, and the solid lines are experimental results from a testbed with an Apache HTTP Server. We see that for MEM, the experimental and simulation results are in good correspondence. However, this is not the case for CPU. Specifically, both settling times and maximum overshoot violate the specifications for CPU.

Why does the controller perform poorly for CPU? One possibility is that the nondominant poles are too close to the dominant poles and hence the former have a significant effect on performance. Rather than iteratively refining the pole placement model, we explore the use of LQR.

Before beginning an LQR design, we must specify the matrices $\mathbf{Q}$ and $\mathbf{R}$. A common approach is first to normalize the terms in the Equation (10.17) cost function. Note that CPU and MEM both have a range of $[0, 1]$. However, the range of values for KeepAlive is 1 to 50, which differs from the range for MaxClients, which is 1 to 1024. We normalize for this difference in value ranges by using

$$\mathbf{R} = \begin{bmatrix} 1/50^2 & 0 \\ 0 & 1/1000^2 \end{bmatrix}$$

where $r_{1,1}$ is the cost associated with KeepAlive control effort and $r_{2,2}$ the cost for MaxClients. For $\mathbf{Q}$, we focus on the diagonal entries. These entries correspond to the state variables $e_1(k)$, $e_2(k)$, $x_{I,1}(k)$, $x_{I,2}$, where the subscript 1 refers to CPU and the subscript 2 refers to MEM. We choose $q_{1,1} = 1 = q_{2,2}$ to

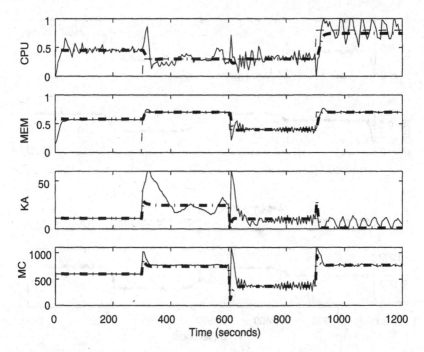

Fig. 10.20 *Tracking performance of a dynamic state feedback controller for the Apache HTTP Server designed using the pole placement method. The dashed lines are the desired values of the output metrics, the dashed-dotted lines are what the model predicts, and the solid lines are experimental results from a testbed with an Apache HTTP Server. Tracking performance is good for* MEM *and poor for* CPU.

provide equal costs for the control errors $(e_1(k), e_2(k))$. A smaller cost is placed on the integrated control errors $x_{I,1}(k)$ and $x_{I,2}(k)$, as indicated by the elements $q_{3,3}$ and $q_{4,4}$:

$$\mathbf{Q} = \begin{bmatrix} 1 & 0 & 0 & 0 \\ 0 & 1 & 0 & 0 \\ 0 & 0 & 0.1 & 0 \\ 0 & 0 & 0 & 0.2 \end{bmatrix}$$

The mechanics of LQR design can be done using the algorithm in Table 10.3 or the MATLAB command dlqr. The resulting feedback gains are

$$\mathbf{K}_P = \begin{bmatrix} 32 & -31 \\ -193 & -890 \end{bmatrix}$$

$$\mathbf{K}_I = \begin{bmatrix} 12 & -9 \\ -75 & -335 \end{bmatrix}$$

Figure 10.21 displays the results of simulation and empirical studies of the LQR controller. The dashed lines are the desired values of the output metrics, dashed-dotted lines are what the model predicts, and the solid lines are experimental results from a testbed with an Apache HTTP Server. We see that much

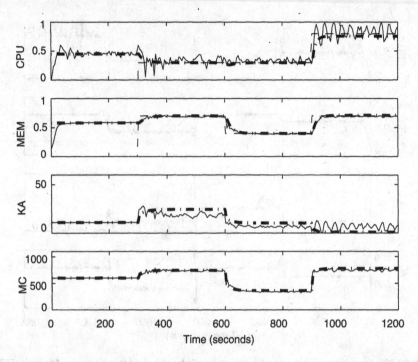

Fig. 10.21 *Tracking performance of a dynamic state feedback controller for the Apache HTTP Server server designed using LQR. The dashed lines are the desired values of the output metrics, the dashed-dotted lines are what the model predicts, and the solid lines are experimental results from a testbed with an Apache HTTP Server. Tracking performance is good for both* MEM *and* CPU.

better tracking performance is achieved. In part, this is due to reducing the control effort for KeepAlive, whose value changes much less in the LQR design than in the pole placement design. The insight here is that LQR provides a fairly easy way to limit control effort through the **R** matrix, something that is difficult to do with a pole placement design.

10.5.2 Effect of the LQR Design Parameters in a Dynamic State Feedback System

In this section we investigate how the LQR parameters **Q** and **R** affect transient response. We do this in the context of Example 10.11, the LQR design for the tandem queue. In that system, the control input is $K(k)$, the size of the buffer of the first queueing system, and the measured output is $R(k)$, the sum of the response times of the two queueing systems. Further, we use

$$\mathbf{Q} = \begin{bmatrix} q_{1,1} & 0 & 0 \\ 0 & q_{2,2} & 0 \\ 0 & 0 & q_{3,3} \end{bmatrix} = \begin{bmatrix} 1 & 0 & 0 \\ 0 & 1 & 0 \\ 0 & 0 & 100 \end{bmatrix}$$

and $R = 1$.

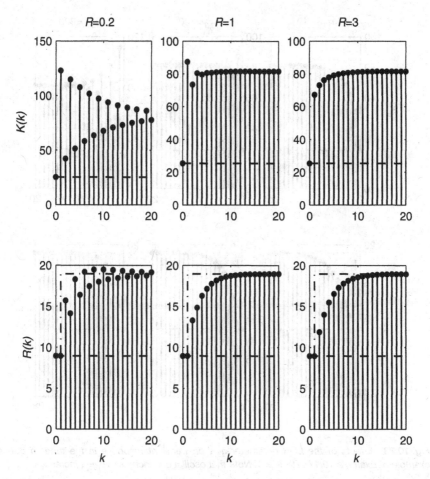

Fig. 10.22 *Effects of the LQR parameter R on transient response in the tandem queue example of Example 10.11 with $q_{3,3} = 100$. Note that overshoot decreases rapidly as R increases.*

First, we consider the effect of R on transient response. Figure 10.22 displays the step response of the control input $K(k)$ and the measured output $R(k)$ as the LQR parameter R increases from 0.2 to 3. We see that overshoot decreases dramatically as R increases. This is a consequence of feedback gains decreasing as R increases because a larger R makes control effort more costly.

Next, we consider the effect of $\mathbf{Q}$ on transient response. We focus on $q_{3,3}$, the cost associated with the integrated control error x_I. Figure 10.23 displays the transient response as $q_{3,3}$ increases from 10 to 300. Here we see that oscillations increase as $q_{3,3}$ increases. This too can be explained in terms of the effect on feedback gains. As $q_{3,3}$ increases, the cost of the control error increases as well, so feedback gains increase. While increasing feedback gains causes an overall decrease in x_I, the larger gains introduce oscillations.

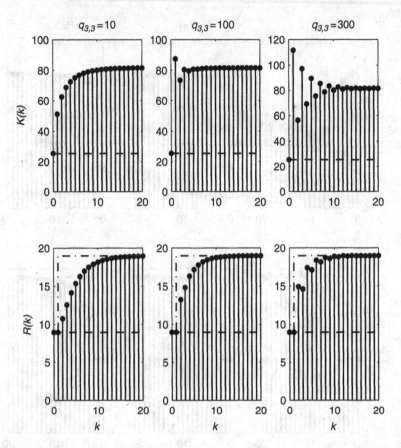

Fig. 10.23 *Effects of the LQR parameter $q_{3,3}$ on transient response in the tandem queue example of Example 10.11 with $R = 1$. Note that oscillations increase as $q_{3,3}$ increases.*

*10.6 DESIGNING STATE-SPACE CONTROLLERS USING MATLAB

In this section we illustrate how to use MATLAB for pole placement and LQR design.

We begin with pole placement design. What follows is a MATLAB approach to Example 10.8. Recall that the state-space model has **A** and **B**. This is expressed in MATLAB as

```
>> A = [0.13    0;   0.46    0.63];
>> B = [0.069; 0];
```

Further, recall that the desired poles are $-0.0091 \pm 0.016j$. That is, the vector of poles, P, is

```
>> P=[-.0091+.016j  -.0091-.016j]
```

We use the MATLAB place command to compute the feedback gains for a pole placement design.

```
>> K = place(A,B,P)

K =

  11.2783   12.8766
```

which is an unrounded version of the result obtained in Example 10.9.

Now consider the LQR design of the dynamic state feedback controller in Example 10.11. Recall that the dynamic state feedback system uses the state-space model parameters

```
>> A = [0.13    0 0;  0.46 0.63 0; 1 1 1];
>> B = [0.069; 0; 0];
```

We construct the LQR parameters **Q** and **R** using the MATLAB commands

```
>> Q = diag([1 1 100]);
>> R = 1;
```

Using the MATLAB command dlqr (discrete time LQR), we compute the feedback gains.

```
>> K = dlqr(A,B,Q,R)

K =

  11.5403   11.9249    6.2095
```

10.7 EXERCISES

1. Consider the system with state-space dynamics $\mathbf{x}(k + 1) = \mathbf{A}\mathbf{x}(k) + \mathbf{B}u(k)$, where $\mathbf{A} = \begin{bmatrix} 0.4 & 0 \\ 0.7 & 0.2 \end{bmatrix}$, $\mathbf{B} = \begin{bmatrix} 0.1 \\ 0 \end{bmatrix}$, and $\mathbf{C} = \begin{bmatrix} 1 & 3 \end{bmatrix}$. We want to construct a controller whose settling time is no larger than 6 and whose maximum overshoot is no greater than 2%.

   (a) What are the desired poles for the closed-loop system and the desired characteristic polynomial?

   (b) Consider the static feedback control architecture with the control law $u(k) = [K_1 K_2]\mathbf{x}(k)$. What is the modeled characteristic polynomial?

   (c) Write the set of equations for K_1 and K_2 based on equating the coefficients of the desired and modeled characteristic polynomials.

   (d) Find K_1 and K_2 using pole placement.

2. Modify the system in Exercise 1 to a precompensated static feedback controller by computing $\overline{N}$.

3. Consider the system with $\mathbf{A} = \begin{bmatrix} 0.8 & 0 \\ 0.3 & 0.2 \end{bmatrix}$ and $\mathbf{B}$ and $\mathbf{C}$ as in Exercise 1. Construct a static state feedback control system with the same settling times and overshoot as in Exercise 1. Why are the feedback gains larger? What is one undesirable implication of larger feedback gains in a computing system?

4. Consider the system in Exercise 1 for which we want to construct a controller whose settling time is no larger than 10 and whose maximum overshoot is no greater than 5%. What are the feedback gains? Why do these feedback gains have a larger magnitude than those in Exercise 1, even though the desired closed-loop system is slower?

5. For the system in Exercise 1, do an LQR design with $\mathbf{Q} = \begin{bmatrix} 1 & 0 \\ 0 & 10 \end{bmatrix}$ and $R = 0.5$. Also, compute the pole locations, settling time, and maximum overshoot. Repeat this exercise with $\mathbf{Q} = \begin{bmatrix} 1 & 0 \\ 0 & 1 \end{bmatrix}$. What is the effect of $\mathbf{Q}$?

6. Consider the system with $\mathbf{A} = \begin{bmatrix} 0.8 & 0 \\ 0.3 & 0.2 \end{bmatrix}$, $\mathbf{B} = \begin{bmatrix} 0.5 \\ 0 \end{bmatrix}$, $\mathbf{C} = \begin{bmatrix} 1 & 1 \end{bmatrix}$ for which we want to construct a dynamic state feedback controller whose settling time is no larger than 10 and whose maximum overshoot is no greater than 5%.

(a) What are the desired poles for the closed-loop system? What is the desired characteristic polynomial?

(b) Consider the dynamic state feedback control architecture with the additional state variable $x_I(k + 1) = x_I(k) + e(k)$ and the control law
$$u(k) = \begin{bmatrix} K_{P,1} & K_{P,2} & K_I \end{bmatrix} \begin{bmatrix} x_1(k) \\ x_2(k) \\ x_I(k) \end{bmatrix}.$$ Write the equations for the dynamics of the augmented state vector.

(c) Compute the feedback gains using pole placement.

(d) Design the feedback control system again using LQR with $R = 0.5$ and $\mathbf{Q} = \begin{bmatrix} 1 & 0 \\ 0 & 1 \end{bmatrix}$. How do the poles obtained compare with those for pole placement design?

11

Advanced Topics

Almost all real-world systems are nonlinear, stochastic, and time varying. Yet linear, deterministic, time-invariant models have met with widespread success in the process control, manufacturing, and aerospace industries. We believe that this confirms the principle we articulated in Chapter 2: "All models are wrong—but some models are useful." Indeed, throughout the book we have demonstrated that many controller design and analysis problems in computing systems can be addressed by relatively simple techniques that assume linear, deterministic, time-invariant systems.

Unfortunately, simple approaches do not always work. In this chapter we provide a brief introduction to several techniques that address nonlinearities, stochastics, and time-varying characteristics such as those encountered in computing systems. The first technique, gain scheduling, addresses nonlinear and/or time-varying systems by using auxiliary measurements (referred to as *scheduling variables*) to switch between controllers; doing so provides a way to use multiple linear controllers for a nonlinear system. Self-tuning regulators, the second technique, make ongoing adjustments to controller parameters based on revised estimates of the model of the target system. Minimum-variance controllers, a third technique, address systems with stochastics. Considered next is fluid flow analysis, an approach to constructing models from first principles. Finally, we describe fuzzy control, an approach to controller construction that uses qualitative rules to describe controller actions.

Feedback Control of Computing Systems, by Joseph L. Hellerstein, Yixin Diao, Sujay Parekh, and Dawn M. Tilbury
ISBN 0-471-26637-X Copyright © 2004 John Wiley & Sons, Inc.

11.1 MOTIVATING EXAMPLE

In this section we illustrate some shortcomings of linear, deterministic models by introducing an example that is used in the remainder of this chapter. Figure 11.1 displays a block diagram of a closed-loop system for controlling an $M/M/1/K$ queueing system using a PI (proportional–integral) controller. The reference input is desired response time, the output is measured response time, and the control input is buffer size. $R(z)$, $Y(z)$, and $U(z)$ are the Z-transforms of the offsets from the operating point. The disturbance input reflects time-varying changes in the arrival rate at the queueing system, a common situation in computing systems.

Figure 11.2 displays the dynamics considered in the example. Figure 11.2(a) depicts how arrival rates change with time. The system begins with an arrival

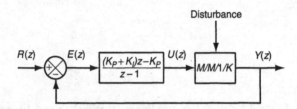

Fig. 11.1 *Closed-loop system used in motivating example. The target system is $M/M/1/K$, which is stochastic and nonlinear. The reference input is desired response time, the measured output is measured response time, and the control input is buffer size. $R(z)$, $Y(z)$, and $U(z)$ are offsets from the operating point. The disturbance is time varying.*

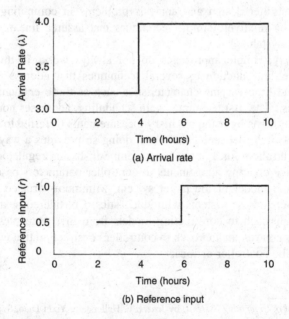

Fig. 11.2 *Summary of input dynamics used in running example. Both the arrival rate and the reference input (R) change.*

rate of $\lambda = 3.2$, which results in a utilization of 0.80. After 4 hours there is a disturbance that causes the arrival rate to jump to 3.96, which corresponds to a utilization of 0.99. Figure 11.2(b) indicates how the reference input changes with time. From hours 2 to 6, the reference input is 0.5 second, at which point the reference is changed to 1.0 second. (Hours 0 to 2 are a "warm-up" period.)

We now consider how to design a controller that can accommodate the changes displayed in Figure 11.2. Intuitively, it seems that a worst-case design might be a good approach. By *worst case*, we mean that the design is done for the high-arrival-rate case. Employing the CHR techniques described in Chapter 9 to this case, we obtain $K_P = 31$ and $K_I = 0.81$. Figure 11.3 displays the results of operating the system in Figure 11.1 with these controller parameters for a simulated $M/M/1/K$ queueing system and applying the dynamics in Figure 11.2. The top plot shows the measured arrival rate in each interval, the middle plot displays the buffer size (which is held constant during the warm-up period), and the bottom plot contains the measured response times with dashed lines indicating the reference input. Observe that settling times are quite long when the arrival rate is lower, and settling times are shorter when the arrival rate is high.

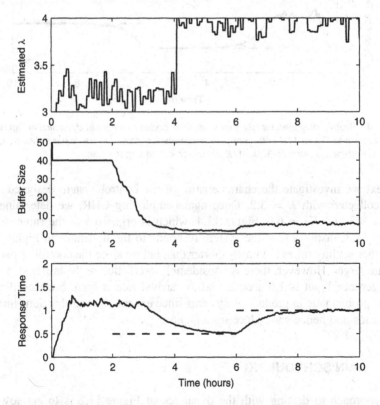

Fig. 11.3 *System designed for high arrival rates. Response to the input dynamics in Figure 11.2 of the system in Figure 11.1 with controller parameters obtained under high arrival rates. The results are obtained using an $M/M/1/K$ simulator as the target system.*

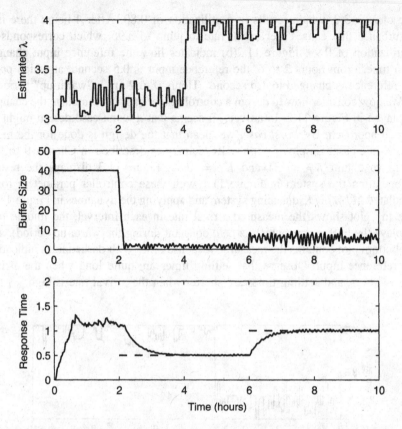

Fig. 11.4 *System designed for low arrival rates: response to the input dynamics in Figure 11.2 of the system in Figure 11.1 with controller parameters obtained under lower arrival rates. The results are obtained using an $M/M/1/K$ simulator for the target system.*

Next we investigate the characteristics of the control system designed using data collected with $\lambda = 3.2$. Once again employing CHR, we determine that $K_P = 143$ and $K_I = 6.0$. Figure 11.4, which is organized in the same way as Figure 11.3, displays how the system responds to the dynamics in Figure 11.2. Note that settling times are much shorter than before since the controller parameters are larger. However, there is considerable oscillation in the buffer size when the reference input is 1.0 second and the arrival rate is high. Such oscillations can be problematic in production systems since excessive control actions increase overheads and hence can reduce throughputs.

11.2 GAIN SCHEDULING

One approach to dealing with the dynamics of Figure 11.2 is to employ *gain scheduling*, a technique that chooses the controller to use dynamically by employing rules that distinguish between operating regimes. Operating regimes are described in terms of *scheduling variables* (e.g., measured arrival rate) that are obtained from the target system. A gain scheduler can be constructed by (1) characterizing the operating regimes in terms of scheduling variables, and (2) doing separate controller designs for each regime.

Figure 11.5 displays a block diagram of a gain scheduling system. The lower part of the diagram contains blocks for the controller and target system. To support gain scheduling, these components differ from those in Figure 11.1 in that (1) the target system must expose the scheduling variables, and (2) the controller must have a means to accept new parameters dynamically. The gain scheduler takes the scheduling variables as input, and it outputs the controller parameters.

Figure 11.6 contains a block diagram of a gain scheduling system for the $M/M/1/K$ queueing system. As before, a PI controller is used. A first-order

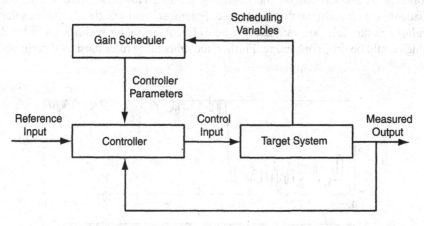

Fig. 11.5 Block diagram of gain scheduling. Scheduling variables measured on the target system are used to adjust controller parameters.

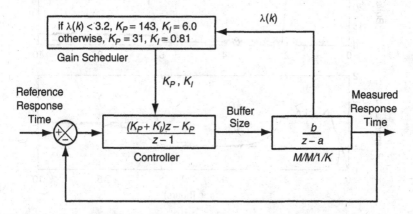

Fig. 11.6 Block diagram of gain scheduling for $M/M/1/K$. The measured arrival rate of the queueing system is used to adjust K_P and K_I.

model is used for the target system. The scheduling variable is $\lambda(k)$, the measured arrival rate of the $M/M/1/K$ system at time k, which is monitored by the gain scheduler. The gain scheduler contains two *scheduling rules* that determine the controller parameters based on measured arrival rates. In essence, this is a way of combining the best characteristics of the controllers presented in Section 11.1.

Figure 11.7 displays the response of the gain scheduling system in Figure 11.6 to the dynamics in Figure 11.2. (As before, an $M/M/1/K$ simulator is used for the target system.) Observe that the gain scheduling system has the desirable characteristics of both of the designs done in Section 11.1, in that (1) there is little or no oscillation in buffer size (as is the case in the design done for high arrival rates), and (2) settling times are short (as is the case in the design done for lower arrival rates).

In principle, the gain scheduler is a meta-controller that chooses a set of controller parameters based on the operating regime. However, there are several challenges with realizing this in practice. Foremost, gain scheduling requires that *multiple* controllers be designed for the different operating regimes considered, which could be time consuming. Further, the scheduling rules must be determined

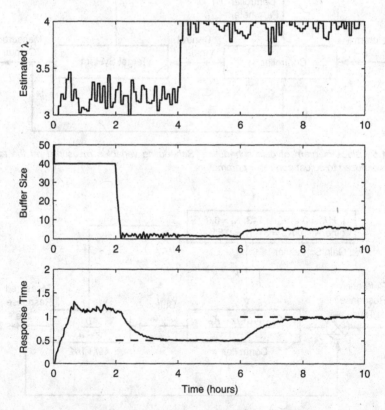

Fig. 11.7 *Response of gain scheduling to the input dynamics in Figure 11.2. The results are obtained using an $M/M/1/K$ simulator for the target system.*

and appropriate interfaces to the target system must be present (or constructed) to obtain the requisite scheduling variables. Care should be taken in the design of the scheduling rules to avoid abrupt shifts in operating regimes (which would probably happen in the system in Figure 11.7). Of particular concern here are undesirable end-user characteristics, such as much larger or more variable response times. Another concern is stability. Specifically, gain scheduling a set of stable controllers may not ensure that the combination of controllers is stable. More details on gain scheduling can be found in [9] and [59].

11.3 SELF-TUNING REGULATORS

In this section we describe *self-tuning regulators*, an approach to adaptation that updates controller parameters at each sample time. There are many different types of self-tuning regulators. One type provides a kind of online pole placement design. This is done by recomputing the controller parameters needed to maintain the desired poles based on updated estimates of the parameters of the target system that are obtained at each sample time.

Figure 11.8 displays a block diagram in which a self-tuning regulator is used for regulatory control. As in gain scheduling, the controller must be capable of dynamically updating its parameters. However, unlike in gain scheduling, there is no need to modify the target system to expose scheduling variables. This is of particular benefit to independent software vendors and customers who assemble end-to-end solutions from commercially available products (e.g., e-commerce systems) since they do not have access to product internals and so cannot modify products to expose additional measurement data.

To better appreciate the foregoing, consider the self-tuning regulator system in Figure 11.9. As before, there is a first-order target system so that

$$G(z) = \frac{b}{z - a}$$

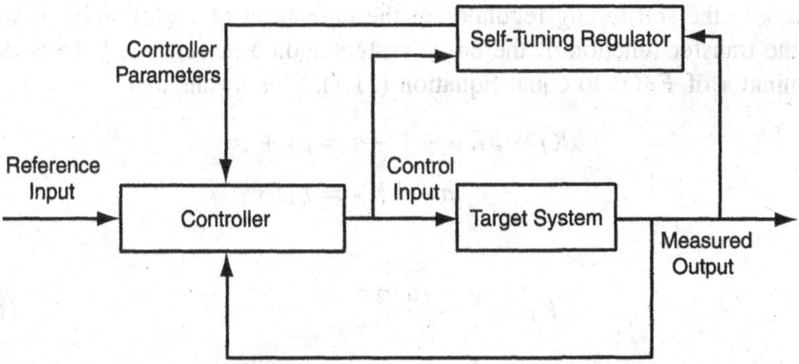

Fig. 11.8 Block diagram of a system employing a self-tuning regulator. The measured output and control inputs are used to adjust the model of the target system and the controller parameters.

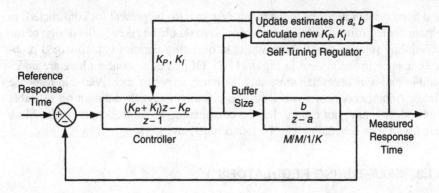

Fig. 11.9 *Block diagram of a self-tuning regulator for the $M/M/1/K$ running example. Parameters a and b of the system model are updated at each sample time based on the measured response time and the buffer size. K_P and K_I are obtained using Equations (11.2) and (11.3), respectively.*

and a PI controller

$$K(z) = K_P + \frac{K_I z}{z - 1}$$

Suppose that we want the closed-loop system to have the poles p_1 and p_2. So the characteristic polynomial is

$$(z - p_1)(z - p_2) = z^2 - (p_1 + p_2)z + p_1 p_2 \tag{11.1}$$

From Figure 11.9, the transfer function from the reference response time to the measured response time is

$$
\begin{aligned}
F_R(z) &= \frac{K(z)G(z)}{1 + K(z)G(z)} \\
&= \frac{bK_I z + bK_P(z - 1)}{z^2 + (bK_I + bK_P - 1 - a)z + a - bK_P}
\end{aligned}
$$

[We ignore the self-tuning regulator in the derivation of $F_R(z)$ since at steady state the transfer function of the target system should not change.] We want the denominator of $F_R(z)$ to equal Equation (11.1). This means that

$$bK_I + bK_P - 1 - a = p_1 + p_2$$

$$a - bK_P = p_1 p_2$$

or

$$K_P = \frac{a - p_1 p_2}{b} \tag{11.2}$$

$$K_I = \frac{1 - p_1 - p_2 + p_1 p_2}{b} \tag{11.3}$$

So if we are given estimates for a and b, we can calculate K_P, K_I.

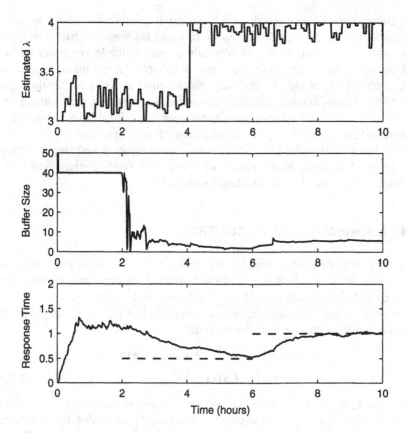

Fig. 11.10 *Response of the self-tuning regulator in Figure 11.9 to the input dynamics in Figure 11.2. The results are obtained using an $M/M/1/K$ simulator for the target system.*

Consider the closed-loop poles 0.88 and 0.51 (which are chosen to provide a middle ground between the closed-loop systems constructed in Section 11.1). Figure 11.10 displays the results of using the system in Figure 11.9 in the presence of the dynamics in Figure 11.2. The results are obtained using an $M/M/1/K$ simulator for the target system. Although this control system avoids significant oscillations, we see that its settling times are long compared with what is obtained for gain scheduling. On the other hand, the self-tuning regulator system can greatly simplify controller design since no CHR tuning is required (because the controller parameters are "learned" online).

Self-tuning regulators require a way to do online estimation of the parameters of the target system. For the target system in Figure 11.9, this means that at the kth sample time, we construct the estimates of the parameters $a(k)$ and $b(k)$. (The parameters are indexed by time since they are assumed to be dynamic.) Typically, this is done using recursive least squares, an online version of the least-squares estimation procedure described in Chapter 2. More details on recursive least squares can be found in [9].

Self-tuning regulators can reduce the complexity of controller design by reducing manual tuning, a process that can be complex (as seen in Chapter 9) and is even more burdensome with gain scheduling since multiple controller designs must be done. However, there are some drawbacks to self-tuning regulators. First, control performance is generally not as good as for a handcrafted gain scheduling system. Second, adjusting controller parameters at each sample time may not be effective for computing systems since it is difficult to determine if the environment has changed (e.g., load has increased) in the presence of stochastics. Further, many of the changes that take place in computing systems are abrupt, such as rapid changes in workloads or changes in configuration. Self-tuning regulators tend to be slow in adapting to such changes.

11.4 MINIMUM-VARIANCE CONTROL

Computing systems have significant stochastics, especially in the interarrival and service-time processes. In this section we describe minimum-variance control, an approach to regulating the variability of the measured output.

Building on the state-space approach described in Chapter 7, we revise the dynamic model to include a stochastic term:

$$\mathbf{x}(k+1) = \mathbf{A}\mathbf{x}(k) + \mathbf{B}\mathbf{u}(k) + \mathbf{w}(k) \tag{11.4}$$

$$\mathbf{y}(k) = \mathbf{C}\mathbf{x}(k) \tag{11.5}$$

$\mathbf{x}(k)$, $\mathbf{u}(k)$, $\mathbf{A}$, $\mathbf{B}$, and $\mathbf{C}$ are defined in the same way as in Equations (7.3) and 7.4. The term $\mathbf{w}(k)$ is a vector of stochastic variables. Observe that by introducing $\mathbf{w}(k)$, $\mathbf{x}(k)$, and $\mathbf{y}(k)$ become stochastic variables. To simplify the following discussion, we assume that $\mathbf{w}(k)$ is a scalar. Further, $w(1), w(2), \ldots, w(k)$ are independent and identically distributed. The expected value of $w(k)$ is denoted by $E[w(k)]$. We assume that $E[w(k)] = 0$. The variance is $\text{var}[w(k)] = \sigma^2$.

Figure 11.11 displays a block diagram of a system in which the disturbance is stochastic. Observe that the controller takes as input both the reference input and the measured output instead of just the control error.

Figure 11.12 displays an instantiation of Figure 11.11 for a first-order target system. For this target system, $C = 1$, so $y(k) = x(k)$. Substituting into

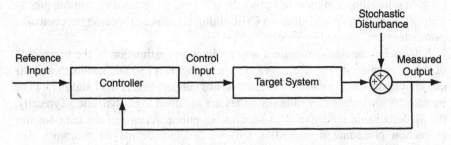

Fig. 11.11   *Block diagram of a stochastic controller. The disturbance is stochastic.*

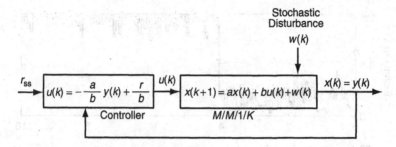

Fig. 11.12 *Block diagram of a simplified stochastic control system. The target system is first order, and all variables are scalars. The controller compensates for the nonstochastic part of the control error.*

Equation (11.4), we obtain

$$y(k+1) = ay(k) + bu(k) + w(k) \qquad (11.6)$$

Ideally, we want $E[y(k+1)] = r_{ss}$. If this is the case, then

$$\text{var}(y(k+1)) = E(y(k+1) - E[y(k+1)])^2$$
$$= E[ay(k) + bu(k) + w(k) - r_{ss}]^2$$
$$= E[ay(k) + bu(k) - r_{ss}]^2 + \sigma^2 \qquad (11.7)$$

Clearly, $u(k)$ affects only the first term in Equation (11.7). So the variance $\text{var}(y(k+1))$ is minimized if $r = ay(k) + bu(k)$. This motivates the following control law:

$$u(k) = -\frac{a}{b}y(k) + \frac{r_{ss}}{b} \qquad (11.8)$$

Substituting Equation (11.8) into Equation (11.6), we have

$$y(k+1) = ay(k) + bu(k) + w(k)$$
$$= ay(k) + b\left(-\frac{a}{b}y(k) + \frac{r_{ss}}{b}\right) + w(k)$$
$$= r_{ss} + w(k) \qquad (11.9)$$

That is, the measured output equals the reference input plus a random variable with a zero mean.

There are several observations of interest about the foregoing. First, the control law in Equation (11.8) is expressed in terms of both the reference input r_{ss} and the measured output $y(k)$ rather than just the control error $r_{ss} - y(k)$. This is why there are two inputs to the controller in Figure 11.11. Second, the settling time of the minimum variance controller is quite short, just one sample time. Exploring this further, we take the expectation of both sides of Equation (11.9), which yields $E[y(k+1)] = r_{ss}$. The transfer function from the reference input

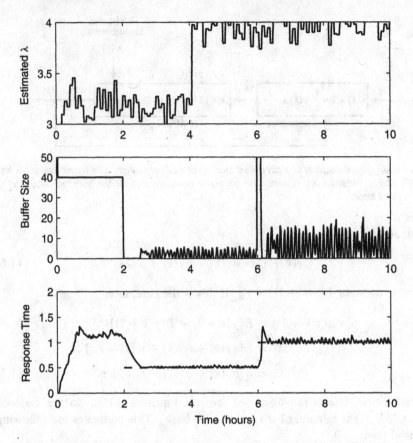

Fig. 11.13 *Response of a stochastic controller to the input dynamics in Figure 11.2.*

to the mean of the measured output is $1/z$. That is, there is a single pole at 0, which is consistent with the very short settling time.

Figure 11.13 displays the response of the controller in Figure 11.12 (with an $M/M/1/K$ simulator as the target system) to the input dynamics in Figure 11.2. We see that settling times are very short, which is consistent with having a pole at 0. However, there still is steady-state variability, especially after hour 6. Also, even though the controller reduces output variability, there is considerable variability in buffer sizes.

11.5 FLUID FLOW ANALYSIS

Successful application of control theory requires a reasonably accurate model of the target system, at least over its operating region. In Chapter 2 we emphasize a black-box approach in which the parameters of ARX models are estimated using empirical techniques. In this section we describe how fluid flow analysis can be used to determine the order of the model of a target system and the factors affecting the parameters of the model.

Fluid flow analysis constructs deterministic, time-varying models based on an analogy to the flow of fluids between containers. Typically, fluid flow analysis is done in continuous time, an approach that involves different mathematical techniques than those used in the book (e.g., systems of differential equations, Laplace transforms). To avoid the need for additional mathematical background, we adapt fluid flow to discrete time.

In a fluid flow analysis, there are one or more containers, each with a finite capacity. Containers are connected by a network of pipes through which fluid flows. One or more containers have an ingress flow in which fluid is delivered from outside the fluid flow network, and some containers have an egress flow in which fluid leaves the fluid flow network. If the capacity of a container is exceeded, fluid spills out. The system is controlled by changing the capacity of the containers and/or the pipes. Doing so affects egress flows, the spill rate, and the volume of fluid in containers. Fluid flow analysis provides a means to calculate the following as a function of time: (1) egress flows, (2) fluid volume in containers, and (3) spill rates.

The analogy to computing systems is as follows. The fluids are types of requests, such as browse and buy requests at an e-commerce site. The containers are computing resources such as CPU and memory. The volume of fluid in a container corresponds to number in system, and an egress flow is a throughput (work completion rate). Spilled fluid corresponds to discarded requests such as dropped packets in network routers. Adjusting the capacity of a pipe is the same as admission control. Limiting container capacity is similar to varying a buffer size. Thus, in fluid flow models, the control inputs are the capacities of pipes and containers; the measured outputs are egress flow, container volume, and spill rates.

We illustrate fluid flow analysis with a simple example. Figure 11.14 displays a cross section of a single container with a single fluid. There is one input and one output pipe. The input pipe can accommodate a capacity of $F_I(k)$ volume per second of fluid, and the capacity of the output pipe is $F_O(k)$. The capacity of the container is denoted by $V(k)$. At time k, the ingress rate is $f_I(k)$, the egress rate is $f_O(k)$, the spill rate is $f_S(k)$, and the volume of fluid in the container is $v(k)$. Throughout, it is assumed that changes made to $F_I(k)$, $F_O(k)$, and $V(k)$ take effect immediately after values are measured for $f_O(k)$, $f_S(k)$, and $v(k)$.

We show how to compute $f_O(k+1)$, $f_S(k+1)$, and $v(k+1)$. This is done by describing the states of a container.

- *Empty:* $0 = v(k)$. No fluid has accumulated. So the output rate is the lesser of the input rate and the output capacity, or $f_O(k) = \min\{f_I(k), F_O(k)\}$. If the container volume is nonzero, $V(k) > 0$, there is no spillage, $f_S(k) = 0$. Otherwise, $f_S(k) = \max\{f_I(k) - F_O(k), 0\}$.
- *Partially full:* $0 < v(k) < V(k)$. Fluid has accumulated, so the output rate is the maximum rate. That is, $f_O(k) = F_O(k)$. Also, there is no spillage $f_S(k) = 0$.

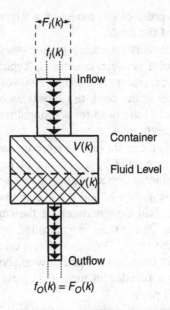

$\leftarrow F_I(k) \rightarrow$

$f_I(k)$

Inflow

Container

$V(k)$

Fluid Level

$v(k)$

Outflow

$f_O(k) = F_O(k)$

Fig. 11.14 *Cross section of an element in a fluid flow network. The top rectangle is the input pipe, the middle is the container, and the bottom is the output pipe. The ingress rate $f_I(k)$ cannot exceed the capacity of the input pipe $F_I(k)$. The container (single-hatched area) has capacity $V(k)$ and contains a fluid (double-hatched area within the hatched area) with volume $v(k) < V$ [which implies that the spill rate $f_S(k) = 0$]. The egress rate $f_O(k)$ cannot exceed the capacity of the output pipe $F_O(k)$. For the situation depicted, the egress rate is at its maximum since the fluid volume is nonzero.*

- *Full:* $v(k) = V(k)$. As with the partially full state, the output rate is the maximum rate. That is, $f_O(k) = F_O(k)$. Fluid spills out at a rate of $\max\{f_I(k) - F_O(k), 0\}$.

Clearly, the input and output flow rates are bounded by the pipe capacities; that is, $f_I(k) \le F_I(k)$ and $f_O(k) \le F_O(k)$. Assuming that sample times and/or dynamics are sufficiently small so that state changes occur only at multiples of the sample time T_S, the volume of fluid at time $k + 1$ is

$$v(k + 1) = \min\{\max\{v(k) + (f_I(k) - F_O(k))\, T_S, 0\}, V(k)\} \qquad (11.10)$$

We can apply Equation (11.10) as follows. Suppose that we want to use admission control to regulate the number of concurrent requests in a computing system. This means that we are adjusting $F_I(k)$ to control $v(k)$ and that the output capacity does not change [i.e., $F_O(k) = F_O$]. Assume that:

1. There is ample buffer space, so that there is no buffer overflow. That is, $V(k) >> v(k)$.
2. There is always sufficient in-flow so that $f_I(k) = F_I(k)$.

Under these conditions, the container is always in the partially full state. So Equation (11.10) becomes

$$v(k + 1) = v(k) + T_S [F_I(k) - F_O] \qquad (11.11)$$

This is a first-order model in which $v(k)$ corresponds to $y(k)$, $F_I(k) - F_O$ corresponds to $u(k)$, and T_S corresponds to b.

Unfortunately, we cannot translate this immediately into a model of the target system since fluid flow analysis only approximates the true input–output behavior of the target system. However, Equation (11.11) does indicate that the functional form of the model of the target system is $y(k + 1) = ay(k) + bu(k)$, where y is the offset value of the measured output and u is the offset value of the control input. Knowing this, we could construct a self-tuning regulator that estimates a and b and then determines the parameters of the controller. In some circumstances, Equation (11.11) provides still more insights. Suppose that T_S is adjusted dynamically (e.g., to reduce measurement overheads during stationary periods). Equation (11.11) indicates that doing so requires a new estimate of b. This suggests that a kind of gain scheduling might be valuable in which a and b are set to values discovered during similar settings of T_S.

An excellent example of fluid flow analysis for control purposes has been done for TCP/IP (Transmission Control Protocol/Internet Protocol). Among other things, TCP/IP controls the flow of packets between senders to receivers across the Internet. The sender has a "window" of bytes that controls what is sent to the receiver. The window is increased at a rate that is inversely proportional to the round-trip time (message transmission plus its acknowledgment), and the window is decreased at a rate proportional to the window size at the time that packets are lost. In fluid terms, the window is a leaky container, where the leaks correspond to packets being discarded by congested routers. The egress rate is the throughput of packets accepted by the receiver. TCP/IP tries to adjust the size of the container so that an appropriate trade-off is achieved between the rate of egress and fluid spill. More details can be found in [48].

Still another example of fluid flow analysis is described in [27]. This work shows how to estimate the parameters of a first-order model from the parameters of an $M/M/1/K$ queueing system. Doing so provides insights into the effects of changes in workload on system dynamics (especially settling times).

Fluid flow analysis can be generalized in many ways. The single-container analysis presented here can be generalized to multiple containers in which a network of pipes connect the containers. Also, there may be multiple types of fluids with different pipe and container capacities, an approach to that is useful in modeling systems with different types of requests. Other examples of fluid flow analysis can be found in [3].

11.6 FUZZY CONTROL

In this section we provide a brief summary of fuzzy control. Our intent is twofold. The first is to expand the scope of techniques used for feedback control to

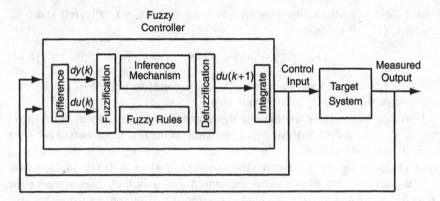

Fig. 11.15 Block diagram of fuzzy control for optimizing the measured output (e.g., finding the lowest response time). The fuzzy controller is driven by the fuzzy rules that use linguistic variables.

include heuristic methods. The second is to address a different control objective—optimization (which is in contrast to the regulation problems that have been the focus of the book).

Figure 11.15 displays a block diagram of the fuzzy control system we consider. As before, there is a controller and a target system. However, there is no reference input since the objective is optimization, not regulation. Second, the feedback consists of both the measured output and the control input.

Before continuing, some background is required. Fuzzy control employs qualitative descriptions of systems so as to make it easier to specify controller actions. Typically, these qualitative descriptions are in the form of directional effects such as *change-in-MaxClients*, *change-in-response-time*, and *next-change-in-MaxClients*. Each of these is an example of a *linguistic variable*. Linguistic variables exist in one-to-one correspondence with numeric variables. For example, *change-in-MaxClients* is a linguistic variable corresponding to the numeric variable for the change in MaxClients. A linguistic variable takes on *linguistic values* such as positive-large (hereafter, *poslarge*) and negative-large (hereafter, *neglarge*). Such variables indicate, among other things, the direction and magnitude of a change.

The fuzzy controller in Figure 11.15 operates as follows. The system computes the differenced control input $du(k) = u(k) - u(k - 1)$ and the differenced measured output $dy(k) = y(k) - y(k - 1)$. The differences are input to the fuzzification component that translates quantitative values into linguistic values. Fuzzy rules are expressed in terms of linguistic variables. These rules, which are interpreted by the inference mechanism, guide the selection of controller actions (which are themselves expressed in the form of directional changes). The defuzzification component translates the linguistic variable for the controller action into a quantitative variable. Typically, these actions are incremental changes in the control input. Thus, the integrator component translates this into an absolute setting. More details on fuzzy control can be found in [55].

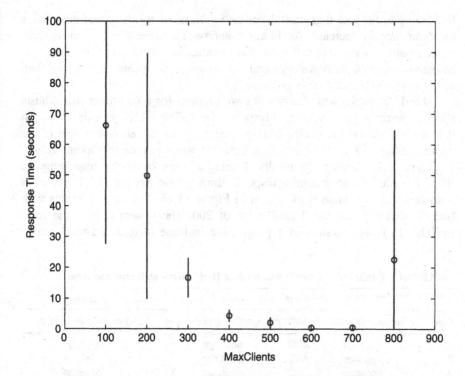

Fig. 11.16 *Effect of* MaxClients *on response times of the Apache HTTP Server for a fixed workload. The circles represent mean values, and the vertical lines indicate standard deviations. Delays for low values of* MaxClients *are due to waits in the TCP accept queue. Delays at high values of* MaxClients *are due to contention for operating system resources.*

We now consider how to optimize the setting of MaxClients in the Apache HTTP Server. Figure 11.16 displays the results of experiments conducted on a testbed for the Apache HTTP Server in which MaxClients is varied for a stationary workload of dynamic pages. We see that response times are quite large if MaxClients is either too small or too large. The former is a consequence of long waits in the TCP accept queue; the latter results from contention between Apache clients for operating system resources (e.g., CPU, memory). We see that setting MaxClients to an intermediate value results in much lower response times.

We illustrate fuzzy control by developing rules that adjust MaxClients to minimize response times in the Apache HTTP Server. In essence, we are seeking the minimum of a concave-upward curve. This could be done using gradient techniques (e.g., [22]). We show that it can also be accomplished using a simple set of fuzzy rules.

Fuzzy rules are if-then statements expressed in terms of linguistic variables and linguistic values. In our case, the if-part of the rule determines what was done last and its effect. For example, "if *change-in-MaxClients* is *poslarge* and *change-in-response-time* is *neglarge*." The then-part specifies the action to take.

For example, suppose that MaxClients is increased at time k and this causes response time to decrease. An intuitive approach at time $k + 1$ is to increase MaxClients some more. Putting this together in a fuzzy rule, we have: "If *change-in-MaxClients* is *poslarge* and *change-in-response-time* is *neglarge*, then *next-change-in-MaxClients* is *poslarge*."

Table 11.1 displays the fuzzy rules we propose for a controller that adjusts MaxClients so as to minimize response times. The if-part provides a way to determine if the minimal value of response time is to the left or the right of the current setting of MaxClients. The then-part prescribes the appropriate action.

Figure 11.17 displays the results of using a fuzzy controller employing the rules in Table 11.1 to minimize response times of the Apache HTTP Server in a testbed with the same workload as in Figure 11.16. The system begins with MaxClients set to the default value of 200. The system applies the rules in Table 11.1. This results in a progressive increase in MaxClients and a

TABLE 11.1   Fuzzy Rules Used in a Controller That Minimizes Response Times

	If		Then
Rule	change-in-MaxClients AND	change-in-response-time	next-change-in-MaxClients
1	neglarge	AND	neglarge	neglarge
2	neglarge	AND	poslarge	poslarge
3	poslarge	AND	neglarge	poslarge
4	poslarge	AND	poslarge	neglarge

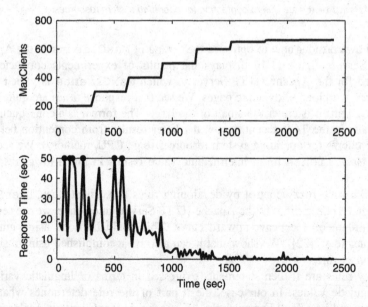

Fig. 11.17 *Operation of the fuzzy controller for the Apache HTTP Server for a fixed workload. The initial setting of MaxClients is 200, one of the Apache HTTP Server defaults.*

corresponding decrease in response time. We see that the ending response time is considerably smaller than the starting value.

One interpretation of the foregoing is that the Apache HTTP Server uses the wrong default setting for MaxClients. That is, the default should be 650 instead of 200, at least for our testbed system. Proceeding in this manner, we compare two control schemes. The first is static control in which MaxClients = 650 throughout the experiment. The second scheme employs fuzzy control with the rules contained in Table 11.1. In both cases, we increase the intensity of the workload at time 600 by adding a large number of requests for static HTML pages. Figure 11.18(a) displays the results for static control and Figure 11.18(b) that for fuzzy control. We see that fuzzy control achieves a substantial reduction in response times compared to static control. More details can be found in [18].

Fuzzy control has the appeal of directly incorporating human intuition in the form of fuzzy rules. Although we have obtained good results using fuzzy control on testbed systems, some caution is advised. In particular, care must be taken in the choice of the increments by which control inputs are increased and/or decreased. Indeed, we use an adaptive scheme whereby the magnitude of the increment changes as the system approaches convergence.

11.7 SUMMARY

1. Although controller designs based on linear, deterministic models often work well in computing systems, sometimes more sophisticated techniques are required. Control theory provides a wealth of such techniques, although their application can require more mathematical sophistication.

2. Gain scheduling provides a way to switch dynamically between controllers using scheduling rules based on scheduling variables that are obtained from the target system. Such an approach provides a framework for using collections of linear controllers to adapt to nonlinearities and stochastics.

3. Self-tuning regulators change controller parameters at each sample time based on updated estimates of the model of the target system. Such regulators can be easier to build than gain schedulers, since they adapt dynamically to the characteristics of the target system. However, the control performance of self-tuning regulators tends to be worse than that for carefully constructed gain schedulers. For example, our studies describe a situation in which self-tuning regulators may have longer settling times.

4. Minimum variance control addresses the variability of the measured output. The underlying model of the target system assumes that state-space dynamics include a random variable, which makes the state variables and measured output stochastic as well. It turns out that minimizing the variance of the measured output also results in very short settling times.

5. Fuzzy control employs heuristic rules to describe when the controller should take what action. The if-part of the rules describes the situation considered in terms of linguistic variables and linguistic values (e.g.,

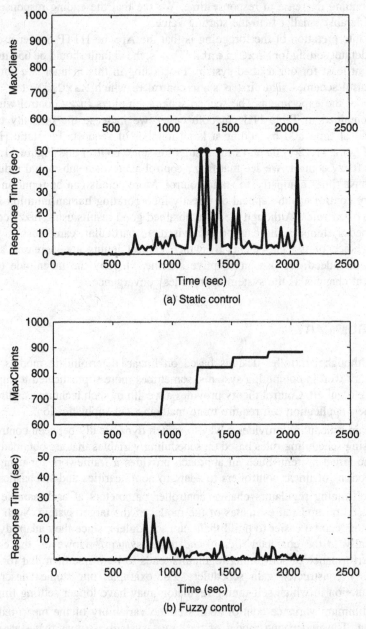

Fig. 11.18 *Operation of static and fuzzy controllers for a second workload. The static controller sets* MaxClients *to the steady-state value obtained for the workload in Figure 11.17. The results suggest that fuzzy control is preferred to static control.*

change-in-MaxClients is *poslarge*). The then-part specifies how control variables should be adjusted (e.g., *next-change-in-MaxClients* is *poslarge*). One application of fuzzy control is to optimization, such as finding the value of `MaxClients` that minimizes the response time of the Apache HTTP Server.

11.8 EXERCISES

1. The gain scheduler developed in Section 11.2 switches between two PI controllers (as specified by their K_P and K_I). What are the advantages and disadvantages of switching among three or more controllers? How should the operating regimes be chosen for the controllers? What scheduling rules should be used?

2. One issue with using self-tuning regulators (as described in Section 11.3) in computing systems is adapting to sudden shifts in workloads. Consider a target system whose control input is buffer size and the measured output is response time. The system is observed online with the input–output data displayed in Table 11.2, in which there is a sudden increase in workload at time $k = 6$. Using the first-order model $y(k + 1) = ay(k) + bu(k)$ to fit the data, estimate a and b for the following: (1) all 10 observations, (2) the first five observations, and (3) the last five observations. Explain why R^2 increases so dramatically from case 1 to cases 2 and 3. What does this suggest in terms of how to manage historical data for self-tuning regulators applied to computing systems?

3. Both minimum-variance control described in Section 11.4 and linear quadratic regulators described in Section 10.3.2 design controllers based on an optimization criteria. Compare and contrast these approaches.

TABLE 11.2   Data Used for Computing Least Squares in Exercise 2

k	Buffer Size	Response Time
1	12	1.3
2	16	1.5
3	10	1.1
4	14	1.4
5	18	1.6
6	12	1.5
7	10	1.3
8	14	1.7
9	18	2.2
10	16	1.9

4. The fluid flow analysis described in Section 11.5 considers only a single container. Extend this to two containers in tandem so that the control input is the volume of the first container and the measured output is the egress rate from the second container.

5. Consider the fuzzy rules in Table 11.1. These rules consider only the linguistic values *poslarge* and *neglarge*. Suppose that we include the linguistic value *nochange* with the interpretation that the underlying quantitative value does not change. Augment the rules in Table 11.1 to consider this linguistic value. How would you expect the behavior of the control system to change as a result of including these additional rules?

Appendix A

Mathematical Notation

Rules

- Boldface lowercase is a vector such as

$$\mathbf{x} = \begin{bmatrix} x_1 \\ x_2 \end{bmatrix}$$

- Boldface uppercase is a matrix such as

$$\mathbf{A} = \begin{bmatrix} a_{11} & a_{12} \\ a_{21} & a_{22} \end{bmatrix}$$

- Bar over a signal gives its operating point, such as $\overline{\text{CPU}}$.
- A signal in the time domain is denoted as $\{x(k)\} = \{x(0), x(1), \ldots\}$, where $x(k)$ is the value of the signal at time k.

Symbols

- a = pole in first-order model
- $\mathbf{A}$ = state-space matrix
- b = coeficient of input signal in first-order model
- $\mathbf{B}$ = state-space input matrix

Feedback Control of Computing Systems, by Joseph L. Hellerstein, Yixin Diao, Sujay Parekh, and Dawn M. Tilbury
ISBN 0-471-26637-X   Copyright © 2004 John Wiley & Sons, Inc.

- $\mathbf{C}$ = state-space output matrix
- $D(z), d(k)$ = disturbance input
- $\det(\mathbf{A})$ = determinant of the matrix $\mathbf{A}$
- $E(z), e(k)$ = control error
- $F(z)$ = transfer function, typically closed-loop transfer function
- $F_D(z)$ = transfer function from the disturbance input to measured output
- $F_{DE}(z)$ = transfer function from the disturbance input to control error
- $F_N(z)$ = transfer function from the noise input to the measured output that includes noise
- $F_{NE}(z)$ = transfer function from the noise input to control error
- $F_R(z)$ = transfer function from the reference input to the measured output
- $F_{RE}(z)$ = transfer function from the reference input to control error
- $G(z)$ = transfer function, typically the open-loop plant
- $H(z)$ = transfer function, typically the sensor or filter transfer function
- $j = \sqrt{-1}$
- k = discrete-time index
- k_s = settling time
- k_s^* = desired settling time used in controller design
- K = buffer size in $M/M/1/K$ queueing system
- $K_P, K_I, K_D = P, I, D$ constants
- $K(z)$ = controller transfer function
- m_I = number of inputs in state space framework
- m_O = number of outputs in state-space framework (if $m_i = m_o$, m is used)
- M_p = maximum overshoot
- M_p^* = desired maximum overshoot used in controller design
- $N(z), n(k)$ = noise input
- n = order of state vector
- $n(k), n(t)$ = number in system as a signal
- N = steady-state number in system
- p, p_i = pole
- q, q_i = zeros
- r = magnitude of complex pole
- $r(k)$ = reference input
- R = steady-state response time
- $R(z), r(k)$ = reference input
- T_s = sample time
- $T(z) = Y(z) + N(z)$ = output of the target system that includes measurement noise
- $\bar{u}$ = operating point of control input

- $\tilde{u}(k) =$ (unnormalized) control input
- $u(k) =$ offset value of control input
- $U(z) =$ Z-transform of the control input
- $V(z), v(k) =$ output of plant (before sensor)
- $W(z), w(k) =$ output of filter
- $\mathbf{X}(z), \mathbf{x}(k) =$ state vector
- $\bar{y} =$ operating point of measured output
- $\tilde{y}(k) =$ (unnormalized) measured output
- $y(k) =$ offset value of measured output
- $Y(z) =$ Z-transform of the measured output
- $\theta =$ angle of complex pole; also, frequency of oscillation
- $\lambda =$ eigenvalue
- $\lambda =$ arrival rate to $M/M/1/K$ queueing system
- $\mu =$ service rate for $M/M/1/K$ queueing system
- $\rho =$ utilization for $M/M/1/K$ queueing system (note that this $\rho < \lambda/\mu$ unless $K = \infty$)
- $\rho(k) =$ utilization at time k

Appendix B

Acronyms

ARX	autoregressive model with a forced input
BFL	buffer fill level
BIBO	bounded input, bounded output
CPU	central processing unit and/or its utilization
HTTP	hypertext transfer protocol
I control	integral control
IT	information technology
KA	KeepAlive
LQR	linear quadratic regulator
MC	MaxClients
MEM	utilization of memory
MIMO	multiple input, multiple output
$M/M/1/K$	single-server queueing system with exponential interarrivals, exponential service times, and a buffer size of K
P control	proportional control
PI control	proportional–integral control
PID control	proportional–integral–derivative control
RED	random early detection of buffer overflow
RIS	number of RPCs in the system
RMSE	root-mean-square error
RPC	remote procedure call

Feedback Control of Computing Systems, by Joseph L. Hellerstein, Yixin Diao, Sujay Parekh, and Dawn M. Tilbury
ISBN 0-471-26637-X   Copyright © 2004 John Wiley & Sons, Inc.

SASO   stability, accuracy, settling times, overshoot properties used in the analysis of closed-loop systems

SISO   single input, single output

SLA   service-level agreement

SLO   service-level objective

TCP/IP   transmission control protocol/Internet protocol

Key Results

C.1 MODELING

C.1.1 Dominant Pole Approximation

Consider

$$G(z) = \frac{b(z - q_1) \cdots (z - q_m)}{(z - p_1) \cdots (z - p_n)}, \qquad \text{where } m \leq n$$

Suppose that p' is the dominant pole. Then, $G(z)$ can be approximated by $G'(z)$, given as

$$G'(z) = \frac{G(1)(1 - p')}{z - p'}, \text{ if } p' \text{ is real} \qquad \text{[Equation (3.30)]}$$

C.1.2 Closed-Loop Transfer Functions

For the closed-loop system shown in Figure 4.1, and repeated in Figure C.1, the various transfer functions are given in Table C.1. Note that $Y(z)$ is used as the output if $N(z) = 0$.

Feedback Control of Computing Systems, by Joseph L. Hellerstein, Yixin Diao, Sujay Parekh, and Dawn M. Tilbury
ISBN 0-471-26637-X Copyright © 2004 John Wiley & Sons, Inc.

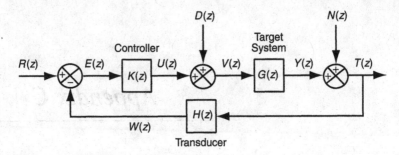

Fig. C.1 Block diagram of a closed-loop system (repeated from Figure 4.5). $R(z)$ is the reference input, $D(z)$ is the disturbance input, $N(z)$ is the noise input, $E(z)$ is the control error, $U(z)$ is the control input, and $Y(z)$ is the system output..

TABLE C.1   Closed-Loop Transfer Functions

Input	Output	
	$Y(z)$ or $T(z)$	$E(z)$
$R(z)$	Equation (4.1)	Equation (4.3)
	$$F_R(z) = \frac{Y(z)}{R(z)}$$ $$= \frac{G(z)K(z)}{1 + K(z)G(z)H(z)}$$	$$F_{RE}(z) = \frac{E(z)}{R(z)}$$ $$= \frac{1}{1 + K(z)G(z)H(z)}$$
$D(z)$	Equation (4.4)	Equation (4.5)
	$$F_D(z) = \frac{Y(z)}{D(z)}$$ $$= \frac{G(z)}{1 + K(z)G(z)H(z)}$$	$$F_{DE}(z) = \frac{E(z)}{D(z)}$$ $$= \frac{-G(z)H(z)}{1 + K(z)G(z)H(z)}$$
$N(z)$	Equation (4.6)	Equation (4.7)
	$$F_N(z) = \frac{T(z)}{N(z)}$$ $$= \frac{1}{1 + K(z)G(z)H(z)}$$	$$F_{NE}(z) = \frac{E(z)}{N(z)}$$ $$= \frac{-H(z)}{1 + K(z)G(z)H(z)}$$

C.2 ANALYSIS

C.2.1 Stability

Theorem 3.2 gives the condition for stability as:

Theorem C.1 (BIBO stability). A system represented by a transfer function $G(z)$ is BIBO stable if and only if all the poles p_i of $G(z)$ are inside the unit circle.

The results in the subsequent sections only apply to systems that are known to be BIBO stable, i.e., $|p_i| < 1$.

C.2.2 Settling Time

The settling time k_s of the system response to a unit step can be approximated by studying its first-order approximation (as in Section C.1.1). The time to settle within 2% of the steady-state value is

$$k_s \approx \frac{-4}{\log r} \qquad \text{[Equation (5.12)]}$$

where $r = \max_i |p_i|$ is the magnitude of the largest closed-loop pole.

In Section 3.3.4 we stated that the approximation is reasonably good if the largest pole (or pair of complex poles) is at least twice as large as the next largest pole(s).

C.2.3 Maximum Overshoot

From Equation (8.8)

$$M_p \approx \begin{cases} 0 & \text{real dominant pole } p_1 \geq 0 \\ |p_1| & \text{real dominant pole } p_1 < 0 \\ r^{\pi/|\theta|} & \text{dominant poles } p_1, p_2 = re^{\pm j\theta} \end{cases}$$

C.2.4 Steady-State Gain

Consider a system with transfer function $G(z)$. For a unit step input, the steady-state output of the system is $y_{ss} = G(1)$ [Equation (3.29)].

C.3 CONTROLLER DESIGN

C.3.1 Control Laws

Consider the feedback system in Figure C.1. Below are the basic control laws and controller transfer functions.

- *Proportional control:*

$$u(k) = K_p e(k) \qquad \text{[Equation (8.1)]}$$

$$K(z) = \frac{U(z)}{E(z)} = K_p \qquad \text{[Equation (8.2)]}$$

Let $r(k)$ be the reference input with steady-state value r_{ss}. As shown in Section 8.3.3, this system has $e_{ss} = 0$ if, and only if, $F_R(1) = 1$. In general,

$$e_{ss} = r_{ss}[1 - F_R(1)] \qquad \text{[Equation (8.5)]}$$

$$= r_{ss}\left[1 - \frac{K_P G(1)}{1 + H(1)K_P G(1)}\right]$$

- *Integral control:*

$$u(k) = u(k - 1) + K_I e(k) \qquad \text{[Equation (9.1)]}$$

$$K(z) = \frac{U(z)}{E(z)} = \frac{K_I z}{z - 1} \qquad \text{[Equation (9.5)]}$$

Integral control can eliminate steady-state error from step changes in either reference or disturbance inputs.

- *Proportional–integral (PI) control:*

$$u(k) = u(k - 1) + (K_P + K_I)e(k) - K_P e(k - 1) \qquad \text{[Equation (9.6)]}$$

$$K(z) = \frac{U(z)}{E(z)} = K_P + \frac{K_I z}{z - 1} \qquad \text{[Equation (9.7)]}$$

- *Proportional–derivative (PD) control:*

$$u(k) = K_P e(k) + K_D(e(k) - e(k - 1)) \qquad \text{[Equation (9.15)]}$$

$$K(z) = \frac{U(z)}{E(z)} = K_P + \frac{K_D(z - 1)}{z} \qquad \text{[Equation (9.16)]}$$

- *Proportional–integral–derivative (PID) control:*

$$u(k) = K_P e(k) + u_I(k - 1) + K_I e(k) + K_D[e(k) - e(k - 1)]$$
$$\text{[Equation (9.17)]}$$

$$K(z) = \frac{U(z)}{E(z)} = K_P + K_I\frac{z}{z - 1} + K_D\frac{z - 1}{z}$$
$$\text{[Equation (9.18)]}$$

C.3.2 Pole Placement Design

In pole placement design, we are given the desired settling time k_s^* and overshoot M_P^*. This information is used to determine values of controller parameters that permit the system to meet these constraints.

PI Controller   Below are the key equations involved in designing a PI controller using the pole placement method from Section 9.2.2, summarized in Table 9.2.

$$r = e^{\frac{-4}{k_s^*}}$$ [Equation (9.9)]

$$\theta = \pi \frac{\log r}{\log M_p^*}$$ [Equation (9.10)]

The desired characteristic polynomial is

$$(z - p_1)(z - p_2) = z^2 - (p_1 + p_2)z + p_1 p_2$$ [Equation (9.11)]

where $p_1 = r \cos \theta + jr \sin \theta$, $p_2 = r \cos \theta - jr \sin \theta$ [Equation (3.19)].

The modeled characteristic polynomial is

$$\frac{[K_P K_I z/(z - 1)]G(z)}{1 + [K_P K_I z/(z - 1)]G(z)}$$

The K_P and K_I are determined by equating the desired and modeled characteristics polynomials.

State Space The procedure is similar to that for the PI controller, and it is discussed in detail in Section 10.3.1. The first two poles are set as noted above; the remaining $n - 2$ poles should have much smaller magnitudes, for example, $0.25r$.

The desired characteristic polynomial is

$$\left[z^2 - (p_1 + p_2)z + p_1 p_2 \right] (z - 0.25r)^{n-2}$$

The modeled characteristic polynomial for static state feedback is

$$\det[z\mathbf{I} - (\mathbf{A} - \mathbf{B}\mathbf{K})]$$ [Equation (10.13)]

where $\mathbf{K} = [K_1, \ldots, K_n]$.

For dynamic state feedback as given in Equation (10.11), the modeled characteristic polynomial is

$$\det \left\{ z\mathbf{I} - \left(\begin{bmatrix} \mathbf{A} & \mathbf{0} \\ -\mathbf{C} & 1 \end{bmatrix} - \begin{bmatrix} \mathbf{B} \\ \mathbf{0} \end{bmatrix} \begin{bmatrix} \mathbf{K}_P & K_I \end{bmatrix} \right) \right\}$$

The full procedure is shown in Table 10.2.

C.3.3 LQR Design

The objective function to minimize is J, given as

$$J = \frac{1}{2} \sum_{k=0}^{\infty} \left(\mathbf{x}^\top(k)\mathbf{Q}\mathbf{x}(k) + \mathbf{u}^\top(k)\mathbf{R}\mathbf{u}(k) \right)$$ [Equation (10.17)]

where $\mathbf{Q}$ is positive semidefinite and $\mathbf{R}$ is positive definite. $\mathbf{Q}$ quantifies the cost of individual (and combinations) of state variables diverge from their operating point. $\mathbf{R}$ specifies the cost of control effort.

The iterative procedure to compute the gain matrix $\mathbf{K}$ manually is given in Figure 10.3.

Appendix D

Essentials of Linear Algebra

In this appendix we provide a brief review of results from linear algebra that are needed for state-space analysis. We state some definitions related to matrices and some properties of matrices without proof. For a deeper understanding, the reader is encouraged to refer to a linear algebra text (e.g., [37]).

D.1 MATRIX INVERSE, SINGULARITY

An $n \times n$ matrix $\mathbf{A}$ is an *invertible matrix* if there exists another $n \times n$ matrix $\mathbf{P}$ such that $\mathbf{AP} = \mathbf{PA} = \mathbf{I}$. If the inverse exists, it is unique and is typically denoted as $\mathbf{A}^{-1}$. Further, it is easy to see that $(\mathbf{A}^{-1})^{-1} = \mathbf{A}$.

If $\mathbf{A}$ does not have an inverse, it is called *singular*.

Theorem D.1 $\mathbf{A}$ is singular if and only if there is a vector $\mathbf{v} \neq 0$ such that $\mathbf{Av} = 0$.

D.2 MATRIX MINOR, DETERMINANT, AND ADJOINT

The minor of an element a_{ij} of an $m \times n$ matrix $\mathbf{A}$ is the matrix, denoted $\mathbf{A}_{ij}$, of size $(m - 1) \times (n - 1)$ formed by deleting row i and column j of $\mathbf{A}$.

The *determinant* of an $n \times n$ matrix $\mathbf{A}$, denoted $\det(\mathbf{A})$ or $|\mathbf{A}|$ is defined recursively as follows, where $a, b, c,$ and d are scalars:

Feedback Control of Computing Systems, by Joseph L. Hellerstein, Yixin Diao, Sujay Parekh, and Dawn M. Tilbury
ISBN 0-471-26637-X   Copyright © 2004 John Wiley & Sons, Inc.

- $n = 1$:

$$|a| = a \tag{D.1}$$

- $n = 2$:

$$\begin{vmatrix} a & b \\ c & d \end{vmatrix} = ad - bc \tag{D.2}$$

- $n > 2$:

$$\det(\mathbf{A}) = \sum_{j=1}^{n} a_{1j}(-1)^{1+j} \det \mathbf{A}_{1,j} \tag{D.3}$$

Theorem D.2 $\det(\mathbf{A}^{-1}) = 1/\det(\mathbf{A})$.

Theorem D.3   If $\mathbf{A}$ is invertible, $\det(\mathbf{A}) \neq 0$.

The *adjoint of a matrix* $\mathbf{A}$ with dimensions $n \times n$ is denoted by $\mathrm{adj}(\mathbf{A})$, which is the matrix whose (i, j)th entry is $(-1)^{i+j} \det(\mathbf{A}_{j,i})$. The determinant and adjoint of a matrix are important, since they can be used to compute the matrix inverse, as follows.

Theorem D.4 (Cramer's rule).   For a nonsingular matrix $\mathbf{A}$, its inverse $\mathbf{A}^{-1}$ can be computed as

$$\mathbf{A}^{-1} = \frac{1}{\det(\mathbf{A})} \mathrm{adj}(\mathbf{A})$$

D.3   VECTOR SPACES

A set of nonzero vectors $V = \{\mathbf{x}_1, \ldots, \mathbf{x}_n\}$ is said to be *linearly dependent* if and only if there exist scalars $a_1, \ldots, a_n$ such that at least two $a_i \neq 0$ and

$$a_1\mathbf{x}_1 + \cdots + a_n\mathbf{x}_n = 0$$

In other words, one of the $\mathbf{x}_i$ can be expressed as a linear combination of the remaining vectors in V. Otherwise, the set of vectors is said to be *linearly independent*.

The set of vectors $S = \{a_1\mathbf{x}_1 + \cdots + a_n\mathbf{x}_n | a_i \in \mathbf{R}\}$ is known as the span of V. S is known as the vector space which is spanned by V. If the members of V are linearly independent, they form a basis for S. The basis of a vector space is not unique—in fact, there are infinitely many bases of any given vector space. However, the following property always holds.

Theorem D.5   For any vector space, the number of vectors in any of its bases is the same.

The *vector space dimension* is defined as the number of vectors in a basis.

D.4 MATRIX RANK

For any matrix, we can consider the rows (or columns) as vectors. The row rank of a $m \times n$ matrix $\mathbf{A}$ is defined as the maximum number of rows which are linearly independent. The *column rank* is defined similarly for the columns of $\mathbf{A}$. Thus, the row (column) rank is also the dimension of the space spanned by the row (column) vectors.

Theorem D.6 For any matrix, the row rank is the same as the column rank.

Hence, we do not distinguish between the row and column ranks, and refer to it simply as the *matrix rank*. If rank($\mathbf{A}$) = min(m, n), $\mathbf{A}$ is called full rank. The determinant and rank are related in that:

Theorem D.7 If $\mathbf{A}$ is a square matrix, det($\mathbf{A}$) $\neq 0$ $\iff$ $\mathbf{A}$ has full rank.

Thus, the determinant, rank and existence of matrix inverse are all interrelated concepts.

D.5 EIGENVALUES

The *eigenvalues* of a matrix is a scalar value λ for which there exists a nonzero vector $\mathbf{v}$ such that

$$\mathbf{A}\mathbf{v} = \lambda\mathbf{v} \tag{D.4}$$

That is, the product of the matrix $\mathbf{A}$ and the vector $\mathbf{v}$ is the same as the product of the scalar λ and the vector $\mathbf{v}$ (such a vector $\mathbf{v}$ is called an eigenvector associated with the eigenvalue λ). We rewrite this equation as follows:

$$(\lambda\mathbf{I} - \mathbf{A})\mathbf{v} = 0$$

Since $\mathbf{v}$ must be nonzero (from the definition of an eigenvalue), it follows that the matrix $(\lambda\mathbf{I} - \mathbf{A})$ must be singular, or equivalently, that its determinant must be zero. Thus, an eigenvalue of $\mathbf{A}$ is any scalar λ such that

$$\det(\lambda\mathbf{I} - \mathbf{A}) = 0 \tag{D.5}$$

The *characteristic polynomial* of $\mathbf{A}$ is the polynomial of λ formed by det($\lambda\mathbf{I} - \mathbf{A}$). The eigenvalues of $\mathbf{A}$ are the roots of the characteristic polynomial. If $\mathbf{A}$ is an $n \times n$ matrix, the polynomial det($\lambda\mathbf{I} - \mathbf{A}$) is nth order and there will be n solutions to the equation and hence n eigenvalues (although some of the eigenvalues may be repeated). Note that if the matrix $\mathbf{A}$ itself is singular, it must have at least one zero eigenvalue.

Let **A** be a *diagnosable matrix*, that is, a matrix that can be expressed as $\mathbf{A} = \mathbf{P}\Lambda\mathbf{P}^{-1}$, where **P** is nonsingular and Λ has all nondiagonal entries set to 0. Then the diagonal entries are the eigenvalues of **A**. This means that

$$\mathbf{A}^m = \left[\mathbf{P}\Lambda\mathbf{P}^{-1}\right]^m$$

$$= \mathbf{P}\Lambda\mathbf{P}^{-1}\mathbf{P}\Lambda\mathbf{P}^{-1}\cdots\mathbf{P}\Lambda\mathbf{P}^{-1}$$

$$= \mathbf{P}\Lambda^m\mathbf{P}^{-1}$$

Appendix E

MATLAB Basics

In this appendix we provide a brief introduction to the features and use of
MATLAB. Parts of this tutorial are borrowed with permission from [47]. Recent
versions of MATLAB have excellent online tutorials and documentation—please
refer to those for more details. At the end of the appendix we list some MATLAB
tutorials that are available on the Web. Readers are encouraged to follow along
by typing the examples into a MATLAB interpreter as they are presented.

In the following, user input to MATLAB follows the MATLAB prompt (">>").
The system response is given in this font.

E.1 VARIABLES AND VALUES

In MATLAB, basic values such as integers and floating-point numbers are entered
directly (e.g., -10, 0.579). Strings are formed by enclosing the characters
in single quotes (e.g., 'A sample string'). Complex numbers can also be
entered directly (e.g., 9.34+7.2j).

Variables can be given any names that are not already reserved or given to
functions. Values are assigned using the "=" sign.

```
>> a = 10
a =
    10
```

Feedback Control of Computing Systems, by Joseph L. Hellerstein, Yixin Diao, Sujay Parekh, and
Dawn M. Tilbury
ISBN 0-471-26637-X   Copyright © 2004 John Wiley & Sons, Inc.

Values of variables are accessed by using them in an expression.

```
>> b = a + 5
b =
    15
```

Variables may be removed from memory by using the clear command.

E.1.1 Vectors

Vectors in MATLAB consist of elements enclosed within square brackets. Row vectors are created by separating the elements with spaces.

```
>> a = [1 2 3 4 5]

a =
    1    2    3    4    5
```

To make it easy to specify sequences, MATLAB provides a convenient syntax of start:increment:end. This generates numbers between start and end, evenly spaced by increment.

```
>> s = 2:3:13
s =
    2    5    8    11
```

The increment value is optional, so the value of a above could also be assigned using a = 1:5.

MATLAB generates row vectors by default, but column vectors may be created directly or converted from row vectors.

```
>> c = [1;2;3;4;5]
c =
    1
    2
    3
    4
    5

>> d = a'
d =
    1
    2
    3
    4
    5
```

where the tick mark (') is the vector (or matrix) transpose operation.

Vector operations are analogous to the operations on scalars as long as the dimensions make sense.

```
>> b = a * 2
b =
    2    4    6    8    10
```

```
>> c = a + b
c =
    3    6    9    12    15
```

Vector elements can be accessed by specifying an array of indices of the elements to be accessed. For example, to retrieve the even-numbered entries of the vector c, one would use

```
>> c([2 4])
ans =
    6    12
```

The special index end refers to the last element of the vector. Thus, accessing the even-numbered entries of any vector can be written as

```
>> c(2:2:end)
ans =
    6    12
```

E.1.2 Matrices

The matrix syntax is an extension of the vector syntax, where rows are separated by semicolons. Thus, a 3×3 matrix is defined as

```
>> m = [1 2 3 ; 4 5 6 ; 7 8 9]
m =
    1    2    3
    4    5    6
    7    8    9
```

by inserting a ";" between each row.

Matrix operations are also defined using the same operators as on scalars and vectors (as long as the dimensions make sense, of course).

```
>> n = [1 2 3] ;
>> n * m
ans =
    30    36    42
```

Here we see that by adding a ";" at the end of the first expression, the normal MATLAB output is suppressed. Further, when the expression result is not assigned to a variable, MATLAB assigns it to a default variable called ans, which may be used in subsequent calculations.

E.2   FUNCTIONS

Beyond the basic unary and binary operations, MATLAB also supports program-
ming-language style procedure calls and functions. These can be built in, provided
by add-ons (called *Toolboxes*) or may even be user defined.

```
>> sin(pi/4)
ans =
    0.7071
```

where we have used the built-in constant pi ($= 3.14159\ldots$).

Thus, functions can take arguments, and these are enclosed in parentheses. In
the case of multiple arguments, they are separated by commas.

```
>> m = round(rand(3) * 1000)
m =

    604     15    932
    272    747    466
    199    445    419
```

To sort the columns of m (its first dimension), use

```
>> sort(m, 1)
ans =
    199     15    419
    272    445    466
    604    747    932
```

Functions can have some arguments be optional as well. Indeed, in the case of
sort, the second argument can be omitted, in which case it defaults to 1.

Like many other functions, sort can actually return multiple values. In MAT-
LAB, multiple values are received by the caller using a vector of variable names
to the left of the "=."

```
>> [sorted, index] = sort(m, 1)
sorted =
    199     15    419
    272    445    466
    604    747    932

index =
      3      1      3
      2      3      2
      1      2      1
```

All built-in and Toolbox functions have detailed documentation that can be accessed using the `help` facility. Just type `help` followed by the function name. For example:

```
>> help inv
```

```
INV    Matrix inverse.
  INV(X) is the inverse of the square matrix X.
  A warning message is printed if X is badly scaled or
  nearly singular.
```

```
See also SLASH, PINV, COND, CONDEST, LSQNONNEG, LSCOV.
```

E.3 PLOTTING

MATLAB provides a nice facility for generating plots and graphs. Here we describe the most basic command, called simply `plot`. It is best illustrated by an example.

```
>> t = 0:360 ;
>> y = sin((pi/180)*x) ;
>> plot(t, y) ;
>> xlabel('Theta (deg)') ;
>> ylabel('Sin(Theta)') ;
>> title('Sine wave') ;
```

This generates the plot shown in Figure E.1. Here we provide the data for the X and Y dimensions of the plot as vectors. The vectors for X and Y must be the same length (see `length`). The other dimension can vary. MATLAB can plot a

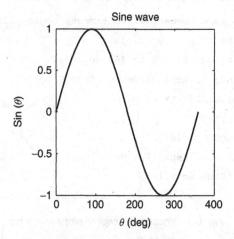

Fig. E.1 *Basic plot example.*

$1 \times n$ vector versus a $n \times 1$ vector, or a $1 \times n$ vector versus a $2 \times n$ matrix (you will get two lines) as long as n is the same for both vectors.

The plot command has many extensions and variants, including customizing the line style and color, plotting multiple functions on one plot, three-dimensional plots, and bar charts. Refer to the online help for more information.

E.4 M-FILES

To avoid repetitive typing of frequently used sequences of commands and function calls, MATLAB provides a way to store these commands in *m-files*. These m-files can then be invoked and the result is equivalent to typing in each of the lines in the m-file at the command prompt. Thus, we could create a file, called, say, 'sineplot.m', as given in Figure E.2. Then, to recreate the plot in Figure E.1, we just type sineplot at the MATLAB prompt. Note that the filename must have the suffix '.m', but this suffix is not used when invoking the m-file. Also, in order that MATLAB is able to locate the right m-file, it must be placed in the MATLAB search path (type help matlabpath).

Another use of m-files is to allow users to define their own functions and subroutines. In fact, many of the Matlab and Toolbox functions are implemented using m-files. The MATLAB code that implements a function is placed in an m-file with the same name as the function (e.g., a function named myfunc would be in a file named myfunc.m). In this m-file, the custom function is then defined using the keyword function. A function taking three arguments and producing two values could be defined as follows:

```
function [output1,output2] = myfunc(input1,input2,input3)
```

```
% This is a comment line.Comments begin with a '%'.
% Script to plot y = sin(x)
% for angles from 0 to 360 degrees.
t = 0:360; % Theta values -- from 0 to 360
y = sin((pi/180)*x);
plot(t,y);
xlabel('Theta (deg)');
ylabel('Sin(Theta)');
title('Sine wave');
```

Fig. E.2 *sineplot.m: script to plot a sine wave.*

This function would be invoked, for example, as follows:

```
>> [x,y] = myfunc(v1,v2,v3)
```

Following the function declaration in the m-file are the MATLAB commands that form the function.

A very simple example of a function that adds two quantities is given in Figure E.3. If this file is saved as add.m, we could add numbers using

```
>> y = add(3, 8)
y =
   11
```

During this execution of add.m, the argument variables (num1, num2) are assigned the values passed as arguments. For example, num1=3 and num2=8. The return value (result) is generated by assigning a value to it, as if it were an ordinary variable. For a function with multiple return values, each return variable *must* be assigned a value before the end of the function. At the command prompt, this return value is then assigned to the designated variable (in this case y).

The function add.m is an overly simplistic function, given for illustrative purposes; typically, functions will be more complex. The best way to learn the intricacies of writing functions is to follow the MATLAB tutorial and study some of the simpler built-in and Toolbox m-files.

We have seen two main types of m-files. The first type is of the form shown in sineplot.m. This type of m-file is called a *MATLAB script*. A script does not define any function; rather, it can be considered to be a macro—or shorthand—for the commands contained within the script. The second type of m-file is given by add.m and is called a *MATLAB function*, since it always contains a function definition. Two key differences between scripts and functions are that (1) scripts do not take arguments, and (2) the variable names used in function m-files are local to that m-file. In other words, even after invoking add.m, the variables num1, num2, and result used in that file are not subsequently available to be used at the command prompt. For a script file, however, the variables (such as t and y in sineplot.m) are available after the script executes. Both types of m-files have their uses, and they can be mixed freely.

```
function [result] = add(num1,num2)
% ADD - Add two numbers

result = num1 + num2 ;
```

Fig. E.3   add.m: A simple MATLAB function that adds its input arguments.

E.5 SUMMARY OF MATLAB FUNCTIONS AND COMMANDS

Type	Function/Command	Description
Basic	'	Matrix transpose
	n = inv(m)	Matrix inverse
	mean(m)	Compute mean values
	sum(m)	Cumulative sum
	diff(m)	Pairwise difference
	zeros(n1, n2)	Create an n1 × n2 matrix of zeros
	ones(n1, n2)	Create an n1 × n2 matrix of ones
	eye(n1, n2)	Create an identity matrix of size n1 × n2
	abs(c), angle(c)	Magnitude (abscissa) and angle (phase) of a complex number
	real(c), imag(c)	Real and imaginary parts of a complex number
	residue(p1, p2)	Partial fraction expansion of polynomial division $p1/p2$
Control Toolbox	tf(np, dp, ts)	Transfer function with numerator np, denominator dp, and sample time ts
	G = feedback(G1, G2)	Transfer function for a feedback loop consisting of feedforward system G1 and with G2 on the feedback path
	dcgain(G)	Gain of transfer function G
	poles(G)	Poles of G
	impulse(G)	Impulse response of system with transfer function G
	step(G)	Step response of system with transfer function G
	rlocus(G)	Plot the root locus of transfer function G
	K = dlqr(F,G,Q,R)	Gains from LQR design for system F,G with LQR criteria Q,R

References

1. T. Abdelzaher and K. G. Shin. QoS provisioning with qContracts in Web and multimedia servers. *Real-Time Systems Symposium*, pp. 44–53, 1999.

2. T. F. Abdelzaher and N. Bhatti. Adaptive content delivery for Web server QoS. *International Workshop on Quality of Service*, London, June 1999.

3. M. Agapie and K. Sohraby. Algorithmic solution to second-order fluid flow. *Proceedings of IEEE INFOCOM '01*, pp. 1–10, Anchorage, AK, April 2001.

4. A. O. Allen. *Probability, Statistics, and Queueing Theory*, 2nd ed. Academic Press, San Diego, CA, 1990.

5. E. Altman, T. Basar, and R. Srikant. Congestion control as a stochastic control problem with action delays. *Automatica*, 35:1936–1950, 1999.

6. J. Aman, C. K. Eilert, D. Emmes, P. Yocom, and D. Dillenberger. Adaptive algorithms for managing a distributed data processing workload. *IBM Systems Journal*, 36(2), 1997.

7. K. Appleby, S. Fakhouri, L. Fong, G. Goldszmidt, M. Kalantar, S. Krishnakumar, D. P. Pazel, J. Pershing, and B. Rochwerger. Oceano—SLA based management of a computing utility. *IEEE/IFIP Integrated Network Management*, pp. 855–868, May 2001.

8. K. J. Astrom and T. Hagglund. *PID Controllers: Theory, Design, and Tuning*, 2nd ed. Instrumentation, Systems, and Automation Society, Research Triangle Park, NC, 1995.

9. K. J. Astrom and B. Wittenmark. *Adaptive Control*, 2nd ed. Addison-Wesley, Reading, MA, 1995.

10. L. Benmohamed and S. M. Meerkov. Feedback control of congestion in packet switching networks: the case of a single congested node. *IEEE Transactions on Networking*, 1(6), December 1993.

11. J. P. Bigus. Applying neural networks to computer system performance tuning. In *IEEE International Conference on Neural Networks*, pp. 2442–2447, 1994.

12. G. E. P. Box. In *Robustness in the Strategy of Scientific Model Building* (R. L. Launer and G. N. Wilkinson, eds.). Academic Press, San Diego, CA, 1979.

13. V. Cardellini, M. Colajanni, and P. S. Yu. Request redirection algorithms for distributed web systems. *IEEE Transactions on Parallel and Distributed Systems*, 14(4):355–368, 2003.

14. K. Chien, J. A. Hrones, and J. B. Reswick. On the automatic control of generalized passive systems. *Transactions of the American Society of Mechanical Engineers*, pages 175–182, February 1952.

15. E. Chung, L. Benini, A. Bogliolo, Y. Lu, and G. De Micheli. Dynamic power management for nonstationary service requests. *IEEE Transactions on Computers*, 51(11):1345–1361, 2002.

16. D. Cuthbert and F. Wood. *Fitting Equations to Data*. Wiley-Interscience, New York, 1971.

17. Y. Diao, N. Gandhi, J. L. Hellerstein, S. Parekh, and D. Tilbury. Using MIMO feedback control to enforce policies for interrelated metrics with application to the Apache Web server. *IEEE/IFIP Network Operations and Management*, April 2002.

18. Y. Diao, J. L. Hellerstein, and S. Parekh. Optimizing quality of service using fuzzy control. *Distributed Systems Operations and Management*, 2002.

19. N. R. Draper and H. Smith. *Applied Regression Analysis*. Wiley, New York, 1968.

20. D. Ferrari, G. Serazzi, and A. Zeigner. *Measurement and Tuning of Computer Systems*. Prentice Hall, Upper Saddle River, NJ, 1983.

21. W. H. Fleming and R. W. Rishel. *Deterministic and Stochastic Optimal Control*. Springer-Verlag, New York, 1996.

22. R. Fletcher. *Practical Methods of Optimization*. Wiley, New York, 2000.

23. S. Floyd and V. Jacobson. Random early detection gateways for congestion avoidance. *IEEE and ACM Transactions on Networking*, 1(4):397–413, August 1993.

24. Apache Software Foundation. *http://www.apache.org*.

25. G. F. Franklin, J. D. Powell, and A. Emani-Naeini. *Feedback Control of Dynamic Systems* 3rd ed. Addison-Wesley, Reading, MA, 1994.

26. A. Goel, M. H. Shor, J. Walpole, D. Steere, and C. Pu. Using feedback control for a network and CPU resource management application. *American Control Conference*, pp. 2974–2980, June 2001.

27. J. L. Hellerstein, Y. Diao, and S. Parekh. A first-principles approach to constructing transfer functions for admission control in computing systems. *Proceedings of the 41st Conference on Decision and Control*, December 2002.

28. C. V. Hollot, V. Misra, D. Towsley, and W. B. Gong. A control theoretic analysis of RED. In *Proceedings of IEEE INFOCOM '01*, Anchorage, AK, April 2001.

29. C. V. Hollot, V. Misra, D. Towsley, and W. B. Gong. On designing improved controllers for AQM routers supporting TCP flows. *Proceedings of IEEE INFOCOM '01*, Anchorage, AK, April 2001.

30. J. Hyun, I. Jung, J. Lee, and S. Maeng. Content sniffer based load distribution in a web server cluster. *IEICE Transactions on Information and Systems*, E86-D(7), 2003.

31. A. Iyengar, J. Challenger, D. Dias, and P. Dantzig. High-performance Web site design techniques. *IEEE Internet Computing*, 4(2):17–26, February 2000.

32. P. Johansson and A. A. Nilsson. Discrete time stability analysis of an explicit rate algorithm for the abr service. In *IEEE ATM Workshop*, pages 229–350, 1997.

33. H. Kameda, E. S. Fathy, I. Ryu, and J. Li. A performance comparison of dynamic vs. static load balancing policies in a mainframe—personal computer network model. In *Proceedings of the 39th IEEE Conference on Decision and Control*. IEEE, 2000.

34. Srinivasan Keshav. A control-theoretic approach to flow control. In *Proceedings of ACM SIGCOMM '91*, September 1991.

35. L. Kleinrock. *Queueing Systems*. 2nd ed. Wiley-Interscience, New York, 1975.

36. L. Kleinrock. *Queueing Systems*, Vol. II, 2nd ed. Wiley-Interscience, New York, 1976.

37. S. J. Leon. *Linear Algebra with Applications*. 6th ed. Prentice Hall, Upper Saddle River, NJ, 2000.

38. P. H. Lewis. A proposed z-plane criterion to expedite transient-performance analyses. *IEEE Transactions on Education*, 43(3):324–329, August 2000.

39. Baochun Li and Klara Nahrstedt. Control-based middleware framework for quality of service applications. *IEEE Journal on Selected Areas in Communication*, 1999.

40. K. Li, M. H. Shor, J. Walpole, C. Pu, and D. C. Steere. Modeling the effect of short-term rate variations on tcp-friendly congestion control behavior. In *Proceedings of the American Control Conference*, pp. 3006–3012, 2001.

41. L. Ljung. *System Identification: Theory for the User*. 2nd ed. Prentice Hall, Upper Saddle River, NJ, 1999.

42. C. Lu, T. F. Abdelzaher, J. A. Stankovic, and S. H. Son. A feedback control architecture and design methodology for service delay guarantees in Web servers. *Technical Report CS-2001-06*. University of Virginia, Department of Computer Science, Charlottesville, VA, 2001.

43. C. Lu, J. A. Stankovic, T. F. Abdelzaher, G. Tao, S. H. Son, and M. Markley. Performance specifications and metrics for adaptive real-time systems. In *Proceedings of the IEEE Real Time Systems Symposium*, Orlando, 2000.

44. Y. Lu, A. Saxena, and T. F. Abdelzaher. Differentiated caching services: a control-theoretic approach. *International Conference on Distributed Computing Systems*, April 2001.

45. H. Marteins, E. Rahm, and T. Stohr. Dynamic query scheduling in parallel data warehouses. *Concurrency Computation Practice and Experience*, 15(11–12), 2003.

46. S. Mascolo, D. Cavendish, and M. Gerla. ATM rate based congestion control using a smith predictor: an EPRCA implementation. In *Proceedings of IEEE INFOCOM '96*, 1996.

47. W. C. Messner and D. M. Tilbury. *Control Tutorials for Matlab and Simulink: A Web-Based Approach*. Addison-Wesley, Reading, MA, 1999.

48. V. Misra, W. B. Gong, and D. Towsley. Fluid-based analysis of a network of AQM routers supporting TCP flows with an application to RED. *Proceedings of ACM SIG-COMM '00*, 2000.

49. T. M. Mitchell. *Machine Learning*. McGraw-Hill, New York, 1997.

50. K. Ogata. *Modern Control Engineering*. 3rd ed. Prentice Hall, Upper Saddle River, NJ, 1997.

51. A. V. Oppenheim, A. S. Willsky, and S. H. Nawab. *Signals and Systems*. 2nd ed. Prentice Hall, London, 1997.

52. M. Parameswaran, A. Susarla, and A. B. Whinston. P2P networking: an information sharing alternative. *IEEE Computer*, 34(7), July 2001.

53. S. Parekh, N. Gandhi, J. Hellerstein, D. Tilbury, J. Bigus, and T. S. Jayram. Using control theory to achieve service level objectives in performance management. *Real-Time Systems Journal*, 23:127–141, 2002.

54. S. Parekh, K. Rose, J. L. Hellerstein, S. Lightstone, M. Huras, and V. Chang. Managing the performance impact of administrative utilities. In *IFIP Conference on Distributed Systems Operations and Management*, 2003.

55. K. M. Passino and S. Yurkovich. *Fuzzy Control*. Addison Wesley Longman, Menlo Park, CA, 1998.

56. A. Pitsillides, Y. A. Sekercioglu, and G. Ramamurthy. Effective control of traffic flow in atm networks using fuzzy explicit rate marking (ferm). *Journal on Selected Areas in Communications*, 15(2):209–225, 1997.

57. A. Robertsson, B. Wittenmark, and M. Kihl. Analysis and design of admission control in Web-server systems. *American Control Conference*, pp. 254–259, June 2003.

58. C. E. Rohrs, R. A. Berry, and S. J. O'Halek. A control engineer's look at ATM congestion avoidance. In *GLOBECOM*, pp. 1089–1094, 1995.

59. W. J. Rugh and J. S. Shamma. Research on gain scheduling. *Automatica*, 36: 1401–1425, 2000.

60. R. Sanz and K. Arzen. Trends in software and control. *IEEE Control Systems Magazine*, June:12–15, 2003.

61. S. Selvakumar and S. V. Raghavan. Differential priority-based adaptive rate service discipline for qos guarantee of video stream. *Computer Communications*, 20(13):1160–1174, 1997.

62. L. Sha, X. Liu, Y. Lu, and T. Abdelzaher. Queueing model based network server performance control. In *IEEE RealTime Systems Symposium*, 2002.

63. N. Sai Shankar and A. P. Shivaprasad. An Instantaneous Control model for Flow Control in an ATM Network. In *International Conference on Information, Communications and Signal Processing*, pp. 878–882, 1997.

64. J.-J. E. Slotine and W. Li. *Applied Nonlinear Control*. Prentice Hall, Upper Saddle River, NJ, 1991.

65. M. R. Stan and K. Skadron. Power-aware computing. *IEEE Computer*, December:35–38, 2003.

66. A. S. Tannenbaum. *Operating Systems: Design and Implementation*. Prentice Hall, Upper Saddle River, NJ, 1987.

67. The Math Works. *MATLAB, The Language of Technical Computing*. The Math Works, Inc., Natick, MA, 1984–2003.

68. L. Zhang, Z. Zhao, Y. Shu, L. Wang, and O. Yang. Load balancing of multipath source routing in ad hoc networks. In *International Conference on Communications*, 2002.

69. R. E. Ziemer, W. H. Tranter, and D. R. Fannin. *Signals and Systems: Continuous and Discrete*, 4th ed. Prentice Hall, Upper Saddle River, NJ, 1998.

Index